Multidisciplinary Perspectives on Grit

Llewellyn Ellardus van Zyl • Chantal Olckers •
Leoni van der Vaart
Editors

Multidisciplinary Perspectives on Grit

Contemporary Theories, Assessments, Applications and Critiques

Springer

Editors
Llewellyn Ellardus van Zyl
Human Performance Management
University of Universiteit Eindhoven
Eindhoven, the Netherlands

Chantal Olckers
Department of Human Resource Management
University of Pretoria
Pretoria, South Africa

Leoni van der Vaart
School of Industrial Psychology and
Human Resource Management
North-West University
Vanderbijlpark, Gauteng, South Africa

ISBN 978-3-030-57388-1 ISBN 978-3-030-57389-8 (eBook)
https://doi.org/10.1007/978-3-030-57389-8

This Springer imprint is published by the registered company Springer Nature Switzerland AG.
The registered company address is: Gewerbestrasse 11, 6330 Cham, Switzerland

This book is dedicated to all those frontline health workers who showed immense GRIT in helping to combat the global COVID-19 health crisis. Your passion for your work and perseverance in these tough times are truly inspiring.

Foreword

Performance in its purest form is more than just the culmination of individuals' cognitive (cap)abilities, potential or "talents"; it has to do with sustained, enduring effort one exerts over time in achieving one's goals (perseverance of effort), the passion one has for one's work/studies (consistency in effort) and the extent towards which one can actively adapt to changing environments (environmental agility)... In effect, it has to do with grit! Originally conceptualized by Duckworth et al. (2007) as a non-cognitive trait associated with the perseverance and passion for long-term goals, grit has shown to be an important explanatory factor in achievement theory as a means to explain why some individuals with lower levels of externally perceived "talent" tend to perform better than their highly cognitively gifted counterparts. Research has shown that gritty individuals are more engaged, motivated, happier, healthier and more successful than those who report low levels of grit. Further, grit has also shown to result in various positive team, family, organization and societal outcomes. As such, it is not surprising that popular media hailed grit as "the new gold standard" for predicting life, school, career and job-related success.

However, despite its widespread popularity within mass media and the popular psychology press, academic studies on grit are still in their infancy. There seems to be little consensus in the literature as to how grit should be conceptualized, measured or managed and how it differs from other constructs such as conscientiousness, diligence or determination. This lack in consensus has resulted in various *specific* criticisms of the construct and led to various new "theories", psychometric instruments and interventions to rapidly emerge in the literature. This rapid emergence of new theories could lead to either seminal advancements in our understanding of grit or could lead grit to becoming yet another victim of the "jingle-jangle fallacy". Therefore, a thorough reappraisal and consolidation as to the nature of grit, how it should or could be measured and how it could be developed is needed. Further, a consolidated narrative as to the criticisms of grit is also required in order to ensure that future research can actively address such in a systematic, rigorous and scientific fashion.

As such, the purpose of this book is to address these challenges through providing a platform to curate contemporary theories of grit, to discuss ways in which it could be rigorously measured and developed, to investigate its relationship with performance-related metrics and to collate the collective criticisms of grit. This book aimed to provide a comprehensive and balanced perspective on grit with the intent to effectively advance the science of achievement.

It is my hope that this book will stimulate further scientific debate on grit and empower gritty researchers to not shy away from criticisms or critiques, but to actively embrace them.

Eindhoven, the Netherlands
February 2021

Llewellyn Ellardus van Zyl

Preface

This volume provides a multidisciplinary perspective on the conceptualization, measurement and development of grit. Specifically, it provides a comprehensive and balanced retort to the criticisms associated with the construct within the contemporary positive psychological literature. Written by a team of multidisciplinary experts in fields ranging from neuroscience, sociology and education to human resource management and psychology, this volume of 13 chapters firmly positions grit within the discipline of positive psychology's nomological lexicon. Each of the 13 chapters of this book makes a unique contribution to our theoretical understanding of grit and aims to provide a retort to contemporary criticisms.

Chapter 1 assesses the association of grit and gratitude on flourishing and how emotion regulation strategies such as cognitive reappraisal and expressive suppression could serve as psychological mechanisms in enhancing this relationship in a collectivist setting. Chapter 2 investigates how grit develops the capacity to regulate better and rebuild personal resources needed for achieving long-term goals through resilience by developing adequate recovery strategies. Chapter 3 examines the role of grit vis-à-vis four psychosocial factors (i.e. conscientiousness, academic self-concept, other-based achievement goals and competence expectancy) in predicting student math performance and subjective well-being in a Chinese context. Chapter 4 explores whether perseverance of effort has the potential to provide compensatory effects in students' engagement, self-perceived gains, time spent studying and GPA for historically underrepresented students to help them overcome obstacles to their student success. Chapter 5 presents the possibility of enhancing grit with longitudinal data and neuropsychological findings on brain development. Intervention strategies are proposed for the cognitive, behavioural and emotional domains of grit. Chapter 6 examines whether high levels of grit may provide a buffer against chronic stress in college students and result in fewer academic problems.

Chapter 7 focuses on determining the effectiveness of a ninth-grade English-language arts curriculum designed to enhance grit at a rural public high school. This chapter also indicates how the task performance of these students can be increased by utilizing multiple motivational theories of achievement to assist students in building grit in their academic careers. Chapter 8 uses item response theory and structural equation modelling approaches to explore whether grit is measured as a higher-order construct comprising two facets: perseverance of effort and consistency of interests or better measured as two separate constructs. Chapter 9 systematically reviews several studies to uncover the neuroanatomical mechanism of grit to explore if differences in grit are caused by underlying structural and functional variations in the brain. Chapter 10 determines whether two potential antecedents of grit, rumination and hope, would predict changes in grit over time by conducting a cross-lag path analysis on a longitudinal dataset. Specifically, this chapter explores if individuals who tend to engage in less rumination, and who are more hopeful, are more likely to become "grittier" over time. Chapter 11 uses data from a national longitudinal study of educational trajectories of school and university leavers in Russia to assess whether grit (i.e. perseverance of effort and consistency of interests) can predict long-term educational outcomes while controlling for several variables. Chapter 12 applies the distal-proximal framework to theoretically explore whether grit, as a trait, could play a role in enhancing employees' task performance and perceptions of career through a proximate, domain-specific flexible psychological construct such as psychological ownership. Chapter 13 argues how self-determination theory (SDT) could be used to create a need-supportive environment that strengthens the effect of grit interventions while enhancing client adherence and engagement for the unemployed.

We hope that these 13 chapters would provide readers with a framework for advancing the science underpinning grit and that it lays the foundation for meaningful scientific debates, scholarly commentary and academic research.

Eindhoven, the Netherlands
Vanderbijlpark, South Africa
Pretoria, South Africa
February 2021

Llewellyn Ellardus van Zyl
Leoni van der Vaart
Chantal Olckers

Acknowledgements

This manuscript is the end result of an 18-month-long collaborative project between our authors, our independent reviewers and Springer. The project would not have been possible without the collective efforts of all those involved and you, our reader. Somewhat ironically, this project was plagued with various challenges throughout the process and was also severely affected by the COVID-19 pandemic. Yet, all of our stakeholders showed tremendous GRIT in pushing through these challenges in order to ensure that we produced a quality manuscript. As the custodians who facilitated the development of this manuscript, we would like to extend our gratitude and appreciation for each of our dedicated authors and our valued peer reviewers who graciously invested their time, energies, wisdom and work into this project.

Firstly, we would like to thank our independent peer reviewers who invested a significant amount of time and effort to aid us in reviewing each chapter of this manuscript. Each of the 13 chapters was subjected to an independent, double-blind peer review process. Two to four independent expert reviewers were assigned to evaluate each chapter based on the focus and scope of its content. These reviewers aided in evaluating each manuscript in order to enhance its credibility, integrity and scientific quality. We would like to thank the following reviewers for investing their valuable time and expertise in enhancing the quality of each manuscript:

Dr Lara Roll:
Prof Ingrid Potgieter:
Dr Melissa du Plessis:
Dr Keeley Webb-Copridge:
Dr Eric Sinclair:
Dr Maartin Renkema:
Prof Leon de Beer:
Dr Johan van der Westhuizen:
Dr Kevin Fosnacht:
Dr Aljoscha Dreisörner:
Prof Claude-Hélène Mayer:
Svenja Frenzel
Prof Yulia Tyumeneva
Dr Buaphrao Raphiphatthana
Dr Sumari O' Neil
Dr Stefanie Richter
Prof Mae Hyang Hwang
Prof Sebastiaan Rothmann
Prof Reinard Tolken
Dr Yulia Kuzmina
Sophia Frick
Lynelle Coxen

Prof Marius Stander:	Prof Elrie Botha
Louise Engelbrecht:	Dr Arrianne Costantini
Prof Jesus Alfonso Datu:	Dr Daphne Pillay
Prof Arien Strasheim:	Dr Inge Hulshof
Prof Ederick Stander:	Dr Leander van der Meij
Prof Mark van Vuuren:	Dr Jeroen Meijerink
Dr Ad Kleingeld:	Dr Piet van Gool

Secondly, we want to express our gratitude to both Springer and Shinjini Chatterjee for their patience and support throughout this process, especially during the COVID-19 pandemic. We are truly grateful for the opportunity to contribute another manuscript to Springer's collection of scientific works.

Finally, we would like to thank Carol-Ann van der Berg for her valuable contributions to the technical editing of this book. We truly value her dedication, diligence and professionalism in finalizing this project.

Contents

Editors and Contributors

About the Editors

Llewellyn Ellardus van Zyl (PhD) holds an extraordinary professorship with the North-West University in South Africa and is employed as an assistant professor of work and organizational psychology with the University of Eindhoven in the Netherlands. He is also affiliated with the Department of Social Psychology at Goethe University in Germany and the Department of Human Resource Management at the University of Twente in the Netherlands. He holds a PhD in industrial psychology, an M.Com in industrial psychology (with honours), a B.Com (Hons) in industrial psychology (with honours), and a B.Com in behavioural sciences (with honours), all obtained at North-West University, South Africa. He is a respected academic, published author and talent management consultant specializing in positive psychological assessment and interventions. During the past decade, he has gained extensive experience in the development, implementation and evaluation of positive psychological interventions for multinational corporations spanning from the Netherlands and Saudi Arabia to South Africa. He has a passion for developing strengths-based, fit-for-purpose positive psychological interventions aimed at the optimization individuals' capability.

Chantal Olckers (PhD) is employed at the University of Pretoria in South Africa as an associate professor in the Department of Human Resource Management. She has completed a Doctorate in the field of human resource management, specializing in psychological ownership. Chantal is a respected researcher and published author of various scientific articles in peer-reviewed journals and chapters in international peer-reviewed books. She has presented several research papers at both national and international conferences. Chantal acted as one of the editors of two scholarly books published by Springer and is a Section Editor of both the *South African Journal of Human Resource Management* and the *South African Journal of Industrial Psychology*. She has extensive experience within the tertiary educational environment (as a lecturer and researcher), as well as within the private sector (as a consultant). Chantal is a registered psychologist (category: industrial) with the Health Professions

Council of South Africa and master human resource practitioner at the South African Board of People Practices (SABPP). Chantal is passionate about enhancing positive organizational behaviour and specifically psychological ownership.

Leoni van der Vaart completed her master's degrees in human resource management and industrial/organizational psychology and a joint PhD in the field of industrial/organizational psychology with KU Leuven (Belgium) and the North-West University (South Africa). She is a senior lecturer and researcher at the North-West University and has a passion for understanding employee/job seeker attitudes and behaviour from a motivational perspective. Leoni is an active researcher with publications in peer-reviewed journals and presentations at international conferences and has experience in the tertiary education environment, both as lecturer and researcher. She is a registered psychological counsellor (category: independent practitioner), a registered psychologist (category: organisational psychology) with the Health Professions Council of South Africa (HPCSA) and human resource professional (category: learning and development) with the South African Board of People Practices (SABPP).

Contributors

Andrea Ceschi Department of Human Sciences, University of Verona, Verona, Italy

Chen Chen Institution of Educational Psychology, School of Psychology, Nanjing Normal University, Nanjing, China

Arianna Costantini Department of Human Sciences, University of Verona, Verona, Italy

Stephan Dickert School of Business and Management, Queen Mary University of London, London, UK

Jesus Alfonso D. Datu Department of Special Education and Counselling, Integrated Centre for Well-Being (i-WELL), The Education University of Hong Kong, Hong Kong, China

Kevin Fosnacht Center for Postsecondary Research, Indiana University, Bloomington, IN, USA

Xinmei Gong Motivation and Social Development Lab, School of Psychology, Nanjing Normal University, Nanjing, China

Mae-Hyang Hwang Department of Education, Gyeongin National University of Education, Incheon, South Korea

Paul E. Jose Victoria University of Wellington, Wellington, New Zealand

Vrinda Kalia Department of Psychology, Miami University, Oxford, OH, USA

JeeEun Karin Nam Ewha Womans University's Graduate School of Education, Seoul, Republic of Korea

Eileen Koekemoer Department of Human Resource Management, University of Pretoria, Pretoria, South Africa

Yulia Kuzmina Institute of Education, National Research University Higher School of Economics, Moscow, Russia
Psychological Institute of Russian Academy of Education, Moscow, Russia

Jingguang Li College of Teacher Education, Dali University, Dali, China

Giorgia Malavasi Milano Cattolica University, Milano, Italy

Chantal Olckers Department of Human Resource Management, University of Pretoria, Pretoria, South Africa

Buaphrao Raphiphatthana Menzies School of Health Research, Charles Darwin University, Darwin, NT, Australia

Riccardo Sartori Department of Human Sciences, Verona University, Verona, Italy

Eric Patrick Sinclair Christel House Academy, Indianapolis, IN, USA

Michael C. Tynan Department of Psychology, Iowa State University, Ames, IA, USA

Yulia Tyumeneva National Research University Higher School of Economics, Moscow, Russia

Jana Patricia M. Valdez Division of Information Technology Studies, The University of Hong Kong, Hong Kong, China

Leoni van der Vaart Optentia Research Focus Area, North-West University, Vanderbijlpark, South Africa

Jessica van Wingerden Center of Excellence for Positive Organizational Psychology, Erasmus University Rotterdam, Rotterdam, the Netherlands

Llewellyn Ellardus van Zyl Human Performance Management, University of Universiteit Eindhoven, Eindhoven, the Netherlands

Song Wang Huaxi MR Research Center (HMRRC), West China Hospital, Sichuan University, Chengdu, China

Keeley Webb-Copridge Indiana University, Bloomington, IN, USA

Chapter 1
How Do Grit and Gratitude Relate to Flourishing? The Mediating Role of Emotion Regulation

Jana Patricia Millonado Valdez and Jesus Alfonso Daep Datu

Abstract Research suggests that grit and gratitude can protect individuals against the hazards of maladaptive outcomes such as suicidal ideation. However, there are scarce investigations on how such positive traits predict wellbeing and the mechanisms underpinning the link of such dispositions to desirable psychological functioning especially in non-Western contexts. Moreover, previous studies relied heavily on the two-factor model of grit in examining the link of grit to psychological outcomes. This research addresses these gaps through assessing the associations of gratitude and triarchic model of grit dimensions (i.e., *perseverance of effort, consistency of interests,* and *adaptability to situations*) with flourishing among 236 high school students in the Philippines. In addition, this study explored the mediating effects of emotion regulation strategies—cognitive reappraisal and expressive suppression—on the hypothesized link of gratitude and grit on psychological flourishing. Results showed that all dimensions of grit and gratitude were associated with higher levels of flourishing. Gratitude and grit dimensions were also positively correlated with both cognitive reappraisal and expressive suppression. Furthermore, bias-corrected bootstrapping analyses at 95% confidence interval based on 5000 bootstrapped resamples demonstrated that cognitive reappraisal mediated the link of gratitude, *perseverance of effort,* and *adaptability to situations* on flourishing. Findings suggest that cognitive reappraisal serves as a psychological mechanism underscoring the relationship of gratitude and grit to wellbeing. Implications of the results to extant grit theorizing and practical initiatives on developing positive characters are elucidated.

Keywords Filipino students · Flourishing · Gratitude · Triarchic model of grit

---

J. P. Millonado Valdez
Department of Management, Hong Kong Baptist University, Hong Kong SAR, China

J. A. Daep Datu (✉)
Department of Special Education and Counselling; Integrated Centre for Well-Being (i-WELL), The Education University of Hong Kong, Hong Kong SAR, China
e-mail: jadatu@eduhk.hk

L. E. van Zyl et al. (eds.), *Multidisciplinary Perspectives on Grit*,
https://doi.org/10.1007/978-3-030-57389-8_1

1.1 Introduction

Psychologists have highlighted the importance of non-cognitive skills such as social-emotional learning, character strengths, and compassion in fostering optimal psychological health in young children and adolescents. There is also an increasing recognition on the educational benefits associated with promoting happiness and positive traits among students in school contexts. Given the growing line of evidence about the beneficial consequences of positive traits on well-being outcomes, this study examines the roles of grit and gratitude in psychological flourishing in selected Filipino high school students.

Grit has been originally operationalized as individual's tendency to show passion and perseverance in achieving long-term goals (Duckworth, Peterson, Matthews, & Kelly, 2007). It has two dimensions namely: *perseverance of effort* (i.e., persisting in achieving ambitions despite the obstacles and difficulties associated with goal pursuit), and *consistency of interests* (i.e., espousing constant interest that can result in goal achievement). Duckworth et al. (2007) demonstrated that grit was linked to optimal academic, career, and performance outcomes.

Grit has been associated with elevated levels of life satisfaction (Clark & Malecki, 2019), school satisfaction (Clark & Malecki, 2019; Ivcevic & Brackett, 2014; Li, Lin, Zhao, Chen, & Wang, 2018), meaning in life (Datu, King, Valdez, & Eala, 2019; Kleiman, Adams, Kashdan, & Riskind, 2013), positive affect (Hill, Burrow, & Bronk, 2016; Li et al., 2018), mindfulness (Li et al., 2018), psychological wellbeing (Salles, Cohen, & Mueller, 2014; Vainio & Daukantaitė, 2015), and satisfaction with peer relationships (Lan & Moscardino, 2019). Moreover, grit was related to lower anxiety (Musumari et al., 2018), depression (Datu et al., 2019; Kleiman et al., 2013; Musumari et al., 2018; Sharkey et al., 2018), and suicidal tendencies (Kleiman et al., 2013). Yet, except for a few studies (Clark & Malecki, 2019; Datu, Yuen, & Chen, 2017, 2018b), previous investigations relied on the two-factor model of grit and its link to wellbeing.

Given that recent literature has criticized the theoretical validity of the two-factor model of grit due to its lack of replicability and problems with its *consistency of interests* dimension (Credé, 2018, 2019; Credé, Tynan, & Harms, 2017), we adopted the *triarchic model of grit* (Datu et al., 2017; Datu, Yuen, & Chen, 2018a) which conceptualizes grit as tendency to show *perseverance of effort, consistency of interests,* and a newly added dimension—*adaptability to situations*. Unlike *consistency, adaptability to situations* encompasses the capacity to modify cognitions, interests, actions, and values based on situational or contextual factors (Datu et al., 2017, 2018a). For instance, even though a student aspiring to become a professional singer had enrolled in a private voice lesson or tutorial for the past few years, his consistent poor performance in local singing competitions where he participated prompted him to shift his focus to playing guitar instead. Studies have shown that *adaptability* was related to increased efficacy in various domains like career exploration, talent development, and performance of academic activities (Datu et al., 2017).

Previous studies have recognized the importance of examining the simultaneous roles of gratitude and grit on wellbeing outcomes (Datu et al., 2019; Kleiman et al., 2013). However, these investigations solely concentrated on meaning in life as a mediator on the link of gratitude and grit to depression which may offer limited insights into other cognitive, affective, and motivational processes explaining why such multiple positive resources may be associated with optimal psychological functioning. Therefore, this research aims to explore the association of gratitude and triarchic model of grit (TMG) dimensions with psychological flourishing via the mediating function of emotion regulation strategies (i.e., cognitive reappraisal and expressive suppression) in selected Filipino high school students.

1.2 Gratitude and Well-Being

Gratitude is defined as "a generalized tendency to recognize and respond with grateful emotion to the roles of other people's benevolence in the positive experiences and outcomes that one obtains" (McCullough, Emmons, & Tsang, 2002, p. 112). It is a positive emotion that commonly results from appreciating the goodness in life, receiving gifts or acts of kindness, or experiencing any desirable event. Gratitude seems to be a prevalent emotion that can be observed in various situations. In fact, there has been numerous studies about the relationship between gratitude and various well-being outcomes.

Previous studies have shown that gratitude was consistently associated with several well-being outcomes such as happiness (Schnitker & Richardson, 2019; Witvliet, Richie, Root Luna, & Van Tongeren, 2019), positive affect (Froh, Kashdan, Ozimkowski, & Miller, 2009; Schnitker & Richardson, 2019), life satisfaction (Wood, Joseph, & Maltby, 2009), hope (Schnitker & Richardson, 2019; Witvliet et al., 2019), and meaning in life (Kleiman et al., 2013). Gratitude was also found to improve quality of sleep (Jackowska, Brown, Ronaldson, & Steptoe, 2016; Southwell & Gould, 2017), and cardiac coherence (Rash, Matsuba, & Prkachin, 2011). More importantly, gratitude has been found to be linked to subjective well-being across the lifespan (Chopik, Newton, Ryan, Kashdan, & Jarden, 2019). There is also growing body of evidence on how gratitude was related to decreased levels of aggression (Deng et al., 2019), anxiety (Flinchbaugh, Moore, Chang, & May, 2012), negative affect (Salces-Cubero, Ramírez-Fernández, & OrtegaMartínez, 2018), pain perception (Yu, Cai, Shen, Gao, & Zhou, 2016), depression (Flinchbaugh et al., 2012; Salces-Cubero et al., 2018), and suicidal risks (Kleiman et al., 2013; Rey, Quintana-Orts, Merida-Lopez, & Extremera, 2019).

Despite the consistent body of research showcasing the psychological benefits of gratitude, it appears that most of these studies focused on its relationship with subjective wellbeing, psychological well-being, and physical health. As Baumsteiger, Mangan, Bronk, and Bono (2019) have shared that "promoting gratitude is a viable route towards advancing human flourishing", it is essential to explore how gratitude tracks psychological flourishing, and pinpoint concrete psychological mechanisms underpinning the positive association of gratitude with optimal mental health outcomes.

1.3 Grit Dimensions and Well-Being

Existing studies have shown that dimensions of grit were differentially linked to various aspects of physical and psychological well-being. Thus far, there has been a relatively robust evidence correlating *perseverance of effort* to increased life satisfaction (Clark & Malecki, 2019; Datu et al., 2018b; Datu, Valdez, & King, 2016), meaning in life, interdependent happiness (Datu et al., 2018b), and optimal neurocognitive functioning (Moore et al., 2018). Perseverance was also negatively correlated to psychological distress (Datu et al., 2018b).

However, there is inconclusive evidence on how consistency of interests relates to well-being outcomes. On one hand, some investigations demonstrated that consistency was significantly associated with increased life satisfaction (Clark & Malecki, 2019), higher meaning in life, greater school satisfaction (Clark & Malecki, 2019), and lower perceived stress (Lee, 2017). On the other hand, other studies indicated that consistency was not significantly related to life satisfaction (Datu et al., 2016, 2018b), and positive affect (Datu et al., 2016, 2018b). Even a previous meta-analytic review (i.e., Credé et al., 2017) has shown that *consistency* was not considerably linked to optimal performance (i.e., academic achievement) outcomes which further exacerbates issues raised against the validity of the two-factor model of grit.

Importantly, few investigations have explored specific psychological mechanisms explaining why grit may be related to higher well-being outcomes. For example, mindfulness mediated the association of grit with happiness (Li et al., 2018). In addition, Jin and Kim (2017) have shown that grit was linked to greater subjective wellbeing due to the mediating role of basic needs satisfaction for competence and autonomy. Clearly, more studies are needed to generate evidence on precise social, cognitive, and emotional processes underscoring the complex link between grit and psychological wellbeing.

1.4 Theoretical Framework

In this research, we adopted the *conservation of resources theory* (Hobfoll, 2002; Hobfoll, Stevens, & Zalta, 2015), and *engine theory of wellbeing* (Jayawickreme, Forgeard, & Seligman, 2012) to rationalize the association of gratitude and grit with psychological flourishing. This section describes how and why positive psychological resources (i.e., gratitude and grit) may be linked to higher psychological wellbeing.

The *conservation of resources theory* (Hobfoll, 2002) argues that individuals experience stress when they are prone to lose valuable social, psychological, and physical resources. As they face challenging situations, they use such resources not only to combat stress but also to gain additional resources necessary for coping with future stressors. In addition, this model emphasizes the importance of continuously accumulating psychological resources in order to shield one against resources loss and optimize mental health (Hobfoll et al., 2015). If gaining resources serves as an essential mechanism to protect individuals against stressful events, it is likely that both gratitude and TMG dimensions may be associated with increased levels of psychological flourishing characterized by purpose in life, efficacy, self-esteem, and positive interpersonal relationships (Diener et al., 2009).

Furthermore, we anticipated that specific psychological resources like gratitude and TMG dimensions (i.e., *perseverance of effort* and *adaptability to situations*) will be linked to elevated levels of flourishing due to the mediating role of emotion regulation strategies (Gross & John, 2003). There are two broad types of emotion regulation namely: (a) cognitive reappraisal which encompasses reinterpreting an emotion-evoking scenario in order to change its meaning and emotional consequences; and (b) expressive suppression which involves attempting to hide or restrict showing of actual emotions felt after an emotion-eliciting event (Gross & John, 2003). Research has shown that cognitive reappraisal is a more adaptive form of emotion regulation approach (Gross, 1999; Gross & Barrett, 2011; Gross & John, 2003). Consistent with the *engine theory of well-being* (Jayawickreme et al., 2012), it is possible that positive intrinsic variables (i.e., gratitude and grit) may be related to well-being outcome (i.e., flourishing) due to the mediating role of process variables or internal subjective states that can affect individuals' actions or behaviors. In this study, we operationalized emotion regulation approaches as process variables as both cognitive reappraisal and expressive suppression are considered internal psychological states that directly impact on emotions and meanings associated with emotion-eliciting events.

Specifically, we proposed the following hypotheses in this study:

Hypothesis 1: Gratitude will positively predict flourishing.
Hypothesis 2: TMG dimensions (i.e., *perseverance* and *adaptability*) will positively predict flourishing.
Hypothesis 2a: *Perseverance* and *adaptability* positively predict flourishing.
Hypothesis 2b: *Consistency* will not predict flourishing.
Hypothesis 3: Gratitude will positively predict cognitive reappraisal.
Hypothesis 4: TMG dimensions (i.e., *perseverance* and *adaptability*) will positively predict cognitive reappraisal
Hypothesis 4a: *Perseverance* and *adaptability* will positively predict cognitive reappraisal.
Hypothesis 4b: *Consistency* will not predict cognitive reappraisal.
Hypothesis 5: Cognitive reappraisal will positively predict flourishing.
Hypothesis 6: Cognitive reappraisal will mediate the associations of gratitude and TMG dimensions (i.e., *perseverance* and *adaptability*) with flourishing.

We did not propose hypotheses on the associations of gratitude, grit, and flourishing with expressive suppression given the scarcity of research on how these variables relate to each other.

1.5 Methods

1.5.1 Participants and Procedures

The sample comprised 213 Filipino high school students from a public school in Quezon City, Philippines. These participants were recruited via convenience sampling approach which involved inviting classes that were available during data collection. Students were advised that they could freely withdraw to participate in the study without facing any consequences on their respective school marks. Students enrolled in public schools commonly cater for students from low-income families. The participants' ages ranged from 10 to 19 ($M_{age} = 15.43$, $SD_{age} = .84$). There were 101 girls and 112 boys who participated in this study.

1.5.2 Measures

Gratitude The 3-item Gratitude Questionnaire (Valdez & Chu, 2019) was used in this research given that criticisms were raised on the original 6-item Gratitude Questionnaire. Items were rated on a 6-point Likert scale (1 = *Strongly disagree*; 6 = *Strongly agree*). The Cronbach's alpha coefficient of this scale was .60. Prior studies also showed that this scale had relatively low reliability estimates especially in Filipino student samples (Datu, 2014; Datu & Mateo, 2015; Valdez & Chu, 2019).

Grit The 10-item Triarchic Model of Grit Scale (Datu et al., 2017) was utilized to measure perseverance, passion, and adaptability for long-term goals in the current sample. Items were rated on a 5-point Likert scale (1 = *Not like me at all*; 5 = *Very much like me*). The Cronbach's alpha coefficients of perseverance of effort, consistency of interests, and adaptability to situation subscales were .67, .50, and .70 respectively. Past studies showed that *consistency of interests* dimension had low reliability estimates in Filipino student samples (Datu et al., 2016, 2017).

Emotion Regulation The 10-item Emotion Regulation Scale (Gross & John, 2003) was used to assess two specific emotion regulation strategies namely: (a) cognitive reappraisal; and (b) expressive suppression. Items were marked on a 7-point Likert scale (1 = *Strongly disagree*; 7 = *Strongly agree*). The Cronbach's alpha coefficients of cognitive reappraisal and expressive suppression dimensions were .71 and .72 respectively.

Flourishing The 8-item Psychological Flourishing Scale (Diener et al., 2009) was used to assess the perceived sense of accomplishment in various areas of life like purpose in life, optimism, positive interpersonal relationship, and self-esteem. Items were rated on a 7-point Likert scale (1 = *Strongly disagree*; 7 = *Strongly agree*). The Cronbach's alpha coefficient of this scale was .84.

The English version of the abovementioned scales were used in this investigation given that English serves as one of the official mediums of instruction in Philippine secondary school educational system.

1.5.3 Procedures

The corresponding author sought the approval of the Human Research Ethics Committee of the Education University of Hong Kong to conduct this study. Next, his research assistant asked permission from the school principal of a government-funded high school to carry out data collection activity. Active consent forms were distributed to participants as well as their parents prior to actual survey administration. After successfully getting an approval to perform data collection in the said school, his research assistant administered the paper-and-pencil version of the survey to 4 classes. On the average, it took her around 15 min to administer the survey packet. All participants voluntarily agreed to participate in this study.

1.5.4 Data Analyses

Cronbach's alpha coefficients of each scale were calculated to provide reliability estimates of the questionnaires used in this research. Then, descriptive statistics like mean and standard deviation of demographic details, explanatory variables, and outcome variable were computed. Next, Pearson-r correlational coefficients were calculated to generate evidence on how explanatory and outcome variables were linked to each other. Then, bias-corrected bootstrapping mediation analysis at 95% confidence interval based on 5000 bootstrapped resamples was conducted to: (a) examine whether gratitude and TMG dimensions would predict flourishing; and (b) emotion regulation strategies like cognitive reappraisal and expressive suppression would mediate the link of gratitude and TMG dimensions to flourishing. These analyses were carried out using the 25th version of the Statistical Package for the Social Sciences.

1.6 Results

The results of reliability, descriptive statistical, and zero-order correlational analyses are shown in Table 1.1. A review of Cronbach's alpha coefficients showed that whereas emotion regulation approaches (i.e., cognitive reappraisal and expressive suppression) and flourishing had good reliabilities, gratitude and selected grit dimensions (i.e., *perseverance* and *consistency*) had relatively low reliability coefficients. Results of correlational analyses showed that gratitude and TMG dimensions were positively correlated with both emotion regulation strategies and flourishing. Both emotion regulation dimensions were positively correlated to flourishing.

Findings of multiple regression analyses are described in Table 1.2. Hypothesis 1 and Hypothesis 2 (i.e., Hypothesis 2a) were supported as gratitude ($\beta = .33$, $t = 4.76$, $p < .001$), perseverance of effort ($\beta = .40$, $t = 8.24$, $p < .001$), and adaptability to situations ($\beta = .37$, $t = 4.37$, $p < .001$) positively predicted flourishing. Hypothesis 2b was confirmed as consistency of interests did not predict flourishing, $\beta = .11$, $t = 1.35$, $p = .08$. Hypothesis 3 was supported as gratitude ($\beta = .33$, $t = 13.49$, $p < .001$) positively predicted flourishing. Corroborating Hypothesis 4a, perseverance of effort ($\beta = .38$, $t = 5.30$, $p < .001$), and adaptability to situations ($\beta = .55$, $t = 6.45$, $p < .001$) positively predicted cognitive reappraisal. Hypothesis 4b was not confirmed as consistency of interests positively predicted cognitive reappraisal, $\beta = .42$, $t = 5.17$, $p < .001$. Gratitude ($\beta = .33$, $t = 4.17$, $p < .001$), perseverance of effort ($\beta = .53$, $t = 6.14$, $p < .001$), consistency of interests ($\beta = .55$, $t = 5.52$, $p < .001$), and adaptability to situations ($\beta = .58$, $t = 5.69$, $p < .001$) positively predicted expressive suppression. Hypothesis 5 was confirmed given that cognitive reappraisal positively predicted flourishing in all hypothesized mediation models.

Table 1.1 Descriptive statistics and correlational analyses among TMG dimensions, gratitude, emotion regulation, and flourishing

				r						
	α	*M*	*SD*	1	2	3	4	5	6	7
1. Gratitude	.60	4.08	.67	–						
2. Perseverance of effort	.67	3.99	.69	.27***	–					
3. Consistency of interests	.50	3.75	.61	.15*	.43***	–				
4. Adaptability to situations	.70	4.02	.59	.35***	.49***	.34***	–			
5. Cognitive reappraisal	.71	5.58	.77	.28***	.34***	.34***	.41***	–		
6. Expressive suppression	.72	5.48	.93	.23***	.39***	.36***	.37***	.66***	–	
7. Flourishing	.84	5.67	.80	.41***	.49***	.27***	.45***	.51***	.45***	–

Note: * $p < .05$, ** $p < .01$, *** $p < .001$

Table 1.2 Standardized regression weights of the regression analyses

Types of paths	Standardized estimates		
Paths	β	SE	*t*
Direct effects			
Gratitude flourishing	.33***	.07	4.76
Perseverance flourishing	.40***	.07	8.24
Consistency flourishing	.11	.08	1.35
Adaptability flourishing	.37***	.09	4.37
Gratitude and grit dimensions predicting mediators			
Gratitude cognitive reappraisal	.33***	.08	13.49
Perseverance cognitive reappraisal	.38***	.07	5.30
Consistency cognitive reappraisal	.42***	.08	5.17
Adaptability cognitive reappraisal	.55***	.08	6.45
Gratitude expressive suppression	.33***	.09	3.48
Perseverance expressive suppression	.53**	.09	6.14
Consistency expressive suppression	.55***	.10	5.52
Adaptability expressive suppression	.58***	.10	5.69
Mediators predicting outcomes			
(Gratitude) cognitive reappraisal flourishing	.33***	.08	4.17
(Perseverance) cognitive reappraisal flourishing	.34***	.08	4.45
(Consistency) cognitive reappraisal flourishing	.38***	.09	4.61
(Adaptability) cognitive reappraisal flourishing	.31***	.08	3.88
(Gratitude) expressive suppression flourishing	.15*	.06	2.38
(Perseverance) expressive suppression flourishing	.09	.06	1.36
(Consistency) expressive suppression flourishing	.15*	.07	2.27
(Adaptability) expressive suppression flourishing	.13*	.07	2.03

Note: $^{*}p < .05$, $^{**}p < .01$, $^{***}p < .001$

Results of bias-corrected bootstrapping analysis at 95% confidence interval based on 5000 bootstrapped resamples demonstrated that cognitive reappraisal mediated the link of gratitude, perseverance of effort, and adaptability to situations to flourishing which corroborated Hypothesis 6. Yet, this emotion regulation strategy mediated the association of consistency with flourishing. Expressive suppression did not mediate the relations of gratitude and TMG dimensions to the said outcome variable. Results of bootstrap analyses were reported in Table 1.3.

Effect sizes were reported based on the coefficient of determination or R-squared coefficients in each hypothesized regression model. The first model revealed that gratitude and emotion regulation approaches to flourishing accounted for 16.51% of the variance in the said outcome variable. Perseverance and emotion regulation dimensions contribute to 37.99% of the changes in psychological flourishing. Further, consistency and emotion regulation dimensions explained 28.82% of the changes in the outcome variable. Lastly, combination of adaptability and emotion regulation dimensions accounted for 34.20% of the variance in flourishing.

Table 1.3 Results of indirect effects of gratitude and TMG dimensions on flourishing via emotion regulation approaches

	Cognitive reappraisals		Expressive suppression	
	Indirect effects	95% CI	Indirect effects	95% CI
Gratitude	.11**	.05, .20	.05	.01, .13
Perseverance of effort	.13***	.06, .24	.05	−.02, .14
Consistency of interest	.17***	.08, .28	.08	−.001, .19
Adaptability to situations	.17***	.08, .29	.08	−.01, .19

Note: ** *p < .01, ****; p < .001*

1.7 Discussion

Existing literature has mostly paid attention to the roles that the two-factor model of grit (Duckworth et al., 2007), and gratitude play in students' mental health outcomes (Datu et al., 2019; Kleiman et al., 2013). However, this model of grit has received considerable criticisms in previous research (Credé, 2018, 2019; Credé et al., 2017) which points to the significance of exploring how alternative grit model predicts psychological wellbeing. Against this backdrop, this research explores the association of TMG dimensions and gratitude with psychological flourishing in selected Filipino high school students. It also assesses the mediating effects of emotion regulation strategies (i.e., cognitive reappraisal and expressive suppression) on the link of both traits to flourishing.

Our research demonstrated that gratitude was linked to increased psychological flourishing and cognitive reappraisal. This result corroborates previous evidence showing how gratitude relates to well-being outcomes (Froh et al., 2009; Kleiman et al., 2013; Schnitker & Richardson, 2019; Witvliet et al., 2019; Wood et al., 2009). To our knowledge, it is the first investigation of its kind to demonstrate the association of gratitude with flourishing and adaptive emotion regulation technique especially in a collectivist setting (i.e., Philippines).

Furthermore, our study revealed that *perseverance of effort* was associated with elevated levels of psychological flourishing which aligned well with what had been found in previous research regarding the positive correlation of *perseverance* to various dimensions of psychological well-being (Clark & Malecki, 2019; Datu et al., 2016, 2018b). It is likely that *perseverance* may relate to social-psychological prosperity as the *invest-and-accrue model of conscientiousness* (Hill & Jackson, 2016) argues that individuals with increased tendencies to show sustained diligence and persistence may prioritize performing actions that result in domain-specific success. As they achieve success in specific domains of life through espousing *perseverance*, they might experience higher levels of psychological wellbeing.

In addition, *adaptability to situations* was related to increased psychological flourishing which corroborated previous research on the positive correlation of this TMG dimension with positive student outcomes (Datu et al., 2017, 2018b). One of the potential reasons accounting for the significant associations of *adaptability to situations* with adaptive emotion regulation strategies and psychological flourishing involves the salience of socially-oriented ambitions in collectivist settings. Further, as collectivist societies (i.e., Philippines) tend to reward calibrating actions or behaviors based on what is needed in various situations (Suh, 2007), it is likely that individuals in such contexts may change their goals contingent on contextual needs.

However, the pattern of association between *consistency of interests* and flourishing was more complex than expected. Whereas *consistency* did not have direct effects on flourishing which corroborated previous studies on lack of relationship between consistency and well-being (Datu et al., 2016, 2018b), result showed that this grit dimension had indirect and positive link to flourishing via the mediator—cognitive reappraisal. This indicates that maintaining consistent set of interests over time may be associated with increased psychological well-being if this tendency provides opportunities to reflect on alternative meanings of emotion-evoking situations and consequently modify emotional responses.

Consistent with our theoretical prediction, cognitive reappraisal was related to increased psychological flourishing. Our result corroborated previous research findings on the beneficial role of adopting cognitive reappraisal when managing emotional reactions (Gross, 1999; Gross & Barrett, 2011; Gross & John, 2003). It is possible that cognitive reappraisal may be associated with greater flourishing as calibrating interpretations of specific emotional events can result in more positive emotional reactions and lesser negative emotional consequences (Gross, 1999, 2002).

Whereas existing literature has allured to the downside of using expressive suppression (Gross, 1999, 2002; Gross & Barrett, 2011; Lu, Tsai, Chu, & Xie, 2018), our study showed that this emotion regulation strategy was positively correlated to flourishing. There is a reason to believe that this emotion regulation technique may not be considered maladaptive in non-Western societies given the evidence on the non-significant or attenuated impacts of this emotion regulation strategy in non-Western samples like Vietnamese Americans (Tsai, Lau, Nguyen, Ngo, & Bahr, 2017). In Asian societies where upholding smooth interpersonal relationships is highly encouraged, directly hiding or inhibiting negative emotional reactions may prevent relational conflicts.

The most important theoretical contribution of our research points to the mediating role of cognitive reappraisal on the link of gratitude, *perseverance*, and *adaptability* to psychological flourishing. Our findings suggest that espousing a sense of gratefulness as well as persistence and adaptability for long-term goals may be related to elevated levels of cognitive reappraisal or capacity to reinterpret meanings of emotional events. In turn, the increased cognitive reappraisal may be associated with higher intensity of psychological flourishing. These results align with the fundamental tenets of *conservation of resources theory* (Hobfoll, 2002) which emphasizes the benefits of accumulating multiple psychological resources to combat the maladaptive effects of variety of stressors in one's life.

However, our study has a few limitations. First, as we used a correlational design, it is not possible to clearly draw causal inferences from the findings of this study.

This shortcoming can be addressed through conducting longitudinal, and experimental research approaches. Second, our reliance on self-reported measures of gratitude, grit, emotion regulation, and flourishing may increase the possibility of social desirability bias. The Cronbach's alpha coefficients of gratitude and TMG's consistency subscales were also low so caution should be observed when interpreting the findings of this study. Future studies can improve this methodological flaw through using alternative techniques in measuring explanatory and outcome variables. Third, we only recruited our sample from a government secondary school in the Philippines so the results of our study may not be generalizable in other non-Western settings.

Nonetheless, our research has implications for the existing grit literature. Although previous studies have shown that grit matters for subjective well-being and meaning in life (Datu et al., 2016, 2018b, 2019; Hill et al., 2016; Jin & Kim, 2017; Kleiman et al., 2013), these studies did not pay attention to how grit relates to other models of psychological well-being. Our study builds on this line of evidence through showing that TMG dimensions (i.e., *perseverance* and *adaptability*) were related to increased psychological flourishing in selected Filipino high school students. Further, this study is the first to demonstrate the mediating role of emotion regulation approaches on the association between TMG dimensions and flourishing. Indeed, results of this study might offer better understanding on the complex psychological mechanisms underlying the complex link of grit to well-being and mental health functioning.

Our research has practical implications. School psychologists and guidance counselors are encouraged to design mental health programs that harness the power of gratitude, *perseverance,* and *adaptability*. School psychologists and teachers can also collaborate on creating low-intensity psychological interventions that aim to cultivate students' capacity to effectively manage their emotions especially in challenging times. For instance, teachers of moral or values education can design diary or journal activities which may require students to identify: (a) undesirable situations they faced throughout the week; (b) their immediate thoughts or interpretations of such experiences; (c) immediate emotional reactions; (d) alternative interpretations that may reduce negative emotional reactions; and (e) emotional consequences of alternative thoughts. In general, findings indirectly point to the psychological rewards associated with cultivating non-cognitive skills in children and adolescents.

Acknowledgements This research was funded by the Internal Research Grant (Grant # RG 90/2017-2018R) from The Education University of Hong Kong awarded to the second author.

References

Baumsteiger, R., Mangan, S., Bronk, K. C., & Bono, G. (2019). An integrative intervention for cultivating gratitude among adolescents and young adults. *Journal of Positive Psychology, 14* (6), 807–819. https://doi.org/10.1080/17439760.2019.1579356.

Chopik, W. J., Newton, N. J., Ryan, L. H., Kashdan, T. B., & Jarden, A. J. (2019). Gratitude across the lifespan: Age differences and links to subjective well-being. *Journal of Positive Psychology, 14*(3), 292–302. https://doi.org/10.1080/17439760.2017.1414296.

Clark, K. N., & Malecki, C. K. (2019). Academic grit scale: Psychometric properties and associations with achievement and life satisfaction. *Journal of School Psychology, 72*, 49–66. https://doi.org/10.1016/j.jsp.2018.12.001.

Credé, M. (2018). What shall we do about grit? A critical review of what we know and what we don't know. *Educational Researcher, 47*, 606–611. https://doi.org/10.3102/0013189X18801322.

Credé, M. (2019). Total grit score does not represent perseverance. *Proceedings of the National Academy of Sciences of the United States of America, 116*, 3941. https://doi.org/10.1073/pnas.1816934116.

Credé, M., Tynan, M. C., & Harms, P. D. (2017). Much ado about grit: A meta-analytic synthesis of the grit literature. *Journal of Personality and Social Psychology, 113*, 492–511. https://doi.org/10.1037/pspp0000102.

Datu, J. A. D. (2014). Forgiveness, gratitude, and subjective wellbeing among Filipino adolescents. *International Journal for the Advancement of Counseling, 36*, 262–273. https://psycnet.apa.org/doi/10.1007/s10447-013-9205-9.

Datu, J. A. D., King, R. B., Valdez, J. P. M., & Eala, M. S. (2019). Grit is associated with lower depression via meaning in life among Filipino high school students. *Youth & Society, 51*, 865–876. https://doi.org/10.1177/0044118X18760402.

Datu, J. A. D., & Mateo, N. J. (2015). Gratitude and life satisfaction among Filipino adolescents: The mediating role of meaning in life. *International Journal for the Advancement of Counseling, 37*, 198–206. https://psycnet.apa.org/doi/10.1007/s10447-015-9238-3.

Datu, J. A. D., Valdez, J. P. M., & King, R. B. (2016). Perseverance counts but consistency does not! Validating the short-grit scale in a collectivist setting. *Current Psychology, 35*, 121–130. https://doi.org/10.1007/s12144-015-9374-2.

Datu, J. A. D., Yuen, M., & Chen, G. (2017). Development and validation of the triarchic model of grit scale (TMGS): Evidence from Filipino undergraduate students. *Personality and Individual Differences, 114*, 198–205. https://doi.org/10.1016/j.paid.2017.04.012.

Datu, J. A. D., Yuen, M., & Chen, G. (2018a). Exploring determination for long-term goals in a collectivist context: A qualitative study. *Current Psychology, 37*, 263–271. https://doi.org/10.1007/s12144-016-9509-0.

Datu, J. A. D., Yuen, M., & Chen, G. (2018b). The triarchic model of grit is linked to academic success and well-being among Filipino high school students. *School Psychology Quarterly, 33*, 428–438. https://doi.org/10.1037/spq0000234.

Deng, Y., Xiang, R., Zhu, Y., Li, Y., Yu, S., & Liu, X. (2019). Counting blessings and sharing gratitude in a Chinese prisoner sample: Effects of gratitude-based interventions on subjective Well-being and aggression. *Journal of Positive Psychology, 14*(3), 303–311. https://doi.org/10.1080/17439760.2018.1460687.

Diener, E., Wirtz, D., Tov, W., Kim-Prieto, C., Choi, D., Oishi, S., & Biswas-Diener, R. (2009). New measures of well-being: Flourishing and positive and negative feelings. *Social Indicators Research, 39*, 247–266. https://doi.org/10.1007/978-90-481-2354-4_12.

Duckworth, A. L., Peterson, C., Matthews, M. D., & Kelly, D. R. (2007). Grit: Perseverance and passion for long-term goals. *Journal of Personality and Social Psychology, 92*, 1087–1101. https://doi.org/10.1037/0022-3514.92.6.1087.

Flinchbaugh, C. L., Moore, E. W. G., Chang, Y. K., & May, D. R. (2012). Student well-being interventions: The effects of stress-management techniques and gratitude journaling in the management education classroom. *Journal of Management Education, 36*(2), 191–219. https://doi.org/10.1177/2F1052562911430062.

Froh, J. J., Kashdan, T. B., Ozimkowski, K. M., & Miller, N. (2009). Who benefits most from a gratitude intervention in children and adolescents? Examining positive affect as a moderator. *Journal of Positive Psychology, 4*, 408–422. https://doi.org/10.1080/17439760902992464.

Gross, J. J. (1999). Emotion regulation: Past, present, future. *Cognition and Emotion, 13*, 551–573. https://doi.org/10.1080/026999399379186.

Gross, J. J. (2002). Emotion regulation: Affective, cognitive, and social consequences. *Psychophysiology, 39*, 281–291. https://doi.org/10.1017/S0048577201393198.

Gross, J. J., & Barrett, L. F. (2011). Emotion generation and emotion regulation: One or two depends on your point of view. *Emotion Review, 3*, 8–16. https://doi.org/10.1177/1754073910380974.

Gross, J. J., & John, O. P. (2003). Individual differences in two emotion regulation processes: Implications for affect, relationships, and well-being. *Journal of Personality and Social Psychology, 85*, 348–362. https://doi.org/10.1037/0022-3514.85.2.348.

Hill, P. L., Burrow, A. L., & Bronk, K. C. (2016). Persevering with positivity and purpose: An examination of purpose commitment and positive affect as predictors of grit. *Journal of Happiness Studies, 17*, 257–269. https://doi.org/10.1007/s10902-014-9593-5.

Hill, P. L., & Jackson, J. J. (2016). The invest-and-accrue model of conscientiousness. *Review of General Psychology, 20*, 141–154. https://doi.org/10.1037/gpr0000065.

Hobfoll, S. E. (2002). Social and psychological resources and adaptation. *Review of General Psychology, 6*, 307–324. https://doi.org/10.1037/1089-2680.6.4.307.

Hobfoll, S. E., Stevens, N. R., & Zalta, A. K. (2015). Expanding the science of resilience: Conserving resources in the aid of adaptation. *Psychological Inquiry, 26*, 174–180. https://doi.org/10.1080/1047840X.2015.1002377.

Ivcevic, Z., & Brackett, M. (2014). Predicting school success: Comparing conscientiousness, grit, and emotion regulation ability. *Journal of Research in Personality, 52*, 29–36. https://doi.org/10.1016/j.jrp.2014.06.005.

Jackowska, M., Brown, J., Ronaldson, A., & Steptoe, A. (2016). The impact of a brief gratitude intervention on subjective well-being, biology and sleep. *Journal of Health Psychology, 21*(10), 2207–2217. https://doi.org/10.1177/1359105315572455.

Jayawickreme, E., Forgeard, M., & Seligman, M. (2012). The engine of well-being. *Review of General Psychology, 16*, 327–342. https://doi.org/10.1037/a0027990.

Jin, B., & Kim, J. (2017). Grit, basic needs satisfaction, and subjective well-being. *Journal of Individual Differences, 38*, 29–35. https://doi.org/10.1027/1614-0001/a000219.

Kleiman, E. M., Adams, L. M., Kashdan, T. B., & Riskind, J. H. (2013). Gratitude and grit indirectly reduce risk of suicidal ideations by enhancing meaning in life: Evidence for a mediated moderation model. *Journal of Research in Personality, 47*, 539–546. https://doi.org/10.1016/j.jrp.2013.04.007.

Lan, X., & Moscardino, U. (2019). Direct and interactive effects of perceived teacher-student relationship and grit on student wellbeing among stay-behind early adolescents in urban China. *Learning and Individual Differences, 69*, 129–137. https://doi.org/10.1016/j.lindif.2018.12.003.

Lee, W. W. S. (2017). Predicting community college students' psychological stress with grit and perception of failure. *Journal of Adolescence, 60*, 148–152. https://doi.org/10.1016/j.adolescence.2017.08.006.

Li, J., Lin, L., Zhao, Y., Chen, J., & Wang, S. (2018). Grittier Chinese adolescents are happier: The mediating role of mindfulness. *Personality and Individual Differences, 131*, 232–237. https://doi.org/10.1016/j.paid.2018.05.007.

Lu, Q., Tsai, W., Chu, Q., & Xie, J. (2018). Is emotion suppression harmful for Chinese American breast cancer survivors? *Journal of Psychosomatic Research, 109*, 51–56. https://doi.org/10.1016/j.jpsychores.2018.03.171.

McCullough, M. E., Emmons, R. A., & Tsang, J. (2002). The grateful disposition conceptual and empirical topography. *Journal of Personality and Social Psychology, 82*, 112–127. https://doi.org/10.1037/0022-3514.82.1.112.

Moore, R. C., Hussain, M. A., Watson, C. W. M., Fazeli, P. L., Marquine, M. J., Yarns, B. C., Jeste, D. V., & Moore, D. J. (2018). Grit and ambition are associated with better neurocognitive and everyday functioning among adults living with HIV. *AIDS and Behavior, 22*, 3214–3225. https://doi.org/10.1007/s10461-018-2061-1.

Musumari, P. M., Tangmunkongvorakul, A., Srithanaviboonchai, K., Techasrivichien, T., Suguimoto, S. P., Ono-Kihara, M., et al. (2018). Grit is associated with lower level of depression and anxiety among university students in Chiang Mai, Thailand: A cross-sectional study. *PLoS One, 13*(12), e0209121. https://doi.org/10.1371/journal.pone.0209121.

Rash, J. A., Matsuba, M. K., & Prkachin, K. M. (2011). Gratitude and well-being: Who benefits the most from a gratitude intervention? *Applied Psychology: Health and Well-being, 3*(3), 350–369. https://doi.org/10.1111/j.1758-0854.2011.01058.x.

Rey, L., Quintana-Orts, C., Merida-Lopez, S., & Extremera, N. (2019). Being bullied at school: Gratitude as potential protective factor for suicide risk in adolescents. *Frontiers in Psychology, 10*, 62. https://doi.org/10.3389/fpsyg.2019.00662.

Salces-Cubero, I. M., Ramírez-Fernández, E., & OrtegaMartínez, A. R. (2018). Strengths in older adults: Differential effect of savoring, gratitude and optimism on well-being. *Aging & Mental Health, 23*(8), 1017–1024. https://doi.org/10.1080/13607863.2018.1471585.

Salles, A., Cohen, G. L., & Mueller, C. M. (2014). The relationship between grit and resident well-being. *American Journal of Surgery, 207*, 251–254. https://doi.org/10.1016/j.amjsurg.2013.09.006.

Schnitker, S. A., & Richardson, K. L. (2019). Framing gratitude journaling as prayer amplifies its hedonic and eudaimonic well-being, but not health, benefits. *Journal of Positive Psychology, 14*(4), 427–439. https://doi.org/10.1080/17439760.2018.1460690.

Sharkey, C. M., Bakula, D. M., Baraldi, A. N., Perez, M. N., Suorsa, K. I., Chaney, J. M., & Mullins, L. L. (2018). Grit, illness-related distress, and psychosocial outcomes in college students with a chronic medical condition: A path analysis. *Journal of Pediatric Psychology, 43*, 552–560. https://doi.org/10.1093/jpepsy/jsx145.

Southwell, S., & Gould, E. (2017). A randomized wait list controlled pre-post-follow-up trial of a gratitude diary with a distressed sample. *Journal of Positive Psychology, 12*(6), 579–593. https://doi.org/10.1080/17439760.2016.1221127.

Suh, E. M. (2007). Downsides of an overly context-sensitive self: Implications from the culture and subjective well-being research. *Journal of Personality, 75*, 1321–1343. https://doi.org/10.1111/j.1467-6494.2007.00477.x.

Tsai, W., Lau, A. S., Nguyen, J., Ngo, V., & Bahr, W. (2017). Cultural differences in the reciprocal relations between emotion suppression coping, depressive symptoms and interpersonal functioning among adolescents. *Journal of Abnormal Child Psychology, 45*, 657–669. https://doi.org/10.1007/s10802-016-0192-2.

Vainio, M. M., & Daukantaitė, D. (2015). Grit and different aspects of well-being: Direct and indirect relationships via sense of coherence and authenticity. *Journal of Happiness Studies, 17*, 1–29. https://doi.org/10.1007/s10902-015-9688-7.

Valdez, J. P. M., & Chu, S. K. W. (2019). Examining the psychometric validity of the five-item gratitude questionnaire: An item response theory approach. *Journal of Psychoeducational Assessment*. https://doi.org/10.1177/0734282918816542.

Witvliet, C. V. O., Richie, F. J., Root Luna, L. M., & Van Tongeren, D. R. (2019). Gratitude predicts hope and happiness: A two-study assessment of traits and states. *Journal of Positive Psychology, 14*(3), 271–282. https://doi.org/10.1080/17439760.2018.1424924.

Wood, A. M., Joseph, S., & Maltby, J. (2009). Gratitude predicts psychological well-being above the big five facets. *Personality and Individual Differences, 45*, 49–54. https://doi.org/10.1016/j.paid.2008.11.012.

Yu, H., Cai, Q., Shen, B., Gao, X., & Zhou, X. (2016). Neural substrates and social consequences of interpersonal gratitude: Intention matters. *Emotion, 17*(4), 589–601. https://doi.org/10.1037/emo0000258.

Jana Patricia Millonado Valdez is a part-time Lecturer in the Department of Management of Hong Kong Baptist University. Broadly speaking, she is a gratitude scientist specializing on interventions that cultivate grateful disposition and emotions among student populations. She also explores how technological platforms can promote well-being and academic success.

Jesus Alfonso Daep Datu is an Assistant Professor in the Department of Special Education and Counselling at The Education University of Hong Kong. He is also an affiliated researcher in the Integrated Centre for Well-being (I-WELL) in the same university. He is a well-being scientist with expertise in *positive psychology* and *positive education*. Currently, he is an Associate Editor of *Journal of Happiness Studies, School Psychology International*, and *International Journal of Disability, Development, and Education*. He is also on the editorial boards of *School Psychology* (formerly *School Psychology Quarterly*), *International Journal of Applied Positive Psychology, Current Psychology*, and *Educational Psychology: An International Journal of Experimental Educational Psychology*.

Chapter 2
A "GRRR" Goal Orientation Process-Model: Workplace Long-Term Relationships Among Grit, Resilience and Recovery

Andrea Ceschi, Francesco Tommasi, Arianna Costantini, Giorgia Malavasi, Stephan Dickert, and Riccardo Sartori

Abstract The spark that ignites passion, tenacity and perseverance is defined as Grit. It encourages individuals to achieve long-term professional goals, especially when they become challenging. Over time, workers develop the main coping ability for reacting quickly to challenging situations: Workplace Resilience is a learnable skill that helps individuals to rebuild the personal resources needed for achieving long-term goals through Recovery strategies. These construct-relationships (i.e., Grit → Resilience → Recovery) are analyzed in the present contribution, with the aim of testing a model named "GRRR", for the better understanding of workplace goal orientation processes. Model testing is based on a three-waves longitudinal data collection (12 months) in which a sample of 582 workers from five Italian companies have been surveyed. Results reveal a mediated relationship among these constructs and a progressive causal enhancement over time. The quasi-trait Grit predicts the development of Resilience, which in turn predicts the development of Recovery strategies. Results and contributions to the scientific literature are discussed in both the frameworks of WOP Psychology and the Personality development paradigm. Practical implications suggest strategies of interventions for enhancing goal orientation through the GRRR process-model.

Keywords Grit · Resilience · Recovery · Goal orientation

A. Ceschi (✉) · F. Tommasi · A. Costantini · G. Malavasi · R. Sartori
Department of Human Sciences, University of Verona, Verona, Italy
e-mail: andrea.ceschi@univr.it

S. Dickert
School of Business and Management, Queen Mary University of London, London, UK

L. E. van Zyl et al. (eds.), *Multidisciplinary Perspectives on Grit*,
https://doi.org/10.1007/978-3-030-57389-8_2

2.1 Introduction

This chapter aims to test the presence of a significant and positive relationship between three psychological constructs: grit, resilience and recovery (abbreviated as "GRRR"). Theoretically, these constructs should relate to each other because they can trigger similar psychological processes, namely goal orientation, preservation of well-being, and managing one's own energies. This investigation finds a suitable application in the workplace domain, considering the extensive ability to manage resources and tackling intensive job demands is vital for the employee's well-being and performance. The study of these energetic processes is not new in the work psychology domain, as it has been studied for centuries. Galton (1869) aimed to collect information on upcoming statesmen, scientists, poets, musicians, and other professionals to prove that talent alone was not enough to reach professional success. The characteristics of efficient people, according to Galton, were enthusiastically skilled individuals who worked hard to reach their long-term goals. Likewise, more than a century later, Feldhusen (1995) concluded that holding IQ constant, the traits that in childhood predicted professional lifetime achievement were: persistence of motive and effort, confidence in abilities and great strength of character. In the twenty-first Century, Galton's (1869) and Feldhusen's (1995) perspective on aptitude is defined as grit, the first of the constructs studied in the present study.

Grit is defined by levels of passion and perseverance toward goals (Duckworth, Quinn, & Seligman, 2009). Grit enhances the significance given to achievements and redefines the extent of efforts that people are willing to accept to reach their goals. Gritty people not only display more stamina in a particular task at a given time, but they do it with permanent strength over the years in seeking their long-term goals (Duckworth et al., 2016). Several studies in the literature show how gritty individuals accomplish—and help others to reach—high achievements at work and in training (Eskreis-Winkler, Duckworth, Shulman, & Beal, 2014). Indeed, grit is a pipeline energetic construct: it has been shown for instance how gritty professors promote the better educational results of their students, by improving students' performance measured after the end of the school year (Duckworth et al., 2009). When a task becomes challenging, gritty individuals push themselves and others to achieve goals, since they considered them worth it. Gritty people do not just outperform because they invest more effort in their work or training, they actually can persevere in tedious and frustrating behaviors (Duckworth et al., 2011). Grit is also associated with psychological regulation processes. By aligning actions and intentions for achieving one's targets, gritty people able to better manage their resources in the long run (Eskreis-Winkler et al., 2014). Such a goal orientation inclination together with the capacity to regulate one's own psychological capital allows the gritty individual to cope with more challenging and tough situations (Ceschi, Sartori, Dickert, & Costantini, 2016).

Successfully coping with these situations is related to the construct of resilience itself, which is the second dimension considered in the GRRR model. Resilience is defined as a successful adaptation despite everyday adversities (Rutter, 1985). It concerns the ability to not succumb to negative events and to continue developing oneself, even after a traumatic event. Etymologically, resilience comes from the Latin word *Resalio*, which means "to spring back". Resilience is defined as the process of adapting well in the face of a psychopathological event, trauma, and tragedy (Joyce et al., 2018). Indeed, the first development of the construct comes from clinical psychology and is associated with reactions to any significant sources of stress, such as health problems or workplace stressors (and finally extended to others psychological domains like I/O psychology). Before finding an application in the psychological domain, the term resilience has been used by the metallurgical sector, indicating the ability of a metal to withstand opposing forces, such as compression or traction. Also, in biology, it represents the ability to self-repair after damage; while in ecology, the more an ecosystem has variability in environmental factors, the more the species that belong to it have a high levels of resilience (Newman, 2005).

Although resilient individuals are able to cope with difficulties, this does not mean that they are immune to the consequences of situations. On the contrary, a resilient person can be deeply touched by a traumatic event and often experience deleterious symptoms, however, this person still carries on with the important aspects of life (Southwick & Charney, 2018). This person does so by developing coping strategies and cognitive reframing processes to give meaning and significance to such events. According to Anthony (1987), it is wrong to reduce the phenomenon to invulnerability, which is associated with the resistance to negative events and paralysis of the subject. The author claims that the construct of "resilience" must be associated with softness, while "resistant" individuals face stressful situations without giving up, resilient individuals are able to adapt better. Consequently, compared to resilient individuals, resistant people will be more exposed to stress and longer recovery times.

In summary, resilient individuals who have an adequate repertoire of resources to deal with life events and the ability to recover from the challenges that they encounter tend to be increasingly flexible and adaptable, qualities that are essential for success (Hiebert, 2006). In the organizational domain, resilience has been applied to the study of those occupational groups more at risk of suffering high stress and who usually experience acute trauma. These populations include firefighters (Freedman, 2004), police officers (Paton & Burke, 2007), disaster relief personnel (Kendra & Wachtendorf, 2003), nurses (Jackson, 2008), and also military personnel (Bowles & Bates, 2010). In the specific case of nurses, resilience has been shown to be fundamental in daily work, because of stressors that a job dedicated to assisting other people entails (Tusaie & Dyer, 2004). Furthermore, resilience plays an even more important role in allowing these health workers to survive and develop within very demanding work situations. Especially for people who go through traumatic experiences in the workplace, primary prevention interventions are needed to build resilience (Tusaie & Dyer, 2004). However, it should be noted that even in circumstances where individuals are subjected to less acute (but more persistent) forms of stress, deleterious consequences, such has cardiovascular complications or eating disorders pathologies may arise (Vanhove, Herian, Perez, Harms, & Lester, 2016).

Therefore, the time of exposure of workers to stressors has to be considered an important factor (Britt, Shen, Sinclair, Grossman, & Klieger, 2016). Although the likelihood of developing burnout increases if stress is experienced at high levels for a long time, resilient individuals usually succeed in overcoming stressors. They are able to interpret situations differently compared to less resilient individuals, which allows them to experience stressful events as motivating and to elicit a sense of personal satisfaction and fulfillment (Finlay-Jones, 2014).

In light of this, the application of grit implies an inclination toward resilience and going the extra mile implies the ability to react positively to difficult and challenging situations. One who is able to cope better with the shocks caused by stressors will also be more motivated to achieve long-term goals (Perkins-Gough, 2013). These two constructs were examined by Incantalupo-Kuhner (2015), who analyzed the role of such dispositions in relation to workplace outcomes. Results suggested a strong causal and positive relationship among the two constructs (i.e., grit and resilience), but with no overlap among them. Moreover, grit and resilience, despite appearing synonymous, are distinguished in the literature because "*grit is not just having resilience in the face of failure, but having deep commitments that you remain loyal to over many years*" (Perkins-Gough, 2013, p. 15).

Finally, in the "GRRR" relationship the last letter applies to recovery strategies. The relationship between resilience and recovery is relatively robust and has been examined for decades. Resilience is likely to help the individual to rebuild the personal resources needed for achieving long-term goals through recovery strategies. Recovery can be defined as a mechanism by which the strain decreases and the functioning of the individual returns to the pre-stressor level (Sonnentag, 2001). Two theoretical models have addressed the theme of recovery, emphasizing the importance of this process in individual well-being as well as health and in countering the negative effects of a difficult work situation. The Effort-Recovery model suggests that work performance involves the development of (negative) emotional, behavioral and cognitive reactions (Meijman, Mulder, Drenth, Thierry, & de Wolff, 1998). Usually these responses are reversible, so that, when a subject is no longer exposed to work demands, his/her psychobiological system can return to the optimal level and recovery begins. However, if the subject remains exposed to job demands even after working hours, recovery cannot take place and fatigue levels remain high. In this way, the worker will start the next day having to apply a compensatory effort, in order to sustain performance. On the contrary, according to the Resource Conservation Theory (Meijman et al., 1998), people struggle to obtain, preserve and protect their resources, which are composed of objects, personal characteristics, and energies useful to the individual. To recover resources, it is necessary to engage in recreational activities, which allow to "recharge" and increase self-esteem. While the Effort-Recovery model argues that moving away from job demands can favor the recovery process, Resource Conservation Theory supports the idea that, in leisure time, the subject can recover lost or threatened resources, through the investment of new resources. However, according to both perspectives, in order for the recovery process to take place it is necessary to move mentally away from one's employment (Sonnentag, 2001). Typically, the best recovery experiences occur during breaks from the workplace (Trougakos, Beal, Green, & Weiss, 2008), free evenings (Rook & Zijlstra, 2006), weekends (Fritz & Sonnentag, 2005) or on vacation (Westman & Eden, 1997).

In conclusion, to detach from work and recover energy, it is important for people to have enough time to recover in order to rebuild their energy. On the other hand, some individual inclinations might boost such processes. Recent research by Hearne (2017) has investigated the causal relationship of individual resilience and recovery within the relationship between stressor, work strain, and performance. Intuitively, the greater the degree of resilience, the lower the need for recovery, as this personal resource moderates the relationship between work demands, exhaustion and low performance (Bakker, Hakanen, Demerouti, & Xanthopoulou, 2007). With the present contribution, we aim to replicate this relationship and to incorporate the construct of grit, since it has a role in rebuilding personal resources, and long-term goal achievement. Indeed, the passionate, perseverant and goal orientated person (i.e., gritty) develops the capacity to regulate the psychological capital allowing the individual to cope with challenging situations (i.e., resilience). In turn, the same individuals who have the ability to rebuild their personal resources from challenges quickly also tend to find moments dedicated to recovery (Hiebert, 2006). Grit, resilience and recovery are constructs which (in this order) could represent a development process that will be tested in the next section.

2.2 Method

2.2.1 Participants, Materials, and Procedure

The present sample belongs to a study designed with multiple research purposes. Since in this study our aim was to examine a development process, three-waves (4 months each) of data collection were conducted. For this study, socio-anagraphic data and measurements of the three constructs was collected from newly hired (<5 years) Italian workers. Five companies, belonging to a North-East Italy industrial district of small-medium dimensions were selected first. The survey deadline was extended online to include more subjects.

A total of 582 employees completed and returned the questionnaire (response rate 62%). Fifty-nine percent of the employees identified as female. Their age ranges between 19 and 54 years with an average of 33 years (SD = 15.82). The educational demographic showed that 24% of this population had higher vocational training (24%) or a high school degree (57%). Most participants worked as clerks (45%) with no qualified profession inside the companies.

Besides the socio-anagraphic data, we also administered three instruments to measure levels of grit, resilience, and recovery over time as follows.

Grit The personality trait Grit was assessed by using the Short Grit Scale, an eight-item self-report questionnaire with established construct and predictive validity.

Participants have endorsed items by indicating consistency of passions "I have been obsessed with a certain idea or project for a short time but later lost interest" (reverse-scored) and consistency of effort "Setbacks don't discourage me," over time, by using a 5-point Likert-type scale (5 = very much like me, 1 = not at all like me). *Resilience:* The Dispositional Resilience Scale (DRS-15) by Bartone (2007) and validated in Italian by Picardi et al. (2012) was used to measure resilience. We selected the five items which concern work activities, such as "By working hard you can nearly always achieve your goals" or "I really look forward to my work activities". The rating is expressed on a 4-point rating scale (1 = *totally disagree*, 4 = *totally agree*). *Recovery:* Recovery strategies were measured using the 16-item Recovery Experience Questionnaire (Sonnentag & Fritz, 2007). Participants were asked to respond to the items with respect to their free time after work. All scales originally included four items, which were rated on a five-point scale ranging from 1 (totally agree) to 5 (totally disagree); e.g. "I use the time to relax" (relaxation), "I distance myself from my work".

2.2.2 Data Testing

All scales present acceptable reliability indexes (Cronbach's $\alpha > .84$). Moreover, we tested the reliability of the aggregate resilience resource score, by carrying out a confirmatory factor analyses (CFA) for each scale. The CFAs show adequate fit indexes for all the three constructs investigated (i.e., grit, resilience, and recovery). Next, we followed the statistical procedure suggested by Hayes, to test the presence of a (partial or full) mediation model. Before proceeding with the modeling of the mediation, we first tested if grit is a predictor of resilience and, in turn, if resilience can predict recovery. Results confirmed a full mediation model, $R^2 = .42$, $p < .001$, $F(494,1) = 26.80$, in the presumed direction, where, except for the main effect between grit and recovery, the other relationships were all significant (Grit → recovery: $t = .61$, $p = .54$; Grit -> resilience: $t = 5.18$, $p < .001$; Resilience → recovery: $t = 3.09$, $p < .001$). The analysis of the direct effect was not significant 95% confidence interval (CI) [−.19, .09], whereas the indirect effect was (CI) [−.21, −.05].

2.3 Discussion

This chapter investigated whether grit, resilience, and recovery can be defined as a process (i.e., GRRR) to rebuild the personal resources needed for achieving long-term goals through recovery strategies. Results show that this process could look like and be conceptualized as a mediation model based on these three interconnected constructs. The proposed order of this process is based primarily on theoretical relationships. Grit develops the capacity to better regulate and rebuild personal resources through resilience, especially during challenging situations, by developing adequate recovery strategies (Hiebert, 2006). The proposed order is also based on their psychological nature. Grit is considered a personality trait characterized by an instinctive need to achieve objectives despite the hurdles that may come along the way. Compared to the classic Big 5 traits, which remain fairly stable for most of us, Duckworth, Gendler, and Gross (2016) suggests that through experience grit develops. Duckworth et al. (2016) found that there are four components processes in particular that occur to develop grit: practice, purpose, interest, and hope. *Practice* is defined as the constant discipline of trying to do things better. Duckworth's research recommends merging moments of deliberate practice in order to build the skills to master. *Purpose* denotes the extent to which the goal matters to the person, their value system, and to others since grit can spread among a group if such values are shared. *Interest* designates the feeling that accompanies or causes special attention to something, followed by development and a lifetime of deepening. *Hope* allows persevering when things get difficult. It allows us to be more optimistic by challenging the reasons for setbacks or failures as nothing permanent (Duckworth et al., 2016).

The processes that define the development of grit are in line also with the five typical characteristics which allow developing resilience: self-esteem, self-efficacy, internal locus of control, awareness, and hope. *Self-esteem* is the evaluation of having a set of certain attributes; *self-efficacy* is based on knowing how to solve problems, which derives from the knowledge of strengths and weaknesses; *internal locus of control* is the tendency to interpret the results and effects of actions as caused by their own behavior; *awareness*, which coincides with an orientation towards acceptance of experiences; and finally, *hope* is already presented above. As for grit, the five components of the model described so far interact dynamically with each other and result in resilient people having the capacity to cope with life events, acquiring the ability to face various situations which enhances their ability to adapt (Oshio, Kaneko, Nagamine, & Nakaya, 2003).

Furthermore, these individuals can increase possibilities of recovery by: (1) adapting the workload; (2) receiving feedback in order to understand the strengths and weaknesses of work; (3) developing psychological detachment conceived as "the individual sense of being far from work situations" despite the fact that new technologies make this increasingly difficult; (4) increasing autonomy, in order to foster the development of the individual's ability to recover and, in turn, increase work productivity (Bakker, Rodríguez-Muñoz, & Derks, 2012). Some of the strategies indicated above can be seen as a conglomerate of experiences which could help to develop resilience. As shown by Ceschi et al. (2017), individuals can develop more resilience through working experiences by adapting their coping strategies and frequently transforming stressful aspects into learning chances. This is done by developing more control over the environment and using cognitive reappraisal to reframe a negative situation in order to moderate its emotional impact. Moreover, if one acquires awareness of such processes, this increases the ability to cope with adversity and to continue to grow resilience. Indeed, compared to grit, the resilience process is considered a coping strategy, and much more developable than a personal trait, but still not completely based on self-awareness. In contrast, recovery strategies are probably considered the most conscious and ductile construct of the entire GRRR model (see Fig. 2.1).

One can choose how to develop its recovery strategies; which can basically be of two types: internal recovery (e.g., work breaks) and external recovery methods, as they occur outside working hours. Among the numerous studies on the holiday-recovery relationship, Caplan and Jones (1975) showed that, following the holiday period, anxiety, depression and heart rate were lower than 5 months before. Furthermore, Etzion (2003) noted that work stress and exhaustion scores had decreased after a holiday break, which can remain low even after 3 weeks later from the break. On the contrary, work-related activities have usually a negative impact on situational well-being, as continuing to think about work commitments prevents the recovery process from starting (Sonnentag, 2001). Domestic and home-related activities, instead, according to the authors, would not favor the Recovery process. Demerouti, Taris, and Bakker (2007) have found that those home-work interferences and the need for recovery influence each other. In this way, strains experienced at home can interfere with work activities, favoring a greater need for Recovery, and vice versa for what concerns work. Finally, when considering only weekend recovery, research by Fritz and Sonnentag (2005) showed that extra-work weekend problems prevented the recovery process from taking place, fostering disengagement and a low level of health after the weekend. Conversely, weekend fatigue levels were lower than weekly ones when people were less involved in work activities and the quality of sleep increased. However, these benefits seemed to fade over time. A real recovery is closely linked to what happens when a person leaves their work environment since it can provide detachment from it.

2.4 Conclusion and Practical Implications

During times of constant changes and impending deadlines, organizations ask employees to face the exposure to frequent stress and overwhelming job demands, which, if prolonged, can result in exhaustion. The scientific literature confirms that these three psychological constructs (i.e., grit, resilience and recovery) are not only beneficial in achieving company goals but that they can also help their employees to prevent, manage, and recover from exhaustion. Connecting them theoretically and practically would be helpful in order to develop training for enhancing awareness levels of grit, resilience and recovery for workers. For instance, resilience is often confused by HRs with the concept of "Psychological Resistance". This distinction can be clarified by presenting some classical definitions of both constructs and by stressing how the resistance culture of "keep going" is replaced by evidence-based practices for the development of organizational resilience. Grit instead is often associated with a short and intense effort in the long run when the original definition presents an exactly opposite construct similar to the capacity of "run a marathon" (Littman-Ovadia & Lavy, 2016). Finally, it would be opportune to realize the effects

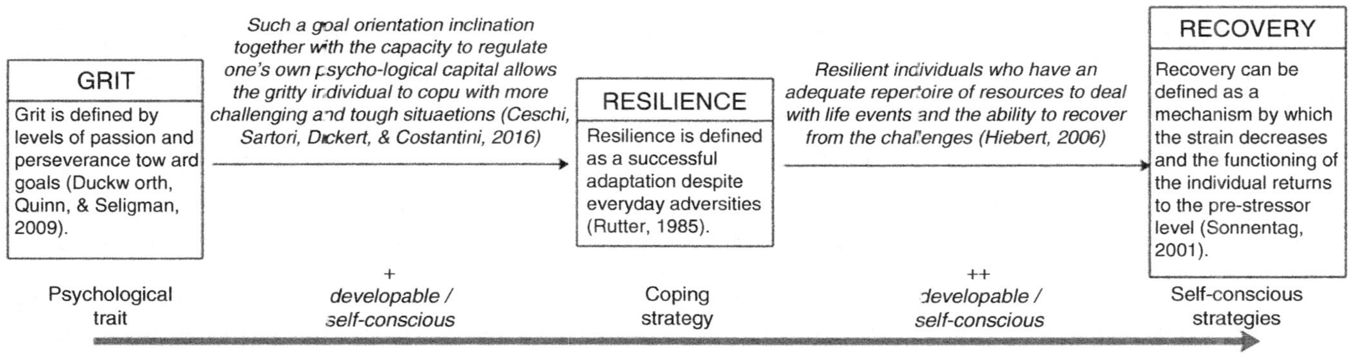

Fig. 2.1 Graphic representation of the process based on an increase of self-consciousness and development between grit, resilience and recovery constructs

of adequate Recovery processes, which should not only be limited to activities during the working day, but they should be related also to levels of detachment from work. Instead of just repeating to employees to 'resist during stressful times', organizations should promote a shared acceptance of workforce limits by instilling the awareness that hard times are momentary experiences and do not last forever. Therefore, the expectations of companies should be informed by and directed towards management strategies that foster coping with stress.

References

Anthony, E. J. (1987). Risk, vulnerability, and resilience: An overview. In *The invulnerable child* (pp. 3–48). New York: Guilford.

Bakker, A. B., Hakanen, J. J., Demerouti, E., & Xanthopoulou, D. (2007). Job resources boost work engagement, particularly when job demands are high. *Journal of Educational Psychology, 99* (2), 274.

Bakker, A. B., Rodríguez-Muñoz, A., & Derks, D. (2012). La emergencia de la psicología de la salud ocupacional positiva. *Psicothema, 24*(1), 66–72.

Bartone, P. T. (2007). Test-retest reliability of the dispositional resilience scale-15, a brief hardiness scale. *Psychological Reports, 101*(3), 943–944.

Bowles, S. V., & Bates, M. J. (2010). Military organizations and programs contributing to resilience building. *Military Medicine, 175*(6), 382–385.

Britt, T. W., Shen, W., Sinclair, R. R., Grossman, M. R., & Klieger, D. M. (2016). How much do we really know about employee resilience? *Industrial and Organizational Psychology, 9*(2), 378–404.

Caplan, R. D., & Jones, K. W. J. J. (1975). Effects of work load, role ambiguity, and type A personality on anxiety, depression, and heart rate. *Journal of Applied Psychology, 60*(6), 713.

Ceschi, A., Fraccaroli, F., Costantini, A., & Sartori, R. (2017). Turning bad into good: How resilience resources protect organizations from demanding work environments. *Journal of Workplace Behavioral Health, 32*(4), 267–289. https://doi.org/10.1080/15555240.2017.1398659.

Ceschi, A., Sartori, R., Dickert, S., & Costantini, A. (2016). Grit or honesty-humility? New insights into the moderating role of personality between the health impairment process and counterproductive work behavior. *Frontiers in Psychology, 7*. https://doi.org/10.3389/fpsyg.2016.01799.

Demerouti, E., Taris, T. W., & Bakker, A. B. (2007). Need for recovery, home–work interference and performance: Is lack of concentration the link? *Journal of Vocational Behavior, 71*(2), 204–220.

Duckworth, A. (2016). *Grit: The power of passion and perseverance* (Vol. 234). New York: Scribner.

Duckworth, A. L., Gendler, T. S., & Gross, J. J. (2016). Situational strategies for self-control. *Perspectives on Psychological Science, 11*(1), 35–55.

Duckworth, A. L., Kirby, T. A., Tsukayama, E., Berstein, H., & Ericsson, K. A. (2011). Deliberate practice spells success: Why grittier competitors triumph at the National Spelling Bee. *Social Psychological and Personality Science, 2*(2), 174–181.

Duckworth, A. L., Quinn, P. D., & Seligman, M. E. (2009). Positive predictors of teacher effectiveness. *The Journal of Positive Psychology, 4*(6), 540–547.

Eskreis-Winkler, L., Duckworth, A. L., Shulman, E. P., & Beal, S. (2014). The grit effect: Predicting retention in the military, the workplace, school and marriage. *Frontiers in Psychology, 5*, 36.

Etzion, D. J. A. (2003). Annual vacation: Duration of relief from job stressors and burnout. *Anxiety Stress & Coping, 16*(2), 213–226.

Feldhusen, J. F. (1995). Talent development: The new direction in gifted education. *Roeper Review, 18*, 92–93.

Finlay-Jones, A. L. (2014). *Self-compassion and psychological health among psychologists*. Bentley WA: Curtin University.

Freedman, T. G. (2004). Voices of 9/11 first responders: Patterns of collective resilience. *Clinical Social Work Journal, 32*(4), 377–393.

Fritz, C., & Sonnentag, S. (2005). Recovery, health, and job performance: Effects of weekend experiences. *Journal of Occupational Health Psychology, 10*(3), 187.

Galton, F. (1869). *Hereditary genius: An inquiry into its laws and consequences* (Vol. 27). London: Macmillan.

Hearne, A. (2017). *Moderating effects of resilience and recovery on the stressor-strain relationship among law enforcement officers*. Mankato: Minnesota State University.

Hiebert, B. (2006). *Creating a resilient workplace*. Division of applied psychology, University of Calgary. NATCON Papers.

Incantalupo-Kuhner, J. (2015). *Teacher dispositions and perceived environment: The relationship among grit, resiliency, and perceptions of school climate*. New York: Hofstra University.

Jackson, D. (2008). Servant leadership in nursing: A framework for developing sustainable research capacity in nursing. *Collegian, 15*(1), 27–33.

Joyce, S., Shand, F., Tighe, J., Laurent, S. J., Bryant, R. A., & Harvey, S. B. (2018). Road to resilience: A systematic review and meta-analysis of resilience training programmes and interventions. *BMJ Open, 8*(6), e017858.

Kendra, J. M., & Wachtendorf, T. (2003). Elements of resilience after the world trade center disaster: Reconstituting New York City's emergency operations Centre. *Disasters, 27*(1), 37–53.

Littman-Ovadia, H., & Lavy, S. (2016). Going the extra mile: Perseverance as a key character strength at work. *Journal of Career Assessment, 24*(2), 240–252.

Meijman, T., Mulder, G., Drenth, P., Thierry, H., & de Wolff, C. (1998). *Handbook of work and organizational psychology. Work Psychology* (Vol. 2). New York: Sage.

Newman, R. (2005). APA's resilience initiative. *Professional Psychology: Research and Practice, 36*(3), 227.

Oshio, A., Kaneko, H., Nagamine, S., & Nakaya, M. (2003). Construct validity of the adolescent resilience scale. *Psychological Reports, 93*(3 suppl), 1217–1222.

Paton, D., & Burke, K. J. (2007). Personal and organizational predictors of posttraumatic adaptation and growth in police officers. *Australasian Journal of Disaster and Trauma Studies*.

Perkins-Gough, D. (2013). The significance of grit: A conversation with Angela Lee Duckworth. *Educational Leadership, 71*(1), 14–20.

Picardi, A., Bartone, P. T., Querci, R., Bitetti, D., Tarsitani, L., Roselli, V., & Flynn, B. (2012). Development and validation of the Italian version of the 15-item dispositional resilience scale. *Rivista di psichiatria, 47*(3), 231–237.

Rook, J. W., & Zijlstra, F. R. (2006). The contribution of various types of activities to recovery. *European Journal of Work and Organizational Psychology, 15*(2), 218–240.

Rutter, M. (1985). Resilience in the face of adversity: Protective factors and resistance to psychiatric disorder. *The British Journal of Psychiatry, 147*(6), 598–611.

Sonnentag, S. (2001). Work, recovery activities, and individual well-being: A diary study. *Journal of Occupational Health Psychology, 6*(3), 196.

Sonnentag, S., & Fritz, C. (2007). The recovery experience questionnaire: Development and validation of a measure for assessing recuperation and unwinding from work. *Journal of Occupational Health Psychology, 12*(3), 204.

Southwick, S. M., & Charney, D. S. (2018). *Resilience: The science of mastering life's greatest challenges*. Cambridge: Cambridge University Press.

Trougakos, J. P., Beal, D. J., Green, S. G., & Weiss, H. M. (2008). Making the break count: An episodic examination of recovery activities, emotional experiences, and positive affective displays. *Academy of Management Journal, 51*(1), 131–146.

Tusaie, K., & Dyer, J. (2004). Resilience: A historical review of the construct. *Holistic Nursing Practice, 18*(1), 3–10.

Vanhove, A. J., Herian, M. N., Perez, A. L., Harms, P. D., & Lester, P. B. (2016). Can resilience be developed at work? A meta-analytic review of resilience-building programme effectiveness. *Journal of Occupational and Organizational Psychology, 89*(2), 278–307.

Westman, M., & Eden, D. (1997). Effects of a respite from work on burnout: Vacation relief and fade-out. *Journal of Applied Psychology, 82*(4), 516.

Andrea Ceschi is Senior (Tenure-Track) Assistant Professor in Work and Organizational Psychology (WOP) at the Human Sciences Department of Verona University. His field of work is organizational behavior, individual differences and decision-making at work, and social dynamics in the applied psychology field.

Arianna Costantini is a Ph.D. in Psychology at Verona University, Department of Human Sciences, Italy. Her field of work is job crafting, behavior change, and work-place innovation.

Giorgia Malavasi is an MPhil student at the Milano Cattolica University. Her field of interest concerns Grit, Resilience and Recovery constructs and interventions in the workplace.

Stephan Dickert is a Reader (Associate Professor) in Marketing at Queen Mary University of London, School of Business and Management. He currently also holds a full Professorship of Psychology at the University of Klagenfurt, Austria. His research focuses on judgment and decision making in social and economic contexts.

Riccardo Sartori is an Associate Professor in Work and Organizational Psychology at Verona University (Italy), Department of Human Sciences. His field of work is organizational innovation and the assessment processes linked to this topic included psycho-logical assessment and human resources management.

Chapter 3
How Does Grit Compare to Other Psychosocial Factors in Predicting University Students' Math Performance and Subjective Wellbeing?

Chen Chen and Xinmei Gong

Abstract This study aimed to examine the role that grit, along with conscientiousness, academic self-concept, other-based achievement goals, and competence expectancy, play in predicting Chinese university students' math performance and subjective wellbeing (i.e., life satisfaction and positive and negative affect). Two hundred and thirty-four university students attended a three-session online survey in their mathematics classes, with their ages ranging from 17 to 24 ($M_{\text{age}} = 18.77$ and $SD = 0.77$) years old. The results showed that independently, grit-PE (perseverance of effort) and other psychosocial factors (i.e., other-approach goals, conscientiousness, academic self-concept, and competency expectancy) all made their significant contributions to math performance; grit-CI (consistency of interest), grit-PE, and other psychosocial variables (i.e., conscientiousness, academic self-concept, and competency expectancy) also had significant contributions to life satisfaction and positive affect. Simultaneously, when grit working with other psychosocial constructs in the model, only grit-CI and other-approach goals significantly contributed to math grades; grit-CI and grit-PE, conscientiousness, and academic self-concept significantly predicted life satisfaction; grit-CI and grit-PE and conscientiousness significantly predicted positive affect; and only other-approach goals significantly and positively contributed to negative affect. More importantly, when grit was entered into the hierarchical regression models in the last step, grit-CI and grit-PE still demonstrated their incremental validity in predicting life satisfaction and positive affect, as well as math grades (though grit-CI only), above and beyond those psychosocial constructs examined. The results indicate that the power of grit in explaining math grades and wellbeing may depend on which psychological constructs grit work together. In addition, the two components of grit are suggested to be examined separately considering their different roles in achievement-relevant and non-achievement-relevant outcomes.

C. Chen (✉) · X. Gong
School of Psychology, Nanjing Normal University, Nanjing, China
e-mail: chenchen@njnu.edu.cn

L. E. van Zyl et al. (eds.), *Multidisciplinary Perspectives on Grit*,
https://doi.org/10.1007/978-3-030-57389-8_3

Keywords Math performance · Subjective wellbeing · Grit · Psychosocial factors · Motivation

3.1 Introduction

Grit, as a trait-like individual difference, has gained widespread attention from researchers around the world in the past decade, given its unique contribution to students' retention and academic achievement above and beyond intelligence and the Big Five personality traits (Chen, Ye, & Hangen, 2018; Credé, Tynan, & Harms, 2017; Datu, Valdez, & King, 2016; Disabato, Goodman, & Kashdan, 2019; Duckworth, Peterson, Matthews, & Kelly, 2007; Duckworth & Quinn, 2009; Jiang, Xiao et al., 2019; Usher, Li, Butz, & Rojas, 2019; Werner, Milyavskaya, Klimo, & Levine, 2019). In recent years, researchers from different perspectives, have advocated unpacking the nature of grit and how grit vis-à-vis other psychological factors (so-called non-cognitive factors) influence individuals' academic and nonacademic outcomes (e.g., Disabato et al., 2019; Dixson, 2019; Hagger & Hamilton, 2019; MacCann & Roberts, 2010; Wolters & Hussain, 2015).

Some have extended outcomes, which might be predicted by grit and its two facets, perseverance of effort and consistency of interest, from academic achievement to academic adjustment, wellbeing and/or personality strengths (e.g., Bowman, Hill, Denson, & Bronkema, 2015; Disabato et al., 2019). Some have addressed the independent and joint effects of grit and various frequently studied psychological constructs on academic achievement, including personality and trait variables (i.e., conscientiousness and self-control, see MacCann & Roberts, 2010; Werner et al., 2019) and motivational variables (e.g., self-efficacy, future-oriented motivation, expectancies for success, and task values, see Dixson, 2019; Muenks, Yang, & Wigfield, 2018; Usher et al., 2019). Others have directed attention towards understanding how grit, along with certain psychological factors, such as effort, need satisfaction, self-regulated learning, and sense of coherence and authenticity may predict academic achievement and wellbeing (Hagger & Hamilton, 2019; Jiang, Jiang et al., 2020; Vainio & Daukantaitė, 2016; Wolters & Hussain, 2015).

Among these researchers, an ongoing debate has called on further research regarding the significant role that grit-PE and grit-CI play in school success (Dixson, Worrell, Olszewski-Kubilius, & Subotnik, 2016; Ivcevic & Brackett, 2014; Muenks et al., 2018; Steinmayr, Weidinger, & Wigfield, 2018), the necessity for educational investment in grit training and/or intervention programs (Dixson, 2019; Usher et al., 2019), and the construct newness of grit distinctive from similar personality traits (e.g., conscientiousness and self-control) and motivation variables (e.g., self-efficacy and self-regulation) (Muenks, Wigfield, Ji Seung, & O'Neal, 2017; Rimfeld, Kovas, Dale, & Plomin, 2016; Vazsonyi et al., 2019; Werner et al., 2019). For example, on one hand, some research supports the assertion that "grit has the potential to be a theoretically and practically separate construct with a unique effect on important outcomes" (Werner et al., 2019, p. 173), on the other hand, others question grit's unique prediction of students' scholastic success, given its little incremental validity (Dixson, 2019; Muenks et al., 2017; Steinmayr et al., 2018).

However, when comparing the role of grit and its subscales with various frequently studied constructs in the personality, motivation, self-regulation, and engagement literatures in school settings, most of the attention has been directed to high school and/or college students' academic achievement. It may not be enough for a deeper understanding of how grit functions in student school success, without taking students' non-academic development, such as wellbeing into account (Ivcevic & Brackett, 2014; MacCann & Roberts, 2010, as exceptions). In addition, when examining how grit vis-à-vis various psychological factors influence students' academic and nonacademic outcomes, most of the research has been conducted in Western societies (e.g., Dixson, 2019; Dixson et al., 2016; Muenks et al., 2018), with less attention being directed towards understanding collectivistic samples, including Chinese students (Datu & McInerney, 2017). As Datu and McInerney (2017) discussed that grit dimensions may exhibit distinct patterns of relationships with academic and nonacademic outcomes in various contexts. In this sense, the replication of the extant research findings mostly revealed in Western societies remains unclear in a sample of Chinese university students. Furthermore, when investigating the association between grit and those constructs in the personality, motivation, self-regulation, and engagement literatures, some variables have been considered less, including academic self-concept and achievement goals, which are relatively powerful predictors for academic achievement (Hulleman, Schrager, Bodmann, & Harackiewicz, 2010; Marsh et al., 2018; Moller & Elliot, 2006; Van Yperen, Blaga, & Postmes, 2014). Taken together, this study aimed to address these issues by investigating how grit vis-à-vis certain psychosocial constructs (i.e., conscientiousness, academic self-concept, achievement goals, and competence expectancy) are related to Chinese university students' math performance and subjective wellbeing (i.e., life satisfaction and positive and negative affect).

3.2 Literature Review

3.2.1 Grit and the Psychosocial Factors of Interest with Academic Achievement

Grit, conscientiousness, academic self-concept, achievement goals, and competence expectancy are all important non-cognitive predictors of educational achievement (e.g., Duckworth et al., 2007; Elliot & Church, 1997; Marsh et al., 2018; Moller & Elliot, 2006; Rimfeld et al., 2016). Defined as trait-like perseverance and passion for long-term goals, grit has been found to be predictive of student performance and retention (Duckworth et al., 2007; Duckworth & Quinn, 2009; Eskreis-Winkler, Shulman, Beal, & Duckworth, 2014). Compared with the facet of grit-CI, grit-PE has been demonstrated to be more salient in predicting academic achievement (Bowman et al., 2015; Credé et al., 2017; Datu et al., 2016). Conscientiousness, as one of the Big Five personality traits, is an attribute of self-control, reflecting people's tendencies of planning, organizing and carrying out a task (Costa & McCrae, 1992; Roberts, Jackson, Fayard, Edmonds, & Meints, 2009). Closely related to but distinctively different from girt (Duckworth et al., 2007; Duckworth & Quinn, 2009; Schmidt et al., 2018; Werner et al., 2019), conscientiousness has long been found to positively predict academic performance at the school, college, university, and even graduate levels (De Raad & Schouwenburg, 1996; Farsides & Woodfield, 2003; O'Connor & Paunonen, 2007).

Academic self-concept refers to students' self-perceptions of their skills and ability in school subjects in general and is widely regarded as "a critical psychological construct that leads to success in educational settings, in social and emotional situations, and in daily life more generally" (Marsh et al., 2018, p. 263). Previous research has evidenced the positive relation between academic self-concept and American high school students' GPA (Prince & Nurius, 2014) and between math self-concept and German students' math scores and school grades (Marsh et al., 2018). A meta-analysis has also identified this association, in which, math and verbal self-concepts are respectively correlated with math ($r = .43$) and verbal ($r = .35$) achievement (Möller, Pohlmann, Köller, & Marsh, 2009).

Motivation constructs, much like grit, also play an important role in academic goal pursuit and achievement (Werner et al., 2019). Among them, achievement goals, the aim that one is committed to in guiding and sustaining his or her behavior in achievement settings (Chen & Zhang, 2011; Elliot & Murayama, 2008; Elliot & Thrash, 2001), have been documented as reliable predictors of students' learning motivation and academic performance (Hulleman et al., 2010; Marsh et al., 2018; Moller & Elliot, 2006; Van Yperen et al., 2014). In general, performance-approach goals (PAP goals) and performance-avoidance goals (PAV goals) are found positively and negatively related to academic achievement. Recently, Elliot and his colleagues (Elliot, Murayama, & Pekrun, 2011) have offered a 3 × 2 achievement goal model to extend and clarify the study of achievement goals, in which, other-approach goals (OAP goals) emphasize the attainment of other-based competence and other-avoidance goals (OAV goals) emphasize the avoidance of other-based incompetence. Their research witnessed the positive relation between OAP goals and exam performance and the negative relation between OAV goals and exam performance. These findings are much like those of PAP and PAV goals in that other-based goals are theoretically identical to performance-based goals (Elliot et al., 2011).

Competence expectancy refers to task-specific competence expectancy and has long been noticed as an important variable in achievement settings by achievement theorists (Atkinson, 1957; Bandura, 1982; Butler, 1992; Harter, 1992; Weiner, 1972). However, as "the 'active ingredient' in achievement motivation and fear of failure" (Kukla, 1972; Meyer, 1987, cited in Elliot & Church, 1997, p. 219)", the relation between competence expectancy and academic achievement is less investigated. Limited research has shown that competence expectancy positively predicted university student grades, mastery and performance-approach goals, and ability-related self-esteem (Elliot & Church, 1997; McGregor & Elliot, 2002). Moreover, math and English competence beliefs were found positively related to German students' math and English effort (Trautwein, Lüdtke, Schnyder, Roberts, & Niggli, 2009).

The relations of academic achievement to grit, conscientiousness, academic self-concept, achievement goals, and competence expectancy have been established, respectively. However, to further answer the question of the relative contribution of grit vis-à-vis those psychological factors to academic achievement necessitates studies on the independent and joint prediction of grit and those personality and motivational constructs. With regard to grit and academic self-concept (ASC there-after), it has been found that the predictive power of grit is far less than academic self-concept in students' GPA, math grades and math test performance, in which only grit-PE is the significant predictor (Dixson, 2019; Steinmayr et al., 2018). Moreover, both grit-PE and grit-CI seemingly did not add any explanatory power for American adolescents' academic achievement above and beyond academic self-concept (Dixson, 2019). As aforementioned, Datu and his colleagues (Datu & McInerney, 2017; Datu et al., 2016) have argued that the nomological network of grit in a collectivist context may be draw with caution, given the cross-cultural similarities and differences in the relationships between grit and educational outcomes.

With regard to grit and conscientiousness, the research findings are inconsistent (Credé et al., 2017; Ivcevic & Brackett, 2014; Muenks et al., 2017; Rimfeld et al., 2016; Steinmayr et al., 2018). Some studies including a meta-analysis have found that grit-PE explains a small amount of incremental variance in UK's GCSE (General Certificate Secondary Education Exams) achievement over and above the Big Five personality traits (0.5%, see Rimfeld et al., 2016), and a substantial amount of incremental variance in college GPA (2.3%), overall academic performance (4.0%), and high school GPA (8.5%) after controlling for conscientiousness (Credé et al., 2017, a meta-analysis). However, other studies have demonstrated that grit and its two facets did not explain additional variance in school outcomes above and beyond the Big Five personality traits (Ivcevic & Brackett, 2014) and conscientiousness, self-regulation and engagement variables (Muenks et al., 2017).

Research on the joint function of grit and achievement goals in academic achievement is rare (Muenks et al., 2018, as an exception), although a group of studies have recently focused on the distinctive role that grit and various motivational variables, such as academic self-efficacy, future-oriented time perspective, expectancies for success, task values, effort regulation and academic engagement, play in students' school success (Dixson, 2019; Dixson et al., 2016; Muenks et al., 2017, 2018; Steinmayr et al., 2018; Usher et al., 2019). Muenks et al. (2018) found that both grit-PE and grit-CI, as well as mastery-approach and performance-approach goals positively and independently predicted junior high school students' grades; however only grit-PE and self-efficacy became significant predictors when these constructs were simultaneously entered into the regression model. Given the inconsistent research findings, we wonder what the result will be in the Chinese context.

To summarize, although the extant research has addressed the issue regarding the significant role that grit-PE and grit-CI play in school success vis-à-vis various frequently studied constructs, at least three research gaps necessitate further investigation. First, the number of the relevant research studies are small (e.g., grit with academic self-concept and achievement goals) and majority of these have been carried out in recent five years. Second, some research findings are inconsistent in the relative power between grit and conscientiousness. Third, up till now, no published research in this field has examined Chinese data. These may impede the better understanding of and a general conclusion on how grit functions in school settings, particularly along with other aforementioned psychological factors, which necessities for the current study.

3.2.2 Grit and the Psychosocial Factors of Interest with Subjective Wellbeing

Compared with those on the prediction of academic achievement, the research on the prediction of subjective wellbeing from grit, conscientiousness, ASC, achievement goals, and/or competence expectancy is far less. The limited studies are centered on the relation of wellbeing to conscientiousness, achievement goals, and grit (e.g., Datu et al., 2016; Moller & Elliot, 2006; Steel, Schmidt, & Shultz, 2008). Specifically, a meta-analysis showed that conscientiousness was positively associated with life satisfaction, quality of life, happiness, and positive affect, and negatively associated with negative affect (Steel et al., 2008). A study conducted among Chinese university students also evidenced that conscientiousness positively predicted life satisfaction and positive affect (Chen, 2015).

Similarly, grit and its two facets may all benefit students' wellbeing (Bowman et al., 2015; Datu et al., 2016; Disabato et al., 2019). For example, general grit was found to be positively related to adolescents' subjective wellbeing and personality strengths in six continents (Disabato et al., 2019). Both grit-PE and grit-CI were found to significantly predict American university students' college sense of belongingness and college satisfaction (Bowman et al., 2015). A study among a group of Asian college students found that grit-PE positively predicted life satisfaction and positive affect, but negatively predicted negative affect; grit-CI negatively predicted students' negative affect (Datu et al., 2016).

With regard to achievement goals, it has been shown that achievement goals that students adopt can influence their wellbeing (Chen, 2015; Elliot et al., 2011; Moller & Elliot, 2006; Senko & Dawson, 2017). PAV goals positively predicted American university students' test anxiety, worry, and emotionality (Moller & Elliot, 2006, as a review); negatively predicted Chinese university students' positive affect (Chen, 2015). PAP goals were not only positively related to positive affect and enjoyment (Chen, 2015; Senko & Dawson, 2017, as a meta-analysis), but also positively related to negative affect and anxiety (Senko & Dawson, 2017), which is in accord with their nature that to exceed others may bring the feelings of pride and happiness, but also create pressure and anxiety for the following action (Elliot, 1999). Considering the newly launching of the 3 × 2 achievement goal model, the research on the relation between other-based goals and wellbeing is rare. One study reported a positive link between OAV goals and worry about exams, which is in line with that of PAV goals (Elliot et al., 2011).

Academic self-concept is regarded as "closely tied to students' economic success and long-term health and wellbeing" (OECD, 2003, p. 9). Several studies with primary and secondary school students have showed the positive correlation between academic self-concept and welling (Chang, McBride-Chang, Stewart, & Au, 2003; Marsh, Trautwein, Lüdtke, Köller, & Baumert, 2006; Westphal, Kretschmann, Gronostaj, & Vock, 2018). For example, Marsh et al. (2006) found that "the entire set of self-concept and esteem factors is able to explain ... between 39.6% and 52.1% (M = 45.1%) of the variance in the three well-being factors" (p. 440), that is, life satisfaction and positive and negative affect. As another example, math self-concept was found to positively and negatively predict German adolescents' enjoyment and anxiety and boredom in math, respectively (Westphal et al., 2018).

Up till now, very little research has attended to the joint predictive power of grit and the personality and motivational variables currently examined in this study. Only two studies were found to examine the effect of grit vis-à-vis conscientiousness on grades and wellbeing. MacCann and Roberts (2010) calculated the partial correlations between grit-PE and grit-CI and wellbeing by controlling for conscientiousness. They found that grit-PE and grit-CI were both positively related to life satisfaction and negatively related to depression; grit-CI was negatively related to anxiety and stress. These results are consistent with the nature of the two grit facets (Duckworth et al., 2007; Duckworth & Quinn, 2009). Interestingly, with conscientiousness controlled for, the positive relation between grit-PE and life satisfaction in the above study still remained significant. However, the other study examined the incremental validity of grit above and beyond conscientiousness, and found that grit had no significant extra contribution to American high school students' GPA and satisfaction with school (Ivcevic & Brackett, 2014).

To sum up, the relations have been evidenced of wellbeing to grit-CI and grit-PE, as well as to conscientiousness, achievement goals, and ASC, separately. However, the extant research centered on the nature of grit, and how grit vis-à-vis various non-cognitive factors affect students' subjective wellbeing is scarce. Although there are limited findings on the prediction of SWB from conscientiousness and achievement goals among Chinese university students (Chen, 2015), the explanation of SWB from grit remains unclear. It is worth extending the research on the prediction of academic outcomes to that of wellbeing outcomes, with which, we can obtain a comprehensive picture of how grit and its facets function in achievement settings.

3.2.3 The Present Study

The objective of the current study is twofold. First, it intended to examine the independent and joint contribution of grit, along with conscientiousness, ASC, other-based achievement goals, and competence expectancy to Chinese university students' math performance and subjective wellbeing (i.e., life satisfaction and positive and negative affect). Second, taking one step further, the current study was also interested in the incremental validity of grit-PE and grit-CI in predicting student math grades and wellbeing above and beyond those psychosocial constructs of interest.

We, based on previous findings, hypothesized that independently, grit-PE, grit-CI, conscientiousness, ASC, OAP goals, and competence expectancy will significantly positively predict math performance and life satisfaction and positive affect, but negatively predict negative affect; OAV goals will significantly negatively predict math performance, life satisfaction and positive affect, but positively predict negative affect (H1.1). Simultaneously, the explanatory power of grit-PE, grit-CI, conscientiousness, ASC, other-based achievement goals, and competence expectancy will greatly decrease, with only the constructs whose correlations being the stronger with math performance and SWB will remain significant (H1.2). With regard to the incremental validity of grit, we anticipated that grit-PE will exhibit its extra contribution to math grades above and beyond other examined constructs (H2). No specific relation was proposed for the incremental validity of grit in predicting SWB, considering the rare empirical work. By answering the two questions, this study may enrich our understanding of the nature of grit and how grit vis-à-vis various psychosocial factors contribute to student school life.

3.3 Method

3.3.1 Participants and Procedures

Two hundred and thirty-four university students attended a three-session online survey in their mathematics classes, with their ages ranging from 17 to 24 ($M_{\text{age}} = 18.77$ and $SD = 0.77$) years old. Among the participants, 185 were female (79.1%) and 49 were male (20.9%); most were freshman (99.1%), with only one sophomore and one junior; and 107 (45.7%) majored in social science and 127 (54.3%) in science. Grit, academic self-concept, competence expectancy, and demographic information were collected in the first session; achievement goals, conscientiousness, and subjective wellbeing, and social desirability were collected in the second session. Students' math grades were provided by instructors in the third session (the end of the semester) after math final exams with their informed consent.

3.3.2 Measures

Some information needs to be noted before the introduction to the measures. First, the Big Five conscientiousness subscale is rated on a 5-point Likert-type scale, with 1 indicating *not at all true of me* and 5 indicating *very true of me*. The other measures are rated on a 7-point Likert-type scale, with 1 representing *not at all true of me* and 7 representing *very true of me*. Second, the questionnaires of grit, conscientiousness, and subjective wellbeing have been validated in the Chinese context, with satisfactory psychometric properties (Chen, 2015, 2016; Chen, Fan, & Jury, 2017; Chen et al., 2018; Chen & Zhang, 2011). The remaining questionnaires of academic self-concept, other-based goals, and competence expectancy went through a standard back translation procedure by the bilingual researchers and professionals. Third, the average scores for each of the variables and dimensions were used for data analysis. Fourth, for the sake of brevity, the measures for predictors and outcomes are separately reported in their corresponding paragraphs.

Measures for Predictors Grit was measured by a validated Chinese version of the Short Grit Scale (Grit-S; Chen et al., 2018; Duckworth & Quinn, 2009). It consists of eight items with four reverse-scored items for grit-CI (e.g., 'I often set a goal but later choose to pursue a different one') and four items for grit-PE (e.g., 'I finish whatever I begin'). Academic self-concept was measured by four items (e.g., 'I am good at most school subjects') from a short version of the Self-Description Questionnaire II (SDQ II-S; Marsh, Ellis, Parada, Richards, & Heubeck, 2005). Conscientiousness was rated by the 12-item Conscientiousness Subscale (e.g., 'I keep my belongings clean and neat') from the Chinese version of NEO-Five Factor Inventory (Chen, 2015; Chen & Zhang, 2011; Costa & McCrae, 1992). The OAP goals (three items; e.g., 'To outperform other students on the exams in this class') and OAV goals (three items; e.g., 'To avoid doing worse than other students on the exams in this class') were adopted from the 3 × 2 Achievement Goal Questionnaire (AGQ; Elliot et al., 2011). Competence expectancy for the math exam (e.g., 'I expect to do well on this exam') was measured by a two-item scale (Elliot & Church, 1997).

Measures for Outcomes The validated Chinese versions of the Satisfaction with Life Scale (SWLS; Diener, Emmons, Larsen, & Griffin, 1985) and Positive and Negative Affect Schedule (PANAS; Watson, Clark, & Tellegen, 1988) were used to measure life satisfaction (e.g., 'So far, I have achieved important things I want in life') and positive and negative affect over the past week (e.g., 'active' and 'upset') (Chen, 2015, 2016; Chen et al., 2017). Students' math grades were provided by instructors in the end of the semester and standardized scores were used in following data analyses.

Control Variables The 20-item Chinese version of the Self-Deceptive Enhancement (SDE; Chen et al., 2018; Paulhus, 1991) was adopted to control the response bias, with 10-item desirable statements (e.g., 'I am a completely rational person') and 10-item undesirable statements (e.g., 'I rarely appreciate criticism'). After reversely coding the undesirable statements, the composite of SDE was an indicator of social desirability. Student social class was indicated by a 10-runged social ladder in the MacArthur Scale of Subjective Social Status (Adler, Epel, Castellazzo, & Ickovics, 2000). The smaller number represents a family's higher subjective SES in relation to others ($M = 6.02$, $SD = 1.55$).

3.3.3 *Data Analysis*

Confirmatory factor analysis (CFA) was carried out via M*plus* 8.2 (Muthén & Muthén, 1998–2017) to examine the factorial validity of the measures. The maximum likelihood (MLR) estimator was used for model testing in that it is more robust to non-normality (Muthén & Muthén, 1998–2017). χ^2, root mean square error of approximation (RMSEA), standardized root mean residual (SRMR), and comparative fit index (CFI) are widely used to evaluate model fit (Byrne, 2012; Iacobucci, 2010). Given that χ^2 test tends to be oversensitive to sample size, multiple indices are adopted for model fit evaluation. RMSEA and SRMR are badness-of-fit indices, whose values close to .08 or lower indicating a good model fit (Hu & Bentler, 1999; Iacobucci, 2010; Kenny, 2014; McDonald & Ho, 2002). CFI is a goodness-of-fit index and the value of .90 (CFI $\geq$ .90) was regarded as the cut-off of a good model fit (Hu & Bentler, 1999).

Three sets of multiple regressions were carried out to examine the contributions of grit, and other psychosocial factors to math grades and SWB (i.e., life satisfaction, positive and negative affect). With gender, subjective SES, and social desirability controlled for, a series of hierarchical regressions were conducted for (a) the effect of each of the predictors and all the predictors simultaneously on math grades and SWB, and (b) the incremental validity of grit to math grades and SWB above the other psychosocial factors.

3.4 Results

3.4.1 *Psychometric Properties of Measures*

The CFA results demonstrated that the psychometric properties of all the measures are satisfactory. As can be seen in Table 3.1, the model fit indices of each models met the criteria, with CFIs higher than .909; RMSEAs lower than .082 (.117 for academic self-concept); SRMRs lower than .065 (.096 for competence expectancy as an exception). All the items loaded on the theoretically constructed factors, with standardized factor loadings higher than .335. The internal consistencies of all the measures ranged from .67 to .94, except for .60 for the social desirability scale (See Table 3.2).

Table 3.1 Model fit of all the measures

Variables	χ^2	*df*	*p*	CFI	RMSEA	SRMR	Factor loading
Grit	33.654	19	.020	.967	.057 [.023, .089]	.065	.335–.895***
Conscientiousness	57.475	27	.006	.909	.080 [.051, .109]	.056	.414–.732***
Other-based goals	17.431	8	.026	.979	.082 [.027, .134]	.036	.590–.980***
Academic self-concept	8.400	2	.015	.979	.117 [.044, .203]	.030	.585–.957***
Competence expectancy	2.380	1	.123	.974	.077 [.000, .208]	.096	.606–.715***
Subjective well-being	435.337	269	<.001	.930	.059 [.049, .069]	.061	.364–.933***

Note. ***$p < .001$. Three items of conscientiousness with factor loadings lower than .30 (*ns*; item 15, 30, 45) were removed

3.4.2 *Intercorrelations Among Key Variables*

As can been seen in Table 3.2, all other predictors except for grit-PE and OAV goals were positively correlated with math grades with correlation coefficients ranging from .16 to .38 (*ps* $< .05$). Among them, OAP goals ($r = .38$, $p < .001$) and academic self-concept ($r = .30$, $p < .001$) had the relatively stronger relations with math grade. All other predictors except for grit-CI were positively correlated with life satisfaction, with correlation coefficients ranging from .19 to .46 (*ps* $< .05$). Among them, conscientiousness ($r = .46$, $p < .001$), academic self-concept ($r = .44$, $p < .001$), and grit-PE ($r = .43$, $p < .001$) exhibited their stronger relations with life satisfaction. Similarly, all other predictors except for grit-CI and OAV goals were positively correlated with positive affect, with correlation coefficients ranging from .25 to .54 (*ps* $< .01$), and conscientiousness ($r = .54$, $p < .001$), grit-PE ($r = .46$, $p < .001$), and academic self-concept ($r = .43$, $p < .001$) exhibited stronger relations with positive affect. Regarding negative affect, conscientiousness ($r = -.38$, $p < .001$), grit-PE ($r = -.32$, $p < .001$) and Grit-CI ($r = -.21$, $p = .005$) were negatively correlated, whereas OAV goals ($r = .19$, $p = .013$) positively correlated with negative affect.

With regard to the correlation among predictors, grit-CI was positively related to grit-PE ($r = .26$, $p < .001$); grit-CI was positively related to conscientiousness ($r = .30$, $p < .001$) and academic self-concept ($r = .22$, $p = .004$); and grit-PE was positively correlated with conscientiousness ($r = .55$, $p < .001$), academic self-concept ($r = .46$, $p < .001$), competence expectancy ($r = .42$, $p < .001$), and OAP goals ($r = .28$, $p < .001$). With the exception of the correlation between conscientiousness and OAV goals, all the other psychosocial predictors were correlated with each other (Table 3.2).

Table 3.2 Intercorrelations among key variables ($n = 176$)

Dimensions	1	2	3	4	5	6	7	8	9	10	11	12	13
1 Subjective social class	-												
2 Social desirability	-.11	-											
3 Math grades	-.15*	.02	-										
4 Life satisfaction	-.19*	.38***	-.12	-									
5 Positive affect	-.21**	.56***	-.08	.62***	-								
6 Negative affect	.03	-.43***	-.06	-.27***	-.23**	-							
7 Consistency of interest	-.24**	.34***	.16*	.07	.11	-.21**	-						
8 Perseverance of effort	-.06	.46***	.11	.43***	.46***	-.32***	.26***	-					
9 Academic self-concept	-.34***	.33***	.30***	.44***	.43***	-.11	.22**	.46***	-				
10 Conscientiousness	-.20**	.58***	.17*	.46***	.54***	-.38***	.30***	.55***	.45***	-			
11 Other-approach goals	-.32***	.15	.38***	.26***	.29***	.08	.06	.28***	.58***	.34***	-		
12 Other-avoidance goals	-.16*	-.09	.13	.19*	.14	.19*	-.12	.12	.35***	.08	.48***	-	
13 Competence expectancy	-.17*	.12	.24**	.33***	.25**	-.13	.03	.42***	.57***	.35***	.45***	.27***	-
M	6.02	4.12	.02	4.31	4.00	2.83	4.06	4.47	4.29	3.69	3.93	4.27	5.18
SD	1.55	0.53	.99	1.01	1.14	1.22	1.11	1.00	1.15	0.50	1.26	1.12	1.13
α	-	.60	-	.83	.93	.93	.79	.70	.83	.80	.94	.80	.67

Note. Listwise deletion; $^{*}p < .05$, $^{**}p < .01$, $^{***}p < .001$

Moreover, both subjective social class and social desirability were correlated with most of psychosocial factors and outcome variables, with the correlation coefficients ranging from −.34 to −.15 ($ps < .05$) for subjective SES and from −.43 to .58 ($ps < .001$) for social desirability. Significant gender difference was only found in negative affect ($t_{(175)} = 2.605$, $p = .010$), with male reporting higher levels of negative affect. Therefore, gender and subjective SES were controlled for in the first step, and social desirability was controlled for in the second step in the following multiple regressions.

3.4.3 *Predicting Math Grades and SWB from Predictors Independently*

As can be seen in Table 3.3, regarding grit, after gender, subjective SES, and social desirability were controlled for, grit-CI was found negatively significantly predicted life satisfaction ($\beta = -.152, p < .05$) and positive affect ($\beta = -.172, p < .01$); grit-PE was found positively significantly predicted math grades ($\beta = .151, p < .05$), life satisfaction ($\beta = .351, p < .001$), and positive affect ($\beta = .289, p < .001$; all R^2s ranging from .031 to .103, $ps < .05$). Except for the negative relation between grit-CI and life satisfaction and positive affect; the null relations between grit-CI and math

Table 3.3 Predicting math grades and SWB from grit and the psychosocial factors of interest independently

Criteria	Predictors	Math grades	Subjective well-being: Life satisfaction	Positive affect	Negative affect
R^2	Grit	.031*	.103***	.079***	.017
	Academic self-concept	.093***	.094***	.048***	.001
	Conscientiousness	.022*	.079***	.065***	.018*
	Other-based goals	.140***	.046**	.036**	.033*
	Competence expectancy	.060***	.069***	.022*	.003
β	Consistency of interest	.058	−.152*	−.172**	−.075
	Perseverance of effort	.151*	.351***	.289***	−.118
	Academic self-concept	.321***	.344***	.245***	.041
	Conscientiousness	.186*	.357***	.323***	−.168*
	Other-approach goals	.433***	.108	.113	.100
	Other-avoidance goals	−.085	.149	.117	.119
	Competence expectancy	.250***	.267***	.152*	−.052

Note. *$p < .05$, **$p < .01$, ***$p < .001$

grades and between grit and negative affect, all the results are consistent with the hypothesis for grit (H1.1).

After gender, subjective SES, and social desirability were controlled for, ASC, competence expectancy, and conscientiousness all positively predicted math grades, life satisfaction and positive affect, with βs ranging from .152 to .433 (ps $< .05$); conscientiousness also negatively predicted negative affect ($\beta = -.168$, $p < .05$). OAP goals only positively predicted math grades ($\beta = .438$, $p < .001$). OAV goals had null relation with all the outcomes. Except for the results of OAV goals, the non-significant prediction of negative affect from ASC, competence expectancy, and OAP goals, as well as the null relation between OAP goals and life satisfaction and positive affect, all the other results are in line with the H1.1.

3.4.4 Predicting Math Grades and SWB from Predictors Simultaneously

When grit working simultaneously with other psychosocial constructs in the model, a great amount of variances in math grades (adjusted $R^2 = .171$, $p < .001$), life satisfaction (adjusted $R^2 = .303$, $p < .001$), positive affect (adjusted $R^2 = .432$, $p < .001$), and negative affect (adjusted $R^2 = .277$, $p < .001$) were explained by grit, other factors, and control variables. Among them, the predictive power for SWB, particularly positive affect and life satisfaction, is much higher than that of math grades (see the bottom of Table 3.4).

Moreover, with gender, SES and social desirability being controlled for, all predictors together explained added variance of math grades ($\Delta R^2 = .171$, $p < .001$), life satisfaction ($\Delta R^2 = .181$, $p < .001$), positive affect ($\Delta R^2 = .131$, $p < .001$), and negative affect ($\Delta R^2 = .084$, $p = .007$). To be specific, grit-CI ($\beta = .166$, $p = .035$) and OAP goals ($\beta = .357$, $p < .001$) significantly positively contributed to math grades. Grit-CI ($\beta = -.150$, $p = .037$), grit-PE ($\beta = .178$, $p = .036$), conscientiousness ($\beta = .226$, $p = .013$), and ASC ($\beta = .205$, $p = .033$) significantly predicted life satisfaction. Grit-CI ($\beta = -.177$, $p = .007$), grit-PE ($\beta = .167$, $p = .029$), and conscientiousness ($\beta = .239$, $p = .004$) significantly predicted positive affect. Only OAP goals ($\beta = .182$, $p = .041$) significantly and positively contributed to negative affect. Except for the negative relation between grit-CI and life satisfaction and positive affect; the prediction of negative affect only from OAP goals, other results are consistent with H1.2.

3.4.5 Incremental Validity of Grit in Predicting Math Grades and SWB

Interestingly, even if other psychosocial factors had strong contributions to math grades and SWB, grit still showed their added contributions to life satisfaction

Table 3.4 Incremental validity of grit in predicting math grades and SWB beyond other psychosocial factors

Criteria		Math grades	Subjective well-being: Life satisfaction	Subjective well-being: Positive affect	Subjective well-being: Negative affect
Step 3	$R^2_{\text{step 3 total}}$ (adjusted R^2)	.194 (.155)	.312 (.279)	.429 (.402)	.310 (.277)
	$R^2_{\text{Gender + Social class}}$ (adjusted R^2)	.047 (.036)	.035 (.024)	.052 (.041)	.038 (.027)
	$R^2_{\text{Social desirability}}$	<.001	.127***	.282***	.196***
	$R^2_{\text{Other psychosocial factors}}$	.147***	.150***	.095***	.076**
	F	5.012***	9.468***	15.681***	9.360***
	df	8, 167	8, 167	8, 167	8, 167
	β_{Gender}	.169*	−.057	−.087	−.179**
	$\beta_{\text{Social class}}$	−.022	−.034	−.058	.028
	$\beta_{\text{Social desirability}}$	−.087	.161	.357***	−.328***
	$\beta_{\text{Academic self-concept}}$	.127	.211*	.130	.029
	$\beta_{\text{Conscientiousness}}$	.023	.251**	.258**	−.208*
	$\beta_{\text{Other-approach goals}}$	.349***	−.086	< .001	.185*
	$\beta_{\text{Other-avoidance goals}}$	−.104	.114	.100	.123
	$\beta_{\text{Competence expectancy}}$	.033	.108	.007	−.139
Step 4	$R^2_{\text{step 4 total}}$ (adjusted R^2)	.218 (.171)	.343 (.303)	.465 (.432)	.318 (.277)
	$R^2_{\text{Gender + Social class}}$ (adjusted R^2)	.047 (.036)	.035 (.024)	.052 (.041)	.038 (.027)
	$R^2_{\text{Social desirability}}$	<.001	.127***	.282***	.196***
	$R^2_{\text{Other psychosocial factors}}$	.147***	.150***	.095***	.076**
	R^2_{Grit}	.024	.031*	.036**	.009
	F	4.598***	8.624***	14.322***	7.707***
	df	10, 165	10, 165	10, 165	10, 165
	β_{Gender}	.182*	−.075	−.106	−.173*
	$\beta_{\text{Social class}}$	.021	−.083	−.111	.033
	$\beta_{\text{Social desirability}}$	−.094	.146	.349***	−.295**
	$\beta_{\text{Academic self-concept}}$	.115	.205*	.131	.057
	$\beta_{\text{Conscientiousness}}$	.024	.226*	.239**	−.173
	$\beta_{\text{Other-approach goals}}$	.357***	−.092	−.007	.182*
	$\beta_{\text{Other-avoidance goals}}$	−.077	.087	.069	.119
	$\beta_{\text{Competence expectancy}}$	.072	.055	−.047	−.122
	$\beta_{\text{Consistency of interest}}$	.166*	−.150*	−.177**	−.042
	$\beta_{\text{Perseverance of effort}}$	−.096	.178*	.167*	−.107

Note. $*p < .05$, $**p < .01$, $***p < .001$

($\Delta R^2 = .031$, $p = .022$), positive affect ($\Delta R^2 = .036$, $p = .005$), and math grades ($\Delta R^2 = .024$, $p = .080$, marginally) (see Table 3.4). More specifically, when working with other psychosocial predictors, grit-CI positively and significantly predicted math grades ($\beta = .166, p = .035$); grit-PE also had positive contribution to life satisfaction ($\beta = .178$, $p = .036$) and positive affect ($\beta = .167$, $p = .029$). Unexpectedly, grit-CI negatively predicted life satisfaction ($\beta = -.150$, $p = .037$) and positive affect ($\beta = -.177, p = .007$), respectively. Surprisingly, the incremental validity of grit-CI to math grades, rather than grit-PE is significant. We then move to the discussion.

3.5 Discussion

The current study examined the role that grit, along with conscientiousness, ASC, other-based achievement goals, and competence expectancy played in predicting Chinese university students' math performance and subjective wellbeing. We hypothesized that with all the constructs included in the predictive model, only those whose correlations are stronger with math performance and SWB will remain as significant predictors, and their explanatory power will in general decrease to a large extent (H1.1 & H1.2). We also hypothesized that grit-PE will exhibit its extra contribution to math grades above and beyond other examined constructs (H2), and we leave the incremental validity of grit in predicting SWB open, given the rare empirical work.

Generally, most of our research results supported the two hypotheses, except that when working alone, (1) grit-CI did not significantly predict math grades (H1.1); (2) the prediction of life satisfaction and positive affect from grit-CI was negative (H1.1); (3) only conscientiousness significantly predicted negative affect (H1.1); and (4) OAV goals did not significantly predict any of the outcomes (H1.1). In simultaneous regressions, (5) only OAP goals became the significant predictor for negative affect (H1.2). (6) The incremental validity of grit-CI to math grades, rather than grit-PE is out of expectation.

3.5.1 Predicting Math Grades and SWB from Predictors Independently

With regard to math grades, grit-PE was a robust and positive predictor, which is consistent with previous research findings (Bowman et al., 2015; Credé et al., 2017; Datu et al., 2016). It seems that persistent effort does benefit math performance. Contrary to H1.1, the prediction of math grades from grit-CI was not significant. There might be three reasons. First, grit-PE is more salient than grit-CI in predicting academic achievement, which is consistent with most previous research (Bowman et al., 2015; Credé et al., 2017; Datu et al., 2016). Second, it may be related to the math subject, which is difficult for many students. To achieve good grades students need long-term hard work and effort. In fact, previous research has found that the non-significant prediction of math grades and/or math test performance from grit-CI

(Steinmayr et al., 2018). Third, this might also be related to the collectivistic culture. Two studies conducted in Asian countries, including China, evidenced that null association between grit-CI, instead of grit-PE, and academic achievement (Datu et al., 2016; Jiang, Xiao, et al., 2019). Of course, the subject- and culture-specific possibilities require further research.

With regard to SWB, the positive association between grit-PE and life satisfaction as well as positive affect was supported and consistent with extant research findings (Bowman et al., 2015; Datu et al., 2016; Disabato et al., 2019). It seems that to put long-term effort in studying math subject, particularly when the effort pays off, students may feel the satisfaction for life and positive feelings like pride and happiness. Contrary to the H1.1, grit-CI negatively predicted life satisfaction and positive affect. Interestingly, in similar fashion, Disabato et al. (2019) found the negative association between grit-CI and beliefs about wellbeing and personality strengths; Bowman et al. (2015) also found that grit-CI negatively predicted college satisfaction, providing support for our findings. An explanation to the unexpected relation may lie in the math subject itself. Many students in the current sample majored social sciences, and mathematics seemed difficult for them (Douglas & Salzman, 2020). Therefore, to maintain consistent interest in math learning requires assertiveness and determination, which may cause emotional anxiety and depression, and weaken current life satisfaction (Bowman et al., 2015; Disabato et al., 2019). Although from a long run, grit-CI may be good for wellbeing, the answer is hard to get with this prospective study. Another explanation may lie in the measure itself. The Grit-S Scale has four reversely worded items measuring grit-CI and the rest positively worded items measuring grit-PE. It may result in acquiescence bias (Bowman et al., 2015), the opposite associations between two facets of grit and wellbeing.

Next, the predictive power of most other psychosocial factors was in line with the H1.1, except that OAV goals had null relations with all the outcomes. This result is consistent with the present null correlations between OAV goals and the outcomes. Perhaps, when working with OAP goals, OAV goals turned to have non-significant effects on all the outcomes. Besides, only conscientiousness independently and negatively predicted negative affect. For one thing, conscientiousness is the most powerful personality trait for SWB (Diener, Suh, & Lucas, 1999). For another, most of the predictors examined, except for OAV goals, may benefit desirable outcomes, such as math grades and positive affect, but not decrease undesirable outcomes, such as negative affect (Credé et al., 2017; Elliot & Church, 1997; Marsh et al., 2018; Senko & Dawson, 2017; Steel et al., 2008).

3.5.2 *Predicting Math Grades and SWB from Predictors Simultaneously*

In line with H1.2, only the constructs whose correlations were stronger with math grades, life satisfaction and positive affect remained significant in the regression model. To begin with, only OAP goals and grit-CI significantly positively predicted math grades. Table 3.2 shows that OAP goals had the strongest correlation with math grades ($r = .38$, $p < .001$). OAP goals also had close relations with ASC ($r = .58$, $p < .001$), competence expectancy ($r = .45$, $p < .001$), conscientiousness ($r = .34$, $p < .001$), and grit-PE ($r = .28$, $p < .001$), but not grit-CI ($r = .06$, *ns*). Thus, at the statistical level, ASC, competence expectancy, conscientiousness, and grit-PE, whose predictions were significant in the simple regressions were removed from the model after the competition with OAP goals. This is why grit-CI, although having moderate correlation with math grades ($r = .16$, $p < .01$), remained as a significant predictor. Dixson (2019) discussed that compared with academic self-concept, grit and engagement explained considerably less of GPA's variance, not supporting the power of grit in predicting high school students' GPA. Our research showed a different story, indicating the power of grit in explaining GPA may depend on which psychological constructs grit works together. In this sense, a general conclusion does require more research.

Next, the predictions of life satisfaction and positive affect from grit and other psychosocial variables support H1.2, and follow a similar pattern that grit-CI, grit-PE, and conscientiousness, remained in the regression models as significant predictors. On one hand, these predictors were positively correlated with each other in a similar fashion (coefficients ranging from .45 to .55, $ps < .001$), on the other hand, these factors were also positively related to life satisfaction (coefficients ranging from .43 to .44, $ps < .001$) and positive affect (coefficients ranging from .43 to .54, $ps < .001$) in a similar degree. Therefore, each of these constructs remained its explanatory power for life satisfaction and positive affect.

Third, in the simultaneous regression, OAP goals were the only positive predictor of negative affect. Although the result is consistent with previous findings in relation to PAP goals (Elliot et al., 2011; Senko & Dawson, 2017), the reason why the other factors whose associations with negative affect were stronger did not enter the model is hard to explain and calls for further investigation.

To sum up, when predicting math grades simultaneously, grit-CI and OAP goals remained as significant predictors. When predicting SWB simultaneously, grit-PE and grit-CI, along with ASC and conscientiousness were the significant predictors of life satisfaction; grit-PE and grit-CI, along with conscientiousness were the significant predictors of positive affect; and only OAP goals remained as a significant predictor of negative effect.

3.5.3 Incremental Validity of Grit in Predicting Math Grades and SWB

Contrary to hypothesis 2, grit-CI, but not grit-PE, showed an extra contribution to math grades above and beyond other examined constructs. This result is inconsistent with previous findings on the incremental validity of grit-PE (Credé et al., 2017;

Rimfeld et al., 2016) or general grit (Dixson, 2019; Ivcevic & Brackett, 2014; Muenks et al., 2017). In the meta-analysis, Credé et al. (2017) discussed, the case that grit-PE explained almost no unique variance in math grades when working with other psychosocial factors may suggest a possible suppressor effect. This happened among Canadian undergraduate students that none of grit, self-control, and conscientiousness, given the high correlations, had significant contribution to students' autonomous motivation for goal pursuit (Werner et al., 2019). In the present study, grit-PE also exhibited much stronger relations with conscientiousness and ASC than with grit-CI, thus, the non-significant incremental validity in predicting math grades may be due to such a suppressor effect. Will the similar result be found among other Chinese university student samples? This is a question necessitating a further investigation.

Moving to SWB, both facets of grit showed their extra contributions to life satisfaction ($\Delta R^2 = .031$, $p = .022$) and positive affect ($\Delta R^2 = .036$, $p = .005$), which enriches previous research findings. It seems that taking SWB into account as outcomes helps us with a better and clear understanding of the function of grit, including those of grit-CI and grit-PE. As mentioned at the very beginning, there is certain questioning on the nature of grit, such as whether schools should invest or stop grit training/intervention programs (Dixson, 2019; Usher et al., 2019) and whether grit is a new label for a traditional construct of similar personality traits and motivation variables (Muenks et al., 2017; Rimfeld et al., 2016; Vazsonyi et al., 2019; Werner et al., 2019). Based on the current research results, any answers are rush without careful investigations. It may be wise to consider more wellbeing variables for seeking the answer.

3.6 Contributions, Limitations and Future Research Directions

This study contributes to the literature in four ways. First, it examined the role of grit vis-à-vis four other psychosocial factors in predicting student math performance and subjective wellbeing. By doing so, we have found grit's different functions in academic achievement and wellbeing, enriching the understanding of the nature of grit. Second, this study provides Chinese students' data for the grit-school success literature, helping with the replication and extension of extant research findings. Third, up till now, no research has examined the four psychosocial constructs simultaneously (i.e., conscientiousness, academic self-concept, other-based achievement goals, and competence expectancy), adding new information into the association between grit and more psychological constructs. Fourth, this study took a prospective research design to collect data in three sessions, rather than a single-session correlational design, which might avoid common method bias (Podsakoff, MacKenzie, Lee, & Podsakoff, 2003).

Of course, the present study has limitations. First, although a prospective design adopted, it is essentially descriptive in nature (Ratelle, Duchesne, Litalien, & Plamondon, 2020; Scherrer, Preckel, Schmidt, & Elliot, 2020), and causal relations between grit and outcome variables can't be drawn. In the future, longitudinal studies are needed to examine the reciprocal relations between grit and academic achievement and SWB. Second, the sample size of this study is small and generalization of the findings has to be cautious. In the future, studies with larger sample size, diverse student groups (e.g., middle and high school students), diverse cultures, and different learning subjects are needed.

In spite of the limitations, this study has its implications for school settings. First, teachers, school administrators, and school counselors need to pay lots of attention to how to cultivate students' grit, both grit-PE and grit-CI. As can be seen in this study, grit showed its contribution to students' math grades and wellbeing in both the independent and joint regression models. Second, the investment of grit cultivation programs at school may not be as effective as possible without taking other psychological factors into account, those that have been proved to be powerful in students' performance and wellbeing (e.g., academic self-concept, achievement goals, and conscientiousness). Just as we discussed, the power of grit in predicting students' academic performance and wellbeing depend on which psychological constructs grit works together.

In the end, if grit has been found to have an effect on academic achievement and SWB, will the effect function through certain processes? As we mentioned at the very beginning, some researchers have already attended their attention to the mechanism that grit interacts with various psychological constructs in the personality and motivational literature. For example, grit-PE was found to influence college students' academic achievement via their self-regulated learning (Wolters & Hussain, 2015). Associated with the variables in the current study, only grit-CI and OAP goals had explanatory power for students' math performance. Based on the hierarchical model of achievement motivation (Elliot & Harackiewicz, 1996; Elliot & Thrash, 2001), may grit-PE affect academic achievement through achievement goals? This deserves future exploration.

Acknowledgements This research was supported in part by grants from the Research Institute of Moral Education at Nanjing Normal University, the Key Research Institute in Humanities and Social Sciences in Universities in China [No. DYS20170602].

References

Adler, N. E., Epel, E. S., Castellazzo, G., & Ickovics, J. R. (2000). Relationship of subjective and objective social status with psychological and physiological functioning: Preliminary data in healthy, White women. *Health Psychology, 19*(6), 586–592. https://doi.org/10.1037/0278-6133.19.6.586.

Atkinson, J. W. (1957). Motivational determinants of risk-taking behavior. *Psychological Review, 64*(6), 359–372. https://doi.org/10.1037/h0043445.

Bandura, A. (1982). Self-efficacy mechanism in human agency. *American Psychologist, 37*(2), 122–147. https://doi.org/10.1037/0003-066X.37.2.122.

Bowman, N. A., Hill, P. L., Denson, N., & Bronkema, R. (2015). Keep on truckin' or stay the course? Exploring grit dimensions as differential predictors of educational achievement, satisfaction, and intentions. *Social Psychological and Personality Science, 6*(6), 639–645. https://doi.org/10.1177/1948550615574300.

Butler, R. (1992). What young people want to know when: Effects of mastery and ability goals on interest in different kinds of social comparisons. *Journal of Personality and Social Psychology, 62*(6), 934–943. https://doi.org/10.1037/0022-3514.62.6.934.

Byrne, B. M. (2012). *Structural equation modeling with Mplus: Basic concepts, applications, and programming*. New York, NY: Routledge/Taylor & Francis Group.

Chang, L., McBride-Chang, C., Stewart, S. M., & Au, E. (2003). Life satisfaction, self-concept, and family relations in Chinese adolescents and children. *International Journal of Behavioral Development, 27*(2), 182–189. https://doi.org/10.1080/01650250244000182.

Chen, C. (2015). Incremental validity of achievement goals in predicting subjective well-being among university students. *Journal of Cognitive Education and Psychology, 14*(1), 38–62. https://doi.org/10.1891/1945-8959.14.1.38.

Chen, C. (2016). The role of resilience and coping styles in subjective well-being among Chinese university students. *Asia-Pacific Education Researcher, 25*(3), 377–387. https://doi.org/10.1007/s40299-016-0274-5.

Chen, C., Fan, J., & Jury, M. (2017). Are perceived learning environments related to subjective well-being? A visit to university students. *Learning and Individual Differences, 54*(1), 226–233. https://doi.org/10.1016/j.lindif.2017.01.001.

Chen, C., Ye, S., & Hangen, E. (2018). Predicting achievement goals in the East and West: The role of grit among American and Chinese university students. *Educational Psychology, 38*(6), 820–837. https://doi.org/10.1080/01443410.2018.1458975.

Chen, C., & Zhang, L. F. (2011). Temperament, personality and achievement goals among Chinese adolescent students. *Educational Psychology, 31*(3), 339–359. https://doi.org/10.1080/01443410.2011.559310.

Costa, P. T., & McCrae, R. R. (1992). *Revised NEO personality inventory (NEO PI-R) and NEO Five-Factor Inventory (NEO FFI): Professional manual.* Odessa, FL: Psychological Assessment Resources.

Credé, M., Tynan, M. C., & Harms, P. D. (2017). Much ado about grit: A meta-analytic synthesis of the grit literature. *Journal of Personality and Social Psychology, 113*(3), 492–511. https://doi.org/10.1037/pspp0000102.

Datu, J. A. D., & McInerney, D. M. (2017). Does culture matter for grit? Mapping cross-cultural directions in grit research programs. In F. Guay, H. W. Marsh, D. M. McInerney, & R. G. Craven (Eds.), *Self: Driving Positive Psychology and Well-Being* (pp. 113–133). Charlotte, NC: IAP Information Age Publishing.

Datu, J. A. D., Valdez, J. P. M., & King, R. B. (2016). Perseverance counts but consistency does not! Validating the Short Grit Scale in a collectivist setting. *Current Psychology, 35*(1), 121–130. https://doi.org/10.1007/s12144-015-9374-2.

De Raad, B., & Schouwenburg, H. C. (1996). Personality traits in learning and education: A review. *European Journal of Personality, 10*(5), 303–336. http://doi.org/10.1002/(SICI)1099-0984(199612)10:5<303::AID-PER262>3.0.CO;2-2.

Diener, E., Emmons, R. A., Larsen, R. J., & Griffin, S. (1985). The Satisfaction With Life Scale. *Journal of Personality Assessment, 49*(1), 71–75. https://doi.org/10.1207/s15327752jpa4901_13.

Diener, E., Suh, E. M., & Lucas, R. E. (1999). Subjective well-being: Three decades of progress. *Psychological Bulletin, 125*(2), 276–302. https://doi.org/10.1037/0033-2909.125.2.276.

Disabato, D. J., Goodman, F. R., & Kashdan, T. B. (2019). Is grit relevant to well-being and strengths? Evidence across the globe for separating perseverance of effort and consistency of interests. *Journal of Personality, 87*(2), 194–211. https://doi.org/10.1111/jopy.12382.

Dixson, D. D. (2019). Is grit worth the investment? How grit compares to other psychosocial factors in predicting achievement. *Current Psychology*. https://doi.org/10.1007/s12144-019-00246-5.

Dixson, D. D., Worrell, F. C., Olszewski-Kubilius, P., & Subotnik, R. F. (2016). Beyond perceived ability: The contribution of psychosocial factors to academic performance. *Annals of the New York Academy of Sciences, 1377*(1), 67–77. https://doi.org/10.1111/nyas.13210.

Douglas, D., & Salzman, H. (2020). Math counts: Major and gender differences in college mathematics coursework. *Journal of Higher Education, 91*(1), 84–112. https://doi.org/10.1080/00221546.2019.1602393.

Duckworth, A. L., Peterson, C., Matthews, M. D., & Kelly, D. R. (2007). Grit: Perseverance and passion for long-term goals. *Journal of Personality and Social Psychology, 92*(6), 1087–1101. https://doi.org/10.1037/0022-3514.92.6.1087.

Duckworth, A. L., & Quinn, P. (2009). Development and validation of the Short Grit Scale (Grit-S). *Journal of Personality Assessment, 91*(2), 166–174. https://doi.org/10.1080/00223890802634290.

Elliot, A. J. (1999). Approach and avoidance motivation and achievement goals. *Educational Psychologist, 34*(3), 169–189. https://doi.org/10.1207/s15326985ep3403_3.

Elliot, A. J., & Church, M. A. (1997). A hierarchical model of approach and avoidance achievement motivation. *Journal of Personality and Social Psychology, 72*(1), 218–232. https://doi.org/10.1037/0022-3514.72.1.218.

Elliot, A. J., & Harackiewicz, J. M. (1996). Approach and avoidance achievement goals and intrinsic motivation: A mediational analysis. *Journal of Personality and Social Psychology, 70*(3), 461–475. https://doi.org/10.1037/0022-3514.70.3.461.

Elliot, A. J., & Murayama, K. (2008). On the measurement of achievement goals: Critique, illustration, and application. *Journal of Educational Psychology, 100*(3), 613–628. https://doi.org/10.1037/0022-0663.100.3.613.

Elliot, A. J., Murayama, K., & Pekrun, R. (2011). A 3 × 2 achievement goal model. *Journal of Educational Psychology, 103*(3), 632–648. https://doi.org/10.1037/a0023952.

Elliot, A. J., & Thrash, T. M. (2001). Achievement goals and the hierarchical model of achievement motivation. *Educational Psychology Review, 13*(2), 139–156. https://doi.org/10.1023/A:1009057102306.

Eskreis-Winkler, L., Shulman, E. P., Beal, S. A., & Duckworth, A. L. (2014). The grit effect: Predicting retention in the military, the workplace, school and marriage. *Frontiers in Psychology, 5*, 36. https://doi.org/10.3389/fpsyg.2014.00036.

Farsides, T., & Woodfield, R. (2003). Individual differences and undergraduate academic success: The roles of personality, intelligence, and application. *Personality and Individual Differences, 34*(7), 1225–1243. https://doi.org/10.1016/S0191-8869(02)00111-3.

Hagger, M. S., & Hamilton, K. (2019). Grit and self-discipline as predictors of effort and academic attainment. *British Journal of Educational Psychology, 89*(2), 324–342. https://doi.org/10.1111/bjep.12241.

Harter, S. (1992). The relationship between perceived competence, affect, and motivational orientation within the classroom: Processes and patterns of change. In A. K. Boggiano & T. S. Pittman (Eds.), *Achievement and motivation: A social-developmental perspective* (pp. 77–114). New York, NY: Cambridge University Press.

Hu, L.-T., & Bentler, P. M. (1999). Cutoff criteria for fit indexes in covariance structure analysis: Conventional criteria versus new alternatives. *Structural Equation Modeling: A Multidisciplinary Journal, 6*(1), 1–55. https://doi.org/10.1080/10705519909540118.

Hulleman, C. S., Schrager, S. M., Bodmann, S. M., & Harackiewicz, J. M. (2010). A meta-analytic review of achievement goal measures: Different labels for the same constructs or different constructs with similar labels? *Psychological Bulletin, 136*(3), 422–449. https://doi.org/10.1037/a0018947.

Iacobucci, D. (2010). Structural equations modeling: Fit Indices, sample size, and advanced topics. *Journal of Consumer Psychology, 20*(1), 90–98. https://doi.org/10.1016/j.jcps.2009.09.003.

Ivcevic, Z., & Brackett, M. (2014). Predicting school success: Comparing conscientiousness, grit, and emotion regulation ability. *Journal of Research in Personality, 52*, 29–36. https://doi.org/10.1016/j.jrp.2014.06.005.

Jiang, W., Jiang, J., Du, X., Gu, D., Sun, Y., & Zhang, Y. (2020). Striving and happiness: Between- and within-person-level associations among grit, needs satisfaction and subjective well-being. *Journal of Positive Psychology, 15*(4), 543–555. https://doi.org/10.1080/17439760.2019.1639796.

Jiang, W., Xiao, Z., Liu, Y., Guo, K., Jiang, J., & Du, X. (2019). Reciprocal relations between grit and academic achievement: A longitudinal study. *Learning and Individual Differences, 71*, 13–22. https://doi.org/10.1016/j.lindif.2019.02.004.

Kenny, D. A. (2014). *Measuring model fit*. Retrieved from http://davidakenny.net/cm/fit.htm

Kukla, A. (1972). Foundations of an attributional theory of performance. *Psychological Review, 79* (6), 454–470. https://doi.org/10.1037/h0033494.

MacCann, C., & Roberts, R. D. (2010). Do time management, grit, and self-control relate to academic achievement independently of conscientiousness? In R. E. Hicks (Ed.), *Personality and individual differences: Current directions* (pp. 79–90). Bowen Hills, QLD: Australian Academic Press.

Marsh, H. W., Ellis, L. A., Parada, R. H., Richards, G., & Heubeck, B. G. (2005). A short version of the self description Questionnaire II: Operationalizing criteria for short-form evaluation with new applications of confirmatory factor analyses. *Psychological Assessment, 17*(1), 81–102. https://doi.org/10.1037/1040-3590.17.1.81.

Marsh, H. W., Pekrun, R., Murayama, K., Arens, A. K., Parker, P. D., Guo, J., & Dicke, T. (2018). An integrated model of academic self-concept development: Academic self-concept, grades, test scores, and tracking over 6 years. *Developmental Psychology, 54*(2), 263–280. https://doi.org/10.1037/dev0000393.

Marsh, H. W., Trautwein, U., Lüdtke, O., Köller, O., & Baumert, J. (2006). Integration of multidimensional self-concept and core personality constructs: Construct validation and relations to well-being and achievement. *Journal of Personality, 74*(2), 403–456. https://doi.org/10.1111/j.1467-6494.2005.00380.x.

McDonald, R. P., & Ho, M.-H. R. (2002). Principles and practice in reporting structural equation analyses. *Psychological Methods, 7*(1), 64–82. https://doi.org/10.1037/1082-989x.7.1.64.

McGregor, H. A., & Elliot, A. J. (2002). Achievement goals as predictors of achievement-relevant processes prior to task engagement. *Journal of Educational Psychology, 94*(2), 381–395. https://doi.org/10.1037/0022-0663.94.2.381.

Meyer, W.-U. (1987). Perceived ability and achievement-related behavior. In F. Halisch & J. Kuhl (Eds.), *Motivation, intention and volition* (pp. 73–86). New York: Springer.

Moller, A. C., & Elliot, A. J. (2006). The 2 × 2 achievement goal framework: An overview of empirical research. In A. V. Mittel (Ed.), *Focus on educational psychology* (pp. 307–326). New York: Nova Science.

Möller, J., Pohlmann, B., Köller, O., & Marsh, H. W. (2009). A meta-analytic path analysis of the internal/external frame of reference model of academic achievement and academic self-concept. *Review of Educational Research, 79*(3), 1129–1167. https://doi.org/10.3102/0034654309337522.

Muenks, K., Wigfield, A., Ji Seung, Y., & O'Neal, C. R. (2017). How true is grit? Assessing its relations to high school and college students' personality characteristics, self-regulation, engagement, and achievement. *Journal of Educational Psychology, 109*(5), 599–620. https://doi.org/10.1037/edu0000153.

Muenks, K., Yang, J. S., & Wigfield, A. (2018). Associations between grit, motivation, and achievement in high school students. *Motivation Science, 4*(2), 158–176. https://doi.org/10.1037/mot0000076.

Muthén, L. K., & Muthén, B. O. (1998–2017). *Mplus user's guide* (8th ed.). Los Angeles, CA: Muthén & Muthén.

O'Connor, M. C., & Paunonen, S. V. (2007). Big five personality predictors of post-secondary academic performance. *Personality and Individual Differences, 43*(5), 971–990. https://doi.org/10.1016/j.paid.2007.03.017.

OECD. (2003). *Literacy skills for the world of tomorrow: Further results from PISA 2000*. Paris: OECD and UNESCO.

Paulhus, D. L. (1991). Measurement and control of response bias. In J. P. Robinson, P. R. Shaver, & L. S. Wrightsman (Eds.), *Measures of personality and social psychological attitudes* (pp. 17–59). San Diego, CA: Academic Press.

Podsakoff, P. M., MacKenzie, S. B., Lee, J.-Y., & Podsakoff, N. P. (2003). Common method biases in behavioral research: A critical review of the literature and recommended remedies. *Journal of Applied Psychology, 88*(5), 879–903. https://doi.org/10.1037/0021-9010.88.5.879.

Prince, D., & Nurius, P. S. (2014). The role of positive academic self-concept in promoting school success. *Children & Youth Services Review, 43*, 145–152. https://doi.org/10.1016/j.childyouth.2014.05.003.

Ratelle, C. F., Duchesne, S., Litalien, D., & Plamondon, A. (2020). The role of mothers in supporting adaptation in school: A psychological needs perspective. *Journal of Educational Psychology*. https://doi.org/10.1037/edu0000455.

Rimfeld, K., Kovas, Y., Dale, P. S., & Plomin, R. (2016). True grit and genetics: Predicting academic achievement from personality. *Journal of Personality and Social Psychology, 111* (5), 780–789. https://doi.org/10.1037/pspp0000089.

Roberts, B. W., Jackson, J. J., Fayard, J. V., Edmonds, G., & Meints, J. (2009). Conscientiousness. In M. R. Leary & R. H. Hoyle (Eds.), *Handbook of individual differences in social behavior* (pp. 369–381). New York, NY: The Guilford Press.

Scherrer, V., Preckel, F., Schmidt, I., & Elliot, A. J. (2020). Development of achievement goals and their relation to academic interest and achievement in adolescence: A review of the literature and two longitudinal studies. *Developmental Psychology, 56*(4), 795–814. https://doi.org/10.1037/dev0000898.

Schmidt, F. T. C., Nagy, G., Fleckenstein, J., Möller, J., Retelsdorf, J., & Back, M. (2018). Same same, but different? Relations between facets of conscientiousness and grit. *European Journal of Personality, 32*(6), 705–720. https://doi.org/10.1002/per.2171.

Senko, C., & Dawson, B. (2017). Performance-approach goal effects depend on how they are defined: Meta-analytic evidence from multiple educational outcomes. *Journal of Educational Psychology, 109*(4), 574–598. https://doi.org/10.1037/edu0000160.

Steel, P., Schmidt, J., & Shultz, J. (2008). Refining the relationship between personality and subjective well-being. *Psychological Bulletin, 134*(1), 138–161. https://doi.org/10.1037/0033-2909.134.1.138.

Steinmayr, R., Weidinger, A. F., & Wigfield, A. (2018). Does students' grit predict their school achievement above and beyond their personality, motivation, and engagement? *Contemporary Educational Psychology, 53*, 106–122. https://doi.org/10.1016/j.cedpsych.2018.02.004.

Trautwein, U., Lüdtke, O., Schnyder, I., Roberts, B. W., & Niggli, A. (2009). Different forces, same consequence: Conscientiousness and competence beliefs are independent predictors of academic effort and achievement. *Journal of Personality and Social Psychology, 97*(6), 1115–1128. https://doi.org/10.1037/a0017048.

Usher, E. L., Li, C. R., Butz, A. R., & Rojas, J. P. (2019). Perseverant grit and self-efficacy: Are both essential for children's academic success? *Journal of Educational Psychology, 111*(5), 877–902. https://doi.org/10.1037/edu0000324.

Vainio, M., & Daukantaitė, D. (2016). Grit and different aspects of well-being: Direct and indirect relationships via sense of coherence and authenticity. *Journal of Happiness Studies, 17*(5), 2119–2147. https://doi.org/10.1007/s10902-015-9688-7.

Van Yperen, N. W., Blaga, M., & Postmes, T. (2014). A meta-analysis of self-reported achievement goals and nonself-report performance across three achievement domains (work, sports, and education). *PLoS One, 9*(4), e93594. https://doi.org/10.1371/journal.pone.0093594.

Vazsonyi, A. T., Ksinan, A. J., Ksinan Jiskrova, G., Mikuška, J., Javakhishvili, M., & Cui, G. (2019). To grit or not to grit, that is the question! *Journal of Research in Personality, 78*, 215–226. https://doi.org/10.1016/j.jrp.2018.12.006.

Watson, D., Clark, L. A., & Tellegen, A. (1988). Development and validation of brief measures of positive and negative affect: The PANAS scales. *Journal of Personality and Social Psychology, 54*(6), 1063–1070. https://doi.org/10.1037/0022-3514.54.6.1063.

Weiner, B. (1972). *Theories of motivation: From mechanism to cognition*. Oxford: Markham.

Werner, K. M., Milyavskaya, M., Klimo, R., & Levine, S. L. (2019). Examining the unique and combined effects of grit, trait self-control, and conscientiousness in predicting motivation for academic goals: A commonality analysis. *Journal of Research in Personality, 81*, 168–175. https://doi.org/10.1016/j.jrp.2019.06.003.

Westphal, A., Kretschmann, J., Gronostaj, A., & Vock, M. (2018). More enjoyment, less anxiety and boredom: How achievement emotions relate to academic self-concept and teachers' diagnostic skills. *Learning and Individual Differences, 62*, 108–117. https://doi.org/10.1016/j.lindif.2018.01.016.

Wolters, C. A., & Hussain, M. (2015). Investigating grit and its relations with college students' self-regulated learning and academic achievement. *Metacognition and Learning, 10*(3), 293–311. https://doi.org/10.1007/s11409-014-9128-9.

Chen Chen (Ph.D.), Professor of Psychology, Head of Institution of Educational Psychology at School of Psychology, Nanjing Normal University, China. Dr. Chen graduated from the University of Hong Kong and has been conducting research in the areas of achievement motivation, parent-child relationship, social development, and well-being. Grounded in the hierarchical model of achievement motivation, Dr. Chen is interested in uncovering the nature of achievement goals from both personal (e.g., grit, temperament, personality, and attachment) and environmental (e.g., parenting, need support, and classroom goal structure) factors. Dr. Chen is an Editorial Board Member for the *Journal of Educational Psychology*, and the director of the Committee of Developmental and Educational Psychology of Psychological Society of Jiangsu Province. Dr. Chen was awarded Middle- and Young-aged Academic Backbone at Nanjing Normal University (2016–2019), Jiangsu Overseas Research and Training Program for University Prominent Young & Middle-aged Teachers and Presidents (2014–2015), Eurasia-Pacific Uninet PhD & Post Doc Scholarship (2008–2009, sponsored by Austrian Exchange Service), and K. P. Tin Visiting Fellowship in Chinese Education (2003–2004, sponsored by The University of Hong Kong).

Xinmei Gong is a Ph.D. candidate and currently under the supervision of Dr. Chen Chen in the Motivation and Social Development Lab at School of Psychology, Nanjing Normal University, China. Miss Gong's major research interests are achievement goals, achievement motivation, need satisfaction and need support. In 2018, she was awarded the honor of Successive Postgraduate and Doctoral Programs by Nanjing Normal University and directly entered the doctoral program from her second year of master program. In 2016 and 2018, she was awarded the First Class Academic Scholarship by Nanjing Normal University. Xinmei Gong is a member of the International Society for the Study of Behavioural Development (ISSBD) and the Society for Research on Adolescence (SRA).

Chapter 4
How Does Perseverance of Effort Influence the University Outcomes of Historically Underrepresented Students?

Kevin Fosnacht and Keeley Webb-Copridge

Abstract Grit has become a popular concept in the education field and is characterised by consistency of interest and perseverance of effort. This study focuses on one dimension of grit, perseverance of effort, to examine if it has compensatory effects for historically underrepresented students. Using a large, diverse sample of undergraduates, the results indicate that perseverance of effort has a stronger relationship with some process indicators of student learning than for traditional students. Additionally, we did not observe any stronger relationships for traditional students relative to non-traditional populations. Consequently, the results suggest that perseverance of effort can have compensatory effects that can help historically underrepresented students overcome obstacles to student success.

Keywords Grit · Perseverance of effort · Non-cognitive traits · Student engagement · Higher education · Racial differences

4.1 Introduction

Grit has become a popular concept in the education field that proponents believe could explain why some students do not succeed in their educational pursuits (Del Giudice, 2014; Duckworth, Peterson, Matthews, & Kelly, 2007; Engber, 2016). Grit is defined as the "perseverance and passion for long term goals" and is a non-cognitive personality trait (Duckworth et al., 2007). This trait contains two constructs: perseverance of effort and consistency of interest (Duckworth, 2016). While grit has various proponents, others have criticised grit as a repackaged concept (Credé, Tynan & Harms, 2016) and a way to justify inequality in our society (Gonzalez-Stokas, 2015; Ris, 2015).

K. Fosnacht (✉) · K. Webb-Copridge
Center for Postsecondary Research, Indiana University, Bloomington, IN, USA
e-mail: kfosnach@indiana.edu

L. E. van Zyl et al. (eds.), *Multidisciplinary Perspectives on Grit*,
https://doi.org/10.1007/978-3-030-57389-8_4

Due to the drastically different opinions on the concept of grit, it is imperative to evaluate how grit influences student outcomes empirically. This study follows up on a previous effort to examine the validity of grit for a large and diverse sample of undergraduates (Fosnacht, Copridge, & Sarraf, 2019). It found partial support for the validity of grit as one of its dimensions, perseverance of effort, was positively associated with a variety of postsecondary outcomes; however, its construct validity needs improvement. Additionally, it found that grit did not exhibit measurement invariance by race, sex, parental education, and class level. This finding indicates that the measurement of grit is not biased against historically marginalised groups, in contrast to the critiques of Gonzalez-Stokas (2015) and Ris (2015). Therefore, we extend our previous analyses and seek to examine if perseverance of effort has the potential to provide compensatory effects for historically marginalised groups.

4.2 Literature Review

The emergence of grit has become a popular concept in the education system. The U. S Department of Education identified grit as one of the non-cognitive factors that were critical for success in the twenty-first century and beyond test scores and intellect (Shechtman, DeBarger, Dornsife, Rosier, & Yarnall, 2013). Grit, a concept developed by Angela Duckworth, is defined as the "perseverance and passion for long term goals" (Duckworth et al., 2007). Grit is a non-cognitive personality trait that includes two lower-order features: perseverance of effort and consistency of interest (Duckworth, 2016; Duckworth et al., 2007). Perseverance of effort is an individual's tendency to work hard regardless of setbacks and obstacles (Duckworth, 2016; Duckworth et al., 2007). Consistency of interest is the propensity not to change goals and interest frequently (Duckworth, 2016; Duckworth et al., 2007). These two constructs work together to positively influence an individual's behaviour and attitude to attain their long-term goals. Grit is often compared to other personality traits such as the Big Five. However, grit differs as it focuses on more long-term goals that require effort and interest. The lack of correlation with intelligence shows that this trait can potentially explain why some students succeed, while others fail (Duckworth, 2016; Duckworth et al., 2007).

Studies have found that grit significantly impacts successful outcomes after conditioning for IQ (Duckworth et al., 2007; Eskreis-Winkler, Duckworth, Shulman, & Beal, 2014). Duckworth et al.'s (2007) study examined the influence of grit and high-achieving populations such as West Point cadets and Scripps Spelling Bee finalists. The study found that grit successfully predicted attrition among the cadets who completed an intense training program and the number of hours Spelling Bee finalists practised.

In the undergraduate setting, studies have shown a positive correlation between grit and students' e-learning success and academic outcomes for at-risk populations. Aparicio, Bacao, and Oliveira (2017) examined grit's impact on e-learning systems success and satisfaction. The findings from this study showed that grittier students were more successful with e-learning systems and reported greater satisfaction than less grittier students. The impact of grit reaches a diverse demographic population as Hodge, Wright, and Bennet (2017) study examined the influence of grit on undergraduate student engagement and productivity. The results from this study found that students who were the first in their family to go to college were associated with increased levels of grit.

Moreover, Eskreis-Winkler et al. (2014) examined the influence of grit and retention in various settings like the military, the workplace, school, and even marriage. Results from this study showed that within the military setting, grittier soldiers were more likely to complete a grueling Special Forces selection program. An analysis of grit and high school graduation found that grittier students were more likely to graduate from high school. Lastly, grit influenced the likelihood of staying married, as the results showed that men with higher levels of grit were more likely to remain married (Eskreis-Winkler et al., 2014).

4.2.1 Grit and University Students

Research on grit has examined its influence on the university student population and has found some promising results. Studies on grit and its constructs have found its impact on student's persistence and success among difficult, long-term tasks (Duckworth et al., 2007; Duckworth & Quinn, 2009). Among university students, grit has been positively correlated with academic adjustment, higher grade point average, increased satisfaction, increased faculty-student interaction, and co-curricular engagement (Bowman, Hill, Denison, & Bronkema, 2015). Grit influences students' self-regulated learning as Wolters and Hussain's (2015) study found that grittier students were less likely to procrastinate on academic tasks. Moreover, Weisskirch's (2018) study examined how self-esteem and grit influence student's estimated and final grade, use of learning strategies, and attitudes about lifelong learning. The findings from this study found that the perseverance of effort construct and self-esteem predicted a student's anticipated course grade.

Within the twentieth and twenty-first century, the United States has become significantly more diverse (Turner, González, & Wood, 2008). The increase in diversity within the country has affected the American postsecondary education system. In response to the change in U.S. university student demographics, research has connected grit with sociocultural factors such as student's race, gender, and parent's educational status. Research examining these factors and grit is essential as minority students remain underrepresented, unsupported, and unsuccessful in attaining their educational aspirations relative to traditional students, students who enroll in college after graduating high school and fall between the ages of 18 and 22 (Adams & Corbett, 2010; Harper & Hurtado, 2007; Milem, Chang, & Antonio, 2005).

Grit has cross-cultural applicability as it has examined its influence on racial/ethnic groups, gender, and first-generation university students. Research shows that grit is associated with mental health, academic success and overall life satisfaction for these demographics (Datu, Valdez, & King, 2015; Strayhorn, 2014; Vela, Lu, Lenz, & Hinojosa, 2015; Wolters & Hussain, 2015).

4.2.2 Grit and Race/Ethnicity

Research examining grit and Black students is sparse but highlights the impact grit has on this demographics' academic success and retention (Strayhorn, 2014; Yates III, Moore, Vairez Jr, Barber-Freeman, Ross, Parker, & Bautista, 2015). Strayhorn's (2014) study examined grit's influence in the academic success of black male students attending a four-year, Predominately White Institution (PWI). Results from this study found that not only did grittier black males students have higher grade point averages in the university, but increased high school grade point averages and ACT scores compared to their less gritty counterparts (Strayhorn, 2014). Further analysis of the data showed that grit was a positive predictor of their university grades even after controlling variables such as age, year in school, engagement activities, transfer status, major aspirations, and prior achievements (Strayhorn, 2014).

Yates and colleagues' (2015) examined how grit influenced African American teachers' academic retention. The results from this study showed that the participants had high grit scores, yet there was a weak or no significant relationship between the participants' age, GPA, and first-generation status and grit. Qualitative findings showed that African-American male pre-service teachers acquired their grit from three sources: their family, life circumstances, and spirituality (Yates et al., 2015).

Studies on grit within the Asian community have focused on undergraduate Asian students enrolled in American and international universities. Research examining grit and Asian university students found that grit positively influenced life satisfaction amongst Filipino students (Datu et al., 2015). Amongst Thailand and Chinese undergraduates, there was a negative relationship between grit and mental health (Zhang, Mou, Tong, & Wu, 2018). Moreover, grit positively influenced the achievement goals of Chinese undergraduate students (Chen, Ye, & Hangen, 2018).

Further analysis of the influence of grit and its constructs, consistency of interest and perseverance of effort, showed that grit predicted four forms of achievement goals in different ways. In this comparative analysis of four forms of achievement goals between American and Chinese undergraduate students, Chen et al. (2018) found that consistency of interest negatively predicted performance-avoidance goals, one of the four forms of achievement goals. Perseverance of effort positively predicted all four goal types with a stronger association among mastery-approach and performance-approach goals compared to the mastery-avoidance and performance-avoidance goals (Chen et al., 2018). Moreover, Slick and Lee's (2014) study examined the influence of grit and attrition for international students enrolled at a Korean university and found a negative correlation between grit and dropping out of university (Slick & Lee, 2014).

4.2.3 Grit and Gender

Scholarship examining the influence of grit and gender have shown mixed results. Duckworth and Quinn's (2009) study validating the Short Grit scale with Scripps Spelling Bee finalists found no significant relationship between gender and grit. Bazelais et al. (2016) came to a similar conclusion using a sample of students enrolled in a science class.

In contrast, studies have shown that females from diverse backgrounds have more grit than their male counterparts (Christensen & Knezek, 2014; Guerrero, Dudovitz, Chung, Dosanjh, & Wong, 2016; Jaeger, Freeman, Whalen, & Payne, 2010). Guerrero et al.' (2016) study examined the association between grit and health behaviours among at-risk Latino adolescents. They found that grit was slightly lower among Latino males relative to Latina females (Guerrero et al., 2016). This was confirmed in Jaeger et al.' (2010) study that sought to examine the grit of first-year engineering students. Their review of the grit constructs found that the most significant difference between gender was with the consistency of interest construct. This insinuates that females were more likely to maintain interest in their major than their male counterparts. Lastly, Christensen and Knezek's (2014) study examined how grit differed based on gender and found that females had significantly higher grit compared to their male counterparts.

4.2.4 Grit and Parental Education Status

Often studies examining grit have demographics that are first-generation but focus on more salient factors such as race, gender, and its impact on grit (O'Neal et al., 2016; Strayhorn, 2014). Research has shown mixed results on how grit influences first-generation college students (Almeida, Byrne, Smith, & Ruiz, 2019; Hodge et al., 2017; Midkiff, Langer, Demetriou, & Panter, 2016; Verdín, Godwin, Kirn, Benson, & Potvin, 2018). For example, Hodge et al. (2017) examined the influence of grit and academic productivity with 395 Australian university. The study found that students who are first-generation were associated with having more grit than their second-generation counterparts (Hodge et al., 2017). The positive influence of grit was further confirmed by Verdín et al. (2018) study which examined how first-generation students' engineering identity and sense of belonging was fostered by grit. Results from the structural equation modeling found that the consistency of interest construct explained 97% of the variance of the student's sense of belonging in the engineering field, while perseverance of effort explained 76% of the variance of the student's engineering identity.

Recognizing the importance of social capital on student educational outcomes, Almeida et al. (2019) sought to examine the relationship between first-generation college student's grit and social capital in their academic success. In this study, first generation juniors and seniors completed a survey inquiring about their mentoring and support systems, GPA, standardized test scores and demographics in addition to the Grit Scale. The results from an ordinary least square regression model showed that grits and its two constructs, consistency of interest and perseverance of effort were not found to be significant predictors of the student's grade point average. However, access to social capital was predictive of a student's grade point average as each additional faculty or staff who a first-generation student received informational support was associated with a .003 unit increase in the college grade point average (Almeida et al., 2019). Moreover, scholars encourage more research on the validity and reliability of grit and first-generation students as Midkiff et al.'s (2016) study found that the constructs of grit, consistency of interest and perseverance of effort, did not load into the higher order construct of grit.

The mixed results on the influence of grit on first-generation students' warrants the need for further research. Additionally, people are multi-faceted individuals who have multiple intersecting identities that consist of privileges and oppression that influence their worldview. Thus, the linear construct of grit is often criticised for being unable to fully incorporate the experiences of gendered, classed, and raced identities.

4.3 Theoretical Framework

Ajzen's Theory of Planned Behavior (Ajzen, 1991) guided our investigation into examining if the relationship between perseverance of effort and student outcomes varied by student characteristics. The Theory of Planned Behavior postulates that an individual's behaviour is influenced by their intention to carry out the behaviour and their perceived behavioural control. The intention to engage in a behaviour is predicted by an individual's attitude towards the behaviour, subjective norms, and perceived behavioural control. Perceived behavioural control is an individual's perception of ease or difficulty in performing the behaviour of interest and is closely related to Bandura's (1977) self-efficacy concept. It is important to note that this perception varies across situations. For example, a student's engagement in seeking tutoring may relate to their belief in their high school preparation and their ability to retain the material. Attitude towards the behaviour is an individual's evaluation (positive or negative) of the behaviour. An example of attitude for this study is if a first-year student expects attending office hours to be beneficial, then this person is more likely to attend office hours. Subjective norms are defined as perceived social pressures to perform or not perform the activity. These social pressures are from other individuals or communities that are important in the individual's life. Thus, the social pressures of being successful from a student's family or community may influence a student's desire to engage in educationally beneficial activities. Alternatively, social norms at their institution may influence students to study collaboratively with friends.

The Theory of Planned Behavior has been incorporated into numerous studies to assist in understanding and modifying student behaviour. One such behaviour that has been investigated is student engagement where Siragusa and Dixon (2009) used the theory to examine undergraduate students' engagement with Information Communication Technology. Burns et al. (2018) incorporated this theory to examine how teacher confirmation or feedback influences an undergraduate student's behavioural intention to communicate with their instructor. Numerous studies using this theory have examined the behavior intentions of university students ranging from drinking (Collins & Carey, 2007), physical activity (Blanchard et al., 2008), and the use of social networking websites (Pelling & White, 2009).

For this study, we seek to examine the constructs of Theory of Planned Behavior (Attitude, Subjective Norms, and Perceived Behavioral Control). This theory will be used to examine how the perseverance of effort construct influenced historically underrepresented student's engagement in educationally purposeful activities compared to their white counterparts.

4.4 Purpose

This study follows up on previous work investigating the validity of the Short Grit Scale, which found a positive relationship between perseverance of effort and a variety of process indicators of student success (Fosnacht et al., 2019). In the current study, we sought to investigate if the grit construct has the potential to provide compensatory effects in students' engagement, self-perceived gains, time spent studying, and GPA for historically marginalised groups. In other words, does grit have a stronger relationship with essential outcomes for historically marginalised populations relative to traditional student populations? If grit does provide compensatory effects, it may be a pathway to help improve outcomes for historically marginalised groups if grit is a malleable trait (Duckworth, 2016).

4.5 Methods

4.5.1 Data

The study used data from the 2016 administration of the National Survey of Student Engagement (NSSE). NSSE is a large, multi-institutional study of undergraduates that inquires the frequency of student engagement in a variety of educationally beneficial activities, student time use, perceptions of the campus environment, and other similar measures. In 2016, students attending a subset of institutions received an additional item set that included a slightly modified version of Duckworth and Quinn's (2009) Short Grit Scale (item wording was lightly edited to comport with the core NSSE instrument). Thus, we focused our analyses on students from these 38 institutions that received the additional items. Our sample included 4668 first-year and 7082 senior students that responded to both NSSE and the additional items.

The response rates were 21% and 24% for the first year and senior samples, respectively.

The students included in our analyses were relatively diverse. About two out of three students were female. Slightly less than 57% of the respondents were White, while Asian/Pacific Islander, Black, Latina/o, multi-racial, and international students represented 6%, 11%, 12%, 7%, and 5% of the respondents, respectively. About half of the students had a parent who completed a bachelor's degree. Over 40% of the respondents attended a public institution. Half of the respondents were enrolled at institutions with a Barron's rating of "competitive". The majority of students attended master's universities, one in four students attended doctoral universities, baccalaureate universities comprised 15% of the sample, and 5% of the respondents attended a special focus institution.

The key variable in our analyses was a modified version of Duckworth and Quinn's perseverance of effort subscale (see Fosnacht et al., 2019 for more detail). We focused on this variable as it was previously found to be related to a variety of outcomes, in contrast to the consistency of interest subscale (e.g., Bowman et al., 2015; Credé et al., 2016; Fosnacht et al., 2019; Muenks et al., 2017). Perseverance of effort represents students' attitudes in our theoretical model. Our dependent variables were process indicators of student learning and development captured on the main NSSE instrument. These variables include 9 of the 10 NSSE Engagement Indicators (Effective Teaching Practices was excluded as it focuses on faculty, not students), NSSE's perceived gains scale, time spent preparing for class, and self-reported grades.

Prior research has found that these measures predict students' learning and college retention and are process indicators of student success (Kuh, Kinzie, Cruce, Shoup, & Gonyea, 2006; National Survey of Student Engagement, n.d.; Pascarella, Seifert, & Blaich, 2010; Sarraf, n.d.). Additionally, they are direct or indirect measurements of behavioural outcomes in the Theory of Planned Behavior. We standardised perseverance of effort, and the dependent variables to all have a mean of 0 and a standard deviation of 1. Three student characteristics were also of focus in this study that indicated membership in a historically marginalised class: race, sex, and parental education. These characteristics were chosen to represent subject norms from students' identity-based community. We collapsed these variables into binary variables to ensure adequate statistical power as, despite our large sample size, many subgroups contained less than 100 students. To control for other factors related to engagement, we also utilised data on the following student characteristics: standardised test score (SAT/ACT), academic major, Greek-life participation, age, athletics participation, transfer status, part-time status, educational aspirations, and on-campus residency. These variables have been previously correlated with student engagement (National Survey of Student Engagement, n.d.; Sarraf, n.d.).

4.5.2 Analyses

We began our analyses by comparing perseverance of effort by our characteristics of interests: sex, parental education, and race, using two-group t-tests. Next, we fitted a series of fixed-effects regression models that predicted each of the dependent variables using perseverance of effort and the student characteristics described in the data section. These models included institution-specific fixed-effects that allowed us to control for both observable and unobservable institution-specific factors. The institution-specific fixed effects allowed us to control for the subjective institutional norms in the Theory of Planned Behaviour. For each dependent variable, we subsequently fit an additional model that added an interaction term between race and perseverance of effort. The interaction term allowed us to assess if the relationship between perseverance of effort and the dependent variable varied by race. We repeated this step for sex and parental education. Finally, if the coefficient associated with an interaction term was significant at $p < .05$, we then graphed the predicted values of the dependent variable by perseverance of effort and the characteristic of interest when all other covariates were held at their mean. These charts allowed us to quickly interpret the interaction term and determine if perseverance of effort has compensatory effects for historically marginalised groups. We repeated all the analyses above for both first year and senior students.

4.5.3 Limitations

Before presenting the study's results, readers should keep some limitations in mind when reviewing the results. First, our dependent variables are process indicators of student learning and development and do not directly measure student learning. Second, the grit scale may be subject to social desirability bias, thus biasing our results. As this study was a secondary analysis of pre-existing data, we were unable to include variables that represented the perceived behavioural control portion of our theoretical model due to a lack of data. Fourth, while our sample is relatively diverse in terms of students and institutions, it is a convenience sample that was not designed to replicate the national population of undergraduates. Therefore, caution should be applied when generalising the results to all undergraduates.

Additionally, our results are correlational and not causal as it is not possible to randomly assign students a non-cognitive trait. Finally, while we hypothesised that the relationship between perseverance of effort and student outcomes would vary by student characteristics, both theory and previous research did not identify specific outcomes that might be subject to this effect. Consequently, we took an exploratory approach that examined a variety of outcomes. A downside of this approach is a high probability of Type I error, where we falsely identified an effect as significant. We considered using adjustments for multiple comparisons like the Bonferoni correction but decided against their use. Effect sizes such as 0.05 SDs, considered *trivial* in disciplines like psychology, are considered *medium* in education research (Kraft, 2020). Adjusting the significance level for multiple comparisons would increase the probability of Type II error (false negatives), which is a greater validity threat to this type of study than Type I error (Nakagawa, 2004). Additionally, as this study is exploratory, the results should be confirmed in a future study before influencing practice, limiting the risk of Type I error. Furthermore, in this study, we are less concerned with the family-wise error within a specific dependent variable than detecting trends across dependent variables, thus a Bonferoni-correction is not appropriate in this scenario (Perneger, 1998).

4.6 Results

4.6.1 First-Year Students

Using two-group t-tests, we observed a significant difference in perseverance of effort scores between female (M = 0.06, SD = 0.97) and male (M = -0.11, SD = 1.04; $t(4663)$ = 5.35, $p < .001$) first-year students. We did not observe a significant difference between White (M = 0.00, SD = 0.97) and non-White (M = -0.00, SD = 1.03; $t(4476)$ = 0.12, p = .901) first-year students. Similarly, we did not observe a significant difference between first-generation (M = 0.01. SD = 1.03) and non-first-generation students (M = -0.00, SD = 0.98; t (4501) = 0.29, p = .769).

Table 4.1 presents the relationship between perseverance of effort and our dependent variables, conditioned on other student and institutional characteristics. Perseverance of effort was positively and significantly related to all of our dependent variables. The magnitude of the coefficients ranged between 0.14 for Discussions with Diverse Others and 0.33 for Learning Strategies. Thus, a standard deviation change in perseverance of effort was expected to result in a 0.33 SD change in Learning Strategies, holding constant other factors. Overall, the results demonstrate that perseverance of effort is positively correlated with engagement in a variety of domains, perceived gains, time spent preparing for class, and GPA.

Table 4.2 summarises the results indicating if the relationship between perseverance of effort and the dependent variables significantly varied by race, sex, and first-generation status. This relationship was assessed by including interaction terms between perseverance of effort and the characteristic of interest into the model. The interaction terms between race and perseverance of effort were only significant at $p < .05$ for Discussions with Diverse Others. Significant interaction terms were found between sex and perseverance of effort for Higher-Order Learning and time spent preparing for class. Additionally, significant interaction terms were observed between first-generation status and perseverance of effort for Reflective and Integrative Learning and GPA.

Figure 4.1 plots the predicted values for Discussions with Diverse Others by race and perseverance of effort. The figure shows that the relationship between

Table 4.1 Relationship between perseverance of effort and student engagement, perceived gains, time spent preparing for class, and GPA

	First-year				Senior			
Dependent variable	Coef.	SE	Sig.	R^2	Coef.	SE	Sig.	R^2
Higher-Order Learning	0.24	0.02	.000	0.09	0.16	0.02	.000	.08
Reflective & Integrative Learning	0.21	0.02	.000	0.11	0.15	0.02	.000	.16
Quantitative Reasoning	0.19	0.02	.000	0.08	0.14	0.02	.000	.13
Learning Strategies	0.33	0.02	.000	0.13	0.23	0.02	.000	.13
Collaborative Learning	0.16	0.02	.000	0.08	0.13	0.02	.000	.14
Discussions w/Diverse Others	0.14	0.02	.000	0.07	0.14	0.02	.000	.07
Student-Faculty Interaction	0.18	0.02	.000	0.07	0.16	0.02	.000	.12
Quality of Interactions	0.17	0.02	.000	0.07	0.11	0.02	.000	.05
Supportive Environment	0.21	0.02	.000	0.06	0.14	0.02	.000	.06
Perceived gains	0.28	0.02	.000	0.10	0.17	0.02	.000	.10
Time spent: Preparing for class	0.19	0.02	.000	0.08	0.19	0.02	.000	.10
GPA	0.28	0.02	.000	0.18	0.25	0.02	.000	.23

Note: The dependent variables and perseverance of effort were standardised with a mean of 0 and a standard deviation of 1. Models controlled for race/ethnicity, sex, age, parental education, SAT I or ACT equivalent, student-athlete status, enrollment intensity, Greek-life participation, transfer status, living on campus, and major field. Models also included institution-specific fixed effects. R^2 is for the full model including all covariates

Table 4.2 Significance tests associated with the interaction term coefficient between perseverance of effort and student characteristics, by race, sex, and parental education and class standing

	First-year			Senior		
	Race	Sex	Par. Ed.	Race	Sex	Par. Ed
Higher-Order Learning	.841	**.003**	.051	.072	.362	.178
Reflective & Integrative Learning	.414	.826	**.035**	**.038**	.227	.104
Quantitative Reasoning	.605	.677	.426	**.049**	.196	.214
Learning Strategies	.222	.153	.098	.773	.615	.168
Collaborative Learning	.219	.195	.998	.151	.060	.406
Discussions w/Diverse Others	**.042**	.891	.143	**.017**	.188	.135
Student-Faculty Interaction	.506	.565	.303	.168	**.002**	**.020**
Quality of Interactions	.060	.705	.589	.397	.373	.526
Supportive Environment	.117	.945	.456	.951	.099	.050
Perceived gains	.775	.218	.198	.174	.187	.062
Time spent: Preparing for class	.279	**.013**	.560	.532	.787	.897
GPA	.842	.199	**.025**	.188	.409	.057

Note: Values less than $p < .05$ are bolded. Models controlled for race/ethnicity, sex, age, parental education, SAT I or ACT equivalent, student-athlete status, enrollment intensity, Greek-life participation, transfer status, living on campus, and major field. Models also included institution-specific fixed effects

perseverance of effort and Discussions with Diverse Others is stronger for non-White students than for White students. Additionally, it shows that non-White students with high levels of perseverance of effort will engage in more frequent

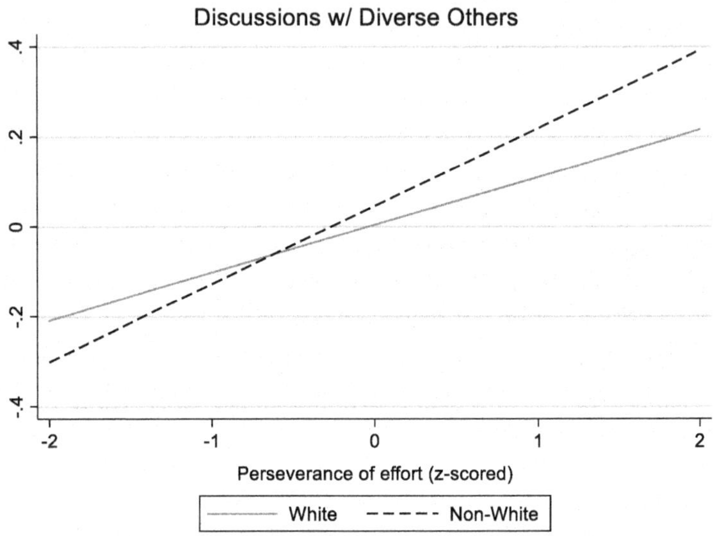

Fig. 4.1 Selected interaction effect results by outcome for race: First-year students

Discussions with Diverse Others than White students, with the opposite being expected for students with low levels of perseverance of effort.

Figure 4.2 contains the same plot, but for the Higher-Order Learning and time spent preparing for class outcomes and sex. The partial correlation between perseverance of effort and Higher-Order Learning is stronger for females compared to males. The bottom panel of the figure shows a similar relationship for time spent studying and perseverance of effort by sex.

Figure 4.3 shows the interaction plots for first-generation university status. It demonstrates a stronger relationship between Reflective & Integrative Learning and perseverance of effort for first-generation students than for non-first-generation students. Similarly, the bottom panel demonstrates a stronger relationship between GPA and perseverance of effort for first-generation students relative to the non-first-generation peers. While not shown, the interaction term for first-generation status and perseverance of effort on our Higher Order Learning measure nearly met our threshold for statistical significance ($p < .05$). The results mirrored the results for the other two interactions for first-generation university status.

4.6.2 Seniors

Using two-group *t*-tests, we observed a significant difference in perseverance of effort scores between senior females ($M = 0.07$, $SD = 0.97$) and males ($M = -0.12$, $SD = 1.04$; $t(5229) = 7.54$, $p < .001$). We did not observe a significant difference between White ($M = 0.00$, $SD = 0.98$) and non-White ($M =$ -0.01, $SD = 1.02$; *t*

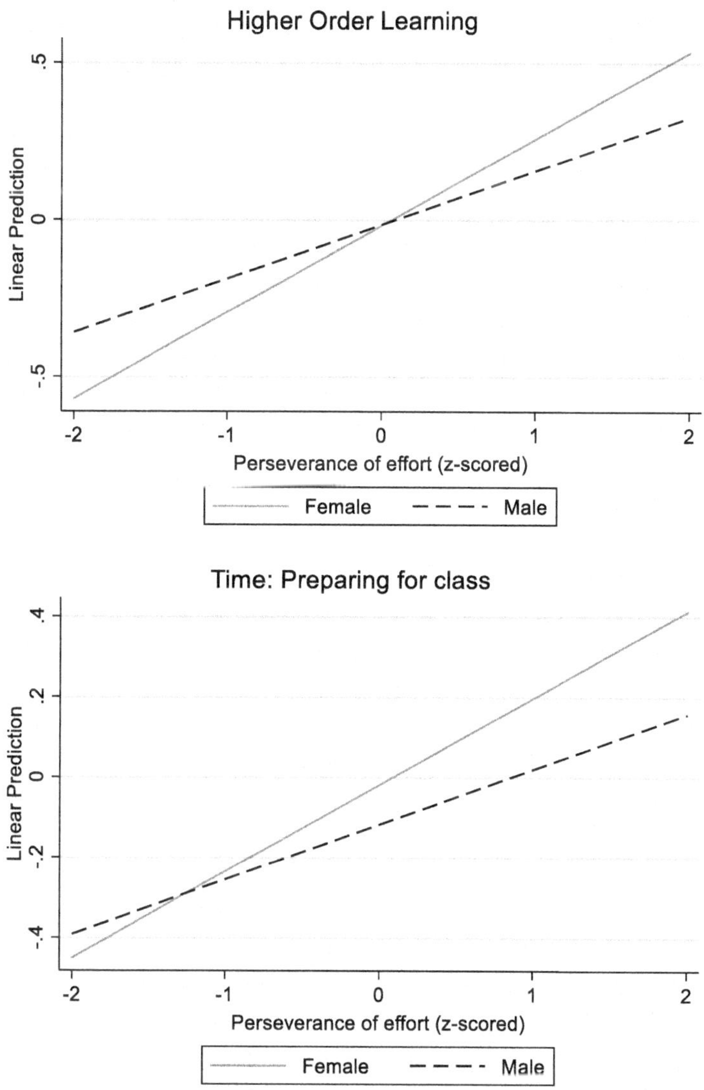

Fig. 4.2 Selected interaction effect results by outcome for sex: First-year students

(5972) = 0.57, $p = .572$) seniors. However, we did observe a significant difference between first-generation ($M = 0.08$. $SD = 0.95$) and non-first-generation seniors ($M = -0.08$, $SD = 1.04$; $t(6894) = 6.94$, $p < .000$).

The main effect results for perseverance of effort in the senior population mirrored the findings for first-year students. Perseverance of effort was positively and significantly related to all of our dependent variables when other student and institutional characteristics were held constant. The magnitude of the relationships varied from 0.11 for Quality of Interactions to 0.25 for GPA. Thus, a SD change in

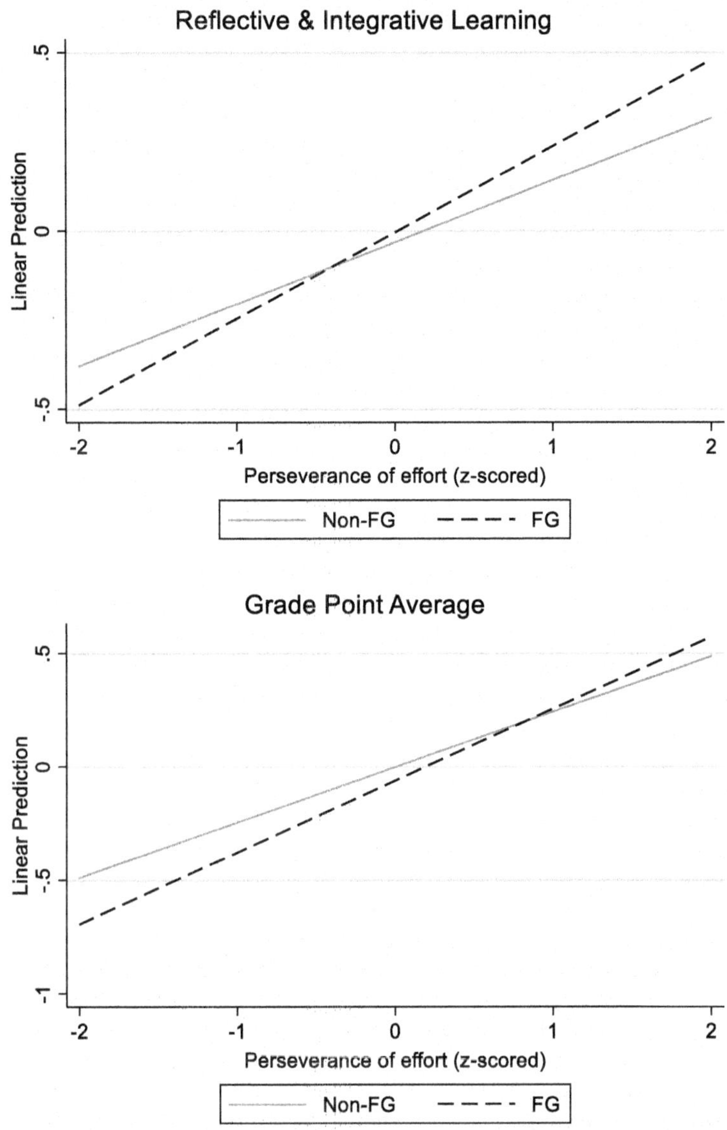

Fig. 4.3 Selected interaction effect results by outcome for parental education: First-year students

perseverance of effort is expected to result in a quarter SD change in GPA. While the senior results were similar to the first-year results, the first-year results were typically slightly higher than the senior coefficients.

Table 4.2 contains the significance values associated with the interaction terms between perseverance of effort and the three demographic groups studied. We observed three significant interactions at $p < 0.05$ for race/ethnicity, one for sex, and two for first-generation status in our senior sample. Figure 4.4 plots the

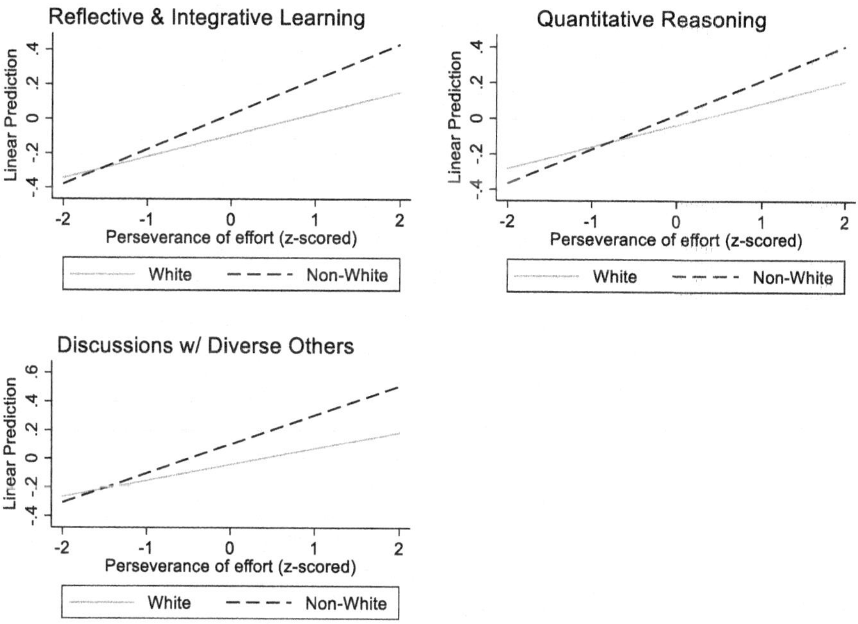

Fig. 4.4 Selected interaction effect results by outcome for race: Seniors

relationship between Reflective & Integrative Learning and perseverance of effort by race. The slope of the line is significantly steeper for non-White students than White students. The middle and bottom panels also demonstrate a similar finding for Quantitative Reasoning and Discussions with Diverse Others in that the estimated relationships are steeper for non-White students than for White students.

Figure 4.5 demonstrates the sole significant interaction effect observed by sex. The partial correlation between Student-Faculty Interaction and perseverance of effort was stronger for females than males.

The top panel of Fig. 4.6 shows that the relationship between perseverance of effort and Supportive Environment was steeper for first-generation students than their peers who had a parent who completed university. Finally, the bottom panel of Fig. 4.6 shows a similar relationship for Student-Faculty Interaction as the relationship for first-generation students was stronger than for non-first-generation students.

4.7 Discussion

Grit has captured the attention of the education community, both proponents and detractors alike. Consequently, it is imperative to better understand the utility of the grit constructs in educational settings. In a previous study, we found that one dimension of grit, perseverance of effort, predicted a variety of educational

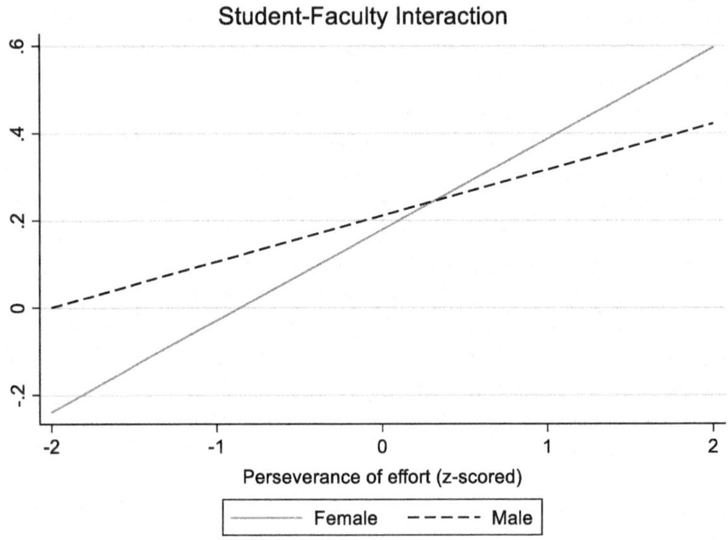

Fig. 4.5 Selected interaction effect results by outcome for sex: Seniors

outcomes, but that its criterion validity could be improved. In this study, we examined if the relationship between perseverance of effort and educational outcomes varied by race, sex, and first-generation status. Understanding how non-cognitive traits like perseverance of effort influence outcomes are critical to their use in educational decisions like admissions. If traits like grit primarily benefit traditional student populations, the use of grit in high stakes decisions could help reproduce inequality and harm non-traditional student populations. However, grit also has the potential to help identify non-traditional students with lower than average academic credentials, but with a high probability of student success.

In our previous work, we demonstrated that grit possesses measurement invariance by race, sex, and first-generation status (Fosnacht et al., 2019). Therefore, grit measures the same construct across these groups, and these groups respond to the grit items similarly. Consequently, claims that grit is biased against particular groups seem unfounded (Gonzalez-Stokas, 2015; Ris, 2015). However, the research community has not yet explored if the relationship between grit and student outcomes varies across subpopulations. As the perseverance of effort dimension of grit focuses on student resilience in the face of barriers to success or negative experiences, we hypothesised that perseverance of effort would be especially beneficial to the success of non-traditional student populations. If our hypothesis were true, it would indicate that grit is an especially important quality for non-traditional students.

Our results demonstrate that perseverance of effort is significantly and positively related to a variety of student outcomes such as engagement, perceived gains, time spent studying, and GPA. The estimates were uniformly positive, substantial, and broad. A standard deviation change in perseverance of effort was associated with a 0.14 to 0.33 SD change in our dependent variables for first-year students and a 0.11

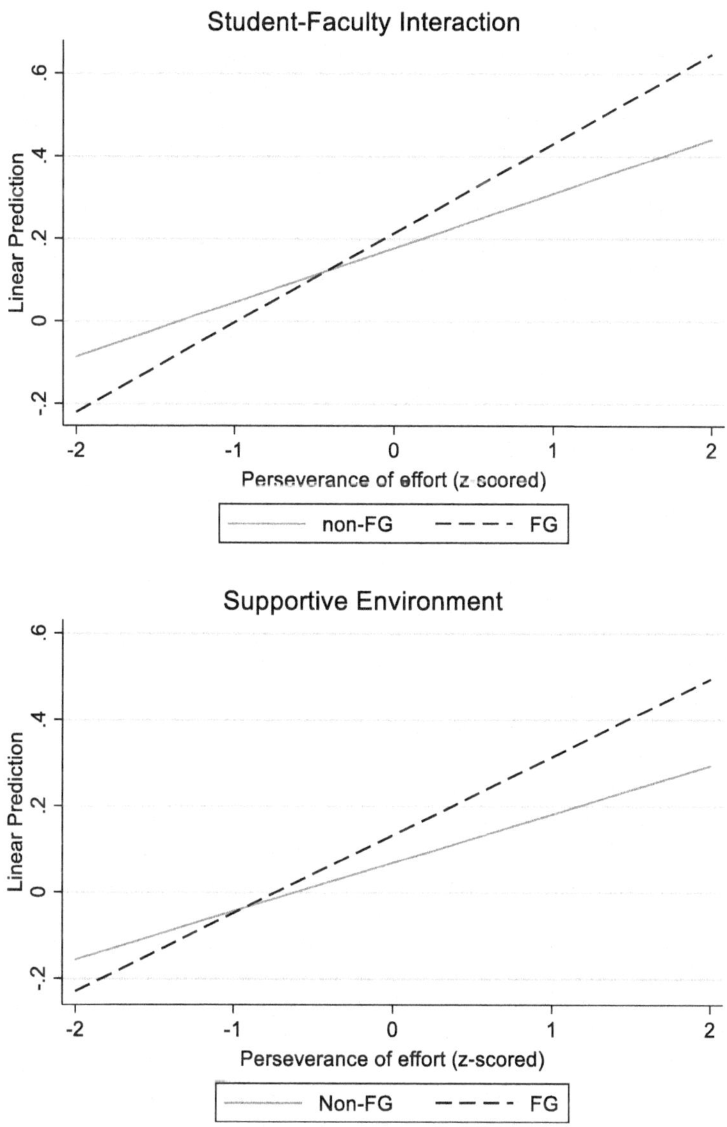

Fig. 4.6 Selected interaction effect results by outcome for parental education: Seniors

to 0.25 SD change for seniors. Consequently, perseverance of effort appears to be a factor that leads to engagement in effective educational practices.

Next, we examined if the relationship between perseverance of effort and our dependent variables varied by student characteristics. While the relationship was statistically constant for many dependent variables, we observed 11 situations where the relationship varied significantly by subgroup. A uniform pattern emerged in these significant relationships. The partial correlation between perseverance of effort and our dependent variables was stronger for non-traditional student populations (female, non-White, first-generation) than for traditional students (male, White, non-first-generation). Therefore, the results suggest that perseverance of effort has compensatory effects on important university outcomes. In other words, perseverance of effort helps non-traditional student populations achieve success despite the additional barriers these students encounter. Consequently, resilience and overcoming obstacles appear to be particularly salient to the success of non-traditional student populations.

Ajzen's (1991) Theory of Planned Behavior explains why perseverance of effort may be more salient for marginalised student populations. We conceptualise perseverance of effort as an attitude students use to motivate their desire to engage in educational activities (behavioural intention). Non-traditional students are aware of their marginalised identities (women, first-generation, and minorities) and use their identities to motivate their engagement in the behaviour of interest. Students' attitudes are also informed by social pressures from their family and home communities. For example, a first-generation student may feel intense pressure from their family and high school teachers to be successful in university and return to their home community. This pressure may foster resilience to overcome setbacks and inspire students to work harder to achieve a university degree (Bryan & Simmons, 2009). Consequently, perseverance of effort is particularly important for non-traditional groups. This construct helps students to overcome gaps in college knowledge and push through obstacles inherent in the college-going process.

Our findings have implications for policy and practice. First, our results suggest that an avenue for institutions to close gaps in student success would be to identify and target students who have qualitatively demonstrated traits like perseverance of effort or resilience. We do not recommend using the grit scale to directly identify these students as the scale does not meet accepted psychometric standards for high-stakes decisions and the scale could be "gamed" if students are cognizant of its use in admissions decisions. Second, our findings also suggest that non-traditional students face additional barriers to student success or did not possess the cultural capital specific to postsecondary education needed to navigate higher education. Therefore, non-traditional students required specific non-cognitive attributes to be successful.

Consequently, higher education institutions should look to proactively identify programs and practices that have a disparate impact on non-traditional students and reformulate them to eliminate their disparate features. Furthermore, institutions should work with faculty, staff, and administrators to ensure that their university is welcoming to all students. While we call for the reduction in barriers to student success for non-traditional students, this call should not be construed as advocating for a less rigorous curriculum or not challenging students academically. Academic challenge is an important aspect of student learning and development and critical to student success.

Our results also have implications for future research. Student engagement is positively related to student persistence and is especially important for historically underrepresented students (Kuh et al., 2006). Therefore, future research should examine the differential impacts of perseverance of effort by student characteristics on persistence. As perseverance of effort has compensatory effects on student engagement and student engagement has compensatory effects on persistence, perseverance of effort is likely to have a larger than average effect on persistence for non-traditional student populations. Our findings also call for continued research into identifying barriers historically underrepresented students face in their pursuit of a degree. While much effort has been given to identifying these barriers, continued vigilance is needed due to the changing nature of higher education.

References

Adams, J., & Corbett, A. (2010). Experiences of traditional and non-traditional college students. *Perspectives, 2*(1), 2.

Ajzen, I. (1991). The theory of planned behavior. *Organizational Behavior and Human Decision Processes, 50*(2), 179–211.

Almeida, D. J., Byrne, A. M., Smith, R. M., & Ruiz, S. (2019). How relevant is grit? The importance of social capital in first-generation college students' academic success. *Journal of College Student Retention: Research, Theory & Practice*. https://doi.org/10.1177/1521025119854688.

Aparicio, M., Bacao, F., & Oliveira, T. (2017). Grit in the path to e-learning success. *Computers in Human Behavior, 66*, 388, 399.

Bandura, A. (1977). Self-efficacy: Toward a unifying theory of behavioral change. *Psychological Review, 84*(2), 191–215.

Bazelais, P., Lemay, D. J., & Doleck, T. (2016). How does grit impact college students' academic achievement in science? *European Journal of Science and Mathematics Education, 4*(1), 33–43.

Blanchard, C., Fisher, J., Sparling, P., Nehl, E., Rhodes, R., Courneya, K., & Baker, F. (2008). Understanding physical activity behavior in African American and Caucasian college students: An application of the theory of planned behavior. *Journal of American College Health, 56*(4), 341–346.

Bowman, N. A., Hill, P. L., Denison, N., & Bronkema, R. (2015). Keep on truckin' or stay the course? Exploring grit dimensions as differential predictors of educational achievement, satisfaction, and intentions. *Social Psychology and Personality Science, 6*, 639–645. https://doi.org/10.1177/1948550615574300.

Bryan, E., & Simmons, L. A. (2009). Family involvement: Impacts on post-secondary educational success for first-generation Appalachian college students. *Journal of College Student Development, 50*(4), 391–406.

Burns, M. E., Houser, M. L., & Farris, K. L. (2018). Theory of planned behavior in the classroom: An examination of the instructor confirmation-interaction model. *Higher Education, 75*(6), 1091–1108.

Chen, C., Ye, S., & Hangen, E. (2018). Predicting achievement goals in the east and west: The role of grit among American and Chinese university students. *Educational Psychology, 38*, 820–837.

Christensen, R., & Knezek, G. (2014). Comparative measures of grit, tenacity, and perseverance. *International Journal of Learning, Teaching and Educational Research, 8*(1), 16–30.

Collins, S. E., & Carey, K. B. (2007). The theory of planned behavior as a model of heavy episodic drinking among college students. *Psychology of Addictive Behaviors, 21*(4), 498–507.

Credé, M., Tynan, M. C., & Harms, P. D. (2016). Much ado about grit: A meta-analytic synthesis of the grit literature. *Journal of Personality and Social Psychology, 111*, 492–511. https://doi.org/10.1037/pspp0000102.

Datu, J. F., Valdez, J. P., & King, R. B. (2015). Perseverance counts but consistency does not! Validating the short grit scale in a collectivist setting. *Current Psychology, 35*, 121–130.

Del Giudice, M. (2014). *Grit trumps talent and IQ: A Story every parent (and educator) should read*. Retrieved from http://news.nationalgeographic.com/news/2014/10/141015-angela-duckworth-success-grit-psychology-self-control-science-nginnovators/

Duckworth, A. L. (2016). *Grit: The power of passion and perseverance*. New York: Simon & Schuster.

Duckworth, A. L., Peterson, C., Matthews, M. D., & Kelly, D. R. (2007). Grit: Perseverance and passion for long-term goals. *Journal of Personality and Social Psychology, 92*(6), 1087–1101. https://doi.org/10.1037/0022-3514.92.6.1087.

Duckworth, A. L., & Quinn, P. D. (2009). Development and validation of the short grit scale (grit-S). *Journal of Personality Assessment, 9*, 166–174. https://doi.org/10.1080/00223890802634290.

Engber, D. (2016). Is "grit" really the key to success? *Slate*. Retrieved from http://www.slate.com/articles/health_and_science/cover_story/2016/05/angela_duckworth_says_grit_is_the_key_to_success_in_work_and_life_is_this.html

Eskreis-Winkler, L., Duckworth, A. L., Shulman, E. P., & Beal, S. (2014). The grit effect: Predicting retention in the military, the workplace, school, and marriage. *Frontiers in Psychology, 5*, 36.

Fosnacht, K., Copridge, K., & Sarraf, S. A. (2019). How valid is grit in the postsecondary context? A construct and concurrent validity analysis. *Research in Higher Education, 60*, 803–822. https://doi.org/10.1007/s11162-018-9524-0.

Gonzalez-Stokas, A. (2015). A genealogy of grit: Education in the new gilded age. *Educational Theory, 65*, 513–528. https://doi.org/10.1111/edth.12130.

Guerrero, L. R., Dudovitz, R., Chung, P. J., Dosanjh, K. K., & Wong, M. D. (2016). Grit: A potential protective factor against substance use and other risk behaviors among Latino adolescents. *Academic Pediatrics, 16*(3), 275–281.

Harper, S. R., & Hurtado, H. (2007). Nine themes in campus racial climates and implications for institutional transformation. *New Directions for Student Services, 120*, 7–24.

Hodge, B., Wright, B., & Bennet, P. (2017). The role of grit in determining engagement and academic outcomes for university students. *Research in Higher Education, 59*(4), 448–460.

Jaeger, B., Freeman, S., Whalen, R., & Payne, R. (2010). Successful students: Smart or tough. In *Proceedings, ASEE Annual Convention, Paper AC* (Vol. 1033).

Kraft, M. A. (2020). Interpreting effect sizes of education interventions. *Educational Researcher, 49*(4), 241–253.

Kuh, G. D., Kinzie, J., Cruce, T., Shoup, R., & Gonyea, R. M. (2006, July). *Connecting the dots: Multi-faceted analyses of the relationships between student engagement results from the NSSE, and the institutional practices and conditions that foster student success: Final report prepared for Lumina Foundation for education*. Bloomington, IN: Indiana University, Center for Postsecondary Research.

Midkiff, B., Langer, M., Demetriou, C., & Panter, A. T. (2016, July). Measuring grit among first-generation college students: A psychometric analysis. In A. van der Ark, M. Wilberg, S. Culpepper, J. Douglas, & W. Wang (Eds.), *Quantitative psychology: The 81st annual meeting of the psychometric society* (pp. 407–420). Cham: Springer.

Milem, J. F., Chang, M. J., & Antonio, A. L. (2005). *Making diversity work on campus: A research-based perspective*. Washington, DC: Association American Colleges and Universities.

Muenks, K., Wigfield, A., Yang, J. S., & O'Neal, C. R. (2017). How true is grit? Assessing its relations to high school and college students' personality charcteristics, self-regulations, engagement, and achievement. *Journal of Educational Psychology, 109*(5), 599–620. https://doi.org/10.1037/edu0000153.

Nakagawa, S. (2004). A farewell to Bonferroni: The problems of low statistical power and publication bias. *Behavioral Ecology, 15*(6), 1044–1045.

National Survey of Student Engagement. (n.d.). *Validity: 2009 known groups validation*. Bloomington, IN: Indiana university center for postsecondary research.

O'Neal, C. R., Espino, M. M., Goldthrite, A., Morin, M. F., Weston, L., Hernandez, P., & Fuhrman, A. (2016). Grit under duress: Stress, strengths, and academic success among non-citizen and citizen Latina/o first-generation college students. *Hispanic Journal of Behavioral Sciences, 38*, 446–466. https://doi.org/10.1177/0739986316660775.

Pascarella, E. T., Seifert, T. A., & Blaich, C. (2010). How effective are the NSSE benchmarks in predicting important educational outcomes? *Change: The Magazine of Higher Learning, 42*(1), 16–22.

Pelling, E. L., & White, K. M. (2009). The theory of planned behavior applied to young people's use of social networking web sites. *Cyberpsychology & Behavior, 12*(6), 755–759.

Perneger, T. V. (1998). What's wrong with Bonferroni adjustments. *BMJ, 316*(7139), 1236–1238.

Ris, E. W. (2015). Grit: A short history of a useful concept. *Journal of Educational Controversy, 10* (1), Article 3. Retrieved from http://cedar.wwu.edu/cgi/viewcontent.cgi?article=1246&context=jec.

Sarraf, S. A. (n.d.). *NSSE predictive validity study*. Retrieved from https://nsse.indiana.edu/nsse/psychometric-portfolio/predictive.html.

Shechtman, N., DeBarger, A., Dornsife, C., Rosier, S., & Yarnall, L. (2013). *Promoting grit, tenacity, and perseverance: Critical factors for success in the 21st century*. US Department of Education Office of Educational Technology. Retrieved from www.ed.gov/edblogs/technology/files/2013/02/OET-Draft-Grit-Report-2-17-13.pdf

Siragusa, L. & Dixon, K. (2009). Theory of planned behaviour: Higher education students' attitudes towards ICT-based learning interactions. In *Same places, different spaces. Proceedings ascilite Auckland 2009*. Retrieved from http://www.ascilite.org.au/conferences/auckland09/procs/siragusa.pdf

Slick, S. N., & Lee, C. S. (2014). The relative levels of grit and their relationship with potential dropping-out and university adjustment of foreign students in Korea. *Journal of Digital Convergence, 12*(8), 61–66.

Strayhorn, T. L. (2014). What role does grit play in the academic success of black male collegians at predominately-white institutions? *Journal of African American Studies, 18*, 1–10. https://doi.org/10.1007/s12111-012-9243-0.

Turner, C. S. V., González, J. C., & Wood, J. L. (2008). Faculty of color in academe: What 20 years of literature tells us. *Journal of Diversity in Higher Education, 1*(3), 139–168. https://doi.org/10.1037/a0012837.

Vela, J. C., Lu, M. T. P., Lenz, A. S., & Hinojosa, K. (2015). Positive psychology and familial factors as predictors of Latina/o students' psychological grit. *Hispanic Journal of Behavioral Sciences, 37*(3), 287–303.

Verdín, D., Godwin, A., Kirn, A., Benson, L., & Potvin, G. (2018). Understanding how engineering identity and belongingness predict grit for first-generation college students. In *2018 CoNECD - The Collaborative Network for Engineering and Computing Diversity Conference*. Retrieved from https://www.asee.org/public/conferences/113/papers/24218/download

Weisskirch, R. S. (2018). Grit, self-esteem, learning strategies and attitudes and estimated and achieved course grades among college students. *Current Psychology, 37*(1), 21–27.

Wolters, C. A., & Hussain, M. (2015). Investigating grit and its relations with college students' self-regulated learning and academic achievement. *Metacognition and Learning, 10*(3), 293–311. https://doi.org/10.1007/s11409-014-9128-9.

Yates, L., III, Moore, J., Vairez, M. R., Jr., Barber-Freeman, P. T., Ross, W., Parker, W. H., & Bautista, R. (2015). The grit of African American male pre-service teachers. *Journal of the Texas Alliance of Black School Educators The Grit of African American, 1*(2), 11–38.

Zhang, M., Mou, N., Tong, K., & Wu, A. (2018). Investigation of the effects of purpose in life, grit, gratitude, and school belonging on mental distress among Chinese emerging adults. *International Journal of Environmental Research and Public Health, 15*(10), 2147.

Kevin Fosnacht (Ph.D.) is Associate Research Scientist at the Indiana University, Bloomington. Center for Postsecondary Research, where he works on the National Survey of Student Engagement. Kevin's research focuses on postsecondary policies and practices that can promote undergraduates' student engagement, learning, and development.

Keeley Webb-Copridge is a Doctoral Candidate in the Higher Education and Student Affairs program at Indiana University in Bloomington, Indiana. Keeley's research focuses on the college access and preparation of historically marginalized student populations and student retention.

Chapter 5
Enhancing Grit: Possibility and Intervention Strategies

Mae-Hyang Hwang and JeeEun Karin Nam

Abstract This chapter suggests intervention strategies for enhancing grit. Since Duckworth's introduction, grit has been demonstrated to be a critical personal characteristic in predicting positive educational, vocational, and well-being outcomes across many cultures. However, it is still unclear whether grit can be increased through interventions and how it could be achieved. While grit has been largely regarded as an unchanging personal trait, research in brain development, neuroscience, and psychological resources have indicated that grit may be malleable and teachable throughout the lifespan. This chapter presents the possibility of enhancing grit with longitudinal data and neuropsychological findings on brain development. Intervention strategies are then proposed for the cognitive, behavioral, and emotional domains of grit. In the cognitive domain, teaching grit, reflecting on one's own and vicarious experiences of grit, adopting a growth mindset, and setting both long-term and short-term goals are suggested. In the behavioral domain, promoting brain development, increasing deliberate practices, and preventing the overuse of media are proposed. Lastly, in the emotional domain, overcoming negative emotions (e.g. stress and frustration) in the process of exercising grit, and promoting interest discovery through flow experiences are offered.

Keywords Grit enhancement · Brain development · Intervention · Growth mindset · Goal setting · Deliberate practice · Flow

---

M.-H. Hwang (✉)
Department of Education, Gyeongin National University of Education, Incheon, South Korea
e-mail: maehyang@ginue.ac.kr

J. K. Nam
Graduate School of Education, Ewha Womans University, Seoul, South Korea
e-mail: jkarin@ewha.ac.kr

L. E. van Zyl et al. (eds.), *Multidisciplinary Perspectives on Grit*,
https://doi.org/10.1007/978-3-030-57389-8_5

5.1 Introduction

Defined as the 'perseverance and passion for long-term goals,' grit refers to the energy to prevail without giving up despite any situational difficulties (Duckworth, Peterson, Matthews, & Kelly, 2007). Grit involves various individual traits known to predict success such as self-control (resisting the momentary temptations for long-term goals), self-regulation (regulating thoughts, emotions, behaviors that get in the way of task performance), and task persistence (persisting in a task already started). As such, consistency of interest (the tendency to maintain a steadfast interest in a target task) and perseverance of effort (the tendency to exert long-lasting efforts) are two distinct dimensions that are thought to comprise grit (Duckworth & Quinn, 2009). A more recent meta-analytic study has attested to these two dimensions of grit (Credé, Tynan, & Harms, 2017).

Grit made its first appearance in 2004 when the Grit Scale was administered at West Point, a U.S. military academy, with scale items derived from Duckworth's interviews with successful people from various fields. Grit received greater attention upon the scale's 2007 academic publication, as well as the U.S. Department of Education's development of a grit-promoting program (Shechtman, DeBarger, Dornsife, Rosier, & Yarnall, 2013). Soon, grit was discussed as a solution to underachievement of vulnerable groups (Tough, 2012), and was made known to the larger public. Grit has drawn steady interest in the field of education research and practice ever since. Grit significantly predicted various achievement outcomes such as high education levels, high college GPA, and even awards at the National Spelling Bee Contest, after controlling for other factors (Duckworth et al., 2007). Its close relationship with the learning process and academic achievement has been reported repeatedly in many different national contexts (e.g., Choi, 2018; Duckworth & Eskreis-Winkler, 2013; Ha, Lim, & Hwang, 2015; Hwang, Ha, & Kim, 2017; Lee & Sohn, 2013; Strayhorn, 2014; Wolf & Jia, 2015). In 2016, Duckworth's University of Pennsylvania team published their research in a book form, which has been translated into various languages. A grit-based educational support website Character LAB (https://www.characterlab.org/) has been under operation since then as well.

Nonetheless, given that grit is still a relatively new concept in the field, much of the existing studies have focused on exploring its dimensions and relationships with other variables. Studies that have directly dealt with enhancing grit are still scarce. This is unfortunate, as grit appears to be better conceptualized behaviorally than innately. Rather than seen as a congenital tendency, grit is being examined as an individual's behavior manifested during task performance. In this view, grit is a characteristic that can be developed as individuals interact with their environment. In fact, a twin study has revealed that individuals' unique environment accounted for more than two-thirds of the variance in grit's consistency of interest and perseverance of effort factors (Rimfeld, Kovas, Dale, & Plomin, 2016). As such, developing educational interventions that promote grit has become a part of an important agenda. In the United States, educational programs that seek to promote grit as a character trait (e.g., Baruch-Feldman, 2017; Character Lab, 2018; Shechtman et al.,

2013) have suggested intrapersonal conditions (interest, practice, goals, hope) as well as environmental conditions (parents, learning experience, cultural context) for the development of grit (Duckworth, 2016). In order to gain further insight into intervention strategies of enhancing grit, this chapter reviews existing studies that directly deal with grit enhancement, along with those that examined the predictors of grit.

5.2 The Possibility of Enhancing Grit

Educators are drawn to grit enhancement because grit is considered an individual characteristic that can be changed through educational interventions. How malleable is grit? To what extent is change possible? Considerable variability exists among human characteristics in terms of their likelihood for change. While there are ongoing debates about how changeable grit might be as a personal characteristic, not many empirical studies have directly examined grit development. A notable study that investigated grit development is the twin study by Rimfeld et al. (2016). They administered the Grit Scale to 4642 16-year-olds (2321 twin pairs) and found a heritability estimate of 37% for perseverance and 20% for consistency. This finding is significant in that it shows how grit may in part be genetically determined, but is largely affected by the environment. Considering that changes occur in the process of gene expression through interactions with the environment, it would be safe to assume that grit can be enhanced in children and adolescents through effective interventions.

Further, Duckworth and Eskreis-Winkler (2013) analyzed cross-sectional data collected from adults and found that grit increased steadily from their twenties to sixties. The results show that grit continues to develop beyond the age of children and adolescents into adulthood. Duckworth and Eskreis-Winkler (2013) interpreted these findings as a function of individuals' learning the importance of effort over time while solidifying their identities, which enables them to pursue more specific goals.

Seen from the neuroscientific perspective, grit also appears to develop steadily during childhood and adolescence. Neuroscience describes the neurological processes underlying grit via executive functioning. Executive functioning is the mental activity that occurs while delaying immediate response to stimuli, and includes self-directed behavior, behavioral organization over time, use of self-directed language, rules, and planning, delayed gratification, goal orientation, future orientation, as well as goal-directed, intentional behavior (Barkley, 2005). Executive functioning mainly involves the frontal cortex of the cerebral cortex and engages the processes of inhibition and decision making. In other words, the control processes that undergird grit can be said to be supported by executive functioning.

Executive functioning is associated with the maintenance of focus on a given task rather than responding to new stimuli, and consists of four elements: goal formation, planning, carrying out goal-directed plans, and effective performance (Jurado &

Rosselli, 2007). Goal-oriented actions implicate the executive functioning processes of setting goals, developing effective plans to achieve them, taking purposive action, and improving effectiveness through self-examination.

These executive functions are also related to the acquisition and use of various strategies to optimize their function. In other words, since grit is closely related to executive function, the development of the frontal lobe (basis for the development of executive function) and the acquisition of various strategies used for executive functioning also become the basis of grit development. Acquisition of strategies necessary for grit, including impulse inhibition and delaying gratification, continues all the way through the development of abstract thinking. In recent brain development studies, the development of the nervous system involved in response inhibition, decision making, and goal pursuit does not become complete until late adolescence (Casey, Tottenham, Liston, & Durston, 2005; Giedd, 2008; Steinberg, 2013). These findings support that childhood and adolescence are important times for increasing grit.

5.3 Grit Promotion Strategies

Although grit is considered to be a personality trait that develops relatively early on in life, the evidence for the possibility of its change during childhood and adolescence is accumulating. Accordingly, there is a growing interest in how to promote grit. However, as grit-related research is still in its infancy, relatively few empirical studies have explored specific ways to promote it or have provided direct evidence for enhanced grit through intervention (Credé et al., 2017).

A representative case where the grit-promoting strategy was first introduced is traced back to Duckworth's (2016) proposal that introduced the very concept of grit. Her character education program included grit-promoting activities, but they still remain as suggestions due to the lack of empirical evidence for their effectiveness. Duckworth suggested that the internal conditions for grit development are the individual's interests, practices, goals, and hopes; parents, learning experiences, and cultural contexts are categorized under environmental conditions (Duckworth, 2016).

Another foray into grit promotion can be found in character education, where grit is taught as a virtue. The Grit Enhancement Program (Shechtman et al., 2013) developed by the US Department of Education and distributed to schools promotes grit through increasing self-control, growth mindset, learning strategies, and resilience. KIPP charter schools include grit in the seven core competencies to teach students (Cohen, 2015). Using the character education materials provided by Character Lab (2018), they discuss the importance of grit, learning role model behavior, and increasing grit through one's experiences of success and failure. The Association for Supervision and Curriculum Development (ASCD) proposes a six-stage curriculum, comprised of creating a supportive environment that recognizes people's efforts, self-understanding through grit testing, teaching the meaning of grit, experiencing failure, examining failure experience, and learning through reflection (Hoerr, 2013). Other grit promotion programs are being proposed, based on the existing empirical research on grit and related variables; however, they are still limited in that their effectiveness has not yet been proven (e.g. Keegan, 2017; Pueschel & Tucker, 2018).

Empirical studies that demonstrate the effectiveness of grit enhancement do exist. DiMenichi and Richmond (2015) found that writing about one's experiences of failure can promote grit, while Major (2013) confirmed that grit and other positive psychological resources can be promoted through the mentoring fitness program. In Turkey, increased grit was achieved through character education consisting of modules that focused on the plasticity of the human brain, the role of effort in achievement, the constructive interpretation of failures, and goal setting (Alan, Boneva, & Ertac, 2019). Although not a study that directly examined grit enhancement, Eskreis-Winkler et al. (2016) developed an intervention strategy that trains participants on deliberate practice—a mediating factor between grit and achievement—and demonstrated the program's effectiveness in improving expectancy-value beliefs, deliberate practice, and academic achievement. The following section further organizes and elaborates on the findings from various grit promoting programs and empirical studies discussed thus far.

5.3.1 *Teaching Grit*

School programs for grit promotion (Baruch-Feldman, 2017; Character Lab, 2018; Shechtman et al., 2013) commonly include grit as an element in the general character education curriculum. Class content and activities include a section on raising the understanding of grit, where knowledge around grit, including the meaning of grit, the importance of grit, and the practice of grit, are directly taught. The meaning of the grit introduces the definition of grit and the two dimensions of grit: sustained effort and interest. The section on the importance of grit deals with the power of grit, closely relating it to successes in various fields, and demonstrate through real cases how effort has a greater, lasting impact than inborn talent. As a way to effectively teach the practice of grit, role models or self-reflection exercises on one's own experiences of grit are used. To help students discover the presence of grit in their daily lives, students are asked to actively use their experiences of achieving success and overcoming failures and solidify what they have learned through tasks that allow them to practice grit themselves. Song (2019) developed and validated a class unit program consisting of learning grit concepts, setting goals, and practicing action. The sixth-grade class that participated in Song's (2019) grit promotion program showed improvement in grit, growth mindset, and self-control.

5.3.2 *Reflecting on the Past Failures*

Considering that grit is the ability to continue towards one's goal despite adversity, grit can be promoted by helping one's process of overcoming failures. Empirical research has substantiated that grit can be enhanced by reflecting on experiences of failure. DiMenichi and Richmond (2015) asked study participants to write about a failure experience (experiment group 1), a successful experience (experiment group 2), or a movie (control group), and then compared the groups' grit scores as well as their performance on a sustained attention to response task. The group who wrote about failure scored high on grit immediately after the experiment and performed with higher accuracy and concentration on the tedious problem-solving task. These results suggested that dealing with failure can directly help to improve grit, contrary to the initial hypothesis of the researchers. The underlying mechanism of the result was explained by the distinction between constructive failure (Clifford, 1984) and productive failure (Kapur, 2008). Clifford noted that some individuals perform better after failure experiences, and that this phenomenon cannot entirely be explained by the extant learned helplessness theory. Clifford proposed the concept of constructive failure, where a failure can bring about positive outcomes (e.g., increased persistence) under certain conditions (e.g., optimally challenging and meaningful goal, self-initiated performance). Kapur further developed the positive outlook on failure by devising a plan to use the failure experiences in classroom activities. Constructive failure and productive failure both challenged the traditional view of linking failures to negative outcomes such as frustration, learned helplessness, reactance, low motivation, and low achievement by highlighting the possibility that failures can improve performance and learning.

5.3.3 *Growth Mindset*

Among beliefs that hinder grit expression or growth is the assumption that abilities are innate and cannot be changed. When people believe that those who are talented and successful are born that way, they have harder time maintaining their interest in something long enough to experience growth. Thus, a representative strategy for increasing grit is to cultivate a growth mindset regarding one's capability (Duckworth, 2016; Duckworth & Eskreis-Winkler, 2013; Perkins-Gough, 2013). The rationale for promoting the belief about changeable ability is supported by the mindset theory proposed by Dweck (2006). Mindset refers to an individual's belief about whether her abilities are mutable or fixed. Mindset theory states that a fixed mindset (believing that one's everyday life abilities, including academic capabilities, are immutable) leads to maladjustments, while a growth mindset (believing that one's abilities can change or improve with effort) leads to an adaptive and successful life (Dweck, 2006). The growth mindset helps students deal with challenges and frustrations at hand by focusing on achieving long-term, high-level goals

(Shechtman et al., 2013). In fact, growth mindset is closely related to 'hope,' a factor Duckworth (2016) has proposed to be one of the intrapersonal conditions for grit. Hope, a belief that one's future will be improved, is highly correlated with a growth mindset, a belief that one can change for the better (Lee & Jang, 2018). Moreover, O'Rourke, Haimovitz, Ballweber, Dweck, and Popović (2014) found that educating students on the growth mindset improved their perseverance of effort. In Korea, empirical studies have identified the growth mindset as a predictor for grit (e.g., Kim, 2018; Kim & Park, 2017; Lee & Kwon, 2016). In other words, grit can be elicited through interventions that instill in students a growth mindset about their abilities.

While Dweck (2006) proposed a number of ways to promote the growth mindset, the main approaches are as follows. First, feedback should be given about the process rather than outcome, on effort rather than ability. Evaluative feedback on performance outcomes or feedback that attribute success to abilities tends to encourage a fixed mindset and lower motivation. On the other hand, commenting on the process of performance itself or effort promotes a growth mindset. Importantly, such feedback should place emphasis on learning, more than the effort itself. If a student is exerting an effort that seems to be ineffective in helping her learn new things or improve skills, for instance, feedback that encourages other methods would be useful (Dweck, 2015). Second, lectures on the mindset should be directly taught. Once the concept of growth mindset is introduced, the students are encouraged to apply both fixed and growth mindsets and experience real-life outcomes before they decide on which mindset to have. For instance, with a growth mindset, one can choose to replace the word "fail" with "learn" and say "I have learned" instead of "I have failed." Research findings illustrated that students' internal monologues changed from a fixed mindset to a growth mindset after listening to the mindset lectures (pp. 217–218, Dweck, 2006). Third, the principles of brain development as well as ways to promote brain development can be directly taught. Dweck's research team developed an effective mindset workshop that focused on brain development and taught students relevant study skills that can be applied in their schoolwork. Blackwell, Trzesniewski, and Dweck (2007) undertook an experimental study to examine the effectiveness of the eight-session growth mindset workshop with 91 seventh graders and found that the workshop participants acquired a growth mindset, as well as an increase in motivation and math grades. Since then, the Dweck team created and widely distributed an online mindset program called the 'Brainology'. Fourth, the role modeling approach can be used to demonstrate the thoughts and actions of people who have a growth mindset. Students come to realize that successful people give personal importance to hard work and value the process of learning. In other words, continuous self-development efforts, not innate talent, are identified as the secrets to success. Given that recent experimental studies have affirmed the efficacy of several growth mindset intervention strategies (e.g., Brougham & Kashubeck-West, 2017; Donohoe, Topping, & Hannah, 2012; Kim, 2016), one could also expect that these efforts would improve grit overall.

5.3.4 Goal Setting

If grit is the characteristic that enables one to progress toward long-term goals, goal setting would be its starting point. Therefore, facilitating goal setting can provide students with opportunities to exercise and enhance grit (Duckworth, 2016; Shechtman et al., 2013). For children, however, career indecision is developmentally expected of their age. Therefore, it would be more helpful to have them set short-term goals rather than career-related long-term goals. In other words, grit-building can begin by setting goals within the time perspective that a child can see, whether it is by day, week, or month. As students enter into adolescence with more of a future orientation, they will be able to set longer-term goals and connect them with their career goals. Grit can be promoted by having students experience successful goal setting and achievement through clarifying why goals are needed, how goals can be set and expressed appropriately; they can be walked through setting specific action plans to achieve goals, as well as anticipating and overcoming barriers in achieving them. You can cultivate the grit steadily toward. Alarcon (2018) created a holistic goal setting model (The G.A.P. Model for Student Success: Goal Setting, Action Planning, and Progress Monitoring) for secondary school students and incorporated goals across social, emotional, academic, life skills domains. The four-part goal setting model has advantages in terms of its wide application across the student life domains but is limited in that its effectiveness has not yet been empirically supported.

Another issue to consider in goal setting is the type of goals that are effective for improving grit. Sociocentric goals have been shown to be more effective in increasing grit, as compared to goals that only involve the self. Duckworth (2016) found that grit paragons, or people who demonstrate grit, commonly set life goals that are aimed at helping others and contributing to society, rather than pursuing personal pleasure. She subsequently suggested that the pursuit of purpose is an important starting point for enhancing grit. Duckworth reported that she found grittier people are more motivated to seek meaningful and other-oriented life through a large-scale survey with 16,000 American adults. Hill, Burrow, and Bronk (2016) demonstrated the causal relationship between purpose commitment and grit through longitudinal analysis with US college student samples. They found initial levels of purpose predicted grit at 3 months later. These findings suggest that helping people to find meaning of life in helping others can promote grit.

5.3.5 Deliberate Practice

Grit manifests itself in behavior that persists in pursuing one's goals or tasks without giving up. Therefore, strategies for directly promoting grit-based behavior have been proposed for grit promotion, a typical example of which is the promotion of deliberate practice. Deliberate practice is identified as a common behavioral characteristic of people with grit and facilitating it would be important for grit cultivation (Duckworth, Kirby, Tsukayama, Berstein, & Ericsson, 2011). MacNamara, Hambrick, and Oswald (2014) viewed Eisenberger's (1992) notion of industriousness to be a grit-like concept, where the process of its formation involves experiencing repeated reinforcement for one's efforts, such that one continues to exert effort even in the absence of external reinforcements. This concept was used to envision a grit enhancing intervention strategy.

Deliberate practice is a concept introduced by a widely-known study that analyzed the process of professional growth and discovered 'Law of 10,000 Hours.' Deliberate practice involves engaging in activities that have been specially designed to maximize the improvement of current skills (Ericsson, Krampe, & Tesch-Romer, 1993, p. 368). Deliberate practice has four main components: (1) a well-defined goal for improving a specific aspect of performance, (2) level of challenge that just exceeds the individual's current skill, (3) the receiving of immediate feedback, and (4) repeated focus on the correction of error (Eskreis-Winkler et al., 2016, p. 729).

Deliberate practice is what mediates the connection between an individual's personal characteristic of grit and the resulting achievement. Increasing deliberate practice behavior can promote grit itself. The brain function that is implicated in grit is executive functioning, which works through the neural networks concentrated in the frontal lobe. Therefore, healthy brain development has been argued to be the first condition that must be met for the development of grit (Barkley, 1997; Carlson, Zelazo, & Faja, 2013). The frontal lobe, which is responsible for cognitive activities required for goal-directed behavior (e.g. planning, response inhibition, working memory, and attention), is a brain region closely related to grit. Longitudinal studies of brain development conducted in the United States have shown that the frontal lobe most actively develops during adolescence, around 11 years of age for girls and 12 years and 6 months for boys. Until then, neurons in the prefrontal cortex form intricately connected networks that continue to become more specialized and efficient over the years (Giedd et al., 1999). This means that the development of grit can depend on the experiences of childhood and adolescence. The brain develops through the "use it or lose it" principle, where functions become strengthened with usage, but dissipate without usage (Giedd, 2015). It can be inferred that the more grit-exercising activities are done, the more grit would be strengthened. Because grit is exercised in the course of the deliberate practice, repeated deliberate practices will also serve to enhance grit.

In Korea, longitudinal data have demonstrated the interaction between learning hours and self-control. Although grit was not measured directly in the study, it provides indirect evidence that self-control is closely related to executive functioning. Students' level of self-control from a previous semester not only predicted their learning hours in the next semester; the previous semester's learning hours also predicted the students' level of self-control in the next semester (Hwang, Lim, & Choi, 2018). The study's finding supports the idea that self-control can be enhanced by increasing learning hours, or that deliberate practice can promote grit. Recently Cho (2020) found deliberate practice had statistically significant effects on their grit in physical education classes. Duckworth concluded "gritty people do more deliberate practice and experience more flow" (Duckworth, 2016, p. 129) through her survey with Ericsson and Csikszentmihalyi. In other words, because exerting consistent, repetitive, and consistent effort toward deliberate practice is the main mechanism through which grit develops, students must be helped to start and maintain deliberate practice. A gradual approach is recommended toward this end, as increasing deliberate practice all at once would be overwhelming. Behavioral modification or self-management techniques can help, as Baruch-Feldman (2017) suggests through a workbook that aims to promote grit by helping people set small goals that can be practiced in everyday life and monitoring practice and habitualizing it.

Increasing grit through deliberate practice is not necessarily limited to academic or cognitive domains. Persisting in structured extracurricular activities can be another area where grit can be cultivated through deliberate practice (Duckworth, 2016). For example, Major (2013) designed a mentoring intervention program that challenges students to give maximum effort through intense physical fitness exercises and deliberate practice activities. The program was found to have improved grit in 32 adolescent participants over the course of 6 months.

5.3.6 Media Overuse

Interventions for behavior that interfere with grit development are also important aspects of grit promotion. The behavior that hinders grit includes the overuse of media, including smartphones or internet gaming. It has not yet been demonstrated that media use directly interferes with grit performance; however, there are many empirical studies that suggest that excessive media use can negatively impact grit performance, such as perseverance effort. It has been found that overuse of media, including video games, is closely related to impaired executive function, a brain function critically involved in grit (Rosselli & Christopher, 2019). Feinstein (2007) cited the finding that during gaming, only the brain areas related to vision and motor movement are activated, but that the frontal cortex becomes activated in the brain while solving simple math problems. He warned that computer games are impairing adolescent brain development, especially in the area of executive functioning. It was also found that students who habitually play video games had lower working memory performance (cognitive self-control) on a given task, as compared to their peers who did not play video games (Bailey, West, & Anderson, 2010). Analysis of Korean panel data also corroborate this finding, as computer use was shown to decrease self-control while engaging in cultural activities increased self-control (Lim & Hwang, 2014). Thus, grit development can be promoted by identifying and monitoring media overuse, which causes deficits in the area of executive functioning.

However, exceptions should be made regarding deliberate use of media for one's goal. For instance, professional gamers use their gaming media 'excessively' in their career pursuit and this behavior in their context will be considered to be grit-driven.

In other words, overuse of media is seen as a hindrance only when media use is not aligned with one's long-term goals.

5.3.7 Emotional Regulation

Grit is also closely related to emotion states, as they relate to the perseverance efforts in the face of adversity, as well as to consistency of interest that sustains one's passion for the task at hand. Emotion regulation is necessary for deliberate practice in regards to perseverance effort. Because deliberate practice, a behavioral mechanism to increase grit, is a lonesome and difficult process, it must be supported by strong motivation and interest to achieve goals and to improve performance (Lee & Sohn, 2013). Therefore, emotional regulation ability is necessary to be able to arouse emotions to keep the motivation and interest going during deliberate practice, while dealing with the frustration and boredom experienced in the process.

Diamond and Lee (2011) reviewed research on the enhancement of executive functioning, the neuropsychological basis of grit. They found that stress relief is an important aspect of improving executive functioning. In a similar vein, Lee (2017) warned that unmanaged stress may weaken one's grit and spark a vicious cycle of influence. The Grit Enhancement Program (Shechtman et al., 2013) developed by the US Department of Education reflects such guidelines and includes stress relief as a major component. Its curriculum also includes resilience enhancement and mindfulness modules. The stress-relieving effects of mindfulness programs have not only been confirmed in people with physical and mental illnesses (Grossman, Niemann, Schmidt, & Walach, 2004), but also in the general population (Chiesa & Serretti, 2009). Mindfulness-based stress reduction programs help individuals to engage in nonjudgmental observations of their here-and-now situations and thoughts by teaching specific techniques such as body scan, and meditation. However, Raphiphatthana et al. (2019)'s study suggested that culture may affect which aspect of mindfulness is associated with grit, calling for further cross-cultural examination of the association. For instance, non-judging aspect of mindfulness predicted the perseverance of effort aspect of grit for New Zealand students but not for Thai students. In brief, a growing emphasis is being placed on helping people overcome their grit-hindering negative emotions.

5.3.8 Interest Discovery and Maintenance

Duckworth (2016) highlights the discovery of interest as the starting point for grit. An important aspect of arousing interest is facilitating immersive peak experiences. Prior to improving executive functioning (neuropsychological basis for grit), it is important to first relieve stress and 'immerse oneself in one's passionate interest' (Diamond & Lee, 2011). Interest strongly predicts success in education and career, and is located at the starting point for the following process: motivation (directionality, vitality, sustainability) → goal-oriented behavior → process of goal achievement (Rounds & Su, 2014). In other words, to promote grit interventions should help people discover and maintain their interest.

Discovering interest requires a variety of experiences. It is, however, important to note that it is not the experience itself, but the quality of the experience that is intimately tied to the development of intriguing interest. For example, experimental studies have shown that the higher the stimulus complexity and understanding, the greater the interest (Silvia, 2005, 2008a; Turner & Silvia, 2006). These findings suggest that interest increases as we come to increasingly understand new, complex, and difficult situations (Silvia, 2008b). In other words, it is not only important to have people obtain experience, but also to have them discover and get to know something new.

As the next step, the interests must be helped to continue. To this end, the discussion around the process of interest development is useful to look at. Literature indicates that enduring interest comes from having accumulated experience in the areas of interest. Everyone is interested in something new, but tends to lose interest once they get used to it; therefore, it is necessary to keep asking questions and paying attention to subtle differences in order to have interests become passions (Duckworth, 2016). An individual's interest develops through the process of discovery, accumulation, and continuation of interest. Interest is often piqued situationally, starting from curiosity about the object; mastery experiences with appropriately challenging tasks help build positive emotional experiences (interest), which then leads to steadier interest in the object. At the later stage of interest development, one begins to feel consistent curiosity, challenge, and enjoyment in the object even without the help of situational and positive emotional experiences (Lepper & Hodell, 1989). The most important process of finding and maintaining interest is the way in which the initial curiosity successfully turns into an enduring interest with the help of positive emotions. In other words, in order to build interest, it is necessary to first accumulate positive experiences in the area of interest. In addition to experiencing positive emotional experiences on one's own, one can be supported through positive feedback from peers, teachers, and parents.

5.4 Future Directions

Ever since grit was proposed as a non-cognitive factor that predicts success in a variety of areas, including academics, grit has received growing attention. Grit is remarkable in that it is changeable through experience, unlike many other cognitive factors such as intelligence. In this chapter, specific intervention strategies were drawn based on the academic discourse on how to improve grit. However, further research is needed to empirically test various ways to improve grit. It is hoped that the effectiveness of the hypothetically proposed grit-promoting measures introduced in this chapter will be verified in the field. Intervention strategies derived from logical reasoning can be expected to promote grit and to help students perform, but the effects should be validated through case studies and experimental studies of students with different characteristics.

In addition, between perseverance effort and consistency of interest that constitute grit, perseverance effort has been discussed for a longer time than the other. Therefore, the intervention strategies tend to include more content relevant to perseverance effort. The maintenance of interest, however, is an important factor that is distinguished from self-control, task continuity, and task obsession.

Finally, the validity of grit-enhancing programs proposed in this chapter must be examined, especially in regards to its cultural universality. Grit is a concept that has been derived from studying adults in the United States, but empirical studies on the applicability of grit to students of different countries and ages are being actively conducted in recent years. A future study that synthesizes results from these studies may help offer useful implications for grit promotion measures that take various cultural characteristics into account.

References

Alan, S., Boneva, T., & Ertac, S. (2019). Ever failed, try again, succeed better: Results from a randomized educational intervention on grit. *The Quarterly Journal of Economics, 134*(3), 1121–1162. https://doi.org/10.1093/qje/qjz006.

Alarcon, S. (2018). The GAP model for student success: Goal setting, action planning, and progress monitoring (Master's thesis, California State University, US).

Bailey, K., West, R., & Anderson, C. A. (2010). A negative association between video game experience and proactive cognitive control. *Psychophysiology, 47*(1), 34–42. https://doi.org/10.1111/j.1469-8986.2009.00925.x.

Barkley, R. A. (1997). *ADHD and the nature of self-control*. New York, NY: Guilford.

Barkley, R. A. (2005). *Attention-deficit hyperactivity disorder: A handbook for diagnosis and treatment* (3rd ed.). New York: The Guilford Press.

Baruch-Feldman, C. (2017). *The grit guide for teens: A workbook to help you build perseverance, self-control, and a growth mindset*. Oakland, CA: New Harbinger Publications.

Blackwell, L. S., Trzesniewski, K. H., & Dweck, C. S. (2007). Implicit theories of intelligence predict achievement across an adolescent transition: A longitudinal study and an intervention. *Child Development, 78*(1), 246–263. https://doi.org/10.1111/j.1467-8624.2007.00995.x.

Brougham, L., & Kashubeck-West, S. (2017). Impact of a growth mindset intervention on academic performance of students at two urban high schools. *Professional School Counseling, 21*(1), 1–9. https://doi.org/10.1177/2156759X18764934.

Carlson, S. M., Zelazo, P. D., & Faja, S. (2013). Executive function. In P. D. Zelazo (Ed.), *Oxford handbook of developmental psychology* (pp. 706–743). New York, NY: Oxford University Press.

Casey, B. J., Tottenham, N., Liston, C., & Durston, S. (2005). Imaging the developing brain: What have we learned about cognitive development? *Trends in Cognitive Science, 9*, 104–110. https://doi.org/10.1016/j.tics.2005.01.011.

Character Lab. (2018). *Grit playbook.* Retrived from https://static1.squarespace.com/static/5980a22e9de4bb9ca8bce449/t/5bbe5c56652dea11f261f1ca/1539202135034/grit_fullcompiled_v2.pdf

Chiesa, A., & Serretti, A. (2009). Mindfulness-based stress reduction for stress management in healthy people: A review and meta-analysis. *The Journal of Alternative and Complementary Medicine, 15*(5), 593–600. https://doi.org/10.1089/acm.2008.0495.

Cho, H.-S. (2020). The relationship between interest, deliberate practice and grit of students in physical education classes. *Korean Journal of Sports Science, 29*(1), 525–537.

Choi, J. A. (2018). The effects of academic self-efficacy, goal-self concordance, grit on academic related efforts. *The Journal of Educational Research (Korea), 16*(1), 41–63.

Clifford, M. M. (1984). Thoughts on a theory of constructive failure. *Educational Psychologist, 19*(2), 108–120. https://doi.org/10.1080/00461528409529286.

Cohen, R. M. (2015). Teaching character: Grit, privilege, and American education's obsession with novelty. *The American Prospect.* Retrieved November 27, 2017 from http://prospect.org/article/can-grit-save-american-education

Credé, M., Tynan, M. C., & Harms, P. D. (2017). Much ado about grit: A meta-analytic synthesis of the grit literature. *Journal of Personality and Social Psychology, 113*(3), 492–511. https://doi.org/10.1037/pspp0000102.

Diamond, A., & Lee, K. (2011). Interventions shown to aid executive function development in children 4-12 years old. *Science, 333*(6045), 959–964. https://doi.org/10.1126/science.1204529.

DiMenichi, B. C., & Richmond, L. L. (2015). Reflecting on past failures leads to increased perseverance and sustained attention. *Journal of Cognitive Psychology, 27*(2), 180–193. https://doi.org/10.1080/20445911.2014.995104.

Donohoe, C., Topping, K., & Hannah, E. (2012). The impact of an online in-tervention (Brainology) on the mindset and resiliency of secondary school pupils: A preliminary mixed methods study. *Educational Psychology, 32*(5), 641–655. https://doi.org/10.1080/01443410.2012.675646.

Duckworth, A. (2016). *Grit: The power of passion and perseverance.* New York: Scribner.

Duckworth, A. L., & Eskreis-Winkler, L. (2013). True grit. *The Observer, 26*(4), 1–3.

Duckworth, A. L., Kirby, T. A., Tsukayama, E., Berstein, H., & Ericsson, K. A. (2011). Deliberate practice spells success: Why grittier competitors triumph at the National Spelling bee. *Social Psychological and Personality Science, 2*(2), 174–181. https://doi.org/10.1177/1948550610385872.

Duckworth, A. L., Peterson, C., Matthews, M. D., & Kelly, D. R. (2007). Grit: Perseverance and passion for long-term goals. *Journal of Personality and Social Psychology, 92*(6), 1087–1101.

Duckworth, A. L., & Quinn, P. D. (2009). Development and validation of the short grit scale (GRIT-S). *Journal of Personality Assessment, 91*(2), 166–174. https://doi.org/10.1080/00223890802634290.

Dweck, C. S. (2006). *Mindset: The new psychology of success.* New York: Random House.

Dweck, C. (2015). Carol Dweck revisits the growth mindset. *Education Week, 35*(5), 20–24.

Eisenberger, R. (1992). Learned industriousness. *Psychological Review, 99*(2), 248–267. https://doi.org/10.1037/0033-295X.99.2.248.

Ericsson, K. A., Krampe, R. T., & Tesch-Romer, C. (1993). The role of deliberate practice in the acquisition of expert performance. *Psychological Review, 100*(3), 363–406.

Eskreis-Winkler, L., Shulman, E. P., Young, V., Tsukayama, E., Brunwasser, S. M., & Duckworth, A. L. (2016). Using wise interventions to motivate deliberate practice. *Journal of Personality and Social Psychology, 111*(5), 728–744. https://doi.org/10.1037/pspp0000074.

Feinstein, S. (2007). *Parenting the teenage brain: Understanding a work in progress.* Lanham, MD: Rowman & Littlefield Education.

Giedd, J. N. (2008). The teen brain: Insights from neuroimaging. *Journal of Adolescent Health, 42*(4), 335–343. https://doi.org/10.1016/j.jadohealth.2008.01.007.

Giedd, J. N. (2015). The amazing teen brain. *Scientific American, 312*(6), 32–37.

Giedd, J. N., Blumenthal, J., Jeffries, N. O., Castellanos, F. X., Lui, H., Zijdenbos, A., Paus, T., Evans, A. C., & Rapoport, J. L. (1999). Brain development during childhood and adolescence: A longitudinal MRI study. *Nature Neuroscience, 2*(10), 861–863.

Grossman, P., Niemann, L., Schmidt, S., & Walach, H. (2004). Mindfulness-based stress reduction and health benefits: A meta-analysis. *Journal of Psychosomatic Research, 57*(1), 35–43. https://doi.org/10.1016/S0022-3999(03)00573-7.

Ha, H. S., Lim, H. J., & Hwang, M. H. (2015). The group difference of grit and self-control and its relations to school maladjustment, academic achievement, and predictability of personality. *Journal of Lifelong Learning Society, 11*(3), 145–166.

Hill, P. L., Burrow, A. L., & Bronk, K. C. (2016). Persevering with positivity and purpose: An examination of purpose commitment and positive affect as predictors of grit. *Journal of Happiness Studies, 17*(1), 257–269. https://doi.org/10.1007/s10902-014-9593-5.

Hoerr, T. R. (2013). *Fostering Grit: How do I prepare my students for the real world? (ASCD arias).* Alexandria, VA: ASCD.

Hwang, M. H., Ha, H. S., & Kim, M. S. (2017). Grit and academic achievement among elementary school students: The mediating role of academic self-regulation. *The Korean Journal of Elementary Counseling, 16*(3), 301–319.

Hwang, M. H., Lim, H. J., & Choi, H. C. (2018). A reciprocal relationship between self-control and learning time among adolescents. *The Journal of Learner-Centered Curriculum and Instruction, 18*, 265–284.

Jurado, M. B., & Rosselli, M. (2007). The elusive nature of executive functions: A review of our current understanding. *Neuropsychology Review, 17*(3), 213–233.

Kapur, M. (2008). Productive failure. *Cognition and Instruction, 26*(3), 379–424.

Keegan, K. (2017). Identifying and building grit in language learners. *English Teaching Forum, 55* (3), 2–9.

Kim, B. (2016). *Effect of mindset change program on mindset, academic self-efficacy and goal orientation of elementary school students* (Master's thesis, Andong University, Korea).

Kim, I.-S. (2018). Structural relationship among growth mind, self-regulation, grit, and intention of athletic participation in elementary school students. *Journal of Korean Society for the Study of Physical Education, 23*(3), 191–203.

Kim, J. G., & Park, D. E. (2017). The longitudinal effects of theory of implicit intelligence on academic achievement: The mediating effect of grit. *Journal of Educational Psychology (Korea), 31*(1), 145–162.

Lee, W. W. S. (2017). Relationships among grit, academic performance, perceived academic failure, and stress in associate degree students. *Journal of Adolescence, 60*, 148–152.

Lee, C. S., & Jang, H. Y. (2018). The roles of growth mindset and grit in relation to hope and self-directed learning. *Journal of the Korea Convergence Society, 9*(1), 95–102.

Lee, J. L., & Kwon, D. H. (2016). An analysis of structural relationship among locus of control, mindset, grit, and academic achievement. *Korean Journal of Youth Studies, 23*(11), 245–264.

Lee, S. R., & Sohn, Y. W. (2013). What are the strong predictors of academic achievement? - deliberate practice and grit. *The Korean Journal of School Psychology, 10*(3), 349–366.

Lepper, M. R., & Hodell, M. (1989). Intrinsic motivation in the classroom. *Research on Motivation in Education, 3*, 73–105.

Lim, H. J., & Hwang, M. H. (2014). The structural relationship among out-of-school activities, self-related constructs, and school satisfaction: Focusing on computer use and cultural activities. *Journal of Educational Studies, 45*(4), 111–132.

MacNamara, B. N., Hambrick, D. Z., & Oswald, F. L. (2014). Deliberate practice and performance in music, games, sports, education, and professions: A meta-analysis. *Psychological Science, 25*, 1608–1618. https://doi.org/10.1177/0956797614535810.

Major, C. (2013). *Youth mentoring partnership's friend fitness program: Theoretical foundations and promising preliminary findings from a new positive psychology intervention for grit and positive youth development.* Master of Applied Positive Psychology (MAPP) Capstone

Pro-jects, 48, University of Pennsylvania. Retrieved from http://repository.upenn.edu/mapp_capstone/48

O'Rourke, E., Haimovitz, K., Ballweber, C., Dweck, C., & Popović, Z. (2014, April). Brain points: A growth mindset incentive structure boosts persistence in an educational game. In *Proceedings of the SIGCHI conference on human factors in computing systems* (pp. 3339–3348). ACM. Retrieved November 29, 2017 from http://grail.cs.washington.edu/wp-content/uploads/2015/08/orourke2014bpa.pdf. https://doi.org/10.1145/2556288.2557157

Perkins-Gough, D. (2013). The significance of grit: A conversation with Angela Lee Duckworth. *Educational Leadership, 71*(1), 14–20.

Pueschel, A., & Tucker, M. L. (2018). Achieving grit through the growth mindset. *Journal of Instructional Pedagogies, 20*, 1–20.

Raphiphatthana, B., Jose, P. E., & Chobthamkit, P. (2019). The association between mindfulness and grit: An east vs. west cross-cultural comparison. *Mindfulness, 10*(1), 146–158.

Rimfeld, K., Kovas, Y., Dale, P. S., & Plomin, R. (2016). True grit and genetics: Predicting academic achievement from personality. *Journal of Personality and Social Psychology, 111* (5), 780–789. https://doi.org/10.1037/pspp0000089.

Rosselli, M., & Christopher, D. M. (2019). Executive dysfunctions associated with the use of information technology. In A. Ardila, S. Fatima, & M. Rosselli (Eds.), *Dysexecutive syndromes* (pp. 177–197). Cham, Switzerland: Springer. https://doi.org/10.1007/978-3-030-25077-5.

Rounds, J., & Su, R. (2014). The nature and power of interests. *Current Directions in Psychological Science, 23*(2), 98–103. https://doi.org/10.1177/0963721414522812.

Shechtman, N., DeBarger, A. H., Dornsife, C., Rosier, S., & Yarnall, L. (2013). *Promoting grit, tenacity, and perseverance: Critical factors for success in the 21st century*. Washington, DC: Department of Education, Office of Education Technology. Retrieved November 27, 2018 from http://pgbovine.net/OET-Draft-Grit-Report-2-17-13.pdf

Silvia, P. J. (2005). What is interesting? Exploring the appraisal structure of interest. *Emotion, 5*, 89–102. https://psycnet.apa.org/record/2005-02259-008.

Silvia, P. J. (2008a). Appraisal components and emotion traits: Examining the appraisal basis of trait curiosity. *Cognition and Emotion, 22*, 94–113. https://doi.org/10.1080/02699930701298481.

Silvia, P. J. (2008b). Interest-the curious emotion. *Current Directions in Psychological Science, 17* (1), 57–60. https://doi.org/10.1111/j.1467-8721.2008.00548.x.

Song, M.-S. (2019). *The effect of grit enhancing program on grit, mindset and self-control of elementary school students* (Master's thesis, Gyeongin National University of Education, Korea).

Steinberg, L. (2013). Does recent research on adolescent brain development inform the mature minor doctrine? *Journal of Medicine and Philosophy, 38*(3), 256–267. https://doi.org/10.1093/jmp/jht017.

Strayhorn, T. L. (2014). What role does grit play in academic success of black male collegians at predominately white institutions? *Journal of African American Studies, 18*(1), 1–10.

Tough, P. (2012). *How children succeed: Grit, curiosity, and the hidden power of character*. Boston, MA: Houghton Mifflin Harcourt.

Turner, S. A., Jr., & Silvia, P. J. (2006). Must interesting things be pleasant? A test of competing appraisal structures. *Emotion, 6*, 670–674. https://doi.org/10.1037/1528-3542.6.4.670.

Wolf, J. R., & Jia, R. (2015). *The role of grit in predicting student performance in introductory programming courses: An exploratory study*. In Proceedings of the Southern Association for Information Systems Conference, Hilton Head Island, SC, USA March 20–21, 2015. Retrieved September 10, 2017, from http://aisel.aisnet.org/sais2015/21

Mae-Hyang Hwang is a professor in the Department of Education at Gyeongin National University of Education in South Korea. And she studied pharmaceutics in undergraduate and worked as a pharmacist at a pharmaceutical company for 5 years. And then she moved to the education undergraduate and completed her PhD in counseling education at Seoul National University, South Korea. She worked as a visiting scholar in United States three times once at University of Missouri at Columbia and two times at University of Missouri at St. Louis. Her research interests include academic counseling focusing on executive function, grit, and academic failure tolerance, career development of marginalized children and adolescents, and brain development and education. She published many articles, wrote book chapters and books, and translated books in her academic area by herself and with her colleagues. Recently she is trying to collaborate with other academic areas especially to expand to mental health care and technology. She is living in Seoul, South Korea with her husband and enjoys reading, listening to music, and watching baseball and other sports games with her husband and friends.

JeeEun Karin Nam is an assistant professor at Ewha Womans University's Graduate School of Education. She identifies herself as a cross-cultural individual as she was born in Korea, spent her childhood in the Czech Republic and her adolescence in the United States. After she received her bachelor's degree in psychology from Wellesley College, she moved back to Korea in hopes to make a difference in enhancing the mental health culture in her motherland. She received her master's and doctoral degrees in educational counseling from Seoul National University. Her research and counseling practice centers around psychological health and resilience of minority groups such as cultural minorities and people with disabilities. She enjoys being a cross-cultural disseminator of important work in the field of counseling psychology and has been translating many books and articles from English to Korean and vice versa. For the time being, she is enjoying her life in Seoul with her husband and her two kids.

Chapter 6
Gritty Goal Pursuit and Perceived Chronic Stress: Exploring Implications for Academic Problems

Vrinda Kalia

Abstract College can be a stressful time for students as they transition to greater independence and increased responsibilities from before. Increased stress levels can have a debilitating effect on their ability to persist with their academic goals. In the psychological literature, researchers believe they have identified a motivation trait that may explain individual differences in persistence and perseverance toward goals. Grit is a motivation orientation characterized by passion and persistence in the pursuit of a long-term goal. Consisting of two facets, Grit-Perseverance and Grit-Consistency, grit has been shown to predict beneficial outcomes in a variety of domains, including academics. Yet, very little work has examined the psychological consequences of gritty goal pursuit. Considering that individuals high on facets of grit are presented as persistently pursuing their goals regardless of setbacks and obstacles it is plausible to speculate that gritty goal pursuit may be associated with increased stress levels. The purpose of this chapter is to present the results of two studies conducted to examine the relations between facets of grit and chronic stress with implications for academic problems in college students. In the first study, 101 participants (72 = Female; 18–24 years) completed the Grit-S Scale and the Perceived Stress Scale (PSS). Bivariate correlations revealed that Grit-Perseverance and Grit-Consistency were negatively correlated with perceived chronic stress. In the second study, 127 participants (88 = Female; 18–32 years) were administered the Academic Problems Subscale of the College Adjustment Scale along with the Grit-S Scale and the Perceived Stress Scale (PSS). Both facets of grit were negatively correlated with perceived chronic stress, thus replicating findings from Study 1. Additionally, regression analysis revealed that Grit-Perseverance and Grit-Consistency predicted fewer academic problems. Finally mediation regression analyses indicated that facets of grit reduced academic problems through decreased stress levels. Overall, these studies suggest that gritty goal pursuit is associated with reduced chronic stress and fewer academic problems in college students.

V. Kalia (✉)
Department of Psychology, Miami University, Oxford, OH, USA
e-mail: kaliav@miamioh.edu

L. E. van Zyl et al. (eds.), *Multidisciplinary Perspectives on Grit*,
https://doi.org/10.1007/978-3-030-57389-8_6

Keywords Grit-perseverance · Grit-consistency · Perceived chronic stress · Academic problems · College students

6.1 Introduction

Conventional wisdom, buttressed by empirical data, suggests that college education has a significant impact on an individual's life. In the United States, college graduates outperform their peers without college degrees on every metric of financial success—employment rates, job satisfaction, and economic wellbeing (Taylor et al., 2014). Yet, concerns about rising personal debt associated with college education have created pessimism about the value of education (Webber, 2016). For instance, a vast majority of American college graduates believe that college has become too expensive (Taylor et al., 2014). In the face of rising cost of a college degree (Webber, 2016) some have questioned whether the connection between college education and success in life is spurious (Hout, 2012). Within this socio-cultural context, identifying the determinants of success in college has become a high stakes endeavor (Dweck, Walton, & Cohen, 2014). According to the American College Health Association—National College Health Assessment II, stress was the variable most frequently reported by students to have a negative impact on their academic performance (ACHA-NCHA, 2019).

Stress is an inevitable aspect of the college experience (Baghurst & Kelley, 2014). Transition to college is also associated with increased academic demands, additional responsibilities associated with autonomous living, and unique personal and social pressures (Baghurst & Kelley, 2014). Some students are able to adapt to the novel demands of a college experience whereas others struggle to cope with the stressors of college. Stress can have a profoundly negative impact on students' health as well their academic achievement (May, Bauer, & Fincham, 2015). For instance, psychological stress has been identified as an important factor in predicting retention and the ability to persist in college (Letkiewicz et al., 2014). As a result, both researchers and educational institutions have begun to recognize the importance of identifying variables that ameliorate the effects of stress on college students (May et al., 2015).

More recently researchers have turned their attention to psychological factors, also known as motivational factors, that might promote long-term learning by allowing the student to view challenges, obstacles, and setbacks as inherent to the learning process (Dweck et al., 2014). In effect, these motivational factors may provide students with a buffer against the stressors of college. One such motivational factor is *persistence in the pursuit of a long-term goal.* It is a commonly held belief that persistence yields rewards; that individuals who persevere despite obstacles are more likely to succeed. Duckworth has found a way to quantify an individual's perseverance toward a long-term goal, calling it *Grit* (Duckworth, Peterson, Matthews, & Kelly, 2007).

Grit, is a personality trait characterized by a motivation orientation (Duckworth et al., 2007). Gritty individuals are defined by a tendency to persevere passionately toward a long-term, superordinate goal. As originally conceptualized, grit is composed of two factors, consistency of interest (Grit-Consistency) and perseverance of effort (Grit-Perseverance) (Duckworth & Quinn, 2009). Consistency of interest reflects an individual's focus on a small set of goals that are related to achieving one's enduring goal (Van Zyl, Olckers, & Roll, 2020). Perseverance of effort reflects effort towards the individual's enduring goal. Although the two facets are correlated ($r = .59$, Duckworth & Quinn, 2009) they are not so highly associated that it would preclude the emergence of distinct effects (Silvia, Eddington, Beaty, Nusbaum, & Kwapil, 2013). Empirical evidence indicates that grit predicts success in various domains including academics (Bowman, Hill, Denson, & Bronkema, 2015), retention in Military Academy (Maddi, Matthews, Kelly, Villarreal, & White, 2012) and the workplace (Eskreis-Winkler, Duckworth, Shulman, & Beal, 2014) and is positively related to well-being (Vainio & Daukantaitė, 2016). This has led some to claim that grit may be personality variable that enhances the role resiliency or protective factors in relation to relevant outcomes (Kleiman, Adams, Kashdan, & Riskind, 2013; Rhodes, Devlin, Steinberg, & Giovannetti, 2017).

In recent years the focus of the research on grit has shifted to an examination of its association with mental health outcomes. For instance, higher levels of grit are associated with reduced risky behaviors (Guerrero, Dudovitz, Chung, Dosanjh, & Wong, 2016) and serve as a buffer against maladaptive behaviors such as disordered eating (Knauft, Ortiz, Velkoff, Smith, & Kalia, 2019) and suicidal ideation (Kleiman et al., 2013). It has been previously documented that stress can exacerbate maladaptive behaviors such as disordered eating (Costarelli & Patsai, 2012) and suicidal ideation (Wilburn & Smith, 2005) in college students. Yet, the relationship between grit and stress is grossly understudied.

6.2 Literature Review

6.2.1 *Stress, Grit, and Academic Problems*

Stress threatens homeostasis by stimulating a series of physiological responses in the human body and brain (Arnsten, 2009). Stress may be of two types, chronic or acute. Chronic stress is long-term stress associated with a continued threat or multiple stressors (e.g. ongoing problems in the workplace). Acute stress, on the other hand, is a transient and recent experience with a single stressor (e.g. getting a speeding ticket). Past research has shown that the body and brain respond quite differently when experiencing acute versus chronic stress (McEwen, 2004). Acute stress responses prepare the body for action ('fight or flight'), allowing the individual to make rapid assessments about threats, respond appropriately within the threatening context, and/or restore homeostasis when the stressor is no longer present (McEwen, 2004). During the acute stress response hormones, such as cortisol, are engaged and can influence cognitive functions (Kalia et al., 2018). However, chronic stress keeps the hypothalamus-pituitary-adrenocortical (HPA) axis and the hormones associated with stress (i.e. cortisol) constantly engaged (McEwen, 2004). This repeated exposure to stress-related hormones is associated with negative health consequences (Pearlin, Schieman, Fazio, & Meersman, 2005), as well as changes in cognition and decision making processes (Liston, McEwen, & Casey, 2009; Schwabe, Tegenthoff, Höffken, & Wolf, 2010). Thus, acute stress is an adaptive response that helps the individual cope with an immediate threat but chronic stress is maladaptive (McEwen, 2004).

The physiological stress response emerges from an interaction of individual characteristics and the environmental context (Danese & McEwen, 2012). Thus, stress is a subjective experience that begins with the recognition, by the individual, of a stressor that poses a threat (McEwen, 2004). The transactional model of stress, proposed by Lazarus and Folkman (1984), identifies stress as a subjective transaction between an individual and their environment. Stress occurs when an individual's appraisal of their available resources do not match the demands of the given situation. Expanding on these ideas, the biopsychosocial model of challenge and threat (Blascovich, 2008) explains individual differences in the experience of stress, by focusing on the person's appraisal of available resources. When demands exceed available resources, the situation is perceived as threatening. But, when one perceives they have sufficient resources to meet contextual demands the stressor is evaluated as challenging, not threatening (Blascovich, 2008). Thus, stressors that are viewed as challenging encourage adaptive responses (e.g. studying harder for a difficult course) whereas stressors that are perceived as threatening evoke negative responses (e.g. dropping out) (Shields, 2001).

The average college student encounters a wide variety of stressors—social, financial, and academic (Baghurst & Kelley, 2014). But, Lazarus and Folkman suggest that it is not the stressor itself but the individual's *appraisal* of the stressor that ultimately initiates the physiological stress response. Therefore, any stressor, whether small or big, could initiate the same physiological stress response if it is perceived as threatening as opposed to challenging. From this emerge two possible scenarios. First, because gritty individuals appear to thrive in challenging circumstances (e.g., National Spelling Bee; Duckworth & Quinn, 2009) it is possible that college students who are high on grit may experience lower levels of stress. Second, if gritty perseverance leads an individual to overestimate their abilities or take on too many responsibilities, this could result in the experience of stress if they are unable to cope effectively.

To the best of my knowledge, only a handful of studies have assessed the relationship between grit and stress in adults and reported inconsistent results. Wong, Anderson, Knorr, Joseph, and Sanchez (2018) investigated the association between grit and perceived stress in 36 emergency physicians. In addition to measuring grit, the researchers also collected data on trait anxiety and perceived stress levels. They found no significant correlation between grit and perceived stress. Similarly, Lee and Park (2018) examined the association between grit and stress in nursing students ($N = 145$) and did not observe a significant association between grit and reported stress levels. However, the small sample size of the study by Wong et al. (2018) and the fact that neither of these studies reported data on the two facets of grit (only overall grit scores) prevent me from making any firm conclusions.

In contrast, Kannangara et al. (2018) observed that overall grit scores were negatively correlated with perceived stress levels in 440 college students from Northwest England. And in another study, Lee (2017) investigated the relationship between grit and stress in community college students (N = 345) from Hong Kong. Lee proposed that the associate degree students in this study were under stress because they had failed to qualify for a seat in traditional colleges in Hong Kong. The data revealed that both facets of grit were negatively correlated with reported stress levels. The author concluded that grit was a psychological resource that protected students from stress (Lee, 2017).

Thus, it appears that more research is needed, on the relationship between grit and stress, before any clarity can be provided, in the literature. In view of the fact that individuals high on facets of grit are presented as persistently pursuing their goals despite challenges it is plausible to speculate that gritty goal pursuit may be associated with increased stress levels. However, the alternative is also possible because emotion regulation is implicated in goal directed behavior (Lowe & Ziemke, 2011) and grit is identified by sustained focus and effort toward a long-term goal (Duckworth et al., 2007), so grittier individuals may be more effective in dealing with stressors. Considering that grit is associated with both increased wellbeing (Goodman, Disabato, Kashdan, & Machell, 2017) and improved academic outcomes (Bowman et al., 2015), researchers and educators have proposed that grit help determine attrition from challenging educational (Hammond, 2017) and professional settings (Burkhart, Tholey, Guinto, Yeo, & Chojnacki, 2014). But, before grit can be utilized in this manner, it is important to establish the nature of the relationship between facets of grit and stress levels.

In contrast to the literature on stress and grit, research on chronic stress in college students is more extensive (Robotham, 2008; Shankar & Park, 2016). Empirical evidence has shown that chronic stress has a negative impact on students' physical (Mouchacca, Abbott, & Ball, 2013) and mental health (Osberg & Eggert, 2012). Additionally, chronic stress levels are associated with poor performance on tests (Bardi, Koone, Mewaldt, & O'Connor, 2011; Wemm, Koone, Blough, Mewaldt, & Bardi, 2010). Bardi et al. (2011) recruited 91 students (45 females and 46 males) enrolled in an organic chemistry course for their study. Cortisol, a key indicator of stress, was assessed through six saliva samples that were collected from students, once in the beginning of the course and then after each test. The authors report that individual differences in physiological stress response to long-term stress predicted, above and beyond GPA, which students passed the challenging chemistry course. The findings of this study suggest that chronic stress levels are associated with academic performance.

However, there are two gaps in the current literature that should be noted. First, majority of the existing research on stress in college students is descriptive in nature with a view toward quantifying the frequency, intensity, and types of stress that a student experiences (Robotham, 2008). Fewer studies have investigated the relationship between chronic stress and academic performance (Bardi et al., 2011), specifically in the United States. This is problematic in view of the fact that the number of American college students who are diagnosed with stress-related disorders, such as depression and anxiety, are rising exponentially (Beiter et al., 2015). Consequently, more research is needed to identify factors that could help mitigate the negative impact of chronic stress in college students.

Second, most of the studies that have explored relations between stress and academic performance have focused on cognitive ability and test performance (Bardi et al., 2011). Academic problems, which indicate bad time management or maladaptive study habits, have been mostly ignored. The focus on academic problems is especially pertinent as recent research studies have shown that the experience of stress and strain related to schoolwork is an independent risk factor for declining academic performance (May et al., 2015). Students who are experiencing chronic stress may be more likely to engage in bad coping strategies (e.g. procrastinate on the internet instead of studying) that could exacerbate their academic problems (Garett, Liu, & Young, 2017).

Because chronic stress has a debilitating effect on the activity of the prefrontal cortex (McEwen, 2004) and the prefrontal cortex regulates goal directed behavior, chronic stress can have a negative impact on an individual's ability to function effectively in daily life (McEwen, 2004). In order to maintain their academic standing in university, college students have to juggle the demands of multiple courses as well as their hectic social lives. Thus, chronic stress could be particularly toxic for academic functioning in college students. One way to identify whether college students are functioning academically is to examine whether they are having problems doing routine course work.

Since grit has been identified as a non-cognitive variable that predicts academic success as well as or better than cognitive ability (Duckworth & Quinn, 2009), it is pertinent to examine whether facets of grit are associated with academic problems. Additionally, as gritty individuals appear to thrive in challenging circumstances (Maddi et al. 2012), and grit serves as a buffer against maladaptive behaviors (Knauft et al., 2019) it is relevant to examine the relationship between facets of grit and perceived stress levels in college students. Therefore, I posed two questions: Q1: What is the relationship between perceived chronic stress and facets of grit in college students? Q2: What is the relationship between facets of grit, chronic perceived stress and reported academic problems in college students?

In order to address these questions I conducted two studies. In the first study I sought to determine the relationship between Grit-Perseverance and Grit-Consistency and perceived chronic stress in students enrolled in a freshman college course. Based on prior research (Kannangara et al., 2018; Lee, 2017) my primary hypothesis was that college students with higher levels of grit would report lower levels of perceived chronic stress. In the second study, I investigated the relationships between facets of grit, chronic stress, and academic problems in a sample of students enrolled in a freshman level course. Based on previous research showing that grit serves as a buffer against maladaptive behaviors (Knauft et al., 2019) my second prediction was that facets of grit would be negatively correlated with academic problems.

6.3 Methodology: Study 1

The procedures used in the following study were approved by the Institutional Review Board at Miami University, Ohio, USA. Participants provided informed consent prior to completing the measures listed below.

6.3.1 *Participants*

One hundred and one undergraduate participants enrolled in a freshman course in Psychology were recruited from a Midwestern university in the US. The participants (Female = 72; $Mean_{age}$ = 19.32) completed several questionnaires online in exchange for research credit. Participants were majority White (71.1%); Asian (18.4%), Hispanic (2.6%), African American (1.8%), Biracial (1.8%), or race or ethnicity not listed (4.4%).

6.3.2 *Measures*

Grit The Short Grit Scale (Grit-S; Duckworth & Quinn, 2009) consists of two facets, each measured by four items: Grit-Perseverance (e.g., *setbacks don't discourage me;* $\alpha = .80$) and Grit-Consistency (e.g., *I have been obsessed with a certain idea or project for a short time but later lost interest*, reversed; $\alpha = .86$). Higher scores indicate higher levels of that facet of grit.

Stress Perceived Stress Scale (PSS; Cohen, Kamarck, & Mermelstein, 1983). Consists of 10 items that measure an individual's perceived chronic stress over the past month. Questions assess how overloaded individuals have generally felt (*e.g., In the last month, how often have you found that you could not cope with all the things you had to do?*). Responses are measured on a five-point likert scale (*never* to *very often*). Items were reverse scored when necessary and summed such that higher scores indicated relatively more perceived stress ($\alpha = 0.86$).

6.3.3 *Data Reduction and Analytic Plan*

Variables were normally distributed with skew and kurtosis coefficients less than 1. No outliers' three standard deviations or more from mean values were present. First bivariate correlations were conducted to examine associations between facets of grit, perceived chronic stress and participant age. Next, in order to investigate whether chronic stress levels varied as a function of grit levels I split participants into high, medium, and low grit groups based on their scores on the two facets of the grit scale.

6.4 Results: Study 1

Prior to conducting any correlation analyses, I examined whether the facets of grit and perceived chronic stress differed as a function of participant gender. One-way ANOVAs with age as a between subjects variable revealed that there was no difference in either facet of grit and reported stress levels between male and female college students, all *ps* $> .20$. Thus, the sample was collapsed for further analyses and did not include gender as a covariate.

Associations Between Facets of Grit and Perceived Chronic Stress Bivariate correlations revealed that Grit-Consistency was positively correlated with Grit-Perseverance. See Table 6.1. Further, consistent with our primary prediction, both Grit-Consistency and Grit-Perseverance were negatively correlated with perceived stress levels reported by the participants. Participant's age was not significantly correlated with any of the other variables. Consequently, age was not included as a covariate in any other analyses. See Table 6.1.

Regression Analysis Predicting Perceived Stress Grit-Consistency and Grit-Perseverance were simultaneously entered into a regression model with perceived stress as the outcome variable. The overall model was significant and explained 8% of the variance in perceived stress, $F(2, 98) = 4.26$, $p = .017$. However, despite significant correlations when entered into the regression equation as predictors, neither Grit-Consistency nor Grit-Perseverance emerged as significant. See Table 6.2.

Table 6.1 Descriptive statistics and correlations between perceived stress, facets of grit, and age (N = 101)

	1.	2.	3.	4.
1. Grit-consistency	–			
2. Grit-perseverance	.45**	–		
3. Perceived stress	−.25*	−.24*	–	
4. Age	.04	−.11	−.00	–
Mean	2.89	3.84	28.11	18.74
Standard deviation	0.71	0.64	5.80	1.05

Note. $*p < .05$, $** p < .001$

Table 6.2 Perceived stress regressed onto Grit-Consistency and Grit-Perseverance (N = 101)

$R^2 = .08$*	B	β	SE
Grit-consistency	−.14	−.18	.09
Grit-perseverance	−.14	−.16	.10

Note. $*p < .05$ $** p < .01$, $*** p < .001$

6.5 Methodology: Study 2

The procedures used in the following study were approved by the Institutional Review Board at Miami University, Ohio, USA. Participants provided informed consent prior to completing the measures listed below. All study procedures were consistent for Study 1 and 2.

6.5.1 Participants

Undergraduate students (N = 127) enrolled in a freshman psychology course were recruited from a university in a Midwestern state of the US in exchange for research credit. The participants (Female = 88; $Mean_{age}$ = 19.17) were majority White (73%); Asian (18.4%), Hispanic (2.6%), African American (1.8%), Biracial (1.8%), or race or ethnicity not listed (2.4%).

6.5.2 Measures

Grit Same as described above in Study 1. Grit-Perseverance (e.g., *setbacks don't discourage me;* $\alpha = .70$) and Grit-Consistency (e.g., *I have been obsessed with a certain idea or project for a short time but later lost interest*, reversed; $\alpha = .77$). Higher scores indicate higher levels of that facet of grit.

Stress Same as described above in Study 1. Items were reverse scored when necessary and summed such that higher scores indicated relatively more perceived stress ($\alpha = 0.85$).

Academic Problems Subscale of the College Adjustment Scale (CAS; Anton & Reed, 1991). Consists of 12 items that provide a measure of the extent of problems related to academic performance that a student is experiencing. Items require responses to statements about specific aspects of academic functioning (e.g. *I have poor study skills*; $\alpha = 0.85$). Responses are measured on a 4-point likert scale (*statement is false* to *statement is very true*). Items are reverse scored when necessary and then summed. Higher scores indicate more academic problems.

6.5.3 Data Reduction and Analytic Plan

Variables were normally distributed with skew and kurtosis coefficients less than 1. No outliers' three standard deviations or more from mean values were present. First I bivariate correlations to examine associations between facets of grit, perceived chronic stress, and academic problems. Next, I conducted a multivariate regression predicting academic problems. Grit-Consistency, Grit-Perseverance, and Perceived Stress were entered as predictor variables into the regression equation.

6.6 Results: Study 2

Prior to conducting any correlation analyses, I examined whether the facets of grit and perceived chronic stress differed as a function of participant gender. One-way ANOVAs with age as a between subjects variable revealed that there was a significant difference in perceived stress levels between male and female college students, ($F(1, 126) = 5.61, p = .02, \eta_p{}^2 = .04$). Examination of means indicated that female students ($M = 27.16$, $SD = 6.11$) reported significantly higher levels of perceived stress than male students ($M = 24.38$, $SD = 6.05$). No other difference emerged significant, all $ps > .20$. As a result, gender was added as a covariate in all further analyses.

Associations Between the Variables Bivariate correlations were conducted to examine the association between facets of grit, perceived chronic stress and academic problems experienced by students. See Table 6.3. Consistent with previous reports (e.g. Duckworth & Quinn, 2009), the analysis revealed that the two facets of grit were positively correlated with one another. Additionally, replicating results from Study 1, both facets of grit were negatively correlated with perceived levels of stress. Students who had high levels of Grit—Perseverance and Consistency also had lower stress levels. Facets of grit were also negatively correlated with academic problems. In contrast, perceived stress was positively correlated with academic problems. Students who reported experiencing higher levels of chronic stress were also more likely to have more academic problems.

Predicting Academic Problems In order to determine whether facets of grit and perceived stress were uniquely associated with academic problems, I conducted hierarchical regression analysis. In the first step of the regression equation gender was added as control variable. In the second step of the regression equation Grit-

Table 6.3 Correlations between facets of grit, perceived stress and academic problems (N = 127)

	1.	2.	3.	4.	5.
1. Grit-perseverance	–				
2. Grit-consistency	.51***	–			
3. Perceived stress	−.36***	−.23**	–		
4. Academic problems	−.52***	−.50***	.51**	–	
5. Age	.06	.09	−.12	−.00	–
Mean	3.70	3.14	26.31	22.05	19.17
Standard deviation	.68	.67	6.20	6.58	1.84

Note. *$p < .05$, ** $p < .01$, *** $p < .001$

Table 6.4 Regression analysis predicting academic problems (N = 127)

Variable	B	SE (B)	β	*t*	*p*
Grit-perseverance	−2.21	.79	−.23	−2.81	.006
Grit-consistency	−2.88	.77	−.29	−3.75	.001
Perceived stress	.41	.08	.38	5.24	.001
R^2 = .46.1***					

Note. *$p < .05$, ** $p < .01$, *** $p < .001$

Perseverance, Grit-Consistency and perceived stress were simultaneously entered as predictor variables. The outcome variable was academic problems. The final model was a significant predictor of academic problems, $R^2 = .46$, $F(3, 126) = 26.11$, $p = .001$. Grit-Perseverance, Grit-Consistency and perceived stress predicted 46.1% of the variance in academic problems. Individuals who were high on either facet of grit were also more likely to report fewer academic problems whereas those with higher levels of perceived stress also had higher number of academic problems. See Table 6.4.

Perceived Stress Mediates the Relationship Between Grit and Academic Problems Since facets of grit were negatively associated with perceived stress, I explored the presence of a mediating effect on academic problems. Specifically, I hypothesized that perceived stress might mediate the relation between grit and academic problems. I conducted a series of regression analyses separately for each facet of grit to support my hypothesis. First I regressed the mediator (perceived stress) on the independent variables (Grit-Perseverance and Grit-Consistency); then regressing the dependent variable (academic problems) on perceived stress; and finally regressing academic problems on both perceived stress and facets of grit (Baron & Kenny, 1986). Participant's gender was added in the first step of all these regression models as a control variable. See Figs. 6.1 and 6.2.

Grit-Perseverance Model Regression analyses revealed that Grit-Perseverance predicted reduced perceived stress ($R^2 = .17$, $F(2, 126) = 13.04$, $p = .000$), and perceived stress predicted increased academic problems ($R^2 = .28$, $F(2, 126) = 24.23$, $p = .000$). The final regression model was also emerged as significant ($R^2 = .40$, $F(3, 123) = 27.21$, $p = .000$). See Table 6.5.

In order to test the significance of the mediation model, I used the online statistical program MedGraph (Jose, 2003), which indicated that a significant Sobel z value of −3.41, $p = .001$ [95% CI [00, −.61]. The unstandardized indirect effect (a*b) was .00 (se = .41) and the total effect (i.e., the sum of both the direct and indirect effects of Grit-Perseverance on academic problems) revealed that 52% of the variance in the students' academic problems was explained by the model (total effect = −.52, se = .26). Thus, the results supported my prediction that perceived stress would mediate the relation between Grit-Perseverance and reported academic problems. An examination of the direct and indirect paths, of the mediation model, indicates that Grit-Perseverance had a negative influence on academic problems partially through reduced perceived stress levels reported by students with high Grit-Perseverance.

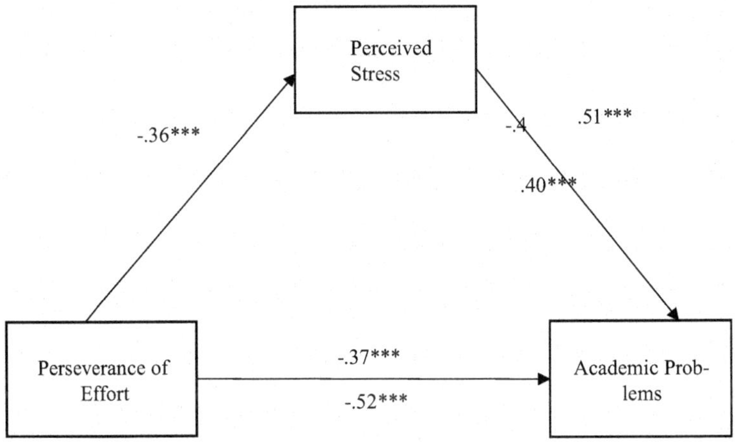

Fig. 6.1 Perceived stress mediates the relationship between perseverance of effort and academic problems $*p < .05$ $**p < .01$ $***p < .0001$. Note: Figure reports unstandardized betas

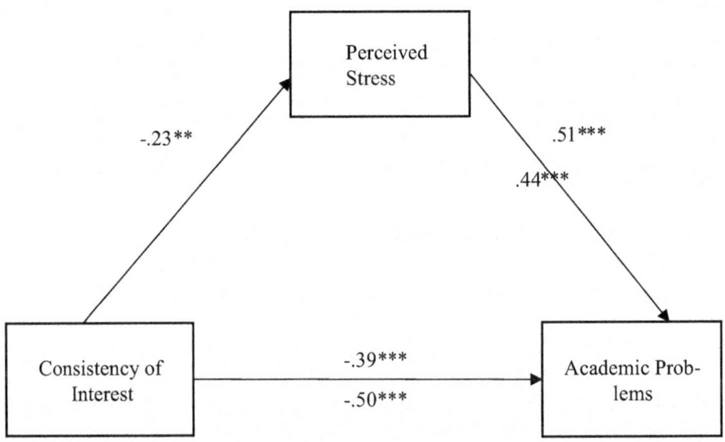

Fig. 6.2 Perceived stress mediates the relationship between consistency of interest and academic problems $*p < .05$ $**p < .01$ $***p < .0001$. Note: Figure reports unstandardized betas

Table 6.5 Regression analysis predicting academic problems (N = 127)

Variable	B	SE (B)	β	*t*	*p*
Gender	−1.39	1.02	−.10	−1.37	.17
Grit-perseverance	−3.60	.73	−.37	−4.91	.001
Perceived stress	.43	.08	.40	5.22	.001
$R^2 = .40^{***}$					

Note. $*p < .05$, $**p < .01$, $***p < .001$

Grit-Consistency Model Regression analyses revealed that Grit-Consistency predicted reduced perceived stress ($R^2 = .10$, $F(2, 126) = 6.81$, $p = .002$), and perceived stress predicted increased academic problems ($R^2 = .28$, F

Table 6.6 Regression analysis predicting academic problems (N = 127)

Variable	B	SE (B)	β	*t*	*p*
Gender	−1.38	.10	−.10	−1.38	.17
Grit-consistency	−3.89	.70	−.39	−5.58	.001
Perceived stress	.47	.08	.44	6.18	.001
R^2 = .43***					

Note. **p* < .05, ***p* < .01, ****p* < .001

(2, 126) = 24.23, p = .000). The final regression model was also emerged as significant (R^2 = .42, F(3, 123) = 30.48, p = .000). See Table 6.6.

In order to test the significance of the mediation model, I used the online statistical program MedGraph (Jose, 2003), which indicated that a significant Sobel z value of −2.52, p = .01 [95% CI [00, −.23]. The unstandardized indirect effect (a*b) was .00 (se = .41) and the total effect (i.e., the sum of both the direct and indirect effects of Grit-Consistency on academic problems) revealed that 50% of the variance in students' academic problems was explained by the model (total effect = .50, se = .21). The results supported my prediction that perceived stress would mediate the relation Grit-Consistency and academic problems. An examination of the direct and indirect paths indicates that Grit-Consistency had a negative association with academic problems partially through reduced stress levels.

6.7 Discussion

Why do some people persist in the face of challenging tasks, when others give up? Researchers are asking this question in a recent resurgence of literature examining the role of motivational factors in determining success in school (Dweck et al., 2014). If a college degree is a long-term goal, then according to Duckworth, gritty individuals will pursue that long-term goal with passion and tenacity despite setbacks, and likely suppress rival short-term and long-term goals that conflict with their pursuit (Duckworth & Gross, 2014). However, challenges and stressors accompany any long-term pursuit. As research has shown pursuing a college education in the US is a stressful experience (Shankar & Park, 2016). The question is whether gritty individuals are better at handling the stressors of college than those who are less gritty?

Across two studies, with two samples of college students from the US, I examined relationships between grit, perceived stress, and academic problems. In both studies, facets of grit were negatively associated with perceived chronic stress. Thus, it appears that being gritty is associated with lower levels of stress in American college students. This is consistent with observations by Lee (2017), who studied in community college students in Hong Kong, and by Kannangara et al. (2018), who studied university students in England. By studying American college students I was able to extend the existing literature on the relationship between grit and stress in college students.

It is important to note that although facets of grit and perceived stress were significantly (negatively) correlated in Study 1, the regression analysis indicated that neither facet of grit was uniquely associated with perceived stress levels. There could be a couple of reasons for this. First, it is possible that the sample size in Study 1 wasn't large enough to capture the effect. The fact that the size of the correlations I observed were consistent with prior reports (e.g. Wong et al., 2018) and that I did observe a predictive relationship between facets of grit and perceived stress in Study 2 provide support for this notion.

Second, it is possible that another variable may account for the relationship between grit and perceived stress. For instance, the development of grit may be associated with enhanced emotion regulation capacities, which allows individuals to cope with stressors more effectively. There is preliminary empirical evidence to indicate that gritty personality traits may be associated with connectivity in the regions of the prefrontal cortex (PFC) implicated in the use of emotion regulation strategies. Resting-state fMRI, within a sample of children ($Mean_{age} = 11.2$ years), has shown that individual level differences in grit were associated with functional connectivity in networks of cognitive and behavioral control in the PFC (Myers, Wang, Black, Bugescu, & Hoeft, 2016). More research is needed before this association between perceived chronic stress and facets of grit can be understood clearly.

The findings of Study 2 indicate that high levels of Grit-Perseverance and Grit-Consistency are associated with fewer academic problems. Students who were goal oriented (i.e. had a long-term goal) and were exhibited consistency in their interests were less likely to report that they were *thinking of dropping some classes* or were *inconsistent in their class work*. This study adds to the existing literature showing that grit is associated with key indicators of success in education (Almeida, 2016; Duckworth & Quinn, 2009). Academic problems (e.g. *I have difficulty concentrating while studying*) provide an assessment of academic behaviors, both activities and actions, that directly and indirectly influence academic achievement (Almeida, 2016). By focusing on academic problems I was able to extend the current literature on grit.

Additionally, results of mediation regression analyses indicate that grit is implicated in fewer academic problems through reduced stress. This is true of both facets of grit. In effect, college students who are high on either Grit-Perseverance or Grit-Consistency are more likely to report lower stress levels which in turn results in fewer academic problems. My data suggests that grit may serve as a psychological resource that provides a buffer against stressors (Lee, 2017; Rhodes et al., 2017). Considering that stress-related disorders and the stress related to schoolwork is rising in the US (May et al., 2015), the role of grit in mitigating the effects of stress on academic outcomes in college students should be systematically studied. In particular, experimental research conducted in the laboratory that examines the interactive effect of grit under acute stress conditions might be able to provide mechanistic explanations to the relationship between grit and stress.

Recent research has shown that Grit–Perseverance is a more robust predictor of outcomes than Grit–Consistency (Bowman et al., 2015; Kalia, Fuesting, & Cody,

2019). This has prompted some researchers to claim that Grit-Perseverance is the only facet of grit that should be considered when researching academic performance (Credé, Tynan, & Harms, 2017). However, the data that I report here contradict this notion. Both facets of grit were uniquely associated with fewer academic problems. Although Grit-Consistency has been overlooked in favor of Grit-Perseverance, more recent research has indicated Grit-Consistency is associated with outcomes (Disabato, Goodman, & Kashdan, 2019; Knauft et al., 2019) and needs to be considered more carefully.

The results of these studies must be interpreted with a view toward their limitations. First, the studies were correlational in design, so no causal claims about the direction of the relationship between facets of grit, perceived chronic stress, and academic problems can be made. Second, in both the studies the number of female participants outnumbered the male participants. Although gender differences in grit are rarely reported, there have been instances where it has been observed (e.g. Lee, 2017). Gender differences did not emerge in Study 1 but they were a factor in Study 2. Thus, it would be helpful to replicate this work with larger and more gender balanced samples. Finally, our measure of stress is self-reported at a single time point. Future research should consider adding physiological or multiple measures of stress to more comprehensively examine the relationship between stress and facets of grit. Nevertheless, this work adds to the limited literature on the association between stress and facets of grit and enhances our understanding of their role in academic achievement.

6.8 Practical Implications

If grit can help identify those vulnerable to chronic stress, then it has immediate practical implication for college counselors. As the number of college students seeking counseling services has risen dramatically in the US (Prince, 2015), the grit scale could be used by counselors to determine which student needs more emotional and psychological support in their first year of college. Relatedly, as academic problems have been cited as one of the reasons that students disengage from their educational pursuit and drop out of college (Tinto, 2012), academic advising could benefit from using the grit scale to identify students who may require additional support and guidance in their study habits which could potentially prevent attrition.

6.9 Future Directions

Although grit is associated with a multitude of positive outcomes there is also evidence to suggest that gritty individuals may be resistant to changing direction or strategies when they experience failure (Lucas, Gratch, Cheng, & Marsella, 2015).

Additionally, empirical data indicate that gritty individuals expend effort at the cost of cognitive flexibility in challenging tasks (Kalia et al., 2019). In view of the fact that flexibility has been posited as essential to learning (Deci, Vallerand, Pelletier, & Ryan, 1991) and is associated with increased academic achievement (George & Greenfield, 2005), future research should examine whether gritty individuals persist with challenging fields of study (e.g. STEM) at the cost of creativity and flexibility.

6.10 Conclusion

Despite the interest and the recognition that grit is associated with positive life outcomes, very little research has been done to examine the impact of grit in the health domain. The work presented in this chapter suggests that high grit levels may provide a buffer against chronic stress in college students. This is an important finding as chronic stress is implicated in wide variety of physical and mental health disorders (Slavich, 2016). More research needs to be conducted to determine the exact nature of the association between grit and chronic stress. Additionally, the results of the second study in this chapter indicate that grit may be associated with high academic functioning and fewer academic problems. Although exploratory and needing replication, this finding extends the current literature on grit and academic achievement by examining academic problems as opposed to academic performance or achievement.

References

Almeida, D. J. (2016). Understanding grit in the context of higher education. In M. B. Paulsen (Ed.), *Higher education: Handbook of theory and research* (Vol. 31, pp. 559–609). Cham, Switzerland: Springer.

American College Health Association. (2019). *American College Health Association-National College Health Assessment II: Reference Group Executive Summary Spring 2019*. Silver Spring, MD: American College Health Association.

Anton, D. W., & Reed, J. R. (1991). *College adjustment scales: Professional manual*. Odessa, FL: Psychological Assessment Resources.

Arnsten, A. F. (2009). Stress signalling pathways that impair prefrontal cortex structure and function. *Nature Reviews Neuroscience, 10*(6), 410–422.

Baghurst, T., & Kelley, B. C. (2014). An examination of stress in college students over the course of a semester. *Health Promotion Practice, 15*(3), 438–447.

Bardi, M., Koone, T., Mewaldt, S., & O'Connor, K. (2011). Behavioral and physiological correlates of stress related to examination performance in college chemistry students. *Stress, 14*(5), 557–566.

Baron, R. M., & Kenny, D. A. (1986). The moderator–mediator variable distinction in social psychological research: Conceptual, strategic, and statistical considerations. *Journal of Personality and Social Psychology, 51*(6), 1173.

Beiter, R., Nash, R., McCrady, M., Rhoades, D., Linscomb, M., Clarahan, M., & Sammut, S. (2015). The prevalence and correlates of depression, anxiety, and stress in a sample of college students. *Journal of Affective Disorders, 173*, 90–96.

Blascovich, J. (2008). Challenge, threat, and health. In J. Y. Shah & W. L. Gardner (Eds.), *Handbook of motivation science* (pp. 481–493). New York: The Guilford Press.

Bowman, N. A., Hill, P. L., Denson, N., & Bronkema, R. (2015). Keep on truckin' or stay the course? Exploring grit dimensions as differential predictors of educational achievement, satisfaction, and intentions. *Social Psychological and Personality Science, 6*(6), 639–645.

Burkhart, R. A., Tholey, R. M., Guinto, D., Yeo, C. J., & Chojnacki, K. A. (2014). Grit: A marker of residents at risk for attrition? *Surgery, 155*(6), 1014–1022.

Cohen, S., Kamarck, T., & Mermelstein, R. (1983). A global measure of perceived stress. *Journal of Health and Social Behavior, 24*(4), 385–396.

Costarelli, V., & Patsai, A. (2012). Academic examination stress increases disordered eating symptomatology in female university students. *Eating and Weight Disorders-Studies on Anorexia, Bulimia and Obesity, 17*(3), e164–e169.

Credé, M., Tynan, M. C., & Harms, P. D. (2017). Much ado about grit: A meta-analytic synthesis of the grit literature. *Journal of Personality and Social Psychology, 113*(3), 492–511.

Danese, A., & McEwen, B. S. (2012). Adverse childhood experiences, allostasis, allostatic load, and age-related disease. *Physiology & Behavior, 106*(1), 29–39.

Deci, E. L., Vallerand, R. J., Pelletier, L. G., & Ryan, R. M. (1991). Motivation and education: The self-determination perspective. *Educational Psychologist, 26*, 325–346.

Disabato, D. J., Goodman, F. R., & Kashdan, T. B. (2019). Is grit relevant to well-being and strengths? Evidence across the globe for separating perseverance of effort and consistency of interests. *Journal of Personality, 87*, 194–211.

Duckworth, A., & Gross, J. J. (2014). Self-control and grit: Related but separable determinants of success. *Current Directions in Psychological Science, 23*(5), 319–325.

Duckworth, A. L., Peterson, C., Matthews, M. D., & Kelly, D. R. (2007). Grit: Perseverance and passion for long-term goals. *Journal of Personality and Social Psychology, 92*, 1087–1101.

Duckworth, A. L., & Quinn, P. D. (2009). Development and validation of the short grit scale (GRIT–S). *Journal of Personality Assessment, 91*(2), 166–174.

Dweck, C. S., Walton, G. M., & Cohen, G. L. (2014). *Academic tenacity: Mindsets and skills that promote long-term learning*. Bill & Melinda Gates Foundation.

Eskreis-Winkler, L., Duckworth, A. L., Shulman, E. P., & Beal, S. (2014). The grit effect: Predicting retention in the military, the workplace, school and marriage. *Frontiers in Psychology, 5*, 36.

Garett, R., Liu, S., & Young, S. D. (2017). A longitudinal analysis of stress among incoming college freshmen. *Journal of American College Health, 65*, 331–338.

George, J. L., & Greenfield, D. B. (2005). Examination of a structured problem-solving flexibility task for assessing approaches to learning in young children: Relation to teacher ratings and children's achievement. *Journal of Applied Developmental Psychology, 26*, 69–84.

Goodman, F. R., Disabato, D. J., Kashdan, T. B., & Machell, K. A. (2017). Personality strengths as resilience: A one-year multiwave study. *Journal of Personality, 85*(3), 423–434.

Guerrero, L. R., Dudovitz, R., Chung, P. J., Dosanjh, K. K., & Wong, M. D. (2016). Grit: A potential protective factor against substance use and other risk behaviors among Latino adolescents. *Academic Pediatrics, 16*(3), 275–281.

Jose, P. E. (2003). MedGraph-I: A programme to graphically depict mediation among three variables: The internet version, version 2.0. Victoria Univesity of Wellington, Wellington, New Zealand. Retrieved [date] from http://www.victoria.ac.nz/staff/paul-jose-files/medgraph/medgraph.php,1.

Hammond, D. A. (2017). Grit: An important characteristic in learners. *Currents in Pharmacy Teaching and Learning, 9*(1), 1–3.

Hout, M. (2012). Social and economic returns to college education in the United States. *Annual Review of Sociology, 38*, 379–400.

Kalia, V., Fuesting, M., & Cody, M. (2019). Perseverance in solving Sudoku: Role of grit and cognitive flexibility in problem solving. *Journal of Cognitive Psychology, 31*, 1–9.

Kalia, V., Vishwanath, K., Knauft, K. M., Von Der Vellen, B., Luebbe, A., & Williams, A. (2018). Acute stress attenuates cognitive flexibility in males only: An fNIRS examination. *Frontiers in Psychology, 9*, 2084.

Kannangara, C. S., Allen, R. E., Waugh, G., Nahar, N., Khan, S. Z. N., Rogerson, S., & Carson, J. (2018). All that glitters is not grit: Three studies of grit in university students. *Frontiers in Psychology, 9*, 1539.

Kleiman, E. M., Adams, L. M., Kashdan, T. B., & Riskind, J. H. (2013). Gratitude and grit indirectly reduce risk of suicidal ideations by enhancing meaning in life: Evidence for a mediated moderation model. *Journal of Research in Personality, 47*(5), 539–546.

Knauft, K. M., Ortiz, S. N., Velkoff, E. A., Smith, A. R., & Kalia, V. (2019). Keep calm and carry on? Grit buffers against disordered eating unless expressive suppression is used to regulate emotions. *Journal of Social and Clinical Psychology*. https://doi.org/10.1521/jscp.2019.38.4.321.

Lazarus, R., & Folkman, S. (1984). *Stress, appraisal and coping*. New York: Springer.

Lee, W. W. S. (2017). Relationships among grit, academic performance, perceived academic failure, and stress in associate degree students. *Journal of Adolescence, 60*, 148–152.

Lee, S. J., & Park, J. Y. (2018). The effects of grit and stress on nursing student's adjustment to college life. *Journal of Digital Convergence, 16*(2), 269–276.

Letkiewicz, J., Lim, H., Heckman, S., Bartholomae, S., Fox, J. J., & Montalto, C. P. (2014). The path to graduation: Factors predicting on-time graduation rates. *Journal of College Student Retention: Research, Theory & Practice, 16*(3), 351–371.

Liston, C., McEwen, B. S., & Casey, B. J. (2009). Psychosocial stress reversibly disrupts prefrontal processing and attentional control. *Proceedings of the National Academy of Sciences, 106*(3), 912–917.

Lowe, R., & Ziemke, T. (2011). The feeling of action tendencies: On the emotional regulation of goal-directed behavior. *Frontiers in Psychology, 2*, 346.

Lucas, G. M., Gratch, J., Cheng, L., & Marsella, S. (2015). When the going gets tough: Grit predicts costly perseverance. *Journal of Research in Personality, 59*, 15–22.

Maddi, S. R., Matthews, M. D., Kelly, D. R., Villarreal, B., & White, M. (2012). The role of hardiness and grit in predicting performance and retention of USMA cadets. *Military Psychology, 24*(1), 19–28.

May, R. W., Bauer, K. N., & Fincham, F. D. (2015). School burnout: Diminished academic and cognitive performance. *Learning and Individual Differences, 42*, 126–131.

McEwen, B. S. (2004). Protection and damage from acute and chronic stress: Allostasis and allostatic overload and relevance to the pathophysiology of psychiatric disorders. *Annals of the New York Academy of Sciences, 1032*(1), 1–7.

Mouchacca, J., Abbott, G. R., & Ball, K. (2013). Associations between psychological stress, eating, physical activity, sedentary behaviours and body weight among women: A longitudinal study. *BMC Public Health, 13*(1), 828.

Myers, C. A., Wang, C., Black, J. M., Bugescu, N., & Hoeft, F. (2016). The matter of motivation: Striatal resting-state connectivity is dissociable between grit and growth mindset. *Social Cognitive and Affective Neuroscience, 11*(10), 1521–1527.

Osberg, T. M., & Eggert, M. (2012). Direct and indirect effects of stress on bulimic symptoms and BMI: The mediating role of irrational food beliefs. *Eating Behaviors, 13*(1), 54–57.

Pearlin, L. I., Schieman, S., Fazio, E. M., & Meersman, S. C. (2005). Stress, health, and the life course: Some conceptual perspectives. *Journal of Health and Social Behavior, 46*(2), 205–219.

Prince, J. P. (2015). University student counseling and mental health in the United States: Trends and challenges. *Mental Health & Prevention, 3*(1–2), 5–10.

Rhodes, E., Devlin, K. N., Steinberg, L., & Giovannetti, T. (2017). Grit in adolescence is protective of late-life cognition: Non-cognitive factors and cognitive reserve. *Aging, Neuropsychology, and Cognition, 24*(3), 321–332.

Robotham, D. (2008). Stress among higher education students: Towards a research agenda. *Higher Education, 56*(6), 735–746.

Schwabe, L., Tegenthoff, M., Höffken, O., & Wolf, O. T. (2010). Concurrent glucocorticoid and noradrenergic activity shifts instrumental behavior from goal-directed to habitual control. *Journal of Neuroscience, 30*(24), 8190–8196.

Shankar, N., & Park, C. L. (2016). Effects of stress on students' physical and mental health and academic success. *International Journal of School & Educational Psychology, 4*(1), 5–9.

Shields, N. (2001). Stress, active coping and academic performance among persisting and nonpersisting college students. *Journal of Applied Biobehavioural Research, 6*, 65–81.

Silvia, P. J., Eddington, K. M., Beaty, R. E., Nusbaum, E. C., & Kwapil, T. R. (2013). Gritty people try harder: Grit and effort-related cardiac autonomic activity during an active coping challenge. *International Journal of Psychophysiology, 88*, 200–205.

Slavich, G. M. (2016). Life stress and health: A review of conceptual issues and recent findings. *Teaching of Psychology, 43*(4), 346–355.

Taylor, P., Parker, K., Morin, R., Fry, R., Patten, E. & Brown, A. (2014). *The rising cost of not going to college*. Washington, DC: Pew Research Center. Retrieved from https://www.pewsocialtrends.org/2014/02/11/the-rising-cost-of-not-going-to-college/

Tinto, V. (2012). *Completing college: Rethinking institutional action*. Chicago, IL: University of Chicago Press.

Vainio, M. M., & Daukantaitė, D. (2016). Grit and different aspects of well-being: Direct and indirect relationships via sense of coherence and authenticity. *Journal of Happiness Studies, 17* (5), 2119–2147.

Van Zyl, L. E., Olckers, C., & Roll, L. C. (2020). The psychometric properties of the Grit-O scale within the Twente Region in the Netherlands: An ICM-CFA vs. ESEM approach. *Frontiers in Psychology, 11*, 796. https://doi.org/10.3389/fpsyg.2020.00796.

Webber, D. A. (2016). Are college costs worth it? How ability, major, and debt affect the returns to schooling. *Economics of Education Review, 53*, 296–310.

Wemm, S., Koone, T., Blough, E. R., Mewaldt, S., & Bardi, M. (2010). The role of DHEA in relation to problem solving and academic performance. *Biological Psychology, 85*(1), 53–61.

Wilburn, V. R., & Smith, D. E. (2005). Stress, self-esteem, and suicidal ideation in late adolescents. *Adolescence, 40*, 33–45.

Wong, M. L., Anderson, J., Knorr, T., Joseph, J. W., & Sanchez, L. D. (2018). Grit, anxiety, and stress in emergency physicians. *The American Journal of Emergency Medicine, 36*(6), 1036–1039.

Vrinda Kalia is an Assistant Professor in the psychology department at Miami University in Ohio. She studies goal directed behavior and the role contextual forces (i.e. family, culture, language environment, stress) that shape the development of cognitive and emotional processes that enable goal achievement. Professor Kalia's work is interdisciplinary intersecting educational psychology, cultural psychology, and cognitive psychology and her studies often combine behavioral data with physiological measurements (i.e. EEG and fNIRS).

Chapter 7
Grit Lit: An Effort to Cultivate Grit and Task Perseverance Through a High-School Language Arts Curriculum

Eric Patrick Sinclair

Abstract Angela Duckworth's 2013 TED Talk explored her research on the statistical correlation between grit and success in many mentally and physically strenuous situations. Grit is defined as passion and perseverance for long-term goals. Duckworth's speech also contained a subsequent challenge for researchers to explore ways to build grit within young people, and this chapter attempts to meet that challenge. The purpose of this chapter was to develop and determine the effectiveness of a ninth-grade English Language Arts curriculum designed to enhance grit at a rural Midwestern public high school. Specifically, it aimed to increase task perseverance by utilizing multiple motivational theories of achievement to help students build grit in their academic careers and beyond. These tenets were reinforced through several intentional methodologies including, first and foremost, reading grit-themed textual materials with an increased level of rigor, rewarding student effort by allowing revision for assessments, providing effort-based feedback to cultivate growth mindset, and tracking student performance and mastery goals over time. Quantitative data was obtained through a pre- and post-assessment on grit, a pre- and post-assessment on task perseverance in the form of student writing revision attempts. Additionally, posthoc qualitative reflections of the highest-performing participants on the effectiveness of each component of the strategy. Specific within-person changes on the subscales will be evaluated and limitations of the research described. Additionally, suggestions for further study are considered and implications for policy changes in English Language Arts classrooms.

Keywords Growth mindset · High school students · Motivational theories · Task perseverance

---

E. P. Sinclair (✉)
Christel House Academy, Indianapolis, IN, USA

L. E. van Zyl et al. (eds.), *Multidisciplinary Perspectives on Grit*,
https://doi.org/10.1007/978-3-030-57389-8_7

7.1 Introduction

Angela Duckworth's interest in grit research developed after spending time teaching in a public school district. She started to notice a strange phenomenon between her lowest and highest achievers regarding intelligence: "Some of my strongest performers did not have stratospheric IQ scores. Some of my smartest kids weren't doing so well" (TED, 2013). This led her to believe that being successful in school and in life is about much more than being able to learn effortlessly, which led her to the exploration of the relationship between success and effortful persistence over extended periods of time. There was a noncognitive factor at play, which she termed "grit," and defined as "passion and perseverance for long-term goals" (Duckworth, Peterson, Matthews, & Kelly, 2007).

To provide validation to the theory that grit is the most accurate predictor of success and motivation across a wide range of scenarios, Duckworth et al. (2007) studied individuals in some of the most difficult situations to determine which factors of their personalities differentiated them enough to push them through their challenges. When the authors published their 2007 article, "Grit: Passion and Perseverance for Long-Term Goals," a compilation of the results of five different independent but interrelated studies, the implications were quite groundbreaking, with grit showing a significant impact on level of education, consistency in careers, college GPA, and even West Point retention rates (Duckworth et al., 2007; Kelly, Matthews, & Bartone, 2014). Studies replicated results showing the importance of grit in Teach for America success rates (Duckworth, Quinn, & Seligman, 2009), Army Special Operations training retention (Eskreis-Winkler, Shulman, Beal, & Duckworth, 2014), retention in difficult sales careers (Eskreis-Winkler et al., 2014), graduation rates from Chicago Public Schools (Eskreis-Winkler et al., 2014),, African-American school success at predominantly white universities (Strayhorn, 2014), non-traditional doctoral student GPA (Cross, 2014), performance (Van Zyl, Olckers, & Roll, 2020) and even success in marriage (Eskreis-Winkler et al., 2014).

When asked if grit can be taught or built up over time, Duckworth was surprisingly candid. Her response: "The honest answer is, I don't know" (TED, 2013). Because of this obvious gap in the research, researchers have already set out to determine the origins of grit and whether it is more hereditary or malleable in nature. Rimfeld, Kovas, Dale, and Plomin (2016) performed a grit study using 2321 twin pairs born between 1994 and 1996 in England and Wales. Grit was assessed at age 16, and correlation was used to estimate associations between the two twins' results. Their results showed that grit was "moderately heritable, with genetic factors explaining about a third of the variance" (p. 785), while shared environmental factors, such as growing up in the same family and attending the same schools, "explained no significant variance in these scales" (p. 786). While this may seem discouraging, Rimfeld et al. (2016) added that "heritability does not imply immutability," and that "this finding does not limit the possible effect of a novel intervention that is not currently part of the environmental variation" (p. 786). However, few intervention studies exist to determine if grit can be improved over time. This problematic because experimental research is imperative to establish the value-add of constructs under investigation.

This "novel intervention" is exactly what I hypothesized and sought to verify at a rural Midwestern public high school in the United States. Building grit has been "set as a priority by the U.S. Department of Education and the U.K. Department of Education" (Rimfeld et al., 2016, p. 781) with a clear lack of empirical evidence that it is even possible to do so. If, as Franklin Bobbitt (1926) suggested, the purpose of schools and school curriculum is to prepare students for the future, and they should be "influential in shaping character and conduct" (p. 474), then attempts at cultivating this character trait through new and inventive approaches must be endeavored. Though there is some evidence currently to suggest that grit may be a malleable trait and able to be improved with interventions (Eskreis-Winkler, 2015), little to no research has been done with secondary students in an educational setting.

Though grit seems to be a manifestation of goals only through enduring progress and struggle over time, some researchers have also explored its connection to everyday learning activities and challenges to find significant connections (Gerhards & Gravert, 2015; Lucas, Gratch, Cheng, & Marsella, 2015; Suzuki, Tamesue, Asahi, & Ishikawa, 2015; Von Culin, Tsukayama, & Duckworth, 2014). From an educational perspective, it is imperative that students undergo what Bullmaster-Day (2015) calls the "productive struggle—effortful practice that goes beyond passive reading, listening, or watching" (p. 2). When students are challenged, it is important for them to struggle with their work before mastering the material to eventually gain complete command over it. This type of short-term struggle is called "task perseverance," which is defined as the ability to persist in achieving or completing a challenge despite competing goals, difficult distractions, or physical/mental hardships. Only task perseverance will allow students to reach this level of learning and pave the way for their future goals, hence showing a longer-term perseverance (grit).

7.2 Grit-Building Curriculum

7.2.1 The Theoretical Grounding of the Grit-Building Curriculum

The question of why some students lack grit and why they are unsuccessful in the classroom, despite being capable of doing so, has plagued educators for decades. The purpose of this study is to develop a specific curriculum that addresses these concerns and evaluate the effectiveness of that intervention. Despite what some students may outwardly project, they care about being perceived as successful and intelligent by others; yet despite the proven benefits of work ethic, trying harder puts some students at risk (Deci, Vallerand, Pelletier, & Ryan, 1985, p. 326). It is, therefore, not a mystery why some students would rather gladly accept failure without true effort than expose themselves to the vulnerability of failing with it. Several theories form the basis for the grit-building curriculum: attribution theory, goal-setting theory, self-control, locus of control, self-efficacy, and growth mindset. All of these constructs tangentially relate to grit, and thus need to be taken into consideration when formulating an intervention.

The nature of the problem that this intervention addresses can be succinctly explained by Anthony Weiner's attributional theory of achievement motivation and emotion is inextricably tied to the concept of grit, which is shown through its clear influence on more recent motivation philosophy (Bandura, 1989; Dweck, 2006; Schwarzer, 2014). Attribution theory is still relevant because it explains motivation in relation to hypotheticals related to effort and achievement, especially in relation to education. In short, the scenarios can be summed up in the following manner: if students expend effort on a skill or assignment and succeed, they will be more likely to expend a similar amount of effort in the future. If students do not expend effort on a skill or assignment and still succeed, they will likely continue to expend little effort in the future with the prediction of future success based on their past experience. If students do not expend effort and do not succeed, they are likely to expend more effort on the next skill or assignment in an attempt to improve their next results. Finally, if students do expend honest effort but still fail, then they are likely to reach a point of defensive pessimism, holding unrealistically low standards so as not to be disappointed (De Castella, Byrne, & Covington, 2013). Therefore, the goal of educators should be to change the meaning of failure and create instances wherein a true exhibition of grit is the only true path to success. According to Weiner's theory, people attribute both successes and failures to either stable or unstable causes. Stable means that the outcome cannot be controlled by the individual, and therefore he or she is not likely to change if the situation is duplicated (Weiner, 1980). Unstable causes, on the other hand, are those that are likely to yield desired results based on the actions and attitudes of the participant. Unstable attributions mean that the participant sees a personal ability to affect change, and the goal of instruction is to help all students see their ability to change and improve their conditions because of their own effort (Weiner, 1980). Thus, the goal of educators should be to persuade students that their successes and failures can be attributed to unstable causes, and that when students' behaviors are exemplary, then positive, desired results will likely follow.

Goal-setting theory, first expressed by Bandura (1997) outlined a hierarchy of goal systems that every individual possesses in some manner or another. The very definition of grit reinforces the importance of goals, especially long-term ones. In fact, grit has sometimes been referred to as "goal commitment" in some texts—specifically those before Duckworth and her colleagues coined the term. Though grit is primarily centered around distal goals, proximal goals, or those considered closer at hand, have been proven beneficial to reaching as well. Proximal goals can also be described as subordinate goals, if used correctly. This means that proximal goals should be set so that they build up the higher-order goal, the long-term one that inspires students to work toward the future (Bandura & Schunk, 1981). Part of the reason why gritty individuals are so successful because they have the attitude that when one door closes, another door opens. When faced with challenges, these students can invent a new way forward by creating alternative lower-order goals when one path closes (Duckworth & Gross, 2014).

Self-control is crucial for an individual to be considered gritty. Bandura (1997) asserted that people use hierarchical structure to align subordinate task goals to their higher-order goals. For gritty individuals, lower-order goals must align with the dominant goal. These people either are able to push off competing subordinate goals or lack them entirely (Duckworth & Gross, 2014, p. 322). This means that they simply let nothing get in the way of their long-term goal; they are able to avoid distractions, delay gratification, and focus on the main task at hand (Goodwin & Miller, 2013, p. 2). In essence, gritty individuals exhibit this same self-control by pushing off their immediate wants for their eventual needs.

J. B. Rotter's *locus of control* is considered a "belief that individuals create about themselves" and their interactions with the world around them; these can "cause distress or act as an interpersonal resource" (Gifford, Briceno-Perriott, & Mianzo, 2006, p. 19). Locus of control determines if individuals blame their own behavior for what happens in life or whether they attribute those outcomes to external circumstances (Hoerr, 2012, p. 84). The locus of control scale is used to describe students' opinions of how much they can control the circumstances of their own life, specifically their "learning behaviors and achievement" (Bulus, 2011, p. 542). Individuals with an internal locus of control (internals) believe that the outcomes in their lives depend mostly on what they do to control them, while individuals with an external locus of control (externals) believe that most circumstances are beyond their own control (Dollinger, 2000, p. 1). On the other hand, internals more actively exert more control over their lives; they do more to avoid failure, partly because of their knowledge of their environment (Lefcourt, 1976, p. 65). Students with an internal locus of control have also been proven to obtain higher test scores and credit their academic success "to internal factors rather than fate, luck or powerful others used by those with an external locus of control" (Kaiser, 1975, p. 426). Internals do more to help themselves because they feel that the weight of responsibility is on them to find success (Chubb, Fertman, & Ross, 1997); they are more aggressive than passive in gathering information that may prove helpful to them in order to achieve their goals.

Albert Bandura was also a pioneer in the studies on *self-efficacy*. As Bandura (1982), himself, explained, self-efficacy is defined as an evaluation of "how well one can execute courses of action required to deal with prospective situations" (p. 122). Self-efficacy is developed most notably through social support, which involves peer and teacher feedback, and these can also help to determine the outcome expectation for the student involved (Schunk, 1995). A study by Collins (1985) showed that self-efficacy could be a key factor in predicting achievement and motivation in school settings. When students in this study were given a wide range of problems, including some that were unsolvable, and they were also given unlimited opportunities to rework those problems. Those students who identified as having high self-efficacy tried longer on the difficult problems and even reworked more problems that they missed, despite their (lack of) aptitude in the subject areas. Regardless of ability, students with high self-efficacy worked harder and performed better than those who had low self-efficacy (p. 104).

Self-efficacy also plays a large role in developing grit. Students must see that their success is a result of their efforts, not of their skills, or at least as a result of their skills because of their efforts. Erez and Judge (2001) also affirmed that the process of setting goals has clear benefits, but these benefits are lost unless individuals are willing to commit to them (p. 1272), and research has shown that students need self-efficacy to commit to goals. Outcome expectations are crucial to establishing self-efficacy. Students are not usually motivated to succeed if they do not believe it is possible; they are more motivated to protect themselves from the negative outcomes of failure (Schunk, 1989, p. 14). If students do not believe they can be successful in completing their desired goals, based on their past experiences and the experiences of comparable peers, "they have little incentive to undertake activities or to persevere in the face of difficulties of failures" (Caprara, Gerbino, Paciello, Di Giunta, & Pastorelli, 2010, p. 36). This further develops the point: grit cannot exist without self-efficacy.

Not unrelated to self-efficacy is Carol Dweck's emerging trend on building grit called *growth mindset*. Dweck (2006) argued that self-efficacy is important, but only after the student has taken proper preparation has for a specific challenge. In fact, self-efficacious behaviors without first expanding effort can be damaging, if not immediately, then at least in the long-term. In fact, Dweck's (2006) book *Mindset: The New Psychology of Success* is full of examples of former prodigies or young phenomena whose initial talent was eventually exceeded by those who expanded more effort over time, hence demonstrating more grit. Dweck (2006) elaborated: "In the fixed mindset, you don't take control of your abilities and your motivation. You look for your talent to carry you through, and when it doesn't, well then, what else could you have done? You are not a work in progress, you're a finished product. And finished products have to protect themselves, lament, and blame. Everything but take charge" (p. 103). Successful individuals have a growth mindset; they feel that intelligence is not fixed and can improve with effort. They also feel that failure is not permanent and is part of the learning and growing process (Elish-Piper, 2014, p. 59). If every student exhibited this attitude, it is undeniable that educators would see more productivity in the classroom, and as a result, more growth within students.

7.2.2 Tenets and Implementation of the Grit-Building Curriculum

The grit-building curriculum consisted of five core principles. These tenets are the constructs of the attributional retraining process, the process which builds grit in students. These are not only focused on the literature that these students read, but they are also focused on classroom policies and teacher behaviors as well. They are as follows: rigor, ownership, effort, goal-setting, feedback, and, of course, grit-based literature.

The first common theme that has emerged through the research is that curriculum must challenge students, and it must challenge them to the point of failure. This is what Hoerr (2013) calls "creating the frustration" (p. 22), and it is essential for cultivating gritty students. Presumably, as Goodwin and Miller (2013) reinforce, holding higher expectations will lead to higher academic outcomes; providing challenging goals encourages greater effort and determination. Some students, however, simply cannot conquer their own fears that they are inadequate. Fear of failure was positively correlated with "helplessness, self-handicapping, truancy, and disengagement," and though these are perceived as apathy, they may be the consequences of "caring too much about the prospect of failure and what it means" (De Castella et al., 2013, p. 875). Hoerr (2012) argued that we can eliminate some of these consequences of failure avoidance by teaching students that failure is okay, and it is only a small step in the process of accomplishment. We should prepare youths to "anticipate misfortunes and point out that excellence in any discipline requires years and years of time on task" (Duckworth et al., 2007, p. 1100). It is essential to understand that becoming successful at any challenging endeavor takes time and effort, and failure is an essential part of that growth experience.

This is exactly what this unit seeks to accomplish. Though the assignments and performance assessments themselves were not altered from what ninth-grade English has previously used, the students must read at a higher level to reach that level of productive struggle. As a result, they may have to read—and reread—the material to fully grasp it. The reading levels of the assigned readings are included in the curriculum maps that I have provided at the "Committed 2 Learning Blog" (Sinclair, 2020). It is important to note that regular class assignments were used as formative assessments, which means that students understood that they would not be penalized for trying and failing to grasp the content and demonstrate mastery on the regular classwork. This ensures that students are exposed to the *rigor* without it negatively affecting their academic grades.

Another aspect of the curriculum that I employed for this group of students is the classroom policies in place, especially regarding paper rewrites and assessment retakes. In the grit-building curriculum, students had unlimited opportunities to retest or redo pertinent assignments. As long as the students prove that they have learned the material, this is considered the main goal in the process. Therefore, if they complete the retake process, students will be allowed to work to relearn material and have the chance to prove that they have mastered it, or at the very least, shown some progression of learning to reach their goals. This falls in line with Hoerr's (2013) suggestion to "require a student to revise and revise again until his or her work is perfect" (p. 22). In short, these opportunities to improve work and skills provide students an opportunity to counteract the rigor of the assessments.

The students must accept the fact that they are in charge of their own outcomes: that they must take *ownership* of their actions and they must believe that they have the power to change them in a positive manner. Locus of control is a crucial aspect of building grit. To make positive changes in students' lives, they must first believe that they are capable of making these changes. They must know that it is possible to change their own circumstances, however unfavorable they may be. Attributional retraining is a process in which teachers use to shift a student's locus of control from external to internal (Perry, Perry, Stupnisky, Hall, Chipperfield, & Weiner, 2010). In some ways, this is exactly what growth mindset teaching is attempting to accomplish as well. One piece of attributional retraining that was utilized related to the retake and rewrite policy that was set in place. To be able to redo work, students will first have to fill out a "Take Ownership Sheet," which you may also find at the "Committed 2 Learning Blog" (Sinclair, 2020). On this reflection, students were asked to acknowledge their lack of skill, time management, or study habits. In other words, they needed to acknowledge what they should have done better, and what they plan to do better for the redone assignment. The point of this assignment is twofold: (1) to ensure that students put in extra work to earn the privilege of making up the work that they were not responsible or skillful enough to complete the first time, and (2) to make students acknowledge that they did not work hard enough to complete the assignment the first time around. In effect, this mandatory reflection attempts to internalize their locus of control and create clear proximal goals before they are given the opportunity to benefit from the policy.

The concept of growth mindset, the ability to overcome these shortcomings, to adapt and improve their intelligence through their own *effort*, was reflected through the writing assignments during the grit-building unit. The first grit-based writing was a poetry project (Sinclair, 2020), which asked students to reflect on the importance of grit to their distal goals. The other thematically-tied assignment was a narrative in which students were asked to write to a college entrance board about a time that they learned a new skill or trait—or somehow otherwise persevered—because of their hard work (Sinclair, 2020), and it reflects the work of Aronson et al. (2002) in which students were assigned to write about the effects of their efforts on intelligence, which implies that students can be pushed away from a fixed mindset when they reflect on their own intelligence and school experiences.

The curriculum must promote and reward hard work. This directly ties into the next common theme among current research: it is necessary to teach students how to work hard for them to reap the benefits of their consistent effort and self-control. People nearly always perform better if they focus on what they can control—their effort and persistence—rather than what they cannot, like their natural skill or aptitude (Glenn, 2010). Self-control is necessary for this consistent effort because students must work through distractions and competing subordinate goals to reach their ultimate desired destinations. Learning and success must be associated with "hard work, practice, and persistence" (Elish-Piper, 2014, p. 59). However, it is not always safe to assume that students know what it takes to put in the work to succeed, or even what it means to work with stamina and self-control. Some students do not even know where to begin in this regard but teaching to Vygotsky's (1978) zone of proximal development is extremely important. Vygotsky asserts that the skill or material being taught should be situated between what the student can already do by him or herself (which is too easy) and what the student cannot do without help (which is too difficult). The ZPD focuses on what the student can do with help from a more knowledgeable other, like a teacher or peer who can guide the student through the material to find some success. Siegel and Shaughnessy (1996) argued that, eventually, when consistent effort is given, it is necessary to lessen task difficulty, or provide more help from the more knowledgeable other, so that lower-achieving students can find some success, to see that effort will pay off in the end.

Again, the retake and rewrite policy specifically relates to this aspect of class as well. There is one last requirement to be able to redo work in the grit-building curriculum. The requirement is that students spend at least one tutorial session to relearn the material or to discover the necessary changes that need to be made to their work to improve it. The point of this aspect of the policy is that students must put in extra work to reap the rewards of the system. If this class provides them an opportunity for their work to pay off, then hopefully it will carry over into other areas of their lives as well.

The main adaptation in this curriculum is the concept of growth mindset and how it is promoted through the reading and writing throughout this curriculum. All the poetry, non-fiction, and fiction pieces, outlined in Sinclair (2020), that were featured in the "grit lit" unit are based on the theme of hard work and determination despite setbacks or failures. Each text promotes the use of persistence to work toward goal completion. Some of the non-fiction even promotes growth mindset itself, using literature to promote the concept of building intelligence through work ethic.

Another adaptation is that students were allotted time in class to do most assignments and studying. This eliminated the ability for parents to interfere with the learning process, giving some students an unfair advantage in the classroom, those with a solid support system at home. It also eliminated the disadvantage for students who have unstable home environments. Additionally, student success on assignments and on assessments without working for their goals becomes more unlikely because they are being supervised in the classroom and encouraged to practice their skills. In this sense, students could attribute their successes to this obligatory guided practice time in class. If they succeed without effort, this results in negative attributional thinking. Students could begin to see that they can succeed without working and then continue a negative trend that will affect them down the road, when the material becomes more difficult. However, if they see that their successes come after studying or preparing for assessments in class, then attributing their success to skill that does not need maintained becomes much less likely.

The students must set clear, challenging *goals*. The positive effects of goal setting have been proven repeatedly. As Rader (2005) pointed out, "When students write down their goals, they are forced to examine themselves and see their own dreams. This is important because, ultimately, reflecting on why they hope to achieve their goals, rather than simply knowing what their goals are, is what motivates them to pursue their life ambitions" (Rader, 2005, p. 123). Because of the strong evidence that supports the benefits of goal-setting, students in the grit curriculum will be encouraged to set performance, mastery, and boundary goals. Therefore, this curriculum employs all of these. Students also completed a "Student Goal Commitment Sheet" (Sinclair, 2020), to address both performance and mastery goals in accordance with goal theory.

The teacher must provide specified *feedback* toward both performance and mastery goals. The last tenet of the grit-building curriculum is the teacher feedback that must take place for students to find success in attributional retraining. In general, teacher feedback should focus not on the skills of the students, but the work that they put toward their goals. Dweck (2006) reflected the importance of this type of feedback in her book *Mindset: The New Psychology of Success.* When Dweck gave students a nonverbal IQ test, two groups of students were initially equal in ability. But when one group received praise on ability and the other received praise on effort, their behaviors started to differ, especially in the ability-praise group. "As we feared, the ability praise pushed students right into the fixed mindset, and they showed all the signs of it, too: When we gave them a choice, they rejected a challenging new task that they could learn from. They didn't want to do anything that could expose their flaws or call into question all of their talent" (p. 72). This directly contrasts the ability-praise group, 90% of whom wanted to accept the challenge of the new task. Their attitudes were the most impressive part, however, because the effort-praised students found that the challenging problems were the most enjoyable. Schunk (1995) explained this phenomenon clearly: "When persons succeed easily, ability feedback is credible and increases self-efficacy, motivation, and performance. When students have to work hard to succeed, they may discount ability feedback in favor of effort. As they become more skillful, switching to ability feedback is desirable because students believe that their ability is increasing" (Schunk, 1995, p. 119).

However, feedback on everyday events that take place in the classroom is not the only type that is important. As Hoerr (2014) put it, "Setting goals is just a starting point. Progress toward goals must be monitored throughout the year" (p. 84). Therefore, the grit curriculum utilized one-on-one conferences for students every other week of the six-month unit during independent work time. For these classes, students were asked to attach their "Student Goal Sheet" to the front of their class binders. Not only did this provide a constant reminder of what students were striving for in the long-term, but it also provided me with an easy way to assess and share progress toward those goals based on current grades, behaviors, and overall performance.

One of the core principles of this intervention is that the literature and vocabulary of the unit was centered on grit, using the key concepts of the framework listed above. All the poetry, short stories, and non-fiction pieces, along with the drama and novel that the students read were tied thematically, and that theme is that perseverance and determination yield results. The literature and grit-themed vocabulary featured in this instructional section is shown in the "Committed 2 Learning Blog" (Sinclair, 2020). This unit is an adaptation of the science fiction unit, which was previously taught in all 9th grade classrooms and was continued for half of all ninth graders at the high school: those not participating in the experiment.

As Hoerr (2013) argued, teaching the vocabulary of grit is crucial to establishing a culture of it in the classroom. For students to make thematic connections to the literature, they must first understand the vocabulary involved. Once this learning occurs, teachers need to use this vocabulary in functional ways in the classroom and on assignment and assessment feedback. He added, "If your students are occasionally included in parent-teacher conferences, grit would be a wonderful topic for discussion. Having everyone around the table increases the likelihood that parents and educators can work together to help students develop grit" (Hoerr, 2013, p. 21). Therefore, it is 100% necessary to include grit-based vocabulary relating to and included in the literature throughout this unit.

7.3 Methods and Research Design

This was a quantitative study that focuses primarily on an experimental correlational approach. When the grit-building curriculum was employed, using the tenets I outlined above, I examined the effects that the curriculum through a quantitative analysis in a pre- and posttest format. The study first examined whether ninth grade English students completed significantly more essay revisions after receiving the grit-building curriculum than they did before receiving the intervention. The paper revision pre-tests were completed in conjunction with the first essay assignment, which took place before the grit-building curriculum began, and the posttests occurred as the last essay assignment of the unit concluded. Additionally, the study examined whether ninth-grade English students scored significantly higher on the grit self-analysis scale after receiving the grit-building curriculum than they did before receiving it. The pretest grit scale was given before the curriculum was implemented, while the posttest was given after the conclusion of the grit unit. A subsequent research question lies in the ability to establish a connection between grit and task perseverance. For this question, I examined the statistical correlation between Grit-S scale scores and the number of paper rewrites per student. These correlations will examine the correlation between both pre-tests of grit, both post-tests of grit, the change in grit scores, and the change in paper rewrite scores.

Student demographics of the study were as follows (Table 7.1):

Two separate and distinct sets of data were analyzed for statistically significant improvements in the area of grit. The first, the eight-item short grit scale (Grit-S) measures potential change in both the short and long term. The second, the number of paper revisions, indicates a task perseverance as a performance variable with a more practical application to the secondary classroom.

The Grit-S Scale was employed in this experiment because Duckworth and Quinn (2009) found its validity to be higher than the 12-item grit scale. Across four studies, Duckworth and Quinn (2009) found the scale to have an internal consistency range

Table 7.1 Demographic data of the study's participants

Demographic	Gender	Race	Age
	17 (male)	40 (Caucasian)	34 (age 15)
	29 (female)	5 (Latino)	11 (age 14)
		1 A(African-American)	1 (age 13)

of 0.73–0.83 and medium-to-strong predictive validity. Unstandardized regression coefficients associated with grit scores predicted student performance ranging from 0.22 to 0.55, with associated odds ratios ranging from 0.80 to 1.73. Items on the scale were measured using a five-point Likert scale, ranging from "Not at all like me" to "Very much like me." The corresponding point value ranges from 1 ("not gritty at all") to 5 ("extremely gritty"). The point totals for each question are added together and divided by 8, which equates to the mean grit score for all eight items. These scores were rounded to the hundredth and entered into SPSS. Appendix G contains the Grit-S survey taken from Duckworth and Quinn (2009).

Task perseverance was measured using a measure of essay revisions for the pre- and posttest. Each time a student completed the full revision process, this included completion of the "Take Ownership Sheet," the student-teacher conference, and the rewrite turned in with the noted changes and the old copy with associated rubric. When this process was completed, the student was marked as having completed one paper rewrite with the possibility of completing as many as possible to improve their grade on this assignment and overall writing prowess. For each paper revision period, students were also given an eventual time cap of 3 weeks to complete all possible revisions. Though this may seem contrary to the spirit of the unit, in general, teachers still must meet grade period deadlines; thus, an eventual time cap was needed to meet said deadlines.

Students were tested using the two measures outlined above to demonstrate growth from pre- to post-test 6 months later. Both pre-tests were given at the beginning of the grit-building curricular unit, and the posttests were given immediately following the conclusion of the unit. Student information data were coded based on a given number in the order in which students turned in their consent and assent forms to the research assistant. These data codes were then used to enter student information into SPSS to protect student confidentiality throughout the process of this study.

The students in this study were entirely randomized, as they were scheduled into my classes through the administration's selection. Generally, freshman English students are placed into teams (and therefore assigned to designated teachers) based on the alphabetical orientation of their last name.

Every student who stayed in the given English I class for the entirety of the six-month intervention had the opportunity to be a part of this study. Students were excluded if they transferred out of the class because of schedule changes or if they transferred to another school district. This means that all students accounted for experienced the entire unit of instruction and were both pre- and post-tested.

Student data were only analyzed for students who turned in their consent and assent forms to the research assistant before the end of the grit unit, giving informed consent from both the student and his or her guardian to use the data in the study. Data for students who did not complete these forms were destroyed immediately at the conclusion of the study.

All data for this study were analyzed using the SPSS computer program. When comparing the correlation between the results of the paper rewrites and the short grit scale, a Pearson r correlation was employed to establish the relationship between grit and task perseverance. Additionally, a correlational analysis was used to determine if the grit surveys were significantly tied to paper rewrites as a measure of task perseverance. The same analysis was also used to establish a correlation between the change in Grit-S scores and the change in the number of essay revisions. Even though this is clearly not the main purpose of the study, it is still important to analyze because past research (Gerhards & Gravert, 2015; Lucas et al., 2015; Suzuki et al., 2015; Von Culin et al., 2014) has determined that the two are indeed closely related. To establish the statistically significant improvement in grit scores and paper rewrites from pre- to post-test, a paired sample t-test was used. Finally, a partial correlation coefficient was commissioned to control for the initial grit measure, while also determining the correlation between both posttest measures as well.

7.4 Results

The research questions examined in this study were as follows:

- RQ1: Is there a significant difference between the T1 and T2 number of rewrites?
- RQ2: Is there a significant difference between the T1 and T2 grit scores?
- RQ3: Is there a correlation between the T1 grit score and the T1 number of rewrites?
- RQ4: Is there a correlation between the T2 grit score and the T2 number of rewrites?
- RQ5: Is there a correlation between the change in grit scores (T2 − T1) and the change in number of rewrites (T2 − T1)?
- RQ6: Controlling for initial (T1) grit scores, is there a correlation between the T2 grit scores and the number of T2 rewrites?

Research Question 1 is explored in the table below:

The analysis shown in Table 7.2 shows an r value of .00, with a p-value of lower than .05, which means H0 was rejected. In fact, this test provided very strong evidence against the null hypothesis. This indicates that the mean paper rewrites per student after the grit unit intervention was statistically significantly higher than before the grit intervention, $t(46) = -5.51$, $p < .001$ ($r2 = .00$). Students scored higher on the posttest ($M = 1.15$, $SD = 1.17$) than they did on the pretest ($M = .37$, $SD = .57$). The effect size (Cohen's d) was .85.

Research Question 2 is explored in the following table:

Table 7.2 Results of t-test and descriptive statistics for paper rewrites

	Before grit unit		After grit unit			95% CI for mean difference		
Outcome	M	SD	M	SD	n		r	t
	.37	.57	1.15	1.17	46	−1.07, −.50	.000*	−5.51

* p < .05

Table 7.3 Results of t-test and descriptive statistics for Grit-S scores

	Before grit unit		After grit unit			95% CI for mean difference		
Outcome	M	SD	M	SD	n		r	t
	3.41	.57	3.59	.58	46	−.30, −.05	.008*	−2.79

* $p < .05$

Table 7.4 Descriptive statistics: Grit-S pretests and rewrite pretests

	Mean	Standard deviation	*N*
Grit-S pretest	3.42	.57	46
Rewrite pretest	.37	.57	46

Table 7.5 Results of Pearson r correlation: Grit-S pretests and paper rewrite pretests

		Grit-S pretests	Paper rewrite pretests
Grit-S pretests	Pearson Correlation	1	.25
	Sig. (2-tailed)	.	.09
	N	46	46
Paper rewrite pretests	Pearson Correlation	.25	1
	Sig. (2-tailed)	.09	.
	N	46	46

The analysis shown in Table 7.3 shows an r value of .008. The *p*-value was again lower than .05, so H0 was once again rejected. As a result, this proves that the mean grit score per student after the grit-building unit was statistically significantly higher than before the intervention, $t(46) = -2.79$, $p < .05$ (r2 = .01). Students scored higher on the posttest ($M = 3.59$, $SD = .58$) than they did on the pretest ($M = 3.14$, $SD = .57$). The effect size (Cohen's d) was .31.

Research Question 3 asks if there is a significant difference between the T1 grit scores and T1 number of paper rewrites. As previous research has indicated (Gerhards & Gravert, 2015; Lucas et al., 2015), grit scale scores are often statistically correlated with aspects of task perseverance on somewhat menial tasks. This Pearson *r* correlation attempts to connect determination on a more practical classroom task to the Grit-S scale. The descriptive statistics for this correlation are shown below (Table 7.4).

Additionally, the correlational analysis is shown in Table 7.5. The Pearson r correlation represented below does not demonstrate a statistically significant correlation between Grit-S Pretests and Paper Rewrite Pretests, $r = .241$, $p = .088$. Thus, H0 was not rejected. However, the data is approaching significance, which is suggestive evidence against the null hypothesis.

A similar test was necessary to run on the posttests of both the Grit-S scores and the paper rewrites to answer Research Question 4. The descriptive statistics for this correlation are shown in Table 7.6 below.

Furthermore, the correlational analysis is shown in Table 7.7 (below). Again, H0 was not rejected. The Pearson r correlation shown below also does not demonstrate a

Table 7.6 Descriptive statistics: Grit-S pretests and rewrite posttests

	Mean	Standard deviation	*N*
Grit-S posttest	3.59	.58	46
Rewrite posttest	1.15	1.17	46

Table 7.7 Results of Pearson r Correlation: Grit-S posttests and paper rewrite posttests

		Grit-S posttests	Paper rewrite posttests
Grit-S posttests	Pearson Correlation	1	.24
	Sig. (2-tailed)	.	.11
	N	46	46
Paper rewrite posttests	Pearson Correlation	.24	1
	Sig. (2-tailed)	.11	.
	N	46	46

Table 7.8 Descriptive statistics: change in Grit-S and change in rewrites

	Mean	Standard deviation	*N*
Grit-S change	.17	.42	46
Rewrite change	.78	.96	46

Table 7.9 Results of Pearson r Correlation: change in Grit-S scales and change in paper rewrites

		Grit-S change	Paper rewrite change
Grit-S change	Pearson Correlation	1	.14
	Sig. (2-tailed)	.	.37
	N	46	46
Paper rewrite change	Pearson Correlation	.14	1
	Sig. (2-tailed)	.37	.
	N	46	46

statistically significant correlation between Grit-S Posttests and Paper Rewrite Posttests, $r = .241, p = .107$.

Research Question 5 asks if there is a significant correlation between the change in grit scores (T2 - T1) and the change in number of rewrites (T2 – T1). Because there was no significant correlation between both sets of pretests and posttests, one may assume that there was also no significant correlation from the difference between the pre- and posttests. Regardless, it was still necessary to run a Pearson *r* correlation to determine if this was indeed true. The descriptive statistics are included in Table 7.8 below.

Again, the correlational analysis shown in Table 7.9 failed to reject H0. The Pearson r correlation shown below also does not demonstrate a statistically significant correlation between the change in Grit-S scales and the change in paper revisions, $r = .135, p = .370$.

Research Question 6 asks if there is a correlation between the T2 grit scores and the number of T2 rewrites, after controlling for initial (T1) grit scores. The rationale behind this question is that if students were initially gritty, therefore leaving little

Table 7.10 Descriptive statistics: Grit-S posttests and paper rewrite posttests, controlling for Grit pretest

	Mean	Standard deviation	*N*
Grit-S posttest	3.59	.58	46
Rewrite posttest	1.15	1.17	46
Grit-S pretest	3.42	.57	46

Table 7.11 Results of Partial Correlation Coefficient: posttests when controlling for Grit-S pretest

Control variables			Grit posttest	Rewrite posttest
Grit-S pretest	Grit-S posttest	Correlation	1.00	.25
		Sig (2-tailed)	.	.10
		df	0	43
		Correlation	.25	1.00
		Sig (2-tailed)	.10	.
		df	43	0

room to improve, there might possibly be a stronger correlation between the two posttests. The descriptive statistics for this correlation are reported in Table 7.10 below.

Despite controlling for the Grit-S Pretests, the correlational analysis shown in Table 7.11 failed to reject H0.

The partial correlation coefficient shown below also does not demonstrate a statistically significant correlation between the Grit-S scale posttests and the paper revision posttests, $r = .248$, $p = .101$.

7.5 Discussion

The purpose of this study was to develop and determine effectiveness of a ninth-grade English Language Arts curriculum designed to enhance grit at a rural Mid-western public high school. More specifically, effectiveness was evaluated by determining the relationship between grit and paper rewrites (when students were given unlimited opportunities to complete as many revisions as possible in order to earn higher grades and improve writing skills). For a variety of reasons, paper revisions seemed a valid test of task perseverance, one of which could be reflected through student Grit-S scores. However, statistical analysis of the two failed to establish any significant relationship between the two experimental variables. This is likely because grit is long-term in nature, by definition, and the short-term nature of task perseverance did not coincide. More significantly, however, the study aimed to measure significant growth in both Grit- S scales and paper rewrites. The results did, however, show that both paper rewrite and grit scores did significantly improve throughout the course of this study.

Post-hoc interviews were conducted 3 months post-study to examine the specific effects on 12 of the highest-growth students in each measure of grit. I looked for thematic connections between students for the specific tenets of the curriculum outlined above to determine which aspects had the most lasting impact on students; this was the primary reason for waiting 3 months after the study ended. Pertinent student quotations have been included in the conclusion section to add qualitative context to the results of the quantitative study.

When interviewing participants post-study, I focused on each individual tenet of the grit-building curriculum to examine which aspects of the curricular changes made had the most impact on students' mentalities. I have coded them based on their initials to retain their confidentiality. After examining their answers, several prominent themes emerged.

When asked about the impact of the grit-themed literature on students, it was clear that the nonfiction had the largest effect. Several students mentioned that the short stories they read had little effect, as they were unable to see themselves in the literature and relate to it. Conversely, most students found value in the nonfiction. More specifically, they commented on the impact of the growth mindset piece. MC made the following comment: "I thought I had a growth mindset before, until we did the survey. I had a fixed mindset. Now, I feel like I have a more growth mindset because I feel like I have time to reach my goals and I don't have to do it the first time." Of those students interviewed, all of them felt that the texts were valuable in some form or fashion. Even one student, AJ, mentioned the poem "Invictus" as being beneficial: "If you really want to do something, you have to work for it. The line, 'I am the master of my fate, I am the captain of my soul.' It really opened my eyes to that." The fact that AJ still remembered that prominent line almost 6 months after studying the poem indicates that it was heavily impactful.

I then moved on to the idea of effort-based feedback and one-on-one conferencing. As a reminder, students were obligated to conference with me before I gave them the opportunity to revise their essays and receive the updated grade for their essays. Several students found the procedure incredibly valuable. PG stated, "You were helping me know what I needed to correct. You kept pushing me to get better and better and better. I understood better by talking than just reading it on my paper." The motif here was that the time spent on the more specific feedback was especially helpful, as exemplified by RD: "Yes because it helped me understand what you expected specifically from me. It helped clarify a lot of things if I didn't understand something. You'd give specific examples." The consensus seemed to be that audio feedback in a face-to-face fashion was more valuable than effort-based feedback, which is unsurprising, especially when coupled with written feedback on the student work samples as well.

Finally, and perhaps most importantly, were the responses to the question about the impact of the unlimited revision policy. Students generally recognized that the policy placed emphasis on the fact that the learning took place rather than when the learning took place. SA, a student who is musically inclined, commented, "I relate it to music and how you don't just pick up an instrument and play it. It takes a lot of work, and that's really what I got from the grit unit. It takes work to be good at any skill." PG added, "The word unlimited made me want to do it this right the first time. I was upset sometimes when I didn't get it right the first time. But I'd just push myself to make it better; it helped me to know that it didn't have to be right the first time." This, to me, justifies the whole process.

7.6 Practical Implications and Future Directions

The quantitative results showed that the tenets of the grit-building curriculum, including rigor, ownership, effort, goal-setting, feedback, and grit-based literature were effective in their overall goal: to cultivate grit and to cultivate task perseverance in students. This was the main goal of the study and suggests that these methods should be employed in more classrooms across the country to yield similar results.

The purpose of the interviews, in part, was both to determine more specific directions for future research studies and to zero in on the practical implications that one might glean from the study. Given that there were positive aspects to each individual aspect of the grit-building curriculum, it may be beneficial to study each aspect individually. This may help to sort out which alteration was most pertinent in creating the statistical difference between the pre- and post-test on either the task perseverance measure of the Grit-S scale. Clearly, the unit as a whole was effective, but practically speaking, it may be difficult for teachers to implement all aspects at once. Therefore, focusing on the key pieces individually, and then implementing it in stages may be more feasible.

Another clear implication and future direction both would be to make the grit-building curriculum more longitudinal. For the sake of this study, it was a necessity to focus solely on task perseverance, because grit, by nature, is long-term. It would be interesting to see if this curriculum repeated over several years could have a measurable effect on GPA, graduation rate, attendance, or even college admission rates. Perhaps making "grit" a core value of a school, and thus tying most learning back to grit in some manner would have a positive impact on school culture and classroom engagement.

7.7 Conclusion

This study aimed to draw a statistical connection between an intervention designed to improve grit and actual Grit-S self-assessment scales. Additionally, the curriculum attempted to provide a marked improvement in a practical test of task perseverance. Both measures were, in fact, statistically significantly improved. Though the study aimed to provide a statistical relationship between task perseverance and grit, it failed to provide such a correlation.

Paper revisions were used as a measure to test students' task perseverance. In other words, when faced with a difficult task, this test exposed which students would step up to the challenge of putting in effort. It also sought to answer which students would perform this writing task multiple times, if given the adequate opportunity.

Most importantly, it sought to determine if adequate improvements were made in the previous two questions throughout the course of the 6-month study. I hypothesized that pretests in paper revision based on the mean of rewrites completed per student would show significant growth over the course of the six-month grit unit intervention. In reality, based on the paired measures t-test performed in SPSS, paper rewrite production grew quite exponentially, showing an incredibly high statistical significance.

The next hypothesis in this study was that Grit-S scales would significantly increase after the grit unit intervention. Because of the research performed that shows that the Grit-S scale is a strong predictor of success in many different applicable situations, it was important to show that grit is a malleable trait and can be changed with time and effort. Although results were not as strong as the previous hypothesis, students did show statistically significant growth in the eight- item grit scale, based on the average grit score in the same set of students, from before and after the intervention. These results of the paired measures t-test conducted in SPSS proved that this growth was indeed very strong statistically.

The first hypothesis connecting the Grit-S scales to a practical measure of task perseverance showed that the two were not as interconnected as I had assumed initially. Because of research connecting task perseverance on trivial—but statistically measurable—challenges to grit, I sought to tie the Grit-S scale to a more applicable undertaking that many English teachers, and teachers in general, use quite often: task engagement on a writing assignment. It was a venture that students could easily apply to future distal goals, especially since many participants are college-bound students. Despite this encouraging prospect, the null hypothesis was still not rejected for the pretest correlation. Although the results were suggestive that there may have been a connection, they were not closely connected enough to meet statistical standards for correlation.

I also hypothesized that Grit-S scale posttest would be positively correlated to paper revision posttests on the same basis that was mentioned above. However, I was still unable to reject the null hypothesis. This time, the results showed that there was no statistical correlation between Grit-S scales and paper revision tests in the posttest form; not only that, the results were not approaching correlation and did not hint at a statistical relationship.

Though no direct research supported the hypothesis that the change in grit scores would be correlated to the change in paper revision scores, I nevertheless thought it a valuable undertaking to examine these results. The idea here is that if students truly became grittier from the grit-building intervention, this may be reflected in both tests simultaneously. Hence, if students truly improved in their self-perception of grit, reflected by the Grit-S scale score, they might also have demonstrated that grit through the test of task perseverance. Unfortunately, there was again no statistically significant correlation between the change in grit scores and the change in paper rewrite numbers based on the Pearson r correlation performed in SPSS. In fact, there was not even suggestive evidence that the two had any statistical relationship whatsoever. Though students statistically improved overall in both measures of grit and task perseverance, this implies that students more than likely improved in either one test or the other, but not both.

The final hypothesis is an expansion of the posttest correlation evaluated above. I hypothesized that after controlling for Grit-S pretests, there would be a statistically significant correlation between Grit-S posttests and paper revision posttests. Once entering the student data into SPSS and performing a partial correlation coefficient, I was still unable to reject the null hypothesis. This means that there was still no statistically significant correlation between the two posttest measures, even though the data was closer to approaching suggestive evidence of correlation after controlling for the Grit-S pretests.

Overall, this study has helped to establish some groundwork for grit as a malleable characteristic. But like all studies, it needs to be replicated and validated, and I look forward to others in the field making an effort to do so.

References

Aronson, J., Fried, C., & Good, C. (2002). Reducing the effects of stereotype threat on African American college students by shaping theories of intelligence. *Journal of Experimental Social Psychology, 38*(2), 113–125.

Bandura, A. (1982). Self-efficacy mechanism in human agency. *American Psychologist, 37*(2), 122–147.

Bandura, A. (1989). Self-regulation of motivation and action through internal standards and goal systems. In L. A. Pervin (Ed.), *Goals concepts in personality and social psychology* (pp. 19–85). Hillsdale, NJ: Erlbaum.

Bandura, A. (1997). *Self-efficacy: The exercise of control*. New York: Freeman.

Bandura, A., & Schunk, D. H. (1981). Cultivating competence, self-efficacy, and intrinsic interest through proximal self-motivation. *Journal of Personality and Social Psychology, 41*(3), 586–598.

Bobbitt, F. (1926). Character building and the new curriculum. *Religious Education, 21*, 472–476.

Bullmaster-Day, M. L. (2015). Productive struggle for deeper learning. *White Paper.* Retrieved from http://www.wagglepractice.com/app/uploads/2016/03/2131A_Productive_Struggle.pdf

Bulus, M. (2011). Goal orientations, locus of control and academic achievement in prospective teachers: An individual differences perspective. *Educational Sciences, 11*(2), 540–546.

Caprara, G. V., Gerbino, M., Paciello, M., Di Giunta, L., & Pastorelli, C. (2010). Countering depression and delinquency in late adolescence. *European Psychologist, 15*(1), 34–48.

Chubb, N. H., Fertman, C. I., & Ross, J. L. (1997). Adolescent self-esteem and locus of control: A longitudinal study of gender and age differences. *Adolescence, 32*(125), 113–130.

Collins, J. (1985). Self-efficacy and ability in achievement behavior. *Dissertation Abstracts International, 46*(1), 103–104.

Cross, T. M. (2014). The gritty: Grit and non-traditional doctoral student success. *Journal of Educators Online, 11*(3), 1–28.

De Castella, K., Byrne, D., & Covington, M. (2013). Unmotivated or motivated to fail? A cross-cultural study of achievement motivation, fear of failure, and student disengagement. *Journal of Educational Psychology, 105*(3), 861–880.

Deci, E. L., Vallerand, R. J., Pelletier, L. G., & Ryan, R. M. (1985). Motivation and education: The self-determination perspective. *Educational Psychologist, 26*(3), 325–346.

Dollinger, S. J. (2000). Locus of control and incidental learning: An application to college student success. *College Student Journal, 34*(4), 1–4.

Duckworth, A. L., & Gross, J. J. (2014). Self-control and grit: Related but separable determinants of success. *Current Directions in Psychological Science, 23*(5), 319–325.

Duckworth, A. L., Peterson, C., Matthews, M. D., & Kelly, D. R. (2007). Grit: Perseverance and passion for long-term goals. *Journal of Personality & Social Psychology, 92*(6), 1087–1101.

Duckworth, A. L., & Quinn, P. D. (2009). Development and validation of the short grit scale (Grit-S). *Journal of Personality Assessment, 91*(2), 166–174.

Duckworth, A. L., Quinn, P. D., & Seligman, M. E. P. (2009). Positive predictors of teacher effectiveness. *Journal of Positive Psychology, 4*(6), 540–547.

Dweck, C. S. (2006). *Mindset: The new psychology of success*. New York: Random House.

Elish-Piper, L. (2014). Parent involvement in reading: Grit and growth mindset: Building important foundations for literacy learning and success at home. *Illinois Reading Council Journal, 42*(4), 59–63.

Erez, A., & Judge, T. A. (2001). Relationship of core self-evaluations to goal setting, motivation, and performance. *Journal of Applied Psychology, 86*(6), 1270–1279.

Eskreis-Winkler, L. (2015). *Building grit* [Unpublished dissertation]. University of Pennsylvania.

Eskreis-Winkler, L., Shulman, E. P., Beal, S. A., & Duckworth, A. L. (2014). The grit effect: Predicting retention in the military, the workplace, school, and marriage. *Frontiers in Psychology, 5*(36), 1 12.

Gerhards, L., & Gravert, C. (2015). Grit trumps talent? An experimental approach. *Working Papers in Economics, 24*, 1–13.

Gifford, D. D., Briceno-Perriott, J., & Mianzo, F. (2006). *Journal of College Admission, 191*, 18–25.

Glenn, D. (2010). Carol Dweck's mindset. *Chronicle of Higher Education, 56*(35), B6–B9.

Goodwin, B., & Miller, K. (2013). Grit + talent = student success. *Educational Leadership, 71*(1), 1–5.

Hoerr, T. R. (2012). Got grit? *Educational Leadership, 69*(6), 84–85.

Hoerr, T. R. (2013). *Fostering grit: How do I prepare my students for the real world?* Alexandria, VA: ASCD.

Hoerr, T. R. (2014). Goals that matter. *Educational Leadership, 72*(1), 83–84.

Kaiser, D. L. (1975). Internal-external control and causal attributions of own and other's performance. *Psychological Reports, 37*, 423–426.

Kelly, D. R., Matthews, M. D., & Bartone, P. T. (2014). Grit and hardiness as predictors of performance among West Point cadets. *Military Psychology, 26*(4), 327–342.

Lefcourt, H. M. (1976). *Locus of control: Current trends in theory and research*. Hillsdale, NJ: Erlbaum.

Lucas, G. M., Gratch, J., Cheng, L., & Marsella, S. (2015). When the going gets tough: Grit predicts costly perseverance. *Journal of Research in Personality, 59*, 15–22.

Perry, R. P., Stupnisky, R. H., Hall, N. C., Chipperfield, J. G., & Weiner, B. (2010). Bad starts and better finishes: Attributional retraining and initial performance in competitive and achievement settings. *Journal of Social & Clinical Psychology, 29*(6), 668–700.

Rader, L. A. (2005). Goal setting for students and teachers. *Clearing House, 78*(3), 123–126.

Rimfeld, K., Kovas, Y., Dale, P. S., & Plomin, R. (2016). True grit and genetics: Predicting academic achievement from personality. *Journal of Personality and Social Psychology, 111* (5), 780–789.

Schunk, D. H. (1989). Self-efficacy and cognitive achievement: Implications for students with learning problems. *Journal of Learning Disabilities, 22*(1), 14–22.

Schunk, D. H. (1995). Self-efficacy, motivation, and performance. *Journal of Applied Sport Psychology, 7*(2), 112–137.

Schwarzer, R. (2014). *Self-efficacy: Thought control of action*. New York: Taylor & Francis.

Siegel, J., & Shaughnessy, M. F. (1996). An interview with Bernard Weiner. *Educational Psychology Review, 8*(2), 165–175.

Sinclair, E. (2020). *Committed 2 learning blog: Grit lit appendix access*. Retrieved from https://epsinclair2.wixsite.com/committed2learning/post/grit-lit-appendix-access

Strayhorn, T. L. (2014). What role does grit play in the academic success of black male collegians at predominantly white institutions? *Journal of African American Studies, 18*(1), 1–10.

Suzuki, Y., Tamesue, D., Asahi, K., & Ishikawa, Y. (2015). Grit and work engagement: A cross-sectional study. *PLoS One, 10*(9), 1–11.

TED. (2013, April). *Angela Lee Duckworth: Grit: The power of passion and perseverance* [Video file]. Retrieved from https://www.ted.com/talks/angela_lee_duckworth_grit_the_power_of_passion_and_perseverance

Van Zyl, L. E., Olckers, C., & Roll, L. C. (2020). The psychometric properties of the Grit-O scale within the Twente Region in the Netherlands: An ICM-CFA vs. ESEM approach. *Frontiers in Psychology, 11*, 796. https://doi.org/10.3389/fpsyg.2020.00796.

Von Culin, K. R., Tsukayama, E., & Duckworth, A. L. (2014). Unpacking grit: Motivational correlates of perseverance and passion for long-term goals. *The Journal of Positive Psychology, 9*(4), 306–312.

Vygotsky, L. (1978). *Mind in society*. Cambridge, MA: Harvard University Press.

Weiner, B. (1980). *Human Motivation*. New York: Holt Rinehart & Winston.

Eric Sinclair is a tenth-year teacher at the high school level and first-year administrator at the middle school level. He taught English Language Arts for 7 years in rural schools in Illinois, including Vandalia Community High School and Mattoon High School. In 2017–2018, he left Illinois to pursue the challenge of working in a low-income, urban school. Since working at Christel House Academy, a school on the south side of Indianapolis that focuses on the mission of breaking the cycle of poverty. He has worked as a team lead and a team administrator in helping employ cutting-edge, research-based strategies predicated on the concepts of both growth mindset and grit, including standards-based grading and restorative justice. Eric earned his B.A. in English and M.S. in education from Eastern Illinois University, and he earned his Ph.D. in curriculum and instruction from Indiana State University.

Chapter 8
Deconstructing Grit's Validity: The Case for Revising Grit Measures and Theory

Michael C. Tynan

Abstract Current measures of grit misrepresent its original conceptualization. This chapter aims to outline the flaws of extant grit measures, particularly in light of recent updated recommendations for maximizing construct validity during scale development. After reviewing empirical findings regarding grit's construct validity, structure, and association with success outcomes, recommendations for the future development of grit will be proposed. Grit was developed as a higher-order construct consisting of two facets: perseverance of effort and consistency of interests. However, the higher order construct of "overall grit" is not supported by item response theory, factor analytic, or structural equation modeling approaches. Grit is currently better interpreted as two separate constructs, possibly within a bifactor model in which "overall grit" does not consist of perseverance and consistency. After controlling for conscientiousness, perseverance explains little incremental variance in success outcomes. However, perseverance may be related to, but distinct from, lower-order facets of conscientiousness. Consistency is much less associated with success outcomes, and its predictive utility is unclear.

Grit researchers would benefit from revising grit measures. Positively and negatively worded items should be used to capture both constructs. An overinclusive set of new items should be administered to heterogeneous samples before the scales are refined. Further structural analysis is recommended, and similar factor analytic, item response theory, and structural equation modeling techniques used for the original grit scale should be employed for any revised measure. Meaningful inferences about grit may only be drawn after such revisions, as the first conceptual iteration of grit is psychometrically unsatisfactory.

Keywords Grit · Conscientiousness · Construct validity · Discriminant validity · Measurement

---

M. C. Tynan (✉)
Department of Psychology, Iowa State University, Ames, IA, USA
e-mail: mtynan@iastate.edu

L. E. van Zyl et al. (eds.), *Multidisciplinary Perspectives on Grit*,
https://doi.org/10.1007/978-3-030-57389-8_8

8.1 Introduction

8.1.1 Deconstructing Grit's Validity: The Case for Revising Grit Measures and Theory

Grit has received significant attention as a non-cognitive variable associated with academic success. Popularized in part outside the psychological field by a viral TED talk, a best-selling general audience book (Duckworth, 2016), multiple articles in major newspapers, and American educators' renewed interest in "character education," interest in grit seemed to grow at a faster rate than other psychological concepts. Grit's popularity has translated to school policy in some settings. Most notably, a U.S. Department of Education report recommended that grit be taught in schools (Schechtman, DeBarger, Dornsife, Rosier, & Yarnall, 2013), and the Knowledge Is Power Program (KIPP) network of 242 charter schools incorporated grit into educational materials and included the increased grit of students as one of the school's "character strength" goals (KIPP, 2019).

The initial conceptualization of grit attempted to distinguish it from related concepts like conscientiousness (Duckworth, Peterson, Matthews, & Kelly, 2007; Duckworth & Quinn, 2009). Outside the original authors' initial construct validation attempts, few studies have been dedicated to the validity of interpretations of grit measures. Construct validity determines the worth of real-world decisions based on psychological research (Clark & Watson, 2019). Considering the real-world implementation of interventions to increase grit and the popularity of grit research around the world, these oversights in the validity of extant grit scales are worth revisiting. This chapter will outline the validation of grit measures in light of the recent guide to best practices to maximize construct validity (Clark & Watson, 2019). This chapter follows a structure assuming Loevinger's (1957) outline of the three components of construct validity: substantive, structural, and external (Clark & Watson, 1995, 2019) as each pertains to the development and administration of existing grit scales. I will limit discussion to the original grit scale (Grit-O) and short grit scale (Grit-S), while acknowledging that many translations or adapted domain-specific versions of these scales exist. Seeing as translations and adapted versions of the primary grit scales are derivative, they are assumed to be similarly problematic in their use and interpretation, barring substantial differences in structure or scale meaning. One notable example of such deviation from the original scale stems from poor fit of the original grit concept in collectivist cultures (Datu, Valdez, & King, 2015). While not the focus of this chapter, as the Grit-O and Grit-S are by far the most commonly used grit scales and most adapted scales shared their structure, I refer interested readers to the (three-facet) Triarchic Model of Grit Scale (see Datu, Yuen, & Chen, 2017).

By outlining the construct validity considerations ideally made when introducing a new concept in psychology and comparing that ideal to the development of grit, I hope to create a case for significant revisions of grit measures and greater caution in interpreting current findings related to grit. This chapter focuses heavily on the two foundational grit articles (Duckworth et al., 2007; Duckworth & Quinn, 2009), and at the risk of repeating information familiar to grit researchers, I hope the lens of construct validity allows readers to approach these works with a fresh perspective.

8.2 Substantive Validity

Substantive validity is the facet of construct validity concerned with the items generated and the items finalized into a scale being truly indicative of the construct being proposed (Loevinger, 1957). This section will focus on the process of the Grit-O's inception and further reductions in items to produce the Grit-S.

There is seemingly no limit to the number of possible psychological constructs to propose as possible new measures, and to illustrate this idea consider all descriptions of human characteristics in the English language in addition to all similar descriptions in the approximately 7000 existing human languages (Clark & Watson, 1995, 2019). In describing a person who is generally achievement-oriented, determined, and perseverant, one out of myriad options for that description is "grit." Grit was developed as a non-cognitive ability capturing "perseverance and passion for long-term goals" (Duckworth et al., 2007, p. 1087). This conceptualization involves generally working hard to achieve a desired outcome and, importantly, having that outcome take a considerable amount of time (e.g. Duckworth and colleagues offer "years" as a marker of "long-term," p. 1088). Within such time, distractions, discouragement, and disinterest must be overcome. Gritty individuals do not entirely avoid boredom or the desire to quit, but rather continue with their initial intention despite short-term situational hurdles. In developing grit, Duckworth and colleagues set out in attempt to write a detailed description of what a gritty individual looks like, and what behaviors are expected of that person. The conceptualization process described is largely in line with ideal construct validity practices (Clark & Watson, 1995, 2019).

8.2.1 Literature Search and Hierarchical Structure of Constructs

The next step in establishing a distinct construct is to search the extant literature for similar constructs, theoretical positioning against "near-neighbor" constructs, and to be able to describe the construct's level of breadth (Clark & Watson, 1995, 2019). The consideration of grit's place in both its breadth and relation to similar constructs within the nomological network seems to be lacking. One clear goal in developing grit was to establish a construct that had four characteristics: psychometric soundness, generalizability across age groups and achievement domains, low likelihood of ceiling effects for high-achievers, and relevance to the proposed grit definition

(Duckworth et al., 2007). Upon finding no scale that captured all four criteria, the initial literature search to compare grit to neighboring constructs appears to be limited to intelligence (used somewhat interchangeably with the vaguer term "talent"), need for achievement, and conscientiousness (Duckworth et al., 2007). A number of other constructs are plausible near-neighbors to grit, as later research suggests, for example: industriousness, self-control, effort regulation, engagement, and self-efficacy (Credé, Tynan, & Harms, 2017; Muenks, Wigfield, Yang, & O'Neal, 2017; Schmidt, Nagy, Fleckenstein, Möller, & Retelsdorf, 2018). In addition to testing an over-inclusive set of related constructs, Clark and Watson (1995, 2019) emphasize the need to consider the place of a new construct within a hierarchy of similar constructs. The consideration of intelligence, conscientiousness, and need for achievement appear to be assumed to have no hierarchical relation to one another, and it is unclear what level of abstraction grit is supposed to occupy. The inference that grit is at the same conceptual level as conscientiousness in particular ignores the possibility of conscientiousness' lower order facets (competence, order, dutifulness, self-discipline, achievement-striving, deliberation) being more strongly related to grit than global conscientiousness (see Costa, McCrae, & Dye, 1991). Theoretical distinction from self-control is offered by Duckworth et al. (2007), again by emphasizing time frame: "An individual high in self-control but moderate in grit may, for example, . . .resist the urge to surf the Internet at work—yet switch careers annually" (p. 1089). This theoretical distinction is not supported by empirical findings for grit and the self-discipline facet of conscientiousness or another self-control measure. Later work suggests that grit may be fully integrated into the hierarchical structure of conscientiousness, as it is strongly related to general conscientiousness, industriousness, and self-discipline, but the original oversight of grit's conceptual breadth delayed this theoretically germane finding (Schmidt et al., 2018).

Appropriate steps were taken, using multiple measures (SAT scores, Verbal IQ, and Whole Candidate Scores for military cadets), to explore the relation between intelligence and grit (Duckworth et al., 2007). There are sound theoretical reasons why grit is expected to be unrelated to intelligence, namely the variance in achievement between individuals known to have similar levels of intelligence and the content of the construct focusing on effort and interest rather than ability. The lack of relation between grit and intelligence found by Duckworth et al. (2007) has been confirmed by later meta-analytic estimates (Credé et al., 2017). Less establishing evidence for grit is provided in comparison to both need for achievement and conscientiousness. Duckworth et al. (2007) do not test the original grit scale against need for achievement. The evidence for this distinction appears to be primarily theoretical, in that individuals high in need for achievement are thought to require external incentives or positive feedback while gritty individuals do not (Duckworth & Quinn, 2009), but this distinction is not supported empirically.

Conscientiousness seemed to be the nearest conceptual neighbor to grit from its inception. The theoretical justification offered for why conscientiousness and grit ought to be considered separately is that grit emphasizes "long term stamina rather than short-term intensity" (Duckworth et al., 2007, p. 1089). Despite this theoretical distinction, conscientiousness is correlated very highly with grit in both the original, $r = .77$, $r = .64$, and short scale development papers, $r = .77$ (Duckworth et al., 2007; Duckworth & Quinn, 2009). Grit is predictive of outcomes in the original paper after controlling for conscientiousness, but both grit levels and these outcomes are subject to range restriction making the conscientiousness-grit relation unclear in terms of incremental validity. Meta-analytic estimates indicate that grit does not explain additional variance in success outcomes like grades in college after controlling for conscientiousness (Credé et al., 2017).

8.2.2 Creation of an Item Pool

The original grit measure was derived from an initial 27-item pool (Duckworth et al., 2007). Items were written to capture "the ability to sustain effort in the face of adversity" and "the consistency of interests over time" (p. 1090). 10 items were excluded from the original 27 before an exploratory factor analysis (EFA) was conducted on the remaining 17. The available sample size was 1545, and EFA was conducted using the responses of half the sample chosen at random ($N = 772$). Retaining at least 5 items with loadings greater than .40 and examining the scree plot to determine factors, using oblique factor extraction with a promax rotation, yielded a two-factor solution with 6 items per factor.

The cardinal rule of item generation is to be over-inclusive: "*At very least, the items in the pool should be drawn from an area of content defined more broadly than the trait expected to be measured*" (Loevinger, 1957, p. 659, emphasis in original). Any initial item pool should include items assessing tangential content or information only marginally related to the theorized construct, with the intention of possible exclusion later in the scale development process (Clark & Watson, 1995, 2019). Put simply, initial scale items "*should be chosen so as to sample all possible contents which might comprise the putative trait according to all known alternative theories of the trait*" (Loevinger, 1957, p. 659, emphasis in original). Speculating upon what was *not* included in the development of the Grit-O is obviously fraught territory. The original 27 items are not included in supplemental materials or appendices to the original article. Readers should be cautioned against over-weighing inferences from unclear or incomplete information in grit's foundational articles. However, the description of item reduction clearly prioritizes internal consistency over construct breadth, which risks construct distortion via the attenuation paradox (i.e. as the scope of a scale narrows, internal consistency increases through item redundancy, therefore reducing the amount of construct-relevant information provided by the scale; Clark & Watson, 2019; Loevinger, 1954). The first 10 items were eliminated by consulting "item-total correlations, internal reliability coefficients, redundancy, and simplicity of vocabulary" (Duckworth et al., 2007, p. 1090) *before* conducting an EFA on the remaining 17. This mixed method of item reduction muddies the conceptualization of grit as either a single construct or a multidimensional one. Item-total correlations are typically appropriate for reducing the items in a scale proposed to be unidimensional, whereas factor analytic techniques are necessary to reduce items in a scale with multiple proposed subscales (Clark & Watson, 1995, 2019). Grit items were written so as to capture two passion and perseverance subscales, so what may have been more informative was to conduct EFA on all 27 initial items. Guidelines in conducting and interpreting exploratory factor analyses are relatively straightforward (see Russell, 2002), and I will emphasize only one additional point. The interpretation of scree plots to determine the number of factors is subjective. Parallel analysis eliminates this ambiguity by comparing the eigenvalues extracted from the scale in question to eigenvalues extracted from random data with the same parameters (sample size and number of items) and retaining the factors of the scale with eigenvalues greater than those of random data (see Hayton, Allen, & Scarpello, 2004). Eliminating ambiguity in factor retention may reduce questionable scale reduction practices, and parallel analysis is the recommended tool in all early-stage scale development.

The two grit factors retained after item-total correlation reduction and EFA are acknowledged to be confounded with positively and negatively worded items. That is, all perseverance items are positively scored (e.g. "I am a hard worker"), and all consistency items are negatively scored (e.g. "I have been obsessed with a certain idea or project for a short time but later lost interest"). The only justification offered is that the researchers were "convinced the factor structure reflected two conceptually distinct dimensions" (Duckworth et al., 2007, p. 1090). Negatively worded items are known to be able to artificially create a distinct factor within factors analyses because they are more difficult to answer (Credé, 2018; Schmitt & Stults, 1985; Swain, Weathers, & Niedrich, 2008). The implications of factors being confounded with item direction will be discussed further in the context of structural validity.

8.2.3 Derivative Versions

Several questions of substantive validity arise for the Grit-S, considering grit's definition and original justification for distinction from conscientiousness. If the key proposed difference between conscientiousness and grit is the time-frame—grit refers to "long-term stamina,"—then the Grit-O items omitted from the Grit-S appear on their face to eliminate a richer measurement of time-relevant information. The following items are included in the Grit-O but not the Grit-S (emphasis added): "My interests change *from year to year*," "I become interested in new pursuits *every few months*," "I have achieved a goal that took *years of work*" (Duckworth & Quinn, 2009). The only remaining reference to specific long-term time frames in the Grit-S is one consistency item: "I have difficulty maintaining my focus on projects that take *more than a few months* to complete." Losing this lack of depth in item content for only minimal gains in convenience of administration or ease of response distorts the original conceptualization of grit. Development of grit's short version appears to have ignored this and other pitfalls of short scales. Resorting to very short measures of individual difference constructs (e.g. four items per facet) risks attenuating effects and increasing both Type 1 and Type 2 error rates (Credé, Harms, Niehorster, & Gaye-Valentine, 2012). The Grit-S scale not only loses face valid time-frame information but also alters the internal structure of the scale. Meta-analytic estimates indicate that the perseverance and consistency facets are much less similar for the Grit-O, $\rho = .27$, than for the Grit-S, $\rho = .66$ (Credé et al., 2017). This difference indicates that the shortening of the grit scale results in a notable alteration of the construct being measured, such that responses to the original grit scale differentiate the two facets to a greater extent than responses to the short grit scale, with apparent loss of the crucial time-frame content which supposedly separates grit from conscientiousness.

It is unclear from Duckworth and Quinn's (2009) terse introduction what the benefit of the Grit-S ought to be other than an attempt to improve the fit of the higher-order, two-factor grit model and general increased efficiency. Modest affordances in scale efficiency do not seem justified in this case. An 8-item scale would likely take most participants only a few seconds less to complete than a 12-item scale with an equal ratio of positively and negatively worded items. The modest improvement in scale administration efficiency does not appear on its face to be worth the loss in information from the original scale. As will be discussed in the structural validity section, improvements may be made in the structural model of grit, but item reduction in pursuit of these improvements produces more confusion than clarity. Grit may serve as a cautionary tale in the attenuation paradox: the Grit-S is seemingly a psychometric improvement on the Grit-O but is in fact a mischaracterization of grit's proposed definition (Clark & Watson, 2019).

Overall, improvements in substantive validity may be made by returning focus to the Grit-O. If a key component of grit is goal adherence in a long-term time frame, the Grit-O contains notably more information than the Grit-S in this regard. Revisiting the substantive validity of grit will necessitate new item generation and overinclusion of these items encompassing the theoretical spectrum of perseverance and consistency to the fullest extent possible. These items should be both positively and negatively worded, with items content encompassing the full grit concept, with particular emphasis on time frame. Scale reduction and validation against conceptual neighbors like conscientiousness should be informed by current best practices (Clark & Watson, 2019; Hayton et al., 2004; Russell, 2002).

8.3 Structural Validity

Structural validity refers to the element of construct validity concerned with the relations between scale items resembling other manifestations of the construct being proposed (Loevinger, 1957). Some issues with item selection and reduction have already been discussed with regard to substantive validity of grit scales, though they are also relevant for structural validity. This section will primarily focus on the proposed higher-order, two-factor structure of the Grit-O and Grit-S before summarizing more recent findings related to the internal structure of grit measures.

Grit is deemed explicitly by Clark and Watson (2019) to be a structurally problematic *conglomerate* construct, in that the overall grit factor claims to be more than the sum of its parts (perseverance and consistency). Specifically, the higher-order grit factor proposed by its developers is meant to be more predictive of achievement than either of its two lower-order facets. In fact, by meta-analytic estimates, the perseverance facet is more predictive of success outcomes like GPA, $\rho = .26$, than "overall grit," $\rho = .17$ (Credé et al., 2017). Conscientiousness is also approximately equally related to both "overall grit," $\rho = .84$, and the perseverance facet, $\rho = .83$ (Credé et al., 2017). Another large-scale ($N = 11{,}750$) investigation of grit's construct validity concludes that the higher-order model does not fit the data, and most of the predictive power of grit is explained by the perseverance facet (Fosnacht, Copridge, & Sarraf, 2018). Skepticism appears to be warranted toward studies reporting results for "overall grit," especially when the Grit-S is the only measure used, for reasons discussed subsequently. There is growing evidence that perseverance and consistency are two separate constructs, and "overall grit" is not psychometrically meaningful (Credé et al., 2017; Disabato, Goodman, & Kashdan, 2019; Fosnacht et al., 2018; Guo, Tang, & Xu, 2019; Tyumeneva, Kardanova, & Kuzmina, 2017).

Several issues are notable in the identification of a higher order, two-facet solution for the grit scale. The Grit-S is especially problematic in this area, due to the confirmatory factor analysis performed in an attempt to replicate the Grit-O structure. A factor structure with one second-order factor and two first-order factors cannot be identified at the higher-order level (Credé et al., 2017; Kline, 2011). That is, the Grit-S developers attempted to solve the equation $a{*}b = y$, where a and b represent the paths from the first order facets to the second order factor and y is held constant as the correlation between perseverance and consistency (Credé, 2018). There are infinite solutions to this problem of identifying a and b (e.g. any two values between 0 and 1 that produce the correlation coefficient), and the fit of this misidentified model will be identical to a model which keeps perseverance and consistency as separate but correlated constructs with no higher-order factor (see Fig. 8.1; Credé, 2018; Credé & Harms, 2015). Duckworth et al. (2007) tested this two-factor solution and reported poor fit for the model, CFI = .83, RMSEA = .11. The higher-order solution found using confirmatory factor analysis is not meaningfully different from a two-factor solution with no higher-order factor, and therefore it does not support the idea of a higher-order model.

More generally, the proposed higher-order model equates individuals with high levels of perseverance and low levels of consistency with individuals who have low levels of perseverance and high levels of consistency, when these individuals are substantively different from one another (Credé, 2018). An alternative conceptualization of grit is that grit is composed only of high-perseverance combined with high-consistency. Duckworth et al. (2007) hint in their original conceptualization that this combination is optimal and reflective of highly successful people. Gritty individuals may need to fulfill both these requirements, and the failure to meet a

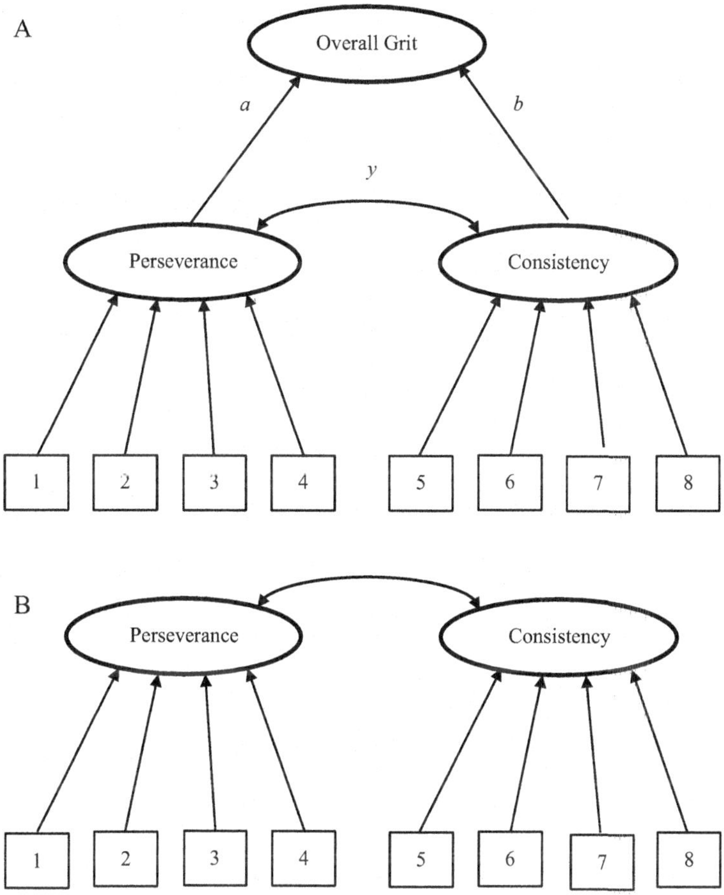

Fig. 8.1 The original proposed factor structure of the Grit-S (**a**) and the empirically supported alternative model (**b**). *Note: a* and *b* are paths calculated between lower order factors and the higher order factor (overall grit) with *y* is held constant. The fit of these two models is equal, and model B is recommended

threshold of either construct means an individual cannot be described as possessing grit. This conceptualization has not been tested empirically but may be using necessary condition analysis (see Dul, 2016) or cluster analytic approaches (Credé, 2018).

8.3.1 Item Response Theory

Item response theory (IRT) has a number of advantages in the course of investigating novel constructs. IRT can calculate probabilities of item response endorsement based on latent trait levels, considering one or more traits at the same time, and clarify the dimensionality of a measure (Clark & Watson, 2019; Smith, 2002; Tyumeneva et al., 2017). Few studies have examined grit using IRT techniques, but findings thereof are briefly discussed here.

The Grit-O measures two distinct constructs as tested by IRT methods, further indicating that skepticism is warranted toward a higher-order, two-factor model (Tyumeneva et al., 2017). After conducting a principal components analysis of the standardized residuals of a Rating Scale Model and confirming the multidimensionality of the Grit-O through IRT model selection, Tyumeneva et al. (2017) conclude that psychometric evidence of a single construct underlying the Grit-O has not been found. Additionally, IRT based findings seem to suggest the Grit-S is more consistent with a unidimensional trait that largely overlaps with self-control (Gonzalez, Canning, Smyth, & Mackinnon, 2019). Item-level analyses point to an item doublet between the perseverance items "I am diligent" and "I am a hard worker," wherein these items are excessively correlated after accounting for a single latent factor (Gonzalez et al., 2019; Schmidt, Fleckenstein, Retelsdorf, Eskreis-Winkler, & Möller, 2019; Tyumeneva et al., 2017). These items are therefore not providing qualitatively different information but are driving the originally hypothesized two-factor solution, when in fact the Grit-S is more aligned with a unidimensional construct more indicative of consistency than perseverance (Gonzalez et al., 2019).

Multidimensional item response theory (MIRT) analyses have been conducted on the Grit-S, allowing for examination of the interaction between the Grit-S and respondents when assumptions of a continuous response format (e.g. Likert-type scales) are violated (Wirth & Edwards, 2007). Muenks et al. (2017) found that participants were not using all five options of the response scale, and responses were not normally distributed for any Grit-S item, indicating that the scale is better examined as having categorical items. Using the same IRT-based methods, perseverance and consistency were found to overlap with neighboring constructs. One factor appears to underlie consistency, effort regulation, and behavioral disaffection; similarly, one factor underlies perseverance and self-control across both high school and college students (Muenks et al., 2017).

8.3.2 *Bifactor Models*

Since critiques of the originally proposed factor structure have surfaced, researchers have paid additional attention to the plausibility of a bifactor model of grit measures. The findings of bifactor analyses and their possible implications are summarized here.

It is possible that grit is structurally variant across age groups or education levels. Using MIRT techniques, a factor structure assuming perseverance and consistency are two separate, correlated constructs with *no* higher-order grit factor fit a high school student sample, whereas a bifactor model fit college students (Muenks et al.,

2017). However, one item, "Setbacks don't discourage me," having an extremely low factor loading led the bifactor model not to converge in the high school sample.[1] When this item was excluded, the bifactor model fit better than competing models in the high school sample as well. In general, if a bifactor model fits older, more educated people better than a two-factor model, the expression or understanding of grit may change such that consistency and perseverance are more easily conceptualized as separate when tasks, such as those of high-school-level work, are clearly defined. Grit may be less informed by perseverance and consistency and more an expression of one underlying general factor as tasks become more difficult or more ambiguous, as is typical in the course of university-level work.

Other researchers have found evidence for the benefit of a bifactor model over the original higher-order model (Gonzalez et al., 2019; van Zyl, Olckers, & Roll, 2020). Using both traditional factor analytic techniques and exploratory structural equation modeling, which imposes less restrictions on factor models and may be provide more distinction between factors in multidimensional constructs, van Zyl et al. (2020) conclude that a bifactor structure is the only appropriate model for the Grit-O in its current form. However, the utility of a bifactor model may as yet be unclear, as one bifactor analysis has shown that the consistency and perseverance subscales contain more common variance within themselves than there is common variance in total scores explained by the general factor (Disabato et al., 2019). An alternative conceptualization may be warranted. Grit's structural problems may be entirely due to artifacts of positively and negatively worded items. The fit of bifactor models may not be describing conceptual differences between perseverance, consistency, and a general factor, but rather positively worded items (perseverance), negatively worded items (consistency), and a unidimensional construct (grit/self-control/conscientiousness). When testing the Grit-O, this very bifactor model fit the data better than alternatives—one general trait factor with positive and negative latent method factors (see Vazsonyi et al., 2019, Appendix B).

While it should be clear to readers at this point that the original proposed higher-order model of grit is not supported, the true structure of grit remains unknown. The Grit-S muddies the waters of the original construct both substantively and structurally. Further examination of grit measures should revert to the Grit-O, and particular attention should be paid to modeling grit as two separate traits or as a bifactor conglomerate, with the possibility of bifactor structure being an artifact of item wording. The structural problems of grit may have been caused by missteps in the original scale validation. Future researchers should consider the following when revising grit measures.

[1]This item in particular has seemed to confuse some respondents because of its double negative wording in conjunction with additional negative terms in the response scale, e.g. "disagree," resulting in low factors loadings and general model improvement if excluded or rewritten (Fosnacht et al., 2018; Tyumeneva et al., 2017). It may be prudent to assume this item in particular is inappropriate for samples with less education or a lower reading level than others. Revisions of the grit scale should avoid similar double-negative wording in the interest of ease for all respondents.

8.3.3 Sample Considerations

Clark and Watson (1995, 2019) recommend validating new scales on several large heterogeneous samples. The original development of grit partially followed this suggestion, as the first study consisted of respondents to a public online posting. Participants were age adults of diverse ages and mostly women (73%), and the sample size was large ($N = 1545$). However, this sample was followed by smaller, much more homogenous ones: Ivy League students ($N = 138$), National Spelling Bee finalists ($N = 175$), and West Point cadets ($N = 1308$). While sample size is clearly not problematic in the West Point sample, all these samples are expected to consist of highly conscientious people. Academically talented students, precocious children, and military trainees are all expected to exhibit range restriction of conscientiousness and achievement, potentially attenuating effects found between close conceptual neighbors describing work ethic and passion. While grit items were not altered according to the responses of any of these samples, examinations of grit's place within the nomological network using these relatively homogenous samples is not advised. Future examination and validation of grit should resemble the original adult sample more than these subsequent samples.

8.3.4 Inclusion of Comparison Scales

As already mentioned, the original grit validation studies included conscientiousness but not need for achievement, though both were discussed as close conceptual neighbors. The step of including measure of related constructs is critical in identifying the boundaries and potential shared information given by a construct and it's "near neighbors" (Clark & Watson, 2019). Informed by findings of potential overlap between grit facets and the following constructs, future examination of grit should measure revised scales against global conscientiousness (Credé et al., 2017), conscientiousness facets including industriousness and self-discipline (Schmidt et al., 2018), and self-control (Gonzalez et al., 2019; Muenks et al., 2017). The theoretical distinction from these constructs—with regards to time frame—must be included in the grit scale, which largely precludes the Grit-S from further analysis in this vein.

8.3.5 Subscales

Scale developers balance between two pitfalls when designing a scale with subscales: creating a measure with items too similar to one another and needlessly breaking them apart, or creating distinct measures and needlessly meshing them together (Clark & Watson, 1995). While apparently desirable—intuitively it seems the inclusion of information assessing diverse elements of a unified construct would make the most robust scale—in the case of grit, it may be useful to remain neutral on the need for a measure with subscales. As both constructs are revised to include positively and negatively worded items, along with time-frame-relevant information, only items which load on a general factor while also loading cleanly on their respective subscales and creating factors moderately correlated with one another can be considered evidence of a grit measure with subscales (Clark & Watson, 2019). Such a measure may not be the ultimate goal of grit research, as perseverance and consistency may simply be differentially related to outcomes of interest.

8.3.6 *Summary*

The original two-factor higher-order structure of grit is clearly unsupported, and the true structure of grit remains unclear. In the pursuit of identifying a better fitting model, researchers should test revised scales using large heterogenous samples, remain impartial to the existence of subscales rather than separate constructs, and include comparison scales such as self-control, conscientiousness facets, and need for achievement to further validate grit or its components against existing constructs.

8.4 External Validity

While substantive and structural validity are mainly concerns surrounding the items within a scale, external validity is the extent to which total scores of a scale are reasonably derived from items and meaningful in terms of discriminative or predictive power (Loevinger, 1957). This section will deal primarily with findings of grit's relations to meaningful outcomes and its place in relation to constructs that occupy similar positions in the nomological network.

8.4.1 *Criterion Validity*

Is grit related to theoretically relevant outcomes? In choosing a criterion relevant to a novel construct, it is beneficial to choose a "risky test," being deliberately difficult for the construct to pass, thereby strengthening the construct if it passes (Meehl, 1978). Relevant outcomes for grit would include performance criteria, and grit appears to have been focused on academic performance since its early development. We should expect grit to be related to high grades. Whether the relation of grit and grades constitutes a "risky test" on its own is not clear, but it may be "risky" to pit grit against well-known predictors of grades in establishing its importance: standardized intelligence tests ($\rho = .54$, Roth et al., 2015), achievement motivation ($\rho = .30$, Robbins et al., 2004), and conscientiousness ($\rho = .23$, Poropat, 2009).

Perseverance and consistency are indeed related to grades, $\rho = .20$, $\rho = .10$ respectively, and comparisons to other constructs will be discussed in the context of incremental validity (Credé et al., 2017).

8.4.2 *Discriminant Validity*

Is grit distinct from other well-known constructs? The primary hurdle of academic success researchers is to study variables orthogonal from intelligence. Intelligence is the best known predictor of grades in high school and college (Kuncel, Hezlett, & Ones, 2004; Roth et al., 2015). One of the original goals of grit research was to support the hypothesis that grit is distinct from intelligence (Duckworth et al., 2007). Meta-analytic estimates support this distinction ($\rho = .05$, Credé et al., 2017). The distinction between grit and intelligence allows for the possibility of grit to explain variance in academic performance over the large amount of variance explained by cognitive ability.

In the case of grit, the next challenge was to distinguish itself from close conceptual neighbors like conscientiousness. For reasons outlined in the substantive and structural validity sections, this is a notable challenge. Substantively, grit and conscientiousness cover very similar information, for example, the perseverance items "I finish whatever I begin" and "I am a hard worker" are very similar to International Personality Item Pool (IPIP) achievement-striving facet items like "I carry out my plans" and "I work hard" (Credé et al., 2017; Goldberg et al., 2006). Structurally, grit's model is misidentified, and theoretically distinctive information is omitted by the commonly used Grit-S. Meta-analytic estimates show a strong relation between conscientiousness and "overall grit," $\rho = .84$; perseverance, $\rho = .83$; and consistency, $\rho = .61$ (Credé et al., 2017). Grit also exhibited a strong relation with self-control, $\rho = .72$, which is considered a facet of conscientiousness (Credé et al., 2017). The strength of these relations indicates that grit and conscientiousness overlap significantly, to the point of valid concern that the two constructs are largely isomorphic. For reference, consider that the relation between grit and conscientiousness is stronger than that of two different global measures of conscientiousness, $\rho = .63$ (Credé et al., 2017; Pace & Brannick, 2010). While grit and conscientiousness may contain very similar information, grit may yet have utility if able to explain variance in outcomes of interest after controlling for conscientiousness.

8.4.3 *Incremental Validity*

Does grit explain variance in relevant outcomes over and above related constructs? After controlling for conscientiousness using hierarchical regression methods, "overall grit" and consistency explained no meaningful additional variance in either high school or college grades (Credé et al., 2017). However, after controlling for conscientiousness and consistency, perseverance explained additional variance in both high school and college grades (Credé et al., 2017). This finding again points to consideration of perseverance and consistency being of more utility as separate constructs. The limitation of this analysis was the reliance on only global measures of conscientiousness as controls. Further research is needed to examine the unique variance explained by perseverance after controlling for lower order conscientiousness facets like self-control and industriousness (Schmidt et al., 2018).

8.4.4 Summary

In the course of exploring relations to academic success, grit passes initial validation tests but fails others. Grit is distinct from intelligence, but not from conscientiousness. The substantive and structural issues with extant grit scales compound difficulties in supporting their external validity. Treating grit in its current iteration as two separate constructs and ultimately revising grit scales is needed before any meaningful relations between grit and academic success may be claimed.

8.5 Conclusion

To this point, the development of grit has been unique as a lesson in the rapid pace of a construct's potential growth, given the speed of modern data collection and dissemination. The goal of this chapter was to pause this process momentarily to reassess what ideals of construct validation grit has met and which it has failed to meet. In approaching this goal, I hope the following points have been made clear. The substance of grit scales is critical for their theoretical meaning and practical utility. The Grit-O and the Grit-S are not equal to the task of reflecting the original definition of grit. Substantively and structurally, the Grit-S is particularly off the mark of the original developers' intentions. Items in current measures do not reflect a theoretically meaningful or predictive construct. "Setbacks don't discourage me" appears to be particularly damaging to meaningful responses to a grit scale by its double-negative framing. The items "I am diligent" and "I am a hard worker" also appear to be redundant. While "overall grit" made up of two subscales may have been intuitively appealing, responses to extant grit measures do not support such a concept's existence. Future work in exploring grit's structure would benefit by treating perseverance and consistency as separate or as unrelated to a general factor underlying grit measures (such as in a bifactor model). Grit's usefulness as a predictor of performance outcome, in part due to these internal inconsistencies, is unclear. Conscientiousness and intelligence, coupled with practical skills such as study habits and class attendance (Credé & Kuncel, 2008; Credé, Roch, & Kieszczynka, 2010) clearly explain most variance in academic performance, and a unified grit construct does not add to this understanding. The future of grit development may lie in examining perseverance against lower-order facets of conscientiousness or domain-specific practical skills.

As scale development and construct validation are iterative processes, there is value in going "back to the drawing board" for grit. The following practical recommendations for revision ought to be considered by future grit researchers. An efficient revision to both the substance of these items and a structural artifact of the grit scale would be to revise items of the Grit-O to be worded both positively and negatively. Having a mix of reverse scored items within both perseverance and consistency scales would eliminate the possibility of misinterpreting factor analytic results as purely artifacts of wording. An over-inclusive set of items based on the Grit-O should be analyzed and reduced using criterion-based and IRT methods to clarify what information is captured by grit items, particularly which items are capturing crucial time-frame information theoretically distinguishing grit from conscientiousness and other near-neighboring constructs. This revised scale should be examined alongside conscientiousness facet scales and other related constructs to determine the discriminant and incremental validity of a revised grit scale.

This continuation of the construct validation process would not establish grit as having passed the scale development phase, as scale development ought to be continuously ongoing (Clark & Watson, 2019), but the next steps in grit research must acknowledge failures to support grit's construct validity to this point. After a reasonable amount of support can be produced in reference to these construct validity questions, more complex psychometric issues such as cross-cultural validation and measurement invariance may be addressed (see van de Vijver, 2002). Until grit, perseverance, and consistency can be supported as psychometrically sound and theoretically meaningful constructs, educational and professional institutions would benefit from devoting attention and resources to more well-established correlates of performance.

References

Clark, L. A., & Watson, D. B. (1995). Constructing validity: Basic issues in objective scale development. *Psychological Assessment, 7*, 309–319. https://doi.org/10.1037/1040-3590.7.3.309.

Clark, L. A., & Watson, D. (2019). Constructing validity: New developments in creating objective measuring instruments. *Psychological Assessment, 31*(12), 1412–1427. https://doi.org/10.1037/pas0000626.

Costa, P. T., McCrae, R. R., & Dye, D. A. (1991). Facet scales for agreeableness and conscientiousness: A revision of the NEO personality inventory. *Personality and Individual Differences, 12*(9), 887–898.

Credé, M. (2018). What shall we do about grit? A critical review of what we know and what we don't know. *Educational Researcher, 47*(9), 606–611. https://doi.org/10.3102/0013189X18801322.

Credé, M., & Kuncel, N. R. (2008). Study habits, study skills, and study attitudes: The third pillar supporting collegiate academic performance. *Perspectives on Psychological Science, 3*, 415–453.

Credé, M., & Harms, P. D. (2015). 25 years of higher order confirmatory factor analysis in the organizational sciences: A critical review and development of reporting recommendations. *Journal of Organizational Behavior, 36*, 845–872.

Credé, M., Harms, P. D., Niehorster, S., & Gaye-Valentine, A. (2012). An evaluation of the consequences of using short measures of the big five personality traits. *Journal of Personality and Social Psychology, 102*, 874–888.

Credé, M., Roch, S. G., & Kieszczynka, U. M. (2010). Class attendance in college: A meta-analytic review of the relationship of class attendance with grades and student characteristics. *Review of Educational Research, 80*, 272–295.

Credé, M., Tynan, M. C., & Harms, P. D. (2017). Much ado about grit: A meta-analytic synthesis of the grit literature. *Journal of Personality and Social Psychology, 113*(3), 492–511. https://doi.org/10.1037/pspp0000102.

Datu, J. A. D., Valdez, J. P. M., & King, R. B. (2015). Perseverance counts but consistency does not! Validating the short grit scale in a collectivist setting. *Current Psychology, 35*, 121–130. https://doi.org/10.1007/s12144-015-9374-2.

Datu, J. A. D., Yuen, M., & Chen, G. (2017). Development and validation of the Triarchic model of grit scale (TMGS): Evidence from Filipino undergraduate students. *Personality and Individual Differences, 114*, 198–205. https://doi.org/10.1016/j.paid.2017.04.012.

Disabato, D. J., Goodman, F. R., & Kashdan, T. B. (2019). Is grit relevant to well-being and strengths? Evidence across the globe for separating perseverance of effort and consistency of interests. *Journal of Personality, 87*, 194–211.

Duckworth, A. L. (2016). *Grit: The power of passion and perseverance*. New York: Scribner.

Duckworth, A. L., Peterson, C., Matthews, M. D., & Kelly, D. R. (2007). Grit: Perseverance and passion for long-term goals. *Journal of Personality and Social Psychology, 92*(6), 1087–1101. https://doi.org/10.1037/0022-3514.92.6.1087.

Duckworth, A. L., & Quinn, P. D. (2009). Development and validation of the short grit scale (grit-S). *Journal of Personality Assessment, 91*(2), 166–174. https://doi.org/10.1080/00223890802634290.

Dul, J. (2016). Necessary condition analysis (NCA): Logic and methodology of "necessary but not sufficient" causality. *Organizational Research Methods, 19*(1), 10–52. https://doi.org/10.1177/1094428115584005.

Fosnacht, K., Copridge, K., & Sarraf, S. (2018). How valid is grit in the postsecondary context? A construct and concurrent validity analysis. *Research in Higher Education*. https://doi.org/10.1007/s11162-018-9524-0.

Goldberg, L. R., Johnson, J. A., Eber, H. W., Hogan, R., Ashton, M. C., Cloninger, C. R., & Gough, H. C. (2006). The international personality item Pool and the future of public-domain personality measures. *Journal of Research in Personality, 40*, 84–96. https://doi.org/10.1016/j.jrp.2005.08.007.

Gonzalez, O., Canning, J. R., Smyth, H., & Mackinnon, D. (2019). A psychometric evaluation of the short grit scale: A closer look at its factor structure and scale functioning. *European Journal of Psychological Assessment*, 1–12. https://doi.org/10.1027/1015-5759/a000535.

Guo, J., Tang, X., & Xu, K. M. (2019). Capturing the multiplicative effect of perseverance and passion: Measurement issues of combining two grit facets. *Proceedings of the National Academy of Sciences, 116*(10), 3938–3940.

Hayton, J. C., Allen, D. G., & Scarpello, V. (2004). Factor retention decisions in exploratory factor analysis: A tutorial on parallel analysis. *Organizational Research Methods, 7*, 191–205.

KIPP. (2019). *Character strengths*. Retrieved November 22, 2019, from http://www.kipp.org/approach/character/

Kline, R. B. (2011). *Principles and practice of structural equation modeling* (3rd ed.). New York: Guilford publications.

Kuncel, N. R., Hezlett, S. A., & Ones, D. S. (2004). Academic performance, career potential, creativity, and job performance: Can one construct predict them all? *Journal of Personality and Social Psychology, 86*(1), 148–161. https://doi.org/10.1037/0022-3514.86.1.148.

Loevinger, J. (1954). The attenuation paradox in test theory. *Psychological Bulletin, 51*, 493–504.

Loevinger, J. (1957). Objective tests as instruments of psychological theory. *Psychological Reports, 3*, 635–694.

Meehl, P. E. (1978). Theoretical risks and tabular asterisks: Sir Karl, Sir Ronald, and the slow progress of soft psychology. *Journal of Consulting and Clinical Psychology, 46*, 806–834.

Muenks, K., Wigfield, A., Yang, J. S., & O'Neal, C. R. (2017). How true is grit? Assessing its relations to high school and college students' personality characteristics, self-regulation, engagement, and achievement. *Journal of Educational Psychology, 109*(5), 599–620.

Pace, V. L., & Brannick, M. T. (2010). How similar are personality scales of the "same" construct? A meta-analytic investigation. *Personality and Individual Differences, 49*, 669–676.

Poropat, A. E. (2009). A meta-analysis of the five-factor model of personality and academic performance. *Psychological Bulletin, 135*, 322–338.

Robbins, S. B., Lauver, K., Le, H., Davis, D., Langley, R., & Carlstrom, A. (2004). Do psychosocial and study skill factors predict college outcomes? A meta-analysis. *Psychological Bulletin, 130*, 261–288.

Roth, B., Becker, N., Romeyke, S., Schäfer, S., Domnick, F., & Spinath, F. M. (2015). Intelligence and school grades: A meta-analysis. *Intelligence, 53*, 118–137. https://doi.org/10.1016/j.intell.2015.09.002.

Russell, D. W. (2002). In search of underlying dimensions: The use (and abuse) of factor analysis in personality and social psychology bulletin. *Personality and Social Psychology Bulletin, 28*, 1629–1646.

Schechtman, N., DeBarger, A. H., Dornsife, C., Rosier, S., & Yarnall, L. (2013). *Promoting grit, tenacity, and perseverance: Critical factors for success in the 21st century*. Washington, DC: U.S. Department of Education, Office of Education Technology. Retrieved from http://pgbovine.net/OET-Draft-Grit-Report-2-17-13.pdf

Schmidt, F. T., Fleckenstein, J., Retelsdorf, J., Eskreis-Winkler, L., & Möller, J. (2019). Measuring grit: A German validation and domain-specific approach to grit. *European Journal of Psychological Assessment, 35*(3), 436–447.

Schmidt, F. T., Nagy, G., Fleckenstein, J., Möller, J., & Retelsdorf, J. (2018). Same same, but different? Relations between facets of conscientiousness and grit. *European Journal of Personality, 32*, 705–720.

Schmitt, N., & Stults, D. M. (1985). Factors defined by negatively keyed items: The result of careless respondents? *Applied Psychological Measurement, 9*, 367–373.

Smith, E. V. (2002). Detecting and evaluating the impact of multidimensionality using item fit statistics and principal component analysis of residuals. *Journal of Applied Measurement, 3*, 205–231.

Swain, S. D., Weathers, D., & Niedrich, R. W. (2008). Assessing three sources of misresponse to reversed Likert items. *Journal of Marketing Research, 45*, 116–131.

Tyumeneva, Y., Kardanova, E., & Kuzmina, J. (2017). Grit: Two related but independent constructs instead of one. Evidence from item response theory. *European Journal of Psychological Assessment, 35*(4), 469–478. https://doi.org/10.1027/1015-5759/a000424.

van de Vijver, F. J. R. (2002). Cross-cultural assessment: Value for money? *Applied Psychology: An International Review, 51*(4), 545–566. https://doi.org/10.1111/1464-0597.00107.

van Zyl, L. E., Olckers, C., & Roll, L. C. (2020). The psychometric properties of the grit-O scale within the Twente region in the Netherlands: An ICM-CFA vs. ESEM approach. *Frontiers in Psychology, 11*, 796. https://doi.org/10.3389/fpsyg.2020.00796.

Vazsonyi, A. T., Ksinan, A. J., Jiskrova, G. K., Mikuška, J., Javakhishvili, M., & Cui, G. (2019). To grit or not to grit, that is the question! *Journal of Research in Personality, 78*, 215–226.

Wirth, R. J., & Edwards, M. C. (2007). Item factor analysis: Current approaches and future directions. *Psychological Methods, 12*, 58–79.

Michael C. Tynan recently earned a PhD in psychology from Iowa State University. He earned a B.S. in psychology from Loyola University Chicago and a M.S. in psychology from Iowa State University. He has published in the *Journal of Personality and Social Psychology*, *Learning and Individual Differences*, and *The Leadership Quarterly*. His research interests include judgment and decision-making, personality trait measurement, academic success antecedents, and predictors of professional well-being

Chapter 9
Neurological Correlates of Grit: A Critical Review

Song Wang and Jingguang Li

Abstract In the long history of identifying factors to predict achievement, grit, a newly explored personality trait involving a person's tendency to pursue long-term goals with continual passion and perseverance, has emerged as a stable predictor for personal achievement and well-being. With the rapid developments of brain imaging techniques and paradigms (particularly within magnetic resonance imaging), an increasing number of studies have begun to explore the neural mechanisms of human personality and behavior. However, few investigations have explored the neural correlates of grit. Examining the neural correlates of grit would deepen our understanding of the neuroanatomical mechanism of grit and broaden our views for future studies in grit. Given that there are stable individual differences in grit trait, differences in grit may be caused by underlying structural and/or functional variations in the brain. In this chapter, we first describe candidate brain regions for grit and then systematically review previous empirical neural studies on grit. We reveal that individual differences in grit are mainly associated with the function and structure of the prefrontal cortex and striatum. These findings may not only increase understanding of grit as a specific construct, as well as the underlying mechanisms of how grit affects personal achievement and well-being, but also provide the empirical evidence that can be used by future researchers to develop targeted programs and strategies to improve grit. Finally, several limitations and future directions are discussed.

Keywords Grit · Achievement · Well-being · Brain · Magnetic resonance imaging

S. Wang (✉)
Huaxi MR Research Center (HMRRC), Department of Radiology, West China Hospital, Sichuan University, Chengdu, China
e-mail: wangs_psych@163.com

J. Li
College of Teacher Education, Dali University, Dali, China

L. E. van Zyl et al. (eds.), *Multidisciplinary Perspectives on Grit*,
https://doi.org/10.1007/978-3-030-57389-8_9

9.1 Introduction

Why do some people achieve more than others? Searching for the secret to success is one major goal in the fields of psychology and education. As prior studies have shown, many psychosocial attributes are found to be linked with achievement, such as family socioeconomic status (Sirin, 2005), general intelligence (Sternberg, Grigorenko, & Bundy, 2001), motivation and personality traits (Poropat, 2009; Robbins et al., 2004). Over the past decade, abundant studies have suggested that a newly explored personality trait named "grit" can predict personal achievement in many professional domains. Grit refers to a person's trait-level perseverance and passion for long-term goals (Duckworth, Peterson, Matthews, & Kelly, 2007). Different from several other related personality constructs (e.g., self-control and conscientiousness), grit emphasizes the indurative stamina (e.g., over months or even years) to pursue a given goal with both passion and perseverance (Duckworth et al., 2007; Duckworth & Gross, 2014).

Increasing evidence has revealed that higher levels of grit are linked to greater achievement in a wide range of contexts, including educational attainment, student academic performance (e.g. grade point average or exam performance), final rank in the US National Spelling Bee competition, performance outcomes in novice teachers, and retention in college, work, marriage and summer training at West Point (Bowman, Hill, Denson, & Bronkema, 2015; Duckworth, Kirby, Tsukayama, Berstein, & Ericsson, 2011; Duckworth et al., 2007, 2019; Duckworth & Quinn, 2009; Duckworth, Quinn, & Seligman, 2009; Eskreis-Winkler, Shulman, Beal, & Duckworth, 2014; Robertson-Kraft & Duckworth, 2014). Furthermore, a number of studies have indicated that grit can predict achievement-related outcomes over and above several other factors such as physical capability, Big Five personality traits, self-control and general intelligence (Duckworth et al., 2007; Eskreis-Winkler et al., 2014; Robertson-Kraft & Duckworth, 2014; Suzuki, Tamesue, Asahi, & Ishikawa, 2015). In addition to achievement, a growing body of studies has shown the crucial role of grit in health and well-being. For instance, it has been reported that grit is negatively linked with body mass index (Thomas, Seiden, Koffarnus, Bickel, & Wing, 2015) and positively linked with exercise adherence (Reed, Pritschet, & Cutton, 2013). Individuals with higher grit demonstrate increased life satisfaction (Li, Lin, Zhao, Chen, & Wang, 2018; Singh & Jha, 2008), show more positive affect and less negative affect (Hill, Burrow, & Bronk, 2016; Li, Lin, et al., 2018), have better psychological well-being (Vainio & Daukantaite, 2016), report lower depression, anxiety and stress (Lee, 2017; Musumari et al., 2018). Moreover, several studies have suggested that grit is a protective factor against suicide risk (Kleiman, Adams, Kashdan, & Riskind, 2013), problematic internet usage (Maddi et al., 2013), and substance use and delinquent behaviors (Guerrero, Dudovitz, Chung, Dosanjh, & Wong, 2016). In summary, grit is an important character strength that contributes to personal achievement and well-being.

Although the research of grit has achieved great progress in the past decade and the concept of grit has gained significant recognition, most studies focus on grit at the behavioral level and less work has examined the neural mechanism underlying grit. Given that grit is a stable personality trait with obvious individual differences (Duckworth et al., 2007; Duckworth & Quinn, 2009), differences in grit may be caused by underlying structural and/or functional variations in the brain. Recently, the rapid development of brain imaging techniques, particularly multimodal magnetic resonance imaging (MRI) techniques (e.g., structural MRI [s-MRI], resting-state functional MRI [rs-fMRI] and diffusion tensor imaging [DTI]), has provided new possibilities to study the underlying neural mechanisms of human mind and behavior (Biswal, 2012; Lerch et al., 2017). Compared to the traditional task-based fMRI, these task-free MRI techniques are more suitable for examining the neural correlates of a personality construct (e.g., grit) because it would be hard to use a single task to tap the cognitive processes involving in a personality construct. Moreover, the personality traits are generally stable within a relatively long time (e.g., several months or years) and are difficult to be measured with a short task (e.g., a few minutes). Additionally, these techniques are not limited to the activity in areas related to a certain task or stimuli during scanning. Given the complex nature of a personality construct, it may be linked to activity in different brain areas related to different tasks or stimulus. Thus, compared to the traditional task-based fMRI with a specific task or stimuli, the task-free multimodal MRI may provide a more unbiased estimate for the neural correlates of a personality construct. Due to these characteristics and advantages, multimodal MRI techniques have been widely used to investigate the neural correlates of human personality and behavior (DeYoung, 2010; Kanai & Rees, 2011; Lai et al., 2019). In recent years, some researchers have also begun to use these techniques to explore the neural correlates of grit. Thus, in this chapter, we aim to systematically review these studies to uncover the neuroanatomical mechanism underlying grit. Specifically, we first state the significance of studying the neural correlates of grit. Then, we describe two brain structures that might be linked to grit. Next, we reveal the existing neural findings on grit. Finally, we discuss the limitations of previous studies and indicate several directions for future research.

9.2 Neural Correlates of Grit

9.2.1 Significance of Neuroimaging Research in Grit

With the enormous growth of personality neuroscience in the past several years (DeYoung, 2010; DeYoung et al., 2010; Lai et al., 2019), an increasing number of studies have been conducted to examine the neural correlates of grit, which may have important theory and practice significance. First, uncovering the neural correlates of grit may help us better understand the essence and connotation of the grit concept, which would increase understanding of grit as a specific construct. Second, the neuroimaging research may help to identify distinct brain regions related to grit and to reveal potential biomarkers for grit. By employing some intervening methods (e.g., transcranial direct current stimulation [tDCS]; Salehinejad, Nejati, & Derakhshan, 2017) and training programs (e.g., neurofeedback procedures; Heinrich, Gevensleben, & Strehl, 2007), experts in the related fields may target these brain regions or biomarkers to manipulate their functions to improve levels of grit in individuals. Third, in light of the critical role of grit in personal achievement and well-being, uncovering the neural correlates of grit may be conducive to explain the mechanism for how grit affects achievement and well-being in the brain. In other words, we can use neuroimaging methods to demonstrate the underlying brain-grit mechanism in the prediction of achievement and well-being (e.g., the mechanism of how brain measures affect achievement and well-being through grit). Fourth, the neuroimaging studies on grit would widen the scope of the grit research and expand the influence of grit research in the neuroscientific field. Overall, investigating the neural correlates of grit would deepen our understanding of the neuroanatomical mechanism of grit and broaden our views for future studies in grit.

9.2.2 Candidate Brain Regions for Searching the Neural Correlates of Grit

As a concept derived from the belief that enduring perseverance and passion is more important than innate talent to achieve long-term goals, grit is generally considered a psychological construct that could be integrated into two broad psychological aspects: self-regulation and motivation (Duckworth et al., 2007; Duckworth & Gross, 2014). Self-regulation is a complex construct, including many subcomponents such as self-control, delayed gratification, impulsivity, planning and conscientiousness (Eisenberg et al., 2019). When facing difficulties, setbacks and distractions on the road to pursue dreams, self-regulation can empower people to persist in the same goals. On the other hand, motivation or drive enables an individual to pursue a given goal lasting a very long time (e.g., several years). Therefore, the neural correlates of grit have been hypothesized to lie in two brain areas, i.e., prefrontal cortex (PFC) and striatum, which are well-known to be linked to self-regulation and motivation, respectively (Nemmi, Nymberg, Helander, & Klingberg, 2016).

The PFC is a part of the frontal lobe that lies in the very front of the brain (e.g., just behind the eyes and forehead). This region is well-known for high-order cognitive functions such as abstract thinking, task planning and management, goal-directed thought and behaviors, and personality and value development (Miller & Cohen, 2001; Stuss & Knight, 2013). In particular, converging evidence has suggested that the PFC plays an extremely important role in self-regulation (Heatherton, 2011; Kelley, Wagner, & Heatherton, 2015). For instance, numerous investigations have shown that the function and structure of the PFC is linked with a variety of self-regulation-related processes such as delayed gratification (Scheres, de Water, & Mies, 2013), impulsivity (Schilling et al., 2013), conscientiousness

(DeYoung et al., 2010) and cognitive control (Ridderinkhof, van den Wildenberg, Segalowitz, & Carter, 2004). When damaged, the PFC would lead to our inability to set and maintain goals, to make plans and to orient our behaviors in line with our goals and values (Szczepanski & Knight, 2014). According to the perspective of trait hierarchy, personality structure starts from a cluster of root traits and extends downward to generate more specific traits, so the higher-order constructs may have influence on the developments of lower-order constructs (Markon, 2009). Because grit is generally considered a lower-order trait developed from the higher-order construct of self-regulation (Duckworth et al., 2007; Eisenberg et al., 2019), the PFC linked with self-regulation may also play a crucial role in grit. Altogether, the PFC may be a candidate region for the neural correlates of grit.

The striatum is a subcortical structure of the human forebrain. As a part of the basal ganglia, this structure contains several sub-structures (e.g., globus pallidus, putamen, nucleus accumbens and caudate). The striatum is mainly in charge of regulating motor behavior and plays an important role in motivation and reward systems (Liljeholm & O'Doherty, 2012; Schultz, 2000). For example, brain lesions evidence has revealed that individuals with striatum damage become less motivated, e.g., be apathetic and insensitive to rewards (Adam et al., 2013), have poor incentive motivation (Schmidt et al., 2008), and have less desire to pleasant stimuli (Vijayaraghavan, Vaidya, Humphreys, Beglinger, & Paradiso, 2008). Moreover, experimental evidence has shown that the striatum is involved in a body of reward-related motivation processes such as reward detection, reward expectancy, reward evaluation and action plan leading to obtain rewards (Liljeholm & O'Doherty, 2012; Shohamy, 2011). Hence, variations in the striatum activity and morphology may bring about individual discrepancy in the potential variations within motivational states, which in turn contribute to individual differences in grit. Specifically, individuals with higher functioning in the striatum may have stronger motivational intensity under a wide range of novel and stressful situations, thus they are more prone to hold positive outlooks (Sharot, Korn, & Dolan, 2011) and motivate themselves to perform persistent coping and goal-directed behaviors (Carver & Scheier, 2014), which are conducive for them to achieve success. In short, the striatum may be the other brain area explaining individual differences in grit.

In summary, based on the existing literature, the PFC and striatum might be the most important candidate brain regions related to individual differences in grit. Nevertheless, there may be other relevant brain regions responsible for grit, because some evidence has suggested that most personality traits are supported by a neural network of multiple brain regions (DeYoung et al., 2010; Lai et al., 2019). However, focusing on the PFC and striatum might be a suitable starting point for exploring the neural correlates of grit.

9.2.3 Extant Empirical Neuroimaging Studies of Grit

In the past several years, a handful of empirical studies have been conducted to examine the neural correlates of individual differences in grit (Myers, Wang, Black, Bugescu, & Hoeft, 2016; Nemmi et al., 2016; Wang et al., 2017, 2018). Notably, the measurement of grit used in these studies was based on self-reported (Myers et al., 2016; Wang et al., 2017, 2018) or teacher-reported (Nemmi et al., 2016) questionnaires (e.g., the grit scale, Duckworth et al., 2007; Duckworth & Quinn, 2009). The findings of these studies have partly confirmed the hypothesis regarding the brain candidates of grit that individual differences in grit are mainly associated with the variations of the activity and morphology in PFC and striatum.

On the one hand, there are two studies that have used rs-fMRI to explore the functional neural correlates of individual differences in grit (Myers et al., 2016; Wang et al., 2017). The rs-fMRI is a crucial and widely used neuroimaging technique that can gauge the intrinsic neural activities reflected in the low-frequency fluctuations (Biswal, 2012), which have a reliable link to neural activities during task performance (Tavor et al., 2016). First, Wang et al. (2017) used the rs-fMRI to investigate the association of grit with local spontaneous brain activity among 217 general high school students aged between 16 and 20. Specifically, in this study, local spontaneous brain activity was assessed using the fractional amplitude of low-frequency fluctuations (fALFF), reflecting the amplitude of regional neural activity (Zou et al., 2008); and the study found that higher levels of grit are linked to lower local spontaneous brain activity in the dorsomedial PFC (Wang et al., 2017). The finding of this study may reflect the role of dorsomedial PFC in goal setting and maintenance and self-regulation-related processes, which are crucial factors for the development of grit (Wang et al., 2017). Interestingly, further analyses showed that the activity of the dorsomedial PFC plays a mediating role in the relationship between grit and academic achievement measured with the score on the Chinese National College Entrance Examination, indicating that there are common variances between grit and academic achievement that can be explained by the dorsomedial PFC spontaneous activity (Wang et al., 2017). Second, in a sample of 20 healthy children aged between 6 and 14, Myers et al. (2016) examined the relationship between individual differences in grit and resting-state functional connectivity (RSFC), another data analysis method of rs-fMRI reflecting the synchronization among multiple brain areas (Lv et al., 2018). By using a seed-to-voxel whole-brain connectivity analysis (selecting ventral and dorsal striatum as regions of interest), the researchers observed that the RSFC between ventral striatum and several PFC regions (e.g., anterior cingulate cortex, medial PFC and dorsolateral PFC) can significantly and positively predict individual differences in grit; this finding might reflect the role of PFC-ventral striatum connectivity in cognitive-behavioral control, perseverance, and receipt and delay of rewards, which are indispensable components of grit concept (Myers et al., 2016). Together, these findings present that the local activity of the PFC and the PFC-striatum connectivity may play an essential role in the development of grit.

On the other hand, two s-MRI studies have been conducted to assess the structural neural correlates underlying individual differences in grit (Nemmi et al., 2016; Wang et al., 2018). Unlike the rs-fMRI technique, which reflects the functional activities of the brain (Biswal, 2012), the s-MRI technique evaluates the structural characteristics of the brain and has been widely employed to examine the neurostructural correlates of human cognition, emotion, personality and behavior (Kanai & Rees, 2011; Lai et al., 2019; Lerch et al., 2017). A study based on 27 six-year-old children first investigated the connection between grit and structural differences (e.g., shape and density) in several striatum regions (e.g., nucleus accumbens, caudate nucleus, and putamen) (Nemmi et al., 2016). Combining an analysis of regions of interest and a leave-one-out cross-validation procedure, individual differences in grit are found to be positively linked only with the variations in the shape and density of the right nucleus accumbens, which is a crucial structure for searching out reward despite obstacles or delays, corresponding to the motivational feature of grit (Nemmi et al., 2016). In another research focusing on a large group of students in late adolescence ($N = 231$), the researchers examined the brain gray matter correlates of grit by estimating cortical gray matter volume utilizing a voxel-based morphometry method (Wang et al., 2018). The gray matter volume evaluated by this method may reflect the number and size of unmyelinated neurons and glial cells, along with the volume of the synapses (Takeuchi et al., 2014). Importantly, this study found that higher grit is positively associated with greater volume in the right putamen, an area mainly responsible for persistence tendency, action planning, and motivation and learning; in contrast, higher grit is negatively associated with smaller volume in the left dorsolateral PFC, a core brain region for self-regulation, which supports the self-regulation account of grit to some degree (Wang et al., 2018). Furthermore, the association between left dorsolateral PFC volume and grit is mediated by growth mindset, a construct referring to the belief that a person's basic attributes (e.g., intelligence) are malleable and can be changed through efforts (Dweck & Leggett,1988). In summary, the current s-MRI findings suggest that the gray matter structure in several PFC-striatum regions (nucleus accumbens, putamen, and dorsolateral PFC) may serve as a neuroanatomical marker for individual differences in grit.

9.3 Limitations and Future Directions

Although an increasing number of researchers have begun to focus on the neural correlates of grit, the neuroimaging research in this field is only in its infancy. Given the various methodological limitations in these studies, the previous findings have not yet been definitive and it may be premature to come to a conclusion about the neural correlates of grit. Further works with more strict and advanced methodology are needed to confirm and clarify the neural correlates of grit.

9.3.1 Methodological Limitations

First, some neuroscientific findings of previous studies on grit relied on relatively small sample sizes (e.g., 20 participants, Myers et al., 2016; 27 participants, Nemmi et al., 2016), which may limit the statistical power of the findings. Due to the high-cost characteristics of the MRI experiments and the early task-based fMRI simulation research indicating that as few as 25 participants are adequate to achieve satisfactory statistical power (e.g., 80%) (Desmond & Glover, 2002), the small sample size seems a prevailing issue in the field of neuroscientific research. For instance, a study has shown that the median statistical power in the area of neuroscience is about 0.21, which is partly caused by the small sample sizes (Button et al., 2013). Given that a replication crisis in psychology and neuroscience has emerged in the past several years (Shrout & Rodgers, 2018), more and more researchers have paid attention to using relatively large sample sizes to achieve sufficient statistical power to observe existing effects. Particularly, in the field of personality neuroscience, some researchers argue that to investigate neural correlates of individual differences in personalities, a sample size of at least 150 participants is recommended (Mar, Spreng, & DeYoung, 2013). Thus, future works may consider using a relatively large sample size to explore the neural correlates of grit, which may not only ensure the adequate statistical power of the study, but also provide the foundation for using some statistical methods (e.g., the randomized grouping validation, Wang et al., 2017; the prediction analysis, Wang et al., 2018) to cross-validate the findings.

Second, in light of the crucial role of grit in student educational outcomes, all of the existing neuroimaging investigations regarding grit focus only on school-aged children or adolescents, which may limit the generalizability of the findings. Prior evidence has revealed that the levels of grit would increase monotonically with age; and importantly, individuals over 25-year-old score higher in grit scale than individuals under 25-year-old, suggesting that life experience may be crucial for the development of grit (Duckworth et al., 2007). Thus, it is necessary and interesting to examine the neural correlates of grit in more diverse populations (e.g., adults and the elderly, and people in special work area with different life experiences) and compare the results with the findings from prior research. Additionally, there is increasing evidence showing an influence of sex on the relations between personality traits and brain structure and function (Lai et al., 2019; Wang et al., 2020). Given that most previous brain studies considered sex as a covariate of no interest without detection of sex-related neural correlates of grit, future studies are invited to explore the sex differences in the association of grit with the brain.

Third, the measure of grit in almost all prior studies has relied on self-reported scale, which may be vulnerable to response bias, although the psychometric properties of the grit scale have been well established in previous studies (Duckworth et al., 2007; Duckworth & Quinn, 2009; Li, Zhao, Kong, et al., 2018). Although the questionnaire method is standard and prevailing to assess a personality trait in the field of personality psychology, it is necessary for future studies to employ other techniques to lessen the impact of response bias and improve measurement accuracy. For instance, in the future investigations of grit, researchers may consider exploring the link between grit and theoretically related behavioral tasks in the experimental conditions. In addition, some other approaches (e.g., qualitative interviewing or implicit testing) are needed to capture the characteristics of grit within the natural conditions. In brief, using multiple measurement techniques might be crucial for advancing the behavioral and neural research in grit.

Fourth, all of the neuroscientific findings on grit were based on cross-sectional data and the correlational nature of these studies makes it impossible to draw causal inferences on the link between grit and the brain. Notably, a recent study using a diary method has revealed that there are intrapersonal differences in the state-level grit, which is sensitive to day-to-day fluctuations (Jiang et al., 2019). This finding suggests that grit may be a construct with malleability and can be manipulated by some intervening or training methods (e.g., tDCS; Salehinejad et al., 2017). Thus, future research should consider utilizing these methods to target the grit-related brain regions to manipulate their functions and observe the changes in grit levels. Moreover, as we mentioned above that grit would increase monotonically with age, longitudinal studies are required to investigate the (neural) development of grit.

9.3.2 Future Directions

First, because only several relatively simple brain measures are employed in previous grit studies, future works are warranted to use multiple brain measures to comprehensively uncover the neural mechanisms of grit. For example, there is a variety of gray matter morphological indicators (e.g., cortical surface area, cortical thickness, cortical folding, and curvature) that have been popularly used in the field of personality neuroscience (DeYoung, 2010; Lai et al., 2019). For the white matter microstructure, the two most widely used measures are fractional anisotropy and mean diffusivity, which evaluate the morphological characteristics of white matter fiber tracts based on DTI (Lai et al., 2019; Lerch et al., 2017) and provide the possibility to reveal the white matter connectivity mechanism underlying grit. Moreover, there are many methods to analyze rs-fMRI data, which can be used to explore the functional neural mechanisms of grit from multiple levels and angles. While fALFF/ALFF analysis assesses the intensity and power of regional neural activity, regional homogeneity analysis evaluates the centrality and coherence of regional brain activity (Lv et al., 2018). However, these methods reflect the features of local brain activity but do not present information on functional connectivity between different brain areas. Functional connectivity could be assessed using a series of approaches such as functional connectivity density analysis, seed-based functional connectivity analysis, independent component analysis and graph analysis (Lv et al., 2018). Overall, the methods mentioned above are complementary and future researchers may consider combining these methods to provide a comprehensive picture of the neural mechanisms underlying grit.

Second, as we discussed at the beginning of this chapter, grit plays a critical and positive role in many developmental outcomes in achievement, health, and well-being. In future studies regarding the neural correlates of grit, researchers are encouraged to incorporate these outcome variables and to explore the neuropsychological mechanism of how grit influences the developmental outcomes in the brain. On the other hand, an increasing number of studies have begun to examine the influential factors of grit and found that grit is affected by several factors including purpose commitment (Hill et al., 2016), belief in free will (Li, Zhao, Lin, Chen, & Wang, 2018) and growth mindset (Wang et al., 2018). Thus, future research is necessary to investigate the underlying neural mechanism linking these influential factors to grit.

Third, although the concept of grit has gained rapid prominence in the past several years, some researchers have suggested that the etiology of grit is highly similar to other related personality constructs (e.g., conscientiousness and self-control) (Rimfeld, Kovas, Dale, & Plomin, 2016). More importantly, several recent studies have revealed that grit does not have sufficient incremental validity over self-control and conscientiousness (Crede, Tynan, & Harms, 2017; Muenks, Wigfield, Yang, & O'Neal, 2017; Schmidt, Nagy, Fleckenstein, Moller, & Retelsdorf, 2018; Vazsonyi et al., 2019). Thus, in the future neuroimaging research of grit, it is necessary to include other variables (e.g., self-control and conscientiousness) highly related to grit. To do so, researchers can explore the common and distinct neural correlates between grit and the other related personality traits (e.g., conscientiousness and self-control). Briefly, neuroimaging research in the future may help to clarify the specific nature of the concept of grit.

Finally, to date, the majority of studies on grit is based on Western participants, and limited investigations focus on grit among participants from East Asia (Li, Lin, et al., 2018; Li, Zhao, Kong, et al., 2018; Li, Zhao, Lin, et al., 2018; Wang et al., 2017, 2018). However, it is possible that culture plays an important role in the development of grit. For instance, in East Asia contexts, being gritty in the face of obstacles takes on a strong moral dimension (Li, 2012), although Western cultures also place value on grit and hard work (Furnham et al., 1993). Meanwhile, it is well-known that cultural differences exist prevalently in human brain structure and function (Park & Huang, 2010). Therefore, it is valuable to simultaneously include participants from countries with different cultures, which may enable researchers to determine both the culturally-specific and culturally-universal neural correlates of grit.

9.4 Practical Applications and Implications for Future Research

In this chapter, we review the intriguing pattern of the neural correlates of grit. Although the research in this field is still in an initial stage of explorations and no definitive conclusion has been obtained, the current work may have some crucial practical applications and implications for future investigations. First, our review may deepen understanding of grit as a specific construct from the neuroscientific perspective, and it also provides possible directions for further studies to examine the neural mechanism underlying grit. Second, the present work reveals primary evidence for the neural correlates of grit, which may help experts in related areas (e.g., education, psychology, and medicine) develop corresponding therapies and strategies to cultivate individuals' grit-linked skills to improve their achievement and well-being. For instance, some intervening and training programs (e.g., neurofeedback procedures, Heinrich et al., 2007; tDCS approaches, Salehinejad et al., 2017) may be developed to target brain regions linked with grit (e.g., PFC and striatum) to manipulate their functions to enhance individuals' grit levels.

Funding This work was supported by the National Natural Science Foundation of China (Grant No. 31800963), the China Postdoctoral Science Foundation (Grant No. 2019M653421), and the Fund for Educational Sciences from the Philosophy and Social Sciences Projects of Yunnan Province (Grant No. AFSZ18030).

References

Adam, R., Leff, A., Sinha, N., Turner, C., Bays, P., Draganski, B., & Husain, M. (2013). Dopamine reverses reward insensitivity in apathy following globus pallidus lesions. *Cortex, 49*(5), 1292–1303.

Biswal, B. B. (2012). Resting state fMRI: A personal history. *NeuroImage, 62*(2), 938–944.

Bowman, N. A., Hill, P. L., Denson, N., & Bronkema, R. (2015). Keep on truckin' or stay the course? Exploring grit dimensions as differential predictors of educational achievement, satisfaction, and intentions. *Social Psychological and Personality Science, 6*(6), 639–645.

Button, K. S., Ioannidis, J. P. A., Mokrysz, C., Nosek, B. A., Flint, J., Robinson, E. S. J., & Munafo, M. R. (2013). Power failure: Why small sample size undermines the reliability of neuroscience. *Nature Reviews Neuroscience, 14*(5), 365–376.

Carver, C. S., & Scheier, M. F. (2014). Dispositional optimism. *Trends in Cognitive Sciences, 18*(6), 293–299.

Crede, M., Tynan, M. C., & Harms, P. D. (2017). Much ado about grit: A meta-analytic synthesis of the grit literature. *Journal of Personality and Social Psychology, 113*(3), 492–511.

Desmond, J. E., & Glover, G. H. (2002). Estimating sample size in functional MRI (fMRI) neuroimaging studies: Statistical power analyses. *Journal of Neuroscience Methods, 118*(2), 115–128.

DeYoung, C. G. (2010). Personality neuroscience and the biology of traits. *Social and Personality Psychology Compass, 4*(12), 1165–1180.

DeYoung, C. G., Hirsh, J. B., Shane, M. S., Papademetris, X., Rajeevan, N., & Gray, J. R. (2010). Testing predictions from personality neuroscience: Brain structure and the big five. *Psychological Science, 21*(6), 820–828.

Duckworth, A., & Gross, J. J. (2014). Self-control and grit: Related but separable determinants of success. *Current Directions in Psychological Science, 23*(5), 319–325.

Duckworth, A. L., Kirby, T. A., Tsukayama, E., Berstein, H., & Ericsson, K. A. (2011). Deliberate practice spells success: Why grittier competitors triumph at the National Spelling Bee. *Social Psychological and Personality Science, 2*(2), 174–181.

Duckworth, A. L., Peterson, C., Matthews, M. D., & Kelly, D. R. (2007). Grit: Perseverance and passion for long-term goals. *Journal of Personality and Social Psychology, 92*(6), 1087–1101.

Duckworth, A. L., & Quinn, P. D. (2009). Development and validation of the short grit scale (grit-S). *Journal of Personality Assessment, 91*(2), 166–174.

Duckworth, A. L., Quinn, P. D., & Seligman, M. E. P. (2009). Positive predictors of teacher effectiveness. *Journal of Positive Psychology, 4*(6), 540–547.

Duckworth, A. L., Quirk, A., Gallop, R., Hoyle, R. H., Kelly, D. R., & Matthews, M. D. (2019). Cognitive and noncognitive predictors of success. *Proceedings of the National Academy of Sciences of the United States of America, 116*(47), 23499–23504.

Dweck, C. S., & Leggett, E. L. (1988). A social cognitive approach to motivation and personality. *Psychological Review, 95*(2), 256–273.

Eisenberg, I. W., Bissett, P. G., Enkavi, A. Z., Li, J., MacKinnon, D. P., Marsch, L. A., & Poldrack, R. A. (2019). Uncovering the structure of self-regulation through data-driven ontology discovery. *Nature Communications, 10*, 2319.

Eskreis-Winkler, L., Shulman, E. P., Beal, S. A., & Duckworth, A. L. (2014). The grit effect: Predicting retention in the military, the workplace, school and marriage. *Frontiers in Psychology, 5*, 36.

Furnham, A., Bond, M., Heaven, P., Hilton, D., Lobel, T., Masters, J., Payne, M., Rajamanikam, R., Stacey, B., & Van Daalen, H. (1993). A comparison of Protestant work ethic beliefs in thirteen nations. *The Journal of Social Psychology, 133*(2), 185–197.

Guerrero, L. R., Dudovitz, R., Chung, P. J., Dosanjh, K. K., & Wong, M. D. (2016). Grit: A potential protective factor against substance use and other risk behaviors among Latino adolescents. *Academic Pediatrics, 16*(3), 275–281.

Heatherton, T. F. (2011). Neuroscience of self and self-regulation. *Annual Review of Psychology, 62*, 363–390.

Heinrich, H., Gevensleben, H., & Strehl, U. (2007). Annotation: Neurofeedback - train your brain to train behaviour. *Journal of Child Psychology and Psychiatry, 48*(1), 3–16.

Hill, P. L., Burrow, A. L., & Bronk, K. C. (2016). Persevering with positivity and purpose: An examination of purpose commitment and positive affect as predictors of grit. *Journal of Happiness Studies, 17*(1), 257–269.

Jiang, W., Jiang, J., Du, X. P., Gu, D., Sun, Y., & Zhang, Y. (2019). Striving and happiness: Between- and within-person-level associations among grit, needs satisfaction and subjective well-being. *Journal of Positive Psychology, 15*, 543–555. https://doi.org/10.1080/17439760.2019.1639796.

Kanai, R., & Rees, G. (2011). The structural basis of inter-individual differences in human behaviour and cognition. *Nature Reviews Neuroscience, 12*(4), 231–242.

Kelley, W. M., Wagner, D. D., & Heatherton, T. F. (2015). In search of a human self-regulation system. *Annual Review of Neuroscience, 38*, 389–411.

Kleiman, E. M., Adams, L. M., Kashdan, T. B., & Riskind, J. H. (2013). Gratitude and grit indirectly reduce risk of suicidal ideations by enhancing meaning in life: Evidence for a mediated moderation model. *Journal of Research in Personality, 47*(5), 539–546.

Lai, H., Wang, S., Zhao, Y., Zhang, L., Yang, C., & Gong, Q. (2019). Brain gray matter correlates of extraversion: A systematic review and meta-analysis of voxel-based morphometry studies. *Human Brain Mapping, 40*(14), 4038–4057.

Lee, W. W. S. (2017). Relationships among grit, academic performance, perceived academic failure, and stress in associate degree students. *Journal of Adolescence, 60*, 148–152.

Lerch, J. P., van der Kouwe, A. J. W., Raznahan, A., Pans, T., Johansen-Berg, H., Miller, K. L., et al. (2017). Studying neuroanatomy using MRI. *Nature Neuroscience, 20*(3), 314–326.

Li, J. (2012). *Cultural foundations of learning: East and West.* Cambridge: Cambridge University Press.

Li, J., Lin, L., Zhao, Y., Chen, J., & Wang, S. (2018). Grittier Chinese adolescents are happier: The mediating role of mindfulness. *Personality and Individual Differences, 131*, 232–237.

Li, J., Zhao, Y., Kong, F., Du, S., Yang, S., & Wang, S. (2018). Psychometric assessment of the short grit scale among Chinese adolescents. *Journal of Psychoeducational Assessment, 36*(3), 291–296.

Li, J., Zhao, J., Lin, L., Chen, J., & Wang, S. (2018). The freedom to persist: Belief in free will predicts perseverance for long-term goals among Chinese adolescents. *Personality and Individual Differences, 121*, 7–10.

Liljeholm, M., & O'Doherty, J. P. (2012). Contributions of the striatum to learning, motivation, and performance: An associative account. *Trends in Cognitive Sciences, 16*(9), 467–475.

Lv, H., Wang, Z., Tong, E., Williams, L. M., Zaharchuk, G., Zeineh, M., et al. (2018). Resting-state functional MRI: Everything that nonexperts have always wanted to know. *American Journal of Neuroradiology, 39*(8), 1390–1399.

Maddi, S. R., Erwin, L. M., Carmody, C. L., Villarreal, B. J., White, M., & Gundersen, K. K. (2013). Relationship of hardiness, grit, and emotional intelligence to internet addiction, excessive consumer spending, and gambling. *Journal of Positive Psychology, 8*(2), 128–134.

Mar, R. A., Spreng, R. N., & DeYoung, C. G. (2013). How to produce personality neuroscience research with high statistical power and low additional cost. *Cognitive, Affective, & Behavioral Neuroscience, 13*(3), 674–685.

Markon, K. E. (2009). Hierarchies in the structure of personality traits. *Social and Personality Psychology Compass, 3*(5), 812–826.

Miller, E. K., & Cohen, J. D. (2001). An integrative theory of prefrontal cortex function. *Annual Review of Neuroscience, 24*, 167–202.

Muenks, K., Wigfield, A., Yang, J. S., & O'Neal, C. R. (2017). How true is grit? Assessing its relations to high school and college students' personality characteristics, self-regulation, engagement, and achievement. *Journal of Educational Psychology, 109*(5), 599–620.

Musumari, P. M., Tangmunkongvorakul, A., Srithanaviboonchai, K., Techasrivichien, T., Suguimoto, S. P., Ono-Kihara, M., & Kihara, M. (2018). Grit is associated with lower level of depression and anxiety among university students in Chiang Mai, Thailand: A cross-sectional study. *PLoS One, 13*(12), e0209121.

Myers, C. A., Wang, C., Black, J. M., Bugescu, N., & Hoeft, F. (2016). The matter of motivation: Striatal resting-state connectivity is dissociable between grit and growth mindset. *Social Cognitive and Affective Neuroscience, 11*(10), 1521–1527.

Nemmi, F., Nymberg, C., Helander, E., & Klingberg, T. (2016). Grit is associated with structure of nucleus accumbens and gains in cognitive training. *Journal of Cognitive Neuroscience, 28*(11), 1688–1699.

Park, D. C., & Huang, C. M. (2010). Culture wires the brain: A cognitive neuroscience perspective. *Perspectives on Psychological Science, 5*(4), 391–400.

Poropat, A. E. (2009). A meta-analysis of the five-factor model of personality and academic performance. *Psychological Bulletin, 135*(2), 322–338.

Reed, J., Pritschet, B. L., & Cutton, D. M. (2013). Grit, conscientiousness, and the transtheoretical model of change for exercise behavior. *Journal of Health Psychology, 18*(5), 612–619.

Ridderinkhof, K. R., van den Wildenberg, W. P. M., Segalowitz, S. J., & Carter, C. S. (2004). Neurocognitive mechanisms of cognitive control: The role of prefrontal cortex in action selection, response inhibition, performance monitoring, and reward-based learning. *Brain and Cognition, 56*(2), 129–140.

Rimfeld, K., Kovas, Y., Dale, P. S., & Plomin, R. (2016). True grit and genetics: Predicting academic achievement from personality. *Journal of Personality and Social Psychology, 111* (5), 780–789.

Robbins, S. B., Lauver, K., Le, H., Davis, D., Langley, R., & Carlstrom, A. (2004). Do psychosocial and study skill, factors predict college outcomes? A meta-analysis. *Psychological Bulletin, 130* (2), 261–288.

Robertson-Kraft, C., & Duckworth, A. L. (2014). True grit: Trait-level perseverance and passion for long-term goals predicts effectiveness and retention among novice teachers. *Teachers College Record, 116*(3) http://www.tcrecord.org/Content.asp?ContentId=17352.

Salehinejad, M. A., Nejati, V., & Derakhshan, M. (2017). Neural correlates of trait resiliency: Evidence from electrical stimulation of the dorsolateral prefrontal cortex (dLPFC) and orbitofrontal cortex (OFC). *Personality and Individual Differences, 106*, 209–216.

Scheres, A., de Water, E., & Mies, G. W. (2013). The neural correlates of temporal reward discounting. *Wiley Interdisciplinary Reviews-Cognitive Science, 4*(5), 523–545.

Schilling, C., Kuhn, S., Paus, T., Romanowski, A., Banaschewski, T., Barbot, A., et al. (2013). Cortical thickness of superior frontal cortex predicts impulsiveness and perceptual reasoning in adolescence. *Molecular Psychiatry, 18*(5), 624–630.

Schmidt, L., D'Arc, B. F., Lafargue, G., Galanaud, D., Czernecki, V., Grabli, D., et al. (2008). Disconnecting force from money: Effects of basal ganglia damage on incentive motivation. *Brain, 131*, 1303–1310.

Schmidt, F. T. C., Nagy, G., Fleckenstein, J., Moller, J., & Retelsdorf, J. (2018). Same same, but different? Relations between facets of conscientiousness and grit. *European Journal of Personality, 32*(6), 705–720.

Schultz, W. (2000). Multiple reward signals in the brain. *Nature Reviews Neuroscience, 1*(3), 199–207.

Sharot, T., Korn, C. W., & Dolan, R. J. (2011). How unrealistic optimism is maintained in the face of reality. *Nature Neuroscience, 14*(11), 1475–U1156.

Shohamy, D. (2011). Learning and motivation in the human striatum. *Current Opinion in Neurobiology, 21*(3), 408–414.

Shrout, P. E., & Rodgers, J. L. (2018). Psychology, science, and knowledge construction: Broadening perspectives from the replication crisis. *Annual Review of Psychology, 69*, 487–510.

Singh, K., & Jha, S. D. (2008). Positive and negative affect, and grit as predictors of happiness and life satisfaction. *Journal of the Indian Academy of Applied Psychology, 34*, 40–45.

Sirin, S. R. (2005). Socioeconomic status and academic achievement: A meta-analytic review of research. *Review of Educational Research, 75*(3), 417–453.

Sternberg, R. J., Grigorenko, E. L., & Bundy, D. A. (2001). The predictive value of IQ. *Merrill-Palmer Quarterly-Journal of Developmental Psychology, 47*(1), 1–41.

Stuss, D. T., & Knight, R. T. (2013). *Principles of frontal lobe function*. New York: Oxford University Press.

Suzuki, Y., Tamesue, D., Asahi, K., & Ishikawa, Y. (2015). Grit and work engagement: A cross-sectional study. *PLoS One, 10*(9), e0137501.

Szczepanski, S. M., & Knight, R. T. (2014). Insights into human behavior from lesions to the prefrontal cortex. *Neuron, 83*(5), 1002–1018.

Takeuchi, H., Taki, Y., Nouchi, R., Hashizume, H., Sassa, Y., Sekiguchi, A., et al. (2014). Anatomical correlates of quality of life: Evidence from voxel-based morphometry. *Human Brain Mapping, 35*(5), 1834–1846.

Tavor, I., Jones, O. P., Mars, R. B., Smith, S. M., Behrens, T. E., & Jbabdi, S. (2016). Task-free MRI predicts individual differences in brain activity during task performance. *Science, 352* (6282), 216–220.

Thomas, J. G., Seiden, A., Koffarnus, M. N., Bickel, W. K., & Wing, R. R. (2015). Delayed reward discounting and grit in men and women with and without obesity. *Obesity Science & Practice, 1* (2), 131–135.

Vainio, M. M., & Daukantaite, D. (2016). Grit and different aspects of well-being: Direct and indirect relationships via sense of coherence and authenticity. *Journal of Happiness Studies, 17* (5), 2119–2147.

Vazsonyi, A. T., Ksinan, A. J., Jiskrova, G. K., Mikuška, J., Javakhishvili, M., & Cui, G. (2019). To grit or not to grit, that is the question! *Journal of Research in Personality, 78*, 215–226.

Vijayaraghavan, L., Vaidya, J. G., Humphreys, C. T., Beglinger, L. J., & Paradiso, S. (2008). Emotional and motivational changes after bilateral lesions of the globus pallidus. *Neuropsychology, 22*(3), 412–418.

Wang, S., Dai, J., Li, J., Wang, X., Chen, T., Yang, X., et al. (2018). Neuroanatomical correlates of grit: Growth mindset mediates the association between gray matter structure and trait grit in late adolescence. *Human Brain Mapping, 39*(4), 1688–1699.

Wang, S., Yang, C., Zhao, Y., Lai, H., Zhang, L., & Gong, Q. (2020). Sex-linked neurofunctional basis of psychological resilience in late adolescence: A resting-state functional magnetic resonance imaging study. *European Child & Adolescent Psychiatry, 29*, 1075–1087.

Wang, S., Zhou, M., Chen, T., Yang, X., Chen, G., Wang, M., & Gong, Q. (2017). Grit and the brain: Spontaneous activity of the dorsomedial prefrontal cortex mediates the relationship between the trait grit and academic performance. *Social Cognitive and Affective Neuroscience, 12*(3), 452–460.

Zou, Q. H., Zhu, C. Z., Yang, Y. H., Zuo, X. N., Long, X. Y., Cao, Q. J., et al. (2008). An improved approach to detection of amplitude of low-frequency fluctuation (ALFF) for resting-state fMRI: Fractional ALFF. *Journal of Neuroscience Methods, 172*(1), 137–141.

Dr. Song Wang is a research fellow in the Huaxi MR Research Center (HMRRC) at West China Hospital of Sichuan University in Chengdu, China. His research interests involve the behavioral and neural mechanism of mental health during adolescence. Currently, he mainly focuses on the neural correlates of self-regulation and positive character strengths and their relationships to adolescent mental health and well-being.

Dr. Jingguang Li is an associate professor in the College of Teacher Education at Dali University in Dali, China. His current research focuses on the antecedents and consequences of individual differences in self-regulation.

Chapter 10
High Hope and Low Rumination Are Antecedents of Grit

Buaphrao Raphiphatthana and Paul Jose

Abstract Grit, passion and perseverance in the service of achieving long term goals is a psychological construct that has been shown to underpin success within different domains, e.g., academic contexts and personal life pursuits such as work and marriage (e.g., Duckworth et al., J Pers Soc Psychol 92(6):1087–1101, 2007). However, to date, little research has been conducted to discern the antecedents of grit. In empirical research described in this chapter, we aimed to determine whether two candidate variables, i.e. rumination and hope, would predict changes in grit over time. First, we provide a literature review of the current findings on the antecedents of grit. Second, we examined two potential antecedents of grit by conducting cross-lag path analyses on a longitudinal subject variable dataset, namely the International Wellbeing Study, involving three times of measurement over the course of 6 months. The sample is large ($N = 755$) and includes individuals across numerous countries, including New Zealand, Australia, US, and UK. Self-report responses were obtained for the Adult Hope Scale (Snyder et al., J Pers Soc Psychol 60:570–585, 1991) and the Ruminative Responses Scale (Treynor et al., Cogn Therapy Res 27(3):247–259, 2003) as well as Duckworth's original Grit Scale (Duckworth et al., J Pers Soc Psychol 92(6):1087–1101, 2007). Structural equation modelling analyses revealed that hope predicted increased levels of grit over time, while rumination predicted decreased levels of grit (with marginal statistical significance). Further, latent profile analyses based on the two predictors corroborated these results: (1) three classes were identified (low hope/high rumination; high hope/low rumination; and high hope/high rumination); and (2) the resulting group means of grit conformed to expectations in that the high hope/low rumination class reported the highest levels of grit whereas the low hope/high rumination class reported the lowest levels of grit. Overall these findings indicate that individuals who tend to engage in less

B. Raphiphatthana (✉)
Menzies School of Health Research, Charles Darwin University, Darwin, Australia

P. Jose
Victoria University of Wellington, Wellington, New Zealand

L. E. van Zyl et al. (eds.), *Multidisciplinary Perspectives on Grit*,
https://doi.org/10.1007/978-3-030-57389-8_10

rumination, and who are more hopeful, are more likely to become 'grittier' over time. These findings provide new insights into the antecedents of grit and advance the current knowledge on what makes someone gritty.

Keywords Gri · Hope · Rumination · Antecedents · Longitudinal study

10.1 Introduction

Grit, the disposition to pursue long-term goals with sustained interest and effort over time (Duckworth et al., 2007), has gained much interest in recent years due to its association with many positive outcomes spanning across different contexts. For instance, it has been found to predict educational attainments, greater academic outcomes, and higher achievements in competitive endeavours, i.e., National Spelling Bee (Duckworth et al., 2007). In regard to marriage, grittier men were found to be less likely to be separated or divorced (Eskreis-Winkler, Duckworth, Shulman, & Ebeal, 2014), and individuals who report higher levels of grit were less likely to change career (Duckworth et al., 2007). Grit has also been found to be associated with various positive psychological outcomes such as psychological wellbeing, positive affect, happiness, and life satisfaction (Salles, Cohen, & Mueller, 2014; Singh & Jha, 2008).

The literature demonstrates numerous benefits of grit, however, not much is known regarding the genesis of grit. Little research has been done to uncover the antecedents of grit, and thus the important question of 'how grit is cultivated?" remains largely unanswered. Emerging evidence suggests that different psychological profiles may be associated with differing levels of grit. Von Culin, Tsukayama, and Duckworth (2014) found that distinct approaches to pursing happiness in life, i.e., orientation towards gaining pleasure, meaning, or engagement, were differentially associated with grit. Individuals who were motivated to find engagement with challenging activities were found to be gritty, while those who were motivated by hedonic pleasure were less gritty. Another study also found that individuals who exhibited greater self-concept clarity, i.e., have formed stable beliefs about the self, also exhibited higher levels of grit (Fite, Lindeman, Rogers, Voyles, & Durik, 2017).

These findings provide interesting insights into the psychological constructs that couple with grit. However, due to their cross-sectional nature, causal and temporal conclusions, i.e., whether the constructs preceded grit, cannot be determined. Among the few studies that have examined longitudinal relationships between grit and other psychological constructs, Hill, Burrow, and Bronk (2016) found that purpose commitment predicted increased levels of grit over time. This result suggests that individuals who are committed to a purpose or direction in life tend to be grittier in the long run. In a more recent study, Raphiphatthana, Jose, and Salmon (2018) found mindfulness to be an antecedent of grit, i.e., present-moment awareness that is non-judgmental and non-reactive in nature predicted increased levels of grit over time. Nonetheless, the literature on the antecedents of grit is still young and much more research is needed to uncover how grit can be cultivated.

The present study aims to address this gap in the literature by investigating potential antecedents of grit. In the literature, hope and rumination are discussed to be important psychological constructs relating to goal pursuit; therefore, they may also have implications for grit development. Using a large international sample (mainly from Western countries, e.g., New Zealand, Australia, the U.S., and the U.K.), the study examined longitudinal relationships among hope, rumination and grit to determine the directions of their relationships over time. Longitudinal cross-lag analyses provide a deeper insight than correlational studies as they can ascertain whether hope and rumination predict higher levels of grit or vice versa. The possible relationships of hope and rumination with grit will now be discussed in more depth.

10.1.1 Hope and Grit

Hope defined as "a cognitive set that is based on a reciprocally derived sense of successful (a) agency (goal-directed determination) and (b) pathways (planning of ways to meet goals)" (Snyder et al., 1991) may be a potential antecedent of grit. Similar to grit, the conceptualization of hope is goal-oriented, such that a hopeful person is defined as someone who has the motivation and belief in their ability to plan and carry out the strategies to achieve their goals. This cognitive set of beliefs regarding goal attainment ability is thought to be reasonably stable over time and therefore may be consistent across situations. Similar to findings relating to grit, individuals with higher levels of dispositional hope tend to do better across various contexts such as exhibiting greater academic achievements, physical health, and psychological adjustment (Snyder, Lopez, Shorey, Rand, & Feldman, 2003). Therefore, it is plausible that an individual who holds a positive outlook and attitude towards his/her ability and motivation to plan and achieve goals may also be more likely to stick to and attain their long term goals.

The importance of hope in relation to grit is discussed at length by Duckworth, who proposed the concept of grit. In her book, she argues that hope is an essential attribute of a gritty person (Duckworth, 2016). A person who has the drive and belief in their ability to strategize ways to achieve their goals is argued to be positioned to better cope with setbacks and challenges, and thus more likely to remain motivated and persevere in working towards their long-term goals. Given that both conceptualization of grit and hope are goal-oriented, it is reasonable to assume that a hopeful person, i.e., someone with a positive goal-oriented attitude, would also be gritty.

Despite the conceptual link between the two constructs, limited studies have empirically examined the relationship between hope and grit. Piña-Watson, López, Ojeda, and Rodriguez (2015) conducted one of the few studies that have examined the association between the two constructs and found them to be positively related within a sample of Mexican American adolescents. However, the relationship was examined cross-sectionally and thus it is unknown whether hope preceded grit. A more recent study found that hope was a significant mediator between mindfulness and grit, such that mindfulness predicted increased levels of hope which in turn predicted enhanced levels of grit over time (Raphiphatthana et al., 2018). This finding suggests that in addition to mindfulness, hope may be another antecedent of grit and lead to greater grittiness over time.

10.1.2 Rumination and Grit

Another psychological construct that may precede and influence levels of grit is rumination. In contrast to hope, rumination may negatively impact grit and lead to lower levels of grittiness. Originally, rumination was conceptualized as a response style to depression involving repetitive self-focused thoughts on one's negative feelings and the causes and consequences of the depressive symptoms (Lyubomirsky & Nolen-Hoeksema, 1993). Since its inception, the conceptualization of rumination has been broadened beyond its relation to depression to a more general nature of repetitive thinking of a particular theme (Martin & Tesser, 1996). In relation to goal pursuit, Martin and Tesser (1996) proposed that rumination is commonly elicited by problems or challenges obstructing goal achievement such that when a person with high rumination tendencies is faced with setbacks, he or she may be more likely to engage in problem-focused ruminative thinking and negative self-referential thoughts, i.e., self-criticism. Supporting this notion, Moberly and Watkins (2010) found that low levels of goal success were associated with ruminative self-focus thinking.

This set of findings has implications for grit because setbacks and challenges are inevitable when pursuing a long-term goal. It may be that individual differences in response style to adverse circumstances may influence the level of focus and persistence in achieving goals. Brooding, an aspect of rumination which refers to the repetitive problem-focused thinking and negative self-referential thoughts such as self-criticism, may be particularly relevant to grit as it may impede the individual from working through the problems. In the literature, brooding rumination has been found to be associated with negative affect, low self-esteem, and negative self-outlook (Moberly & Watkins, 2008; Phillips & Hine, 2016). Self-esteem and positive self-outlook regarding one's abilities to achieve goals (self-efficacy) are important determinants of task motivation and performance across various settings, e.g., sport, work and education (Chen, Gully, & Eden, 2004; Erez & Judge, 2001; Lane, Lane, & Kyprianou, 2004). They are also conceptualized to be important for grit, as they enable the individuals to persevere and problem-solve when facing adversities (Perkins-Gough, 2013; Wolters & Hussain, 2015). Therefore, rumination may impede one's motivation and perseverance in working towards a long-term goal by reducing one's capacity to deal with and overcome challenges.

10.1.3 The Present Study

The aim of the present study was to address the gap in the literature regarding the antecedents of grit by examining whether hope and rumination would influence levels of grit over time. A large international survey was conducted to determine longitudinal relationships between the three constructs: grit, hope and rumination. It was hypothesized that hope would predict increases in grit over time (Hypothesis 1), while rumination would predict decreases in grit over time (Hypothesis 2). A possible bidirectional relationship among the three constructs was also examined to determine whether grit would predict changes in rumination and hope over time. And last, latent profile analyses were conducted to classify profiles based on hope and rumination scores and determine their relations to levels of grit.

10.2 Method

10.2.1 Participants

The International Wellbeing Study dataset (Wellbeingstudy.com, 2019), a subject variable longitudinal dataset including adult individuals recruited from all over the world but chiefly from New Zealand, the U.S., Hungary, Australia and England, was used to test the hypotheses and answer related research questions. The study focused on the first three times of measurement separated by 3 months each. The dataset was composed of 755 individuals who participated in these three times of measurement, although some small amount of missing values occurred in the data. Demographic information of the sample is presented in Appendix 1.

10.2.2 Measures

10.2.2.1 Rumination

Participants self-reported on the revised version of the Rumination Response Style measure (RRS; Nolen-Hoeksema, Larson, & Grayson, 1999) their degree of having ruminative thoughts relating to their negative mood and self-criticisms. The scale was composed of 6 items assessing the brooding aspect of rumination (Treynor et al., 2003). Sample items are: "Thought 'why do I always react this way?'", and "Thought 'why can't I handle things better?'". Participants indicated their responses on a 7-point Likert scale (1 = *strongly disagree* to 7 = *strongly agree*). Internal reliability of the RRS has been found by Schoofs, Hermans, and Raes (2010) to be very good ($\alpha = .92$), and they also demonstrated construct validity with a moderate association with depression ($r = .53$).

10.2.2.2 Hope

Eight items constituting the Adult Hope Scale (Snyder et al., 1991) were used to measure self-reported hope. Four items tapped agency (e.g., "I energetically pursue my goals") and four items tapped pathways (e.g., "I can think of many ways to get out of a jam"). Participants responded to the questions on a 4-point Likert scale from 1 ("*definitely false*") to 4 ("*definitely true*"). The scale has demonstrated internal reliability ($\alpha = .85$) and validity, i.e., moderate associations with positive traits such as positive affect, optimism, and quality of life (Mast, Ludwin, Van Haitsma, & Meeks, 2015).

10.2.2.3 Grit

The construct of grit was assessed with 12 items representing two subscales (Duckworth et al., 2007). Six items composed the *persistence of effort* subscale, e.g., "setbacks don't discourage me", and six items composed the *consistency of interest* subscale, e.g., "my interests change from year to year" (reverse-coded). Respondents recorded their answers on a 5-point Likert scale from 1 ("*not at all like me*") to 5 ("*very much like me*"). Psychometric evaluations of the Grit Scale indicate that it exhibits satisfactory internal consistency ($\alpha = .80$), test-retest reliability ($r = .78$ over 1 month), and construct validity (Li et al., 2018).

10.2.3 Procedure

Participants were recruited through a variety of methods: Facebook announcements, invitations on poster boards, e-mail solicitation by the IWS research team, and personal invitations. Interested individuals visited the IWS website and read a description of the online study. Individuals who agreed to participate recorded contact information (i.e., name and e-mail address) and then completed the online survey, which took about 45–50 min. Participants were then reminded to participate a second and a third time 3 and 6 months later respectively. After participants had completed participation, their identifying information was deleted so the data became anonymous. Participants were told that a lottery would choose a single individual at each time of measurement to receive a $100 Amazon voucher. Ethical approval was obtained from the host institution of the IWS team leader.

10.2.4 Analytic Plan

We initially examined zero-order relationships among the variables to determine whether they conformed to expected directions of association, and we also examined internal reliabilities (Cronbach's alpha) of the scores to ascertain whether the scores tapped homogeneous constructs. Next we constructed a three-variable longitudinal path model to test our predictions that rumination and hope would temporally predict changes in grit over time. The same model also permitted an examination of the reverse-order temporal relationships, i.e., did grit predict changes in rumination and hope over time? Third and last, we conducted a latent profile analysis based on rumination and hope scores to identify a small number of homogeneous clusters of individuals. We sought to determine whether these groups would differ in predictable ways on the variable of grit, i.e., we predicted that groups based on high hope and low rumination would also report higher levels of grit.

10.3 Results

10.3.1 Descriptive Statistics

Table 10.1 reports the raw correlations, means, standard deviations, and Cronbach's alphas of the three constructs over the three time points of measurement. As expected, grit and hope were positively related to each other, and, as expected, rumination was negatively related to grit and hope. Also, all constructs at all time-points evidenced adequate internal reliability.

Table 10.1 Correlations, means, standard deviations, and Cronbach's alphas of hope, rumination, and grit over three times of measurement

	1	2	3	4	5	6	7	8	9
1. Hope T1		−.38	.43	.84	−.37	.42	.81	−.31	.43
2. Rum T1			.39	−.34	.72	−.37	−.34	.65	−.36
3. Grit T1				.38	−.37	.85	.38	−.29	.82
4. Hope T2					−.40	.42	.84	−.32	.42
5. Rum T2						−.40	−.38	.66	−.40
6. Grit T2							.40	−.30	.86
7. Hope T3								−.36	.47
8. Rum T3									−.34
9. Grit T3									
Mean	6.20	4.03	3.61	6.19	4.00	3.60	6.22	3.94	3.62
SD	1.07	1.59	0.62	1.08	1.56	0.62	1.05	1.60	0.63
Cronbach's alpha	.88	.88	.79	.89	.88	.80	.89	.89	.81

Note. All correlations significant at $p < .001$, $N = 755$. Rum = rumination

10.3.2 Did Hope and Rumination Predict Changes in Grit Over Time?

We constructed a three-variable cross-lag longitudinal path model to test Hypotheses 1 and 2. Hypothesis 1 projected that hope would predict increases in grit, and Hypothesis 2 predicted that rumination would predict diminished grit over time. Figure 10.1 depicts the path model that we tested, but reliability coefficients and covariances among exogenous variables and error terms for the endogenous variables were deleted to improve readability. Non-significant cross-lag paths are not shown. To simplify the model's results, we also constrained cross-lags from T1 to T2 to be identical to the same cross-lag from T2 to T3. The model fit indices of the estimated model were found to be excellent: $\chi^2/\mathrm{df} = 3.04$, SRMR $= .033$, CFI $= .995$, RMSEA $= .056$.

The cross-lag that informed Hypothesis 1 was hope to residualized grit, and it yielded a significant positive relationship, $\beta = .04$, $p = .003$. This result provided support for the hypothesis that hope would predict an increase in grit 3 months later. And the cross-lag that informed Hypothesis 2 was rumination to residualized grit, and it yielded a marginally significant negative relationship, $\beta = -.02$, $p = .07$. This result provided partial support for the hypothesis that rumination would predict a decrease in grit 3 months later.

10.3.3 Did Grit Predict Changes in Hope and Rumination Over Time?

Our model also allowed us to determine whether any evidence of a bi-directional relationship might be found between grit and the other two variables. Figure 10.1 shows that one other relationship proved to be statistically significant: grit predicted a diminishment of residualized rumination at the subsequent time point, $\beta = -.03$,

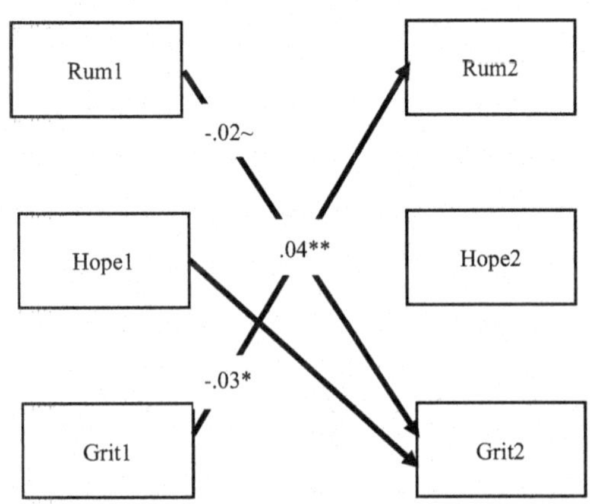

Fig. 10.1 Longitudinal path model of rumination, grit and hope predicting each other 3 month later. Note. Standardized beta weights are super-imposed on each pathway, with ~p. > .05, *p < .05, and **p < .01

$p = .039$. This result suggests that grit and rumination affected each other in a bi-directional relationship over time, namely grit predicted a reduction of subsequent rumination at the same time that rumination predicted a reduction of subsequent grit.

In contrast, the relationship between grit and hope was shown to be uni-directional, i.e., hope predicted an increase in grit over time, but grit failed to predict subsequent levels of hope over time.

Covariances of the concurrent associates between T1 variables and T2 error terms were omitted from the model for clarity.

10.3.4 Do Different Profiles of Hope and Rumination Exhibit Expected Levels of Grit?

As a research question, we next explored whether grit would differ in an expected fashion among profiles based on hope and rumination scores. Given that grit was found to be positively associated with hope and to be negatively associated with rumination, we broadly expected that high levels of grit would be reported by profiles reporting high levels of hope and that low levels of grit would be reported by profiles reporting high levels of rumination.

The first step in this analysis was to identify an optimal number of profiles through latent profile analysis (Nylund-Gibson & Choi, 2018) on our sample of 755 participants. We performed a latent profile analysis based on the indicators of hope and rumination over the three time points (i.e., based on six indicators), and we hoped that the analysis would generate more than one discriminable profile. Mplus syntax used for this analysis are presented in Appendix 2. Table 10.2 reports that the optimal number of profiles was three, based chiefly on the Lo-Mendell-Rubin adjusted LRT test. Figure 10.2 shows that the three profiles were constituted by scores that were: (1) high rumination/low hope; (2) low rumination/high hope; and (3) high rumination/high hope. The first group constituted 20% of the sample, and the latter two groups each constituted 40% of the sample.

Based on the findings of the path model, we estimated that we might find significant differences in levels of self-reported grit among these three groups in the following order: the highest group would be low rumination/high hope; the

Table 10.2 Latent profile analysis statistics for two, three, and four profile solutions

	AIC	BIC	Entropy	Lo-Mendell-Rubin adjusted LRT test	p-value	Any profiles less than 10%?
Two profiles	31436.5	31524.4	.87	1338.32	.0000	no
Three profiles	30768.8	30889.1	.84	667.38	.0264	no
Four profiles	30389.2	30541.9	.86	385.28	.1731	yes

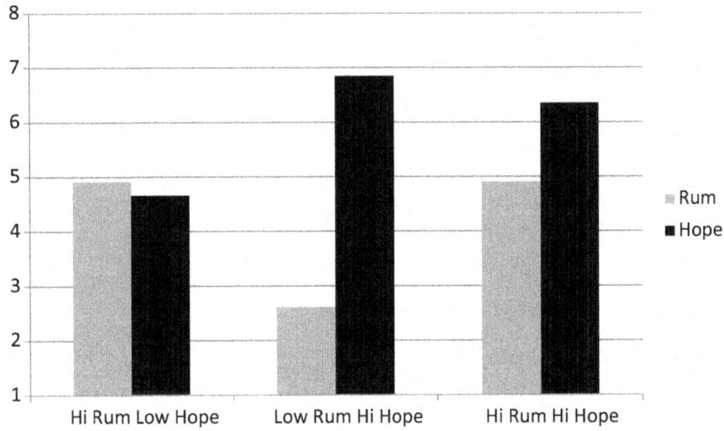

Fig. 10.2 Mean levels of average rumination and hope scores within the three latent profiles of participants across the three time points. Rum = rumination. *N*s of three profiles = 149, 299, and 307 respectively

intermediate group would be high rumination/high hope; and the lowest group would be high rumination/low hope. We performed a repeated measures ANOVA to test this supposition, and we obtained strong support for this prediction. Neither the Time nor the Profile X Time interaction yielded significant main effects, Wilk's $\lambda s = .997$ and .989 respectively, $ps = .35$ and .09 respectively, but the Profile main effect did yield a significant effect, $F(2, 752) = 92.18, p < .001$, partial $\eta^2 = .20$. The three profiles differed from each other significantly using 95% confidence intervals in the predicted order: the highest group was low rumination/high hope (M = 3.90, 95% CI = [3.84, 3.96]); the intermediate group was high rumination/high hope (M = 3.53, 95% CI = [3.47, 3.59]); and the lowest group was high rumination/low hope (M = 3.20, 95% CI = [3.12, 3.29]). Thus, individuals in the profile high in hope and low in rumination reported the highest level of grit, individuals in the mixed profile (high rumination and high hope) reported an intermediate level of grit, and individuals in the profile low in hope and high in rumination reported the lowest level of grit. This result suggests that grit is experienced at higher levels in individuals experiencing low levels of rumination as well as high levels of hope.

10.4 Discussion

The aim of the present work was to examine longitudinal relationships between hope, rumination, and grit. Cross-lag path analysis was conducted on a large international dataset (mainly from Western countries, e.g., New Zealand, Australia, the U.S., and the U.K.). Results showed support for Hypothesis 1, i.e., hope predicted increased levels of grit over time, and partial support for Hypothesis

2, i.e., rumination predicted somewhat decreased levels of grit over time. The model also revealed a bi-directional relationship between rumination and grit such that grit was found to significantly predict lower levels of rumination over time. Latent profile analysis based on the reported levels of hope and rumination yielded three classifications: low hope/high rumination; high hope/low rumination and; high hope/ high rumination. The three profiles differed significantly in their relation to grit. Individuals in the low rumination/high hope group reported the highest levels of grit, followed by those in the high rumination/high hope group. Those individuals in the low hope/high rumination group reported the lowest levels of grit. These findings will now be interpreted in light of the wider literature.

The finding that hope predicted increased levels of grit over time but not vice versa suggests that hope contributes to the cultivation of grit but not the other way around, i.e., being gritty will not typically lead to being more hopeful. This finding is consistent with earlier findings which showed that hope mediated the relationship between mindfulness and grit in a longitudinal study conducted with New Zealand university students (Raphiphatthana et al., 2018). The study's finding suggests that mindful individuals are more likely to also be hopeful, which, in turn, render them grittier over time.

In the literature, hope is conceptualised as a cognitive construct relating to goal pursuit. Snyder et al. (1991) defined a hopeful person as someone who is motivated and believe in their abilities to devise plans in order to achieve their goals. The impact of this positive goal-oriented attitude on performance is well established across different domains including academics (e.g., Onwuegbuzie & Snyder, 2000; Snyder et al., 2003), sports (Curry, Snyder, Cook, Ruby, & Rehm, 1997), and work (Adams et al., 2002). To understand the mechanisms underlying hope and its impact on performance improvement, Peterson, Gerhardt, and Rode (2006) examined the role of learning goal orientation in relation to hope and task performance in a laboratory experiment. They found that learning goal orientation predicted hope, which, in turn, predicted superior task performance. Thus, they concluded that learning goal orientation may serve as an antecedent of hope.

Learning goal orientation is conceptualised as part of the implicit theory which posits that individuals hold basic assumptions regarding the stability of human attributes and its relation to actions and outcomes (Dweck, 1991). Individuals with a growth mindset, i.e., they believe that their attributes are malleable and perceive actions and outcomes to be linked to specific behaviour or psychological mediators (e.g., effort or hard work), are argued to be oriented towards goal mastery through personal development (learning goal orientation). When a person with a growth mindset is faced with a challenging task, he or she would put effort into learning new skills required to master the task because they believe that mastery is achieved from effort and hard work rather than a fixed attribute such as IQ.

With respect to the theory of hope, the growth mindset has implications for both the agency and pathways aspects of hope. The belief that effort will increase abilities to achieve goals has implications for agency cognitions, as with such belief a person would be more motivated to put effort into overcoming challenges and achieving their goals. Additionally, when faced with adversities, a person holding a strong learning goal orientation would approach the challenges as ways to learn new skills, thus evoking a sense of perceived capabilities for generating workable routes to the desired goals.

The growth mindset also has important implications for the construct of grit. In her book, Duckworth (2016) discussed the growth mindset and orientation to learning as an essential foundation for grit development. She argues that what enables a person to be gritty in working towards their long-term goals is their belief that their goal can be achieved by effort and hard-work, and that achievement is not something that is dependent on fixed, innate talent, e.g., IQ. Thus, when setbacks are encountered, a person with a growth mindset would not perceive such adversities as a fault in their personal attributes but rather a challenge to be overcome by effort and learning new skills. Given the shared implicit theory (growth mindset) that underlines both hope and grit, it is unsurprising that the two constructs are also interlinked.

Though a unidirectional relationship was found between hope and grit, i.e., hope led to increased levels of grit over time but not vice versa, the same was not found for rumination and grit. The two constructs were found to influence each other over time, such that rumination predicted lower levels of grit, while grit predicted lower levels of rumination. This bi-directional relationship suggests that a person who tends to ruminate on negative mood states and engage in self-criticisms is more likely to become less gritty in the long run. In contrast, individuals who are focused and persevere in working towards their long- term goals tend to ruminate less over time. However, we found that the direction in which grit predicted lower levels of rumination was stronger than the other way around, because one direction—namely, rumination to grit—was only partially significant. Thus, in regard to the relationship between grit and rumination, grit may more typically serve as a protective factor against rumination rather than rumination serving as a risk factor for grit.

The role of grit as a protective factor against rumination may be explained by grit's relationship with hope. As discussed, hope is a positive goal-oriented attitude that enables a person to keep persevering and working towards one's long-term goals in the face of adversities. In contrast, rumination is a cognitive response to challenges that involves repetitive thinking about negative affect and self-critical thoughts. In essence, hope incorporates positive and forward-thinking attitudes and is problem-solving in nature, while rumination is retrospective and problem-focused. In the literature, many studies have demonstrated a negative association between hope and rumination (e.g., Geiger & Kwon, 2010; Sun, Tan, Fan, & Tsui, 2014; Tucker et al., 2013). Given that a gritty person tends to also be hopeful, when such a person is faced with challenges, he or she would likely respond with a problem-solving attitude. Consequently, he or she would be less likely to dwell on the problem and engage in debilitating self-referential thoughts.

The findings and discussions around the relationships between hope, rumination, and grit also explains the findings gleaned from the latent profile analysis. The results revealed three classifications: low hope/high rumination; high hope/low rumination; and high hope/high rumination, all of which exhibited differing levels of grit. Individuals with high levels of hope and low levels of rumination reported the highest levels of grit, while those individuals with low levels of hope and high levels of rumination reported the lowest levels of grit. This pattern is not surprising given the positive relationship between hope and grit, and the negative relationship between grit and rumination. Consider a situation where a person with high hope and low rumination profile is faced with a goal-related obstacle. Such a person would respond to the challenge with a positive attitude and focus on problem-solving, rather than dwelling on the problem and engaging in negative self-referential thoughts. Thus the positive attitude towards adversities, which is not dampened by the tendencies to ruminate, would encourage perseverance and continuation of efforts in working towards long-term goals.

In contrast, in response to adversities, a person who reports low levels of hope and high levels of rumination would likely get stuck and dwell on the setbacks and the associated negative affect and engage in debilitating self-criticisms. Without the presence of hope to protect against such a negative response, the individual may lose the drive to find ways to overcome the obstacle and be less likely to continue to work towards their goals. Thus, it is unsurprising that such persons in the low hope/high rumination group would report the lowest levels of grit. However, consider a similar person who responds to goal-obstructed problems with rumination, but also exhibit a positive goal-oriented attitude, i.e., the intermediate group. The presence of hope enables the individual to generate a positive self-outlook and strategize plans to address the problem at hand, and thus helps the person to overcome their negative thoughts. Therefore, in comparison to the other two profiles of hope and rumination, a person with high hope and high rumination exhibits an intermediate level of grit as the negative impact of rumination is somewhat dampened by the presence of hope.

10.4.1 Limitations of the Present Study

It is important to note that the effect sizes are quite small, and thus the significance of the findings should not be overstated. However, the analytic strategy used to analyse the data, i.e., crossed-lag path analysis, takes into consideration the stability of the psychological constructs over time, and since levels of hope, grit, and rumination are quite stable over time, this model leaves little variance in intervening variables to be explained by preceding variables (Jose, 2016). Nonetheless, when significant cross-lags are identified after residualization, they very likely indicate significant change in the psychological constructs over time. In the context of the present findings, the analyses provide preliminary evidence that an increased level of hope can lead to an increased level of grit, while an increased level of grit can lead to a decreased level of rumination.

Another important limitation is the survey design of the study. Collecting data through self-reported questionnaires comes with several limitations as reporting accuracy can be influenced by a number of factors such as misunderstanding of the questions, disengaging from the questionnaire, and inaccurate or biased self-perceptions. Regardless, self-report is a widely used method in research and has shown a good level of accuracy. Additionally, the present study used a large sample which can mitigate the effects of extraneous errors associated with self-reporting questionnaires (Jones, Baxter, & Khanduja, 2013).

10.4.2 Future Directions

The present work provides some insights into how grit may be cultivated; nonetheless, many questions are left unanswered. Firstly, as discussed, a growth mindset may play a fundamental role in cultivating both grit and hope, and thus future studies should examine these three constructs to determine whether they are indeed interrelated and investigate the nature and directions of their relationships. Secondly, hope, although treated as a disposition here, can also be conceptualised and measured as a state (Snyder et al., 1996). Given that traits and states may be influenced and interact with other constructs differently, it would be interesting to examine how the different states of hope influence the disposition of hope and grit over time and vice versa. Thirdly, to confidently show causal links, experimental work designed to enhance hope and/or reduce rumination may more powerfully show effects on the development of grit. Lastly, given that grit may function as a protective factor against the tendency to ruminate, which is strongly linked to poor mental health (Smith & Alloy, 2009), investigations into whether a grit-related intervention could be used within mental health settings is worth exploring.

10.5 Conclusion

Many correlates of grit have been found, however, very few studies have examined the relationships between grit and other psychological constructs longitudinally. Since little is known regarding the antecedents of grit, the present study was designed to examine the temporal relationships among hope, rumination, and grit. We found support for the supposition that hope acts as a fostering antecedent of grit and rumination acts as a diminishing antecedent of grit. Further, rumination was found to exist in a bi-directional relationship with grit; however, grit seemed to be a stronger protective factor against rumination than the reverse temporal relationship. Lastly, profile analysis demonstrated that individuals with high levels of hope tended to be grittier than those with low levels of hope, regardless of the level of their rumination, thus, further highlighting the importance of hope for grit. Together, these findings add to the growing body of literature and provide some insights regarding the antecedents of grit.

Appendix 1: Demographic Information

Age: 15–82 years old. M = 39.32, SD = 14.51

Gender: 634 females, 121 males

Top Countries:

1. New Zealand (34.3%)
2. USA (16.6%)
3. Hungary (9.3%)
4. Australia (9.1%)
5. England (5.2%)
6. Slovenia (4.1%)
7. Czech Republic (4.0%)
8. Canada (2.9%)
9. Germany & Slovakia (1.2%)

List of countries

Country	No. of people	Percentage of the sample
Australia	69	9.1
Belarus	1	0.1
Brasil	5	0.7
Bulgaria	1	0.1
Canada	22	2.9
Colombia	8	1.1
Czech Republic	30	4.0
Denmark	2	0.3
England	39	5.2
Estonia	1	0.1
France	4	0.5
Germany	9	1.2
Greece	1	0.1
Guatemala	3	0.4
Hungary	70	9.3
India	2	0.3
Ireland	7	0.9
Italy	2	0.3
Japan	2	0.3
Kuwait	1	0.1
Lithuania	1	0.1
Malaysia	1	0.1
Mexico	8	1.1
Moldova	1	0.1
Netherlands	1	0.1
New Zealand	259	34.3

(continued)

Country	No. of people	Percentage of the sample
Norway	7	0.9
Philippines	1	0.1
Portugal	3	0.4
Russia	8	1.1
Saudi Arabia	1	0.1
Scotland	7	0.9
Singapore	1	0.1
Slovakia	9	1.2
Slovenia	31	4.1
South Africa	4	0.5
Sweden	2	0.3
Switzerland	4	0.5
Ukraine	2	0.3
USA	125	16.6
Total	755	100.0

Appendix 2: Mplus Syntax Used to Perform the Latent Profile Analysis

```
Title: Latent Class Analysis Grit Rum Hope;
    Data: file is
    C:\Users\grit book\Rum grit.dat;
    Variable: Names are ID hope1 rum1 hope2 rum2 hope3 rum3;
    usevar = ID hope1 rum1 hope2 rum2 hope3 rum3;
    IDVARIABLE is ID;
    missing = all (-99);
    classes = c(3);
    Analysis: type = mixture;
    starts = 1000 50;
    iterations = 20;
    Output: sampstat standardized tech1
    tech8 tech11 tech14;
    Savedata: file is
    C:\Users \grit book\profiles.sav;
    save is cprob;
    format is free;
```

References

Adams, V. H., Snyder, C. R., Rand, K. L., King, E. A., Sigman, D. R., & Pulvers, K. M. (2002). Hope in the workplace. In R. A. Giacolone & C. L. Jurkiewicz (Eds.), *Handbook of workplace spirituality and organization performance* (pp. 367–377). New York: Sharpe.

Chen, G., Gully, S. M., & Eden, D. (2004). general self-efficacy and self-esteem: Toward theoretical and empirical distinction between correlated self-evaluations. *Journal of Organizational Behavior, 25*(3), 375–395. https://doi.org/10.1002/job.251.

Curry, L. A., Snyder, C. R., Cook, D. L., Ruby, B. C., & Rehm, M. (1997). Role of hope in academic and sport achievement. *Journal of Personality and Social Psychology, 73*, 1257–1267. https://doi.org/10.1037//0022-3514.73.6.1257.

Duckworth, A. (2016). *Grit: The power of passion and perseverance*. New York, NY: Scribner.

Duckworth, A. L., Peterson, C., Matthews, M. D., & Kelly, D. R. (2007). Grit: Perseverance and passion for long-term goals. *Journal of Personality and Social Psychology, 92*(6), 1087–1101. https://doi.org/10.1037/0022-3514.92.6.1087.

Dweck, C. S. (1991). Self-theories and goals: Their role in motivation, personality, and development. In R. Dienstbier (Ed.), *Perspectives on motivation: Nebraska symposium on motivation 1990* (Vol. 38, pp. 199–235). Lincoln, NE: University of Nebraska Press.

Erez, A., & Judge, T. A. (2001). Relationship of core self-evaluations to goal setting, motivation, and performance.(Abstract). *Journal of Applied Psychology, 86*(6), 1270. https://doi.org/10.1037/0021-9010.86.6.1270.

Eskreis-Winkler, L., Duckworth, A. L., Shulman, E. P., & Ebeal, S. (2014). The grit effect: Predicting retention in the military, the workplace, school and marriage. *Frontiers in Psychology, 5*. https://doi.org/10.3389/fpsyg.2014.00036.

Fite, R. E., Lindeman, M. I. H., Rogers, A. P., Voyles, E., & Durik, A. M. (2017). Knowing oneself and long-term goal pursuit: Relations among self-concept clarity, conscientiousness, and grit. *Personality and Individual Differences, 108*, 191–194. https://doi.org/10.1016/j.paid.2016.12.008.

Geiger, K. A., & Kwon, P. (2010). Rumination and depressive symptoms: Evidence for the moderating role of hope. *Personality and Individual Differences, 49*(5), 391–395. https://doi.org/10.1016/j.paid.2010.04.004.

Hill, P., Burrow, A., & Bronk, K. (2016). Persevering with positivity and purpose: An examination of purpose commitment and positive affect as predictors of grit. An interdisciplinary forum on subjective well-being. *Journal of Happiness Studies, 17*(1), 257–269. https://doi.org/10.1007/s10902-014-9593-5.

Jones, T. L., Baxter, M. A. J., & Khanduja, V. (2013). A quick guide to survey research. *Annals of the Royal College of Surgeons of England, 95*, 5–7. https://doi.org/10.1308/003588413X13511609956372.

Jose, P. E. (2016). The merits of using longitudinal mediation. *Educational Psychologist, 51*(3–4), 331–341. https://doi.org/10.1080/00461520.2016.1207175.

Lane, J., Lane, A. M., & Kyprianou, A. (2004). Self-efficacy, self-esteem and their impact on academic performance. *Social Behavior and Personality, 32*(3), 247–256. https://doi.org/10.2224/sbp.2004.32.3.247.

Li, J., Zhao, Y., Kong, F., Du, S., Yang, S., & Wang, S. (2018). Psychometric assessment of the Short Grit Scale among Chinese adolescents. *Journal of Psychoeducational Assessment, 36*(3), 291–296. https://doi.org/10.1177/0734282916674858.

Lyubomirsky, S., & Nolen-Hoeksema, S. (1993). Self-perpetuating properties of dysphoric rumination. *Journal of Personality and Social Psychology, 65*(2), 339–349. https://doi.org/10.1037/0022-3514.65.2.339.

Martin, L. L., & Tesser, A. (1996). Some ruminative thoughts. In R. S. Wyer (Ed.), *Advances in social cognition* (Vol. 9, pp. 1–47). Mahwah, NJ: Lawrence Erlbaum Associates.

Mast, B. T., Ludwin, B., Van Haitsma, K. V., & Meeks, S. (2015). Reliability and validity of the adule hope scale in nursing home residents. *The Gerontologist, 55*(2), 705. https://doi.org/10.1093/geront/gnv355.02.

Moberly, N. J., & Watkins, E. R. (2008). Ruminative self-focus, negative life events, and negative affect. *Behaviour Research and Therapy, 46*(9), 1034–1039. https://doi.org/10.1016/j.brat.2008.06.004.

Moberly, N. J., & Watkins, E. R. (2010). Negative affect and ruminative self-focus during everyday goal pursuit. *Cognition and Emotion, 24*(4), 729–739. https://doi.org/10.1080/02699930802696849.

Nolen-Hoeksema, S., Larson, J., & Grayson, C. (1999). Explaining the gender difference in depressive symptoms. *Journal of Personality and Social Psychology, 77*(5), 1061–1072. https://doi.org/10.1037/0022-3514.77.5.1061.

Nylund-Gibson, K., & Choi, A. Y. (2018). Ten frequently asked questions about latent class analysis. *Translational Issues in Psychological Science., 4*, 440–461. https://doi.org/10.1037/tps0000176.

Onwuegbuzie, A. J., & Snyder, C. R. (2000). Relations between hope and graduate students' coping strategies for studying and examination-taking. *Psychological Reports, 86*(3), 803–806. https://doi.org/10.2466/pr0.2000.86.3.803.

Perkins-Gough, D. (2013). The significance of grit: A conversation with Angela Lee Duckworth. *Educational Leadership, 71*, 14–20. Retrieved from http://www.ncpdf.org/pdf/steering/2013-09-06/14.0%20Grit.pdf.

Peterson, S. J., Gerhardt, M. W., & Rode, J. C. (2006). Hope, learning goals, and task performance. *Personality and Individual Differences, 40*(6), 1099–1109. https://doi.org/10.1016/j.paid.2005.11.005.

Phillips, W. J., & Hine, D. W. (2016). En route to depression: Self-esteem discrepancies and habitual rumination. *Journal of Personality, 84*(1), 79–90. https://doi.org/10.1111/jopy.12141.

Piña-Watson, B., López, B., Ojeda, L., & Rodriguez, K. M. (2015). Cultural and cognitive predictors of academic motivation among Mexican American adolescents: Caution against discounting the impact of cultural processes. *Journal of Multicultural Counselling and Development, 43*, 109–121. https://doi.org/10.1002/j.2161-1912.2015.00068.x.

Raphiphatthana, B., Jose, P., & Salmon, K. (2018). Does dispositional mindfulness predict the development of grit? *Journal of Individual Differences, 39*(2), 76–87. https://doi.org/10.1027/1614-0001/a000252.

Salles, A., Cohen, G. L., & Mueller, C. M. (2014). The relationship between grit and resident well-being. *American Journal of Surgery, 207*(2), 251–254. https://doi.org/10.1016/j.amjsurg.2013.09.006.

Schoofs, H., Hermans, D., & Raes, F. (2010). Brooding and reflection as subtypes of rumination: Evidence from confirmatory factor analysis in nonclinical samples using the Dutch ruminative response scale. *Journal of Psychopathology and Behavioral Assessment, 32*(4), 609–617. https://doi.org/10.1007/s10862-010-9182-9.

Singh, K., & Jha, S. D. (2008). Positive and negative affect, and grit as predictors of happiness and life satisfaction. *Journal of the Indian Academy of Applied Psychology, 34*, 40–45.

Smith, J. M., & Alloy, L. B. (2009). A roadmap to rumination: A review of the definition, assessment, and conceptualization of this multifaceted construct. *Clinical Psychology Review, 29*(2), 116–128. https://doi.org/10.1016/j.cpr.2008.10.003.

Snyder, C. R., Harris, C., Anderson, J. R., Holleran, S. A., Irving, L. M., Sigmon, S. T., et al. (1991). The will and the ways: Development and validation of an individual differences measure of hope. *Journal of Personality and Social Psychology, 60*, 570–585. https://doi.org/10.1037/0022-3514.60.4.570.

Snyder, C. R., Lopez, S. J., Shorey, H. S., Rand, K. L., & Feldman, D. B. (2003). Hope theory, measurements, and applications to school psychology. *School Psychology Quarterly, 18*(2), 122–139. https://doi.org/10.1521/scpq.18.2.122.21854.

Snyder, C. R., Sympson, S. C., Ybasco, F. C., Borders, T. F., Babyak, M. A., & Higgins, R. L. (1996). Development and validaton of the State Hope Scale. *Journal of Personality and Social Psychology, 70*, 321–3.35.

Sun, H., Tan, Q., Fan, G., & Tsui, Q. (2014). Different effects of rumination on depression: Key role of hope. *International Journal of Mental Health Systems, 8*(1), 53. https://doi.org/10.1186/1752-4458-8-53.

Treynor, W., Gonzalez, R., & Nolen-Hoeksema, S. (2003). Rumination reconsidered: A psychometric analysis. *Cognitive Therapy and Research, 27*(3), 247–259. https://doi.org/10.1023/A:1023910315561.

Tucker, R. P., Wingate, L. R., O'keefe, V. M., Mills, A. C., Rasmussen, K., Davidson, C. L., & Grant, D. M. (2013). Rumination and suicidal ideation: The moderating roles of hope and optimism. *Personality and Individual Differences, 55*(5), 606–611. https://doi.org/10.1016/j.paid.2013.05.013.

Von Culin, K. R., Tsukayama, E., & Duckworth, A. L. (2014). Unpacking grit: Motivational correlates of perseverance and passion for long-term goals. *The Journal of Positive Psychology, 9*(4), 306–312. https://doi.org/10.1080/17439760.2014.89832.

Wellbeingstudy.com (2019). http://www.wellbeingstudy.com/.

Wolters, C., & Hussain, M. (2015). Investigating grit and its relations with college students' self-regulated learning and academic achievement. *Metacognition and Learning, 10*(3), 293–311. https://doi.org/10.1007/s11409-014-9128-9.

Dr. Buaphrao Raphiphatthana completed her PhD in Positive Psychology, under the supervision of Professor Paul Jose, at Victoria University of Wellington, receiving her degree in 2018. In her thesis, she examined the relationship between mindfulness and grit across different cultures. In addition to her research interest in positive psychology, Dr. Raphiphatthana is also interested in researching ways to enhance mental health and well-being. She is currently a research fellow at Menzies School of Health Research, Darwin, Australia, as part of the mental health team, examining the role of e-mental health in addressing mental health concerns in community members.

Paul Jose teaches and conducts research at Victoria University of Wellington, New Zealand. He obtained his PhD in developmental psychology at Yale University in 1980, and has a long-standing research interest in maladaptive emotion regulation strategies in adolescents and young adults, particularly the use of rumination by anxious and depressed individuals. In the last decade, however, he has begun to examine adaptive emotion regulation strategies such as savoring, mindfulness, and hope. The construct of grit seems to be an adaptive strategy as well, and the work reported here considers how it should be positioned between the opposing poles of adaptive and maladaptive emotion regulation strategies. Prof Jose also seeks to examine these relationships with advanced statistical methods such as longitudinal path models in structural equation modelling.

Chapter 11
Can the Components of Grit Predict the Long-Term Educational Outcomes?

Yulia Tyumeneva, Yulia Kuzmina, and Tatiana Chirkina

Abstract Grit is widely considered a trait composed of perseverance of effort (PE) and consistency of long-term interests (CI) that is positively associated with educational and professional attainments. However, because of unclear relations between the two elements that compose grit, PE and CI, the theoretical model of the construct of grit is still questionable. On the one hand, we have extensive evidence that the overall score for grit can predict important life outcomes. On the other hand, predictive ability does not necessarily indicate that a measure reflects a unitary psychological trait. In the case of the Grit scale, a number of works have shown that treating grit as a whole or higher-order construct is psychometrically and psychologically unsound. In this work, we aimed to explore the relationship of PE and CI with long-term educational outcomes in desired educational trajectories while controlling for potentially confounding factors. We hypothesized that if PE and CI are facets of a unified grit construct, we would find consistent patterns in these facets for a range of educational outcomes. Our study was conducted on a large sample of students (N = 3110) from a national longitudinal study of school and university graduates. These students were also participants in both the TIMSS-2011 and PISA-2012 studies. When the students were in ninth grade, we assessed their grit, academic achievement, and educational aspiration. The next year, we obtained information about the choices students made after completing compulsory education: staying in high school vs. obtaining vocational training. Two years later, we again assessed the students' educational and life outcomes. We run two regression models. The first model was a model with PE and CI as predictors only. In the second model, SES, gender, cognitive ability scores and educational aspirations were added as covariates. To test the mediation hypotheses, we also run regression

Y. Tyumeneva (✉) · T. Chirkina
National Research University Higher School of Economics, Moscow, Russia
e-mail: jtiumeneva@hse.ru

Y. Kuzmina
National Research University Higher School of Economics, Moscow, Russia

Psychological Institute of Russian Academy of Education, Moscow, Russia

L. E. van Zyl et al. (eds.), *Multidisciplinary Perspectives on Grit*,
https://doi.org/10.1007/978-3-030-57389-8_11

models for possible mediators (educational aspirations and achievement) as outcomes. The results showed that perseverance was a better predictor than interests, although the effects of perseverance on long-term educational outcomes were more often indirect. Consistency of interests did not predict educational trajectories or achievement. Accordingly, we failed to find any consistent patterns in perseverance and interests with long-term educational outcomes. These findings are discussed in terms of the nature of the grit construct and the validity of the Grit scale. We conclude that grit, as a unique trait conjoining perseverance and stability (or consistency) of interests, rather failed to manifest itself. The findings so far reflect that it is only perseverance that matters. The consistency of interests construct looks very promising for the future research, but for now it is too ill-defined and cannot be properly measured.

Keywords Grit · Perseverance · Consistency of interests · Long-term educational outcomes · Construct validity

11.1 Introduction

A range of personality traits involving perseverance, tenacity, firmness, and willpower, is widely believed to impact the successful attainment of established goals. Empirical research has generally supported these expectations and shown that these goal-oriented traits help people resist failure, overcome drawbacks, address stressful and discouraging situations, and ultimately reach their aims (Hough, 1992; McClelland, 1961; Mega, Ronconi, & De Beni, 2014; Muenks, Yang, & Wigfield, 2018). According to this line of research, many appropriate psychometric instruments have been developed, including the Tenacity Scale (Baum & Locke, 2004), the Motivational Persistence Scale (Constantin, Holman, & Hojbotă, 2011), the Scale for Measuring Persistence (Lufi & Cohen, 1987) and others.

Some time ago, a new scale was proposed: the Grit scale (Duckworth, Peterson, Matthews, & Kelly, 2007). This scale differs from other measures of this repertoire in that in addition to perseverance, the scale contains a subscale to measure long-term interests. Thus, the theoretical model underlying the Grit scale assumes that there is a psychological construct, grit, which is two-faceted and consists of the perseverance of effort dimension (PE) and the consistency of long-term interest dimension (CI). The Grit scale has become a popular measure in research in a wide range of domains, from educational to clinical psychology. In most previous studies, researchers have constructed the overall grit score by summing the scores of the PE and CI subscales (as proposed by the Grit scale developers). The "grit construct" has been used to explain various life outcomes, and it could really predict some important ones, such as educational attainment, academic and sport careers, the completion of various training programmes (Duckworth et al., 2007), retention in the military, workplace, school, and marriage (Eskreis-Winkler, Shulman, Beal, & Duckworth, 2014), teachers' efficiency (Duckworth et al., 2009; Robertson-

Kraft & Duckworth, 2014), well-being in the domain of general surgery (Salles, Cohen, & Mueller, 2014) and job satisfaction among doctors (Reed, Schmitz, Baker, Nukui, & Epperly, 2012). These results have led to the acceptance of the two-faceted grit construct. In other words, the overall grit score has been explicitly interpreted as if grit was a substantive psychological trait that allows people to achieve their goals.

However, despite the wide adoption of this scoring and interpretation of grit, there is still little basis for this construct. To ascertain that grit is a unitary psychological trait that produces scores for the facets of grit, it is necessary to confirm at least that the structure of the test scores fits the theoretical model of this trait and that there are consistent associations with other psychological traits and behavioural outcomes predicted by the model. Unfortunately, in the case of the Grit scale, a number of works have shown that these expectations are not met. In the next section we consider them in detail.

11.2 Does the Grit Scale Structure Fit the Theoretical Model of Grit?

Originally, the developers of the Grit scale proposed that there are individuals who approach "achievement as a marathon; his or her advantage is stamina". They referred to some early biographical research (Galton, 1892; Cox, 1926; Terman & Oden, 1947) as a source for the idea that "ability combined with zeal and with capacity for hard labour" predict lifetime achievement, as well as to more recent research on traits influencing success. The scale developers generated a pool of items based on their interviews with professionals (lawyers, businesspeople, academics, etc.) describing "the attitudes and behaviours characteristic of the high-achieving individuals" (Duckworth et al., 2007, p. 1090). Importantly, however, that the authors also added some other items focusing on consistency of interests rather than on characteristics of high achievers. They did this to identify the people who "sustain effort not because of subjective interest but rather because they are afraid of change, compliant with the expectations of others, or unaware of options" (Duckworth et al., 2007, p. 1090). Thus, they collected items laden with two different ideas: one was about "high achieving people", the other was about "people with constant interests". Factor analysis elicited the two-dimensional structure of their item pool. As their approach was theory-free, the authors interpreted this quite straightforwardly, as a structure of a personal trait: grit, as they called it. However, even if their interpretation was right, there might be an alternative one: these two dimensions could reflect two different personal characteristics: perseverance and consistency of interests. And even though both characteristics are thought to facilitate success, they can still be different traits.

So, these two dimensions were independent "by birth". To obtain a multidimensional factor structure of a scale which combines descriptions of different traits is by no means to measure a new trait. It might be, but not necessarily, and it should have been kept as a hypothesis. The question is whether we have enough evidence to talk about grit as a certain personal trait, as the developers argue, or whether we talk about grit as a label for the beneficial composition of perseverance and long-lasting interests. After the first publication a large number of studies have reported the same two-factor structure as the developers found initially (Abuhassàn & Bates, 2015; Arco-Tirado, Fernández-Martín, & Hoyle, 2018; Datu, Valdez, & King, 2015; Li et al., 2018; Schmidt, Fleckenstein, Retelsdorf, Eskreis-Winkler, & Möller, 2017; Tedesqui & Young, 2017; Zhong et al., 2018). Moreover, in some studies, the single factor structure fitted data better than the two-factor one, after controlling for highly similar items (Arco-Tirado et al., 2018; Gonzalez, Canning, Smyth, & MacKinnon, 2019). Interestingly, however, the studies on two-factor structure reported correlations between PE and CI in the range from 0.16. (Datu et al., 2015) to 0.45 (Duckworth et al., 2007), which was not strong enough to conclude that these two factors present a substantial general dimension (Credé, Tynan, & Harms, 2016).

At the same time, some studies exploring the dimensionality of the Grit scale with IRT modelling showed that PE and CI present independent dimensions rather than a unidimensional scale (e.g., Tyumeneva, Kardanova, & Kuzmina, 2019), while others did not find a clear factor structure at all, especially, in relation to CI dimensionality (Credé, 2019; Hatchimonji, 2016; Jachimowicz, Wihler, Bailey, & Galinsky, 2019; Sheehan, 2014). Apart from this, findings have not distinguished the grit structure from other personality measures, such as self-control (Vazsonyi et al., 2019). All in all, results on the Grit scale structure are rather mixed and, taken together, cast doubt on the concept of grit as a unitary trait.

11.3 Do the Grit Scale Facets Form Consistent Patterns with Other Traits and Behaviours?

Regarding the associations of grit with other psychological traits, a few criterion-related studies have explored patterns in which PE and CI combine with other constructs or behaviours. If certain facets or dimensions underlie the same psychological construct, they are expected to predict similar outcomes; otherwise, there is no reason to treat these dimensions as belonging to a unitary construct. For example, to show that math anxiety is a one–dimensional trait with two facets (math learning anxiety and math evaluation anxiety), the bi-factorial structure of the scale was confirmed, and the consistency of the patterns formed by these two facets in addition to mathematical achievement, motivation for learning math, age and gender was demonstrated (Sadiković, Milovanović, & Oljača, 2018). In this sense, the two facets of grit seem to exist independently.

Indeed, empirical results have shown that PE and CI are not conjoined intrinsically but rather are independent constructs. In the educational domain, a systematic review of 29 studies on the role of grit in education (Christopoulou, Lakioti,

Pezirkianidis, Karakasidou, & Stalikas, 2018) concluded that these two facets of grit play different roles, with perseverance being a stronger positive predictor of many academic achievements. A number of other works have found that PE is a consistent predictor of a range of educational outcomes, such as academic engagement and well-being (Datu et al., 2015); academic achievement (Bowman, Hill, Denson, & Bronkema, 2015; Chang, 2014; Hatchimonji, 2016; Rimfeld, Kovas, Dale, & Plomin, 2016; Wolters & Hussain, 2014), self-regulated learning (Wolters & Hussain, 2014), academic adjustment, college satisfaction, sense of belonging and faculty-student interactions (Bowman et al., 2015). However, CI is not.

In addition to the education domain, PE and CI have been associated with distinct life outcomes and behaviours. For example, PE, but not CI, predicted subjective well-being (Datu et al., 2015) and problem-solving capacity (Kalia, Fuesting, & Cody, 2019). CI and PE also showed diverse patterns of correlations with certain personal traits (Weston, 2014) and physical activities (Hein, Kalajas-Tilga, Koka, Raudsepp, & Tilga, 2019). Even at the psycho-physiological and neurological levels, PE and CI manifested themselves independently (Kalia, Thomas, Osowski, & Drew, 2018; Silvia, Eddington, Beaty, Nusbaum, & Kwapil, 2013; Wohleber, Matthews, Reinerman-Jones, Panganiban, & Scribner, 2015).

In summary, an increasing body of studies has repeatedly indicated that PE and CI factors form inconsistent nomological networks; they predict life outcomes differently and are associated with different behaviours. Indeed, the substantial independence of the two factors of PE and CI can be easily grasped. We could reasonably imagine a person who is quite persistent for short periods of time but then is keen on doing something in a different domain (a high PE and low CI person). The opposite pattern is also possible, in which a person can have long-lasting interests in some domains but avoid pursuing any demanding goals. In both cases, PE and CI should be treated as different constructs that can be combined in a number of different ways, like any other personal traits.

11.4 Where to Look for the Effects of Grit?

These facets of grit may work consistently as a unitary trait only in specific situations. In what situations could we look for grit? Grit has been conceptualized as the pursuit of **long-term goals;** therefore, consistency between the two facets might be found only from a **long-term** perspective and only when **personal goals** are pursued.

Surprisingly, the correspondence of research designs to the theoretical model of grit has not been discussed in previous literature. The vast majority of studies on the predictive ability of perseverance and consistency of interests have implemented cross-sectional designs that are inappropriate for exploring long-term effects. We found only three longitudinal studies involving grit as a predictor. Two of them addressed the short-term (3 and 4 months) effects of grit as a whole construct and did not provide data on the PE and CI facets separately (O'Neal, Goldthrite, Weston

Riley, & Atapattu, 2018; Saunders-Scott, Braley, & Stennes-Spidahl, 2018). The third study is of greater interest to us because the authors explored the separate effects of perseverance and stable interests in a large sample of 6th–9th graders (Tang, Wang, Guo, and Salmela-Aro, 2019). Their results showed that only the PE facet of grit measured in the 8th grade predicted educational outcomes measured in the 9th grade (specifically, school achievement and learning involvement). It seems that the facets of grit are inconsistent from a long-term perspective.

Certainly, the results of a single study are not sufficient to make conclusions about patterns of perseverance and interest with long-term outcomes, especially because the latter study seems to omit another crucial feature of grit: both perseverance and interests are supposed to affect outcomes that were desired and planned by a person. Obviously, there is little point in searching for their effects outside the domain of personal interests. In this sense, most criterion-related studies, including the study by Tang et al. (2019), do not and cannot find real effects of perseverance and stable interests on outcomes because they have not constrained the range of outcomes to be planned or desired by participants.

Thus, the school achievements of the 8- to 12-year-old children in the study by Tang et al. (2019) are probably not an appropriate domain to explore the effects of grit, particularly because of its CI component. Interests (that are more or less stable) may appear in domains that are irrelevant to school learning. For example, interests in music, arts, sport, or IT may have little in common with school learning, and in this case, school achievements cannot reflect any of these interests. On the other hand, perseverance (the PE component of grit) is required to move along an educational trajectory without grade repetition and dropping out. We believe this may be why the researchers found effects of PE, but not CI, on school achievements.

We assume that to assess the effects of both PE and CI properly, we must focus only on the long-term activities people consider personally desirable instead of those they are obliged to do. Because the existing literature has completely overlooked these constraints, it remains unclear what patterns of relations PE and CI form with long-term outcomes. If these two facets affect long-term and planned outcomes in a consistent manner, they can be considered to underlie the same psychological construct. Otherwise, there is no reason to treat PE and CI as facets of a substantial single construct. In the last case, treating grit as a substantive construct is rather pointless.

Departing from previous studies, we examine whether the two facets, perseverance of effort and consistency, can predict outcomes that are in line with the theory behind grit. Specifically, we focus only on outcomes that are long-term that lie in the domain of individuals' interests. We claim that if perseverance and consistency of interests can be found to be facets of the unitary concept of grit, they should involve only activities that are both long-term and planned by individuals. Another discrepancy between our approach to grit and many other studies is that we take the facets of grit—perseverance of effort and consistency of interests—as separate and independent personal traits without a higher-order trait such as grit. In this approach, we rely on results from a large number of previous studies that failed to confirm a higher-order structure of grit, its one-dimensionality or consistency between criterion-related patterns of PE and CI (Bowman et al., 2015; Credé et al., 2016; Tyumeneva et al., 2019).

11.5 Current Study

In this study, we used data from a national longitudinal study of educational trajectories of school and university leavers (https://trec.hse.ru/en/). PE and CI (as separate facets of grit) were measured with the long version of the Grit scale, when the participants were in 9th grade (the last year of compulsory education in the Russian Federation) along with other characteristics of the participants, such as their cognitive abilities, educational achievement and aspirations, as well as socio-economic status. Every second year, the participants were surveyed about their educational outcomes, among which factual educational trajectories and academic achievement were of particular interest to the current study.

Trajectories Students can take several educational trajectories (Fig. 11.1). In Russia, basic (or lower) secondary education consists of Grades 5–9 (this is compulsory education), while upper secondary education covers Grades 10–11. Alternatively, after finishing basic education (Grade 9), students can choose to attend vocational school, where they study both general education subjects (equivalent to Grades 10–11, but at a basic level) as well as vocational education subjects and training. This is the first fork in students' educational trajectories. For those who remain in general secondary school, standardized national exams, known as the

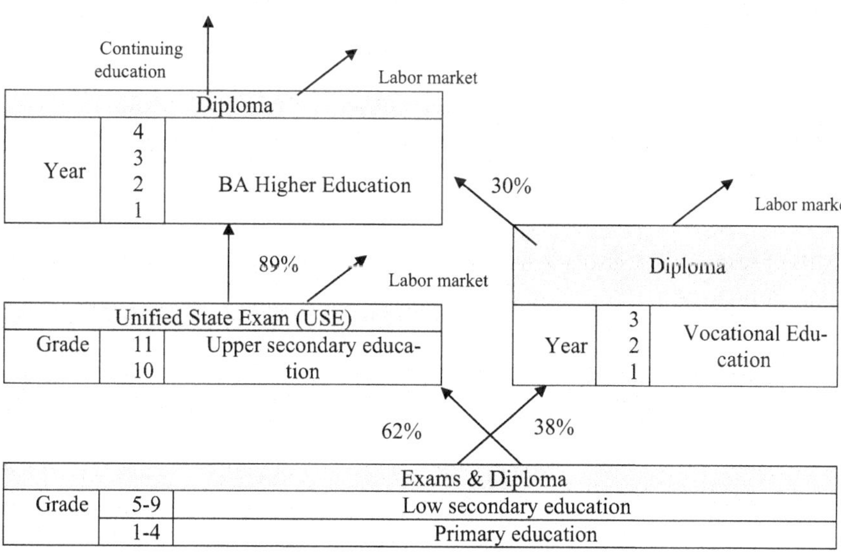

Fig. 11.1 The educational levels and tracks in Russian Federation. *Note.* Even at the psycho-physiological and neurological levels, PE and CI manifested themselves independently

Unified State Examinations (USE), must be taken after Grade 11. The USE combines the general secondary education graduate examinations with higher education entrance examinations; therefore, the USE scores have high priority for students planning to enter university, especially for entrance to some selective universities. Alternatively, after finishing general school (Grade 11), students can choose to obtain vocational training or to start work. This is the second fork in students' educational trajectories.

Another less direct way to enter university is to leave low-secondary school after Grade 9, obtain 3-year-vocational training, and enter university without the USE because, by the federal Law on Education, the USE is not required after the completion of vocational training. This is the main reason why less academically successful pupils take this path to enter university. We expect that the facets of grit play a role in the choice between the direct way to university through the demanding USE and the longer but less demanding vocational training.

Presuming that perseverance and consistency of interest are required to graduate university, we expected that these traits would be associated with aspirations for university and would predict graduation. Accordingly, in terms of educational trajectories, we could expect that perseverance and consistency of interest are predictors of staying in general school after Grade 9, entering university (especially selective universities), and the absence of dropping out until the fourth year of university (i.e., bachelor's level).

Achievements Academic achievements were measured as important outcomes that are affected by students' perseverance and consistency of interests based on USE results measured after Grade 11, as well as academic achievements in university.

Some student characteristics, such as educational aspirations, cognitive abilities and socio-economic status, were measured either as controlling variables or as mediators of the effects of perseverance and consistency of interest.

Overall, this design allowed us to assess whether PE and CI can predict long-term outcomes in desired educational trajectories while controlling for potentially confounding factors.

11.6 Method

11.6.1 Sample

A total of 3110 students (51% were girls, and the mean age was 15.90, SD = 0.49) in Grade 9 answered questions from the Russian version of the Grit scale. Due to the attrition of the sample, a smaller number of students participated in subsequent waves. The number of participants, their demographic characteristics and the measures applied in each wave are presented in Table 11.1. Because this sample was based on the sample of students participating in the PISA survey (the Program of

Table 11.1 Cohort characteristics and measures applied in each wave

Year	Sample size	Level of education	Grade level	Mean age (SD)	Proportion of girls	Measures
2012	3110	Secondary education	9	15.90 (0.49)	51%	The grit scale Educational aspiration Cognitive abilities SES index[a]
2013	3011	Higher education/vocational school	10 grade or 1-year vocational school	16.85 (0.48)	57%	Educational trajectories
2014	1503	High education/vocational school	11 grade or 2-year vocational school	17.85 (0.48)	59%	Educational aspiration USE
2015	1399	University	Sophomores/second year of BA	18.86 (0.47)	58%	Educational trajectories Selectivity
2017	1222	University	Seniors /fourth year of BA	20.86 (0.47)	59%	Academic achievement

[a]Socio-economic index is based on the PISA 2012 survey (OECD, 2013)

International Student Assessment) in 2012 (OECD, 2013), we were able to implement some indicators derived in PISA in our study.

11.7 Predictor Measures

11.7.1 Consistency of Interest and Perseverance of Effort

A previous study of the 12-item grit scale conducted on a Russian sample (Tyumeneva et al., 2019) revealed that the PE and CI subscales reflect related but independent constructs rather than one integrated trait. Accordingly, we used the scores on these subscales as two distinct variables.

The scores on each scale were calculated as the sum of weighted item scores. The weight was obtained for each item as a standardized factor loading for the item on the relevant latent variable from confirmatory factor analysis:

$$CI = CI1 * L1 + CI2 + L2 + CI3 * L3 + CI4 * L4 + CI5 * L5 + CI6 * L6 + CI7 * L7$$

$$PE = PE1 * L1 + PE2 * L2 + PE3 * L3 + PE4 * L4 + PE5 * L5.$$

The model in which PE was represented by five items and CI was represented by seven items had appropriate GOF indices ($\chi^2 = 463.5$, df $= 53$, RMSEA $= 0.06$

(90% CI 0.055–0.065), CFI = 0.92, SRMR = 0.055). Standardized factor loadings are shown in Appendix 1.

11.8 Outcome Measures

11.8.1 Educational Trajectories

Educational trajectories were measured after the end of basic school in Grade 10 or at the first year of vocational school (staying in general school vs. leaving for vocational training); and after the end of general secondary education (entering university vs. going to vocational training or the labour market); and retaining vs. dropping out during the fourth year of university.

In addition, we took into account whether a student entered university via general school and passing the USE or, alternatively, by bypassing the USE through vocational training. We also considered whether a student entered a selective vs. a non-selective university (Dobryakova & Kuzminov, 2016).

11.8.2 Academic Achievement

USE scores. The first indicator of academic achievement was the USE scores achieved by the participants and reported 2 months after they had taken the USE. The USE scores are standardized on a 0–100 point scale with mean = 60 and SD = 13.65.

University Academic Achievements The second indicator of academic achievement was the students' marks in university. Fourth-year university students were asked to report their academic achievement by selecting one of two options. A binary variable was created: the value "1" corresponded to the option when the student had only excellent or good marks, and the value "0" corresponded to the option when students had satisfactory marks and consistently or occasionally unsatisfactory marks.

11.9 Covariates

We used several variables as covariates.

Gender and SES In each model, we added the "gender" variable (0—boy, 1—girl) and socioeconomic status (SES) as covariates. Socioeconomic status is a complex index that is derived in PISA based on information about students' families: parents' education, the number of books at home and the index of home possession (OECD, 2013).

Cognitive Abilities Based on previous findings about the very high proportion of shared dispersion between PISA cognitive test scores and measures of general cognitive abilities, we also used PISA scores as an indicator of general cognitive abilities (Meisenberg & Woodley, 2013; Rindermann, 2007). To obtain a "general" cognitive ability measure, all available subject scores (reading, mathematics and science) were combined using factor analysis, and a general latent factor was created. Weighted individual scores were then derived.

Educational Aspirations Educational aspirations were measured in Grade 9 and Grade 11. Students were asked about the level of education they expected to achieve in the future. A binary variable was created: 1—higher education, 0—lower level. The reason for using aspirations as covariates (and as mediators) was their potentially mediating role between the facets of grit on the one hand and outcomes on the other. Specifically, students with higher perseverance and more consistent interests may have higher educational aspirations, and aspirations rather than perseverance or interests may affect educational outcomes.

USE Scores For university outcomes, we used USE scores as mediators between the facets of grit on the one hand and outcomes on the other. Specifically, students with higher perseverance and more consistent interests may have higher USE scores, and these USE scores, rather than perseverance and interests, may have affected educational outcomes.

11.10 Statistical Approach

For each outcome, we ran two regression models. The first model was a model with PE and CI as predictors only. In the second model, SES, gender, cognitive ability scores and educational aspirations were added as covariates.

To test the mediation hypotheses, we also ran regression models for possible mediators as outcomes. The possible mediators were educational aspirations in Grade 9 and Grade 11 and USE scores. The indirect effects were calculated as a product of the coefficients of PE or CI from the model where the mediators were dependent variables and the coefficients of corresponding mediators were from models with relevant outcomes. Before all continuous variables were included in the analyses, they were transformed into Z-scores. The analysis was performed using the Stata 15.0 package (StataCorp, 2017).

11.11 Results

All descriptive statistics on the predictor and outcome variables are presented in Appendix 2.

11.11.1 How PE and CI Predict Educational Trajectories after Grade 9

After the end of basic school (Grade 9), students might continue education in general schools or transfer to vocational schools. We conducted a logistic regression analysis to estimate to what extent CI and PE were associated with an increasing probability of continuing education in general school adjusted for educational aspirations, SES, cognitive abilities and gender (Table 11.2).

After the end of basic school (Grade 9), students might continue education in general schools or transfer to vocational schools. We conducted a logistic regression analysis to estimate to what extent CI and PE were associated with an increasing probability of continuing education in general school adjusted for educational aspirations, SES, cognitive abilities and gender (Table 11.2).

Our analysis revealed that the probability of continuing education in general school was positively associated with the level of PE and CI, however, these associations became non-significant when controlling for educational aspirations. Taking into account cognitive abilities, SES, gender and educational aspiration, the predicted probability to continue education in general school did not significantly vary for pupils with different level of PE or CI.

11.11.2 How PE and CI Predict Educational Trajectories after the End of Secondary Education (AFTER Grade 11 in General School)

After Grade 11, students may enter universities or go to vocational schools. We estimated whether high levels of PE and CI were associated with a higher probability of university entry while controlling for students' SES, USE scores, educational aspirations, cognitive abilities and gender (Table 11.3).

Table 11.2 Results of logistic regression analysis for educational track after Grade 9

Variables	(1) Odds Ratio (s.e.)	(2) Odds Ratio (s.e.)
Perseverance of effort (in Z-scores)	1.21***(0.06)	1.06 (0.06)
Consistency of interest (in Z-scores)	1.15**(0.05)	1.10(0.06)
Educational aspirations at grade 9 (1 = higher education)		3.98*** (0.56)
Cognitive abilities		2.34*** (0.18)
SES (in Z-scores)		1.52*** (0.18)
Female		1.22 (0.15)
Constant		0.64*** (0.09)
N	3011	3011

***$p < .001$, **$p < .01$

Table 11.3 Results of logistic regression analysis for educational track after Grade 11

Variables	(1)	(2) Odds Ratio (s.e.)
Perseverance of effort (in Z-scores)	1.14 (0.16)	0.96 (0.14)
Consistency of interest (in Z-scores)	1.17 (0. 13)	1.07 (0.15)
Educational aspirations at grade 11 (1 = higher education)		4.69***(1.25)
Cognitive abilities		1.56* (0.30)
USE scores (in Z-scores)		3.46*** (0.57)
SES (in Z-scores)		2.03*** (0.39)
Female		0.61* (0.12)
Constant		4.34*** (1.30)
N	1399	1399

***$p < .001$, *$p < .05$

Table 11.4 Results of logistic regression analysis for entrance into selective universities after Grade 11

Variables	(1)	(2) Odds Ratio (s.e.)
Perseverance of effort (in Z-scores)	1.17*(0.08)	1.04 (0.09)
Consistency of interest (in Z-scores)	0.93(0.08)	0.95 (0.10)
Educational aspirations at grade 11 (1 = higher education)		0.94 (0.34)
Cognitive abilities		1.70*** (0.21)
USE scores (in Z-scores)		1.72*** (0.18)
SES (in Z-scores)		1.77** (0.33)
Female		1.83** (0.32)
Constant		0.13*** (0.05)
N	1276	1276

***$p < .001$, **$p < .01$, *$p < .05$

Our analysis revealed that PE and CI were not associated with the probability of university entry in either model with or without covariates.

We also estimated whether PE or CI predicted the probability to be accepted into a selective university (in comparison with a non-selective university) (Table 11.4).

The analysis demonstrated that PE was positively associated with the probability of entering selective universities, although this effect became non-significant after covariates were controlled. CI did not predict the probability of entering selective universities.

In addition, we checked whether PE and CI affected the probability to enter into universities for students who leaved general school after Grade 9 and finished vocational school (Table 11.5).

The results showed that both PE and CI did not associate with probability to enter into university after vocational school.

Table 11.5 Results of logistic regression analysis for university entry after vocational school

Variables	(1) Odds Ratio (s.e.)	(2) Odds Ratio (s.e.)
Perseverance of effort (in Z-scores)	1.09 (0.09)	1.05 (0.09)
Consistency of interest (in Z-scores)	0.88(0.07)	0.92 (0.10)
Educational aspirations at grade 9 (1 = higher education)		1.62 (0.41)
Cognitive abilities		1.55*** (0.18)
SES (in Z-scores)		2.67*** (0.44)
Female		1.61* (0.31)
Constant	0.37***(0.04)	0.24*** (0.05)
N	844	844

***$p < .001$, **$p < .01$, *$p < .05$

Table 11.6 Predicted probability of various educational tracks for pupils with different level of PE or CI (adjusted for educational aspirations, cognitive abilities, SES and gender)

	Predicted probability [95% CI]			
	Level of PE		Level of CI	
Educational track	Low (– 1 SD)	High (+1 SD)	Low (– 1 SD)	High (+1 SD)
Continuation of education in general school after grade 9	.59 [.55; .62]	.61 [.57; .64]	.58 [.55; .61]	.61 [.58; .64]
Entering into university after grade 11	.88 [.82; .91]	.87 [.84; .90]	.87 [.84; .89]	.88 [.84; .91]
Entering into selective university after grade 11	.25 [.20; .29]	.26 [.22; 30]	.26 [.21; .31]	.24 [.20; .29]
Entering into university after vocational school	.27 [.23; .30]	.28 [.23; .33]	.28 [.24; .33]	.26 [.20; .31]

In addition, for each outcome the predicted probability to success was calculated regarding to level of PE or CI (Table 11.6).

11.11.3 How PE and CI Predict Academic Achievement for Students in General School

We ran a regression analysis for USE scores as a dependent variable to estimate the extent to which PE and CI predicted academic achievement in high school. The results are presented in Table 11.7.

The results of the analysis revealed that PE was positively associated with USE scores; this effect remained significant even when controlling for SES, gender, educational aspirations and cognitive abilities. CI did not significantly correlate with USE scores.

Table 11.7 Results of regression analysis for USE scores (in Z–sores) as dependent variable

Variables	(1) B (s.e.)	(2) B (s.e.)
Perseverance of effort (in Z-scores)	0.10**(.03)	0.05* (.03)
Consistency of interest (in Z-scores)	−0.00(0.02)	−0.00 (0.02)
Educational aspirations at grade 1 (1 = higher education)		0.24***(0.09)
Cognitive abilities		0.59*** (0.03)
SES (in Z-scores)		0.24*** (0.05)
Female		0.16***(0.05)
Constant		−0.64*** (0.03)
N	1503	1503

***$p < .001$, **$p < .01$, *$p < .05$

Table 11.8 Results of logistic regression analysis for academic achievement in universities

Variables	(1)	(2) Odds Ratio (s.e.)
Perseverance of effort (in Z-scores)	1.20**(0.08)	1.15 (0.09)
Consistency of interest (in Z-scores)	1.02(0.072)	1.09 (0.08)
Cognitive abilities		1.03 (0.10)
USE scores (in Z-scores)		1.50*** (0.13)
SES (in Z-scores)		0.76* (0.10)
Female		2.17*** (0.26)
Constant		0.77* (0.10)
N	1222	1222

***$p < .001$, **$p < .01$, *$p < .05$

11.11.4 How PE and CI Predict Academic Achievement in Universities

We estimated to what extent PE and CI predicted academic achievement in universities while controlling for SES, gender and cognitive abilities. The results are presented in Table 11.8.

Our analysis revealed that PE is positively associated with the probability of having only excellent or good marks at universities, even when the covariates were controlled. CI had no effect on academic achievement at universities. The probability to have an excellent marks at university was 0.52 (95% CI, 0.47–0.56) for students with low level of PE (− 1 SD) and 0.58 (95% CI, 0.53–0.63) for pupils with high level of PE (+1 SD). For pupils with low level of CI the probability to have excellent and good marks was 0.53 (95% CI, 0.48–0.58) while for pupils with high level of CI it was 0.57 (95% CI, 0.52–0.61).

11.12 Mediation Analyses

Because the effects of the facets of grit on educational outcomes were often diminished after controlling for USE scores and educational aspirations, we explored in detail the paths transferring these effects. We hypothesized that educational aspirations and academic achievement measured in school might mediate the effects of PE and CI. We ran mediation analyses to test this hypothesis.

At the first step of the mediation analysis, the effects of CI and PE on possible mediators were assessed (Table 11.9).

The analysis revealed that CI (in Grade 9) was positively associated with educational aspirations measured in Grade 9 and Grade 11, while PE was positively associated with educational aspirations measured in Grade 9 as well as with USE scores.

In the next step, the direct effects of PE and CI and the effects of mediators (aspirations and USE scores) on educational outcomes were estimated (Figs. 11.2 and 11.3). As can be seen, that neither PE nor CI had a direct effect on educational trajectories after Grade 9.

Table 11.9 The effects of CI and PE on possible mediators

Variables	Mediators Educational aspiration at Grade 9	 Educational aspirations at Grade 11	 USE scores
	Log odds (s.e.)	Log odds (s.e.)	B (s.e.)
Consistency of interest	0.25*** (0.04)	0.20* (0.10)	0.04 (0.03)
Perseverance of effort	0.39*** (0.04)	0.22 (0.12)	0.13*** (0.03)
N	3011	1412	1399

***p < .001, *p < .05

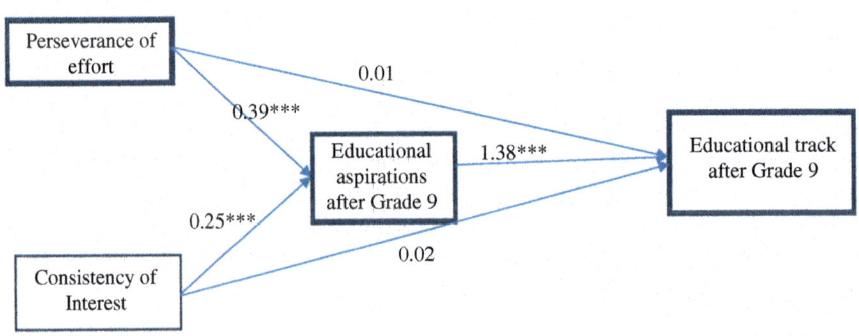

Fig. 11.2 Direct effects of PE and CI on educational trajectories after Grade 9 (log odds). *** *p < .001*

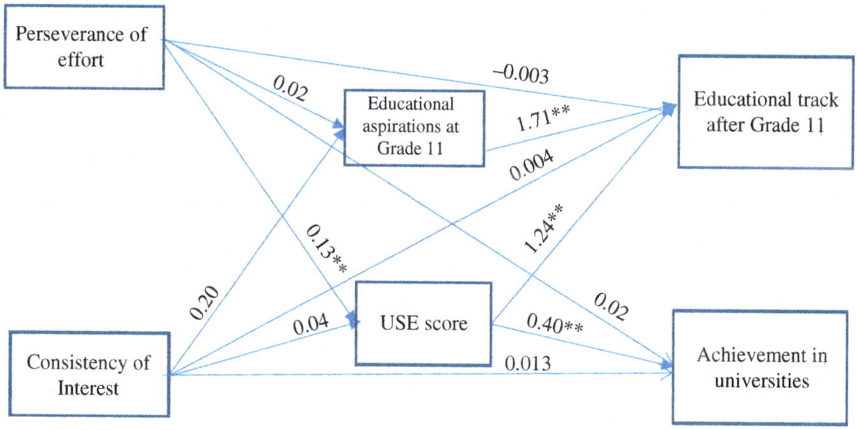

Fig. 11.3 Direct of PE and CI on educational trajectories after Grade 11 (log odds). *** *p < .001*, ***p < .01*

Next, the indirect effects of PE and CI were calculated as a product of the coefficients of PE or CI from the model in which the mediators were the dependent variable and the coefficients of corresponding mediators from models with different outcomes. In Table 11.10 we show direct, indirect and total effects of PE and CI on educational trajectories after Grade 9 via educational aspirations at Grade 9, and on educational trajectories after Grade 11 via educational aspirations and USE scores at Grade 11 (log odds), as well as on educational achievement in universities via USE scores.

The results indicated that PE and CI had only indirect effects, via educational aspirations in Grade 9, on trajectories after Grade 9. Students with higher PE or CI had a higher probability of having higher educational aspirations and, consequently, had a higher probability of continuing their education in general school.

Similarly, PE and CI had only indirect effects, via aspirations, on the trajectory after Grade 11. However, their direct and total effects were insignificant. The results also demonstrated that USE scores were another significant mediator, apart from aspirations, but only for PE. CI had neither direct nor indirect effects via the USE on educational trajectories after Grade 11.

Regarding PE and CI effects on educational achievement in university, as can be seen from Table 11.9, PE, but not CI, had significant indirect and total effects on academic grades in universities via USE scores, although the direct effect was not significant.

Table 11.10 Direct, indirect and total effects of PE and CI on educational trajectories after Grade 9 via educational aspirations at Grade 9, on Grade 11 via educational aspirations at Grade 11 and USE scores (log odds),on educational achievement in universities via USE scores

Predictors	Direct effect	Indirect effect	Total effect	Proportion of total effect mediated
	Log odds [95% CI]		Log odds (s.e.)	
	Trajectories after Grade 9			
	Via Educational aspirations at Grade 9th			
Consistency of interest (CI)	0.02 [−.001; 0.04]	0.013 [0.01; 0.02]	0.03 [0.01; 0.05]	0.43
Perseverance of effort (PE)	0.01 [−0.01; 0.03]	0.02 [0.01; 0.03]	0.03 [0.01; 0.05]	0.66
	Trajectories after Grade 11			
	Via Educational aspirations at Grade 11			
Consistency of interest (CI)	0.005 [−0.02; 0.03]	0.006 [0.002; 0.009]	0.01 [−0.01; 0.03]	0.38
Perseverance of effort (PE)	0.002 [−0.02; 0.03]	0.006 [0.002; 0.009]	0.009 [−0.02; 0.03]	0.37
	Via USE scores			
Consistency of interest (CI)	0.004 [−0.017; 0.02]	0.004 [−0.001; 0.001]	0.008 [−0.013; 0.027]	0.29
Perseverance of effort (PE)	−0.003 [−0.02; 0.02]	0.011 [0.006; 0.019]	0.008 [−0.01; 0.03]	0.78
	Educational achievement in universities			
	Via USE scores			
Consistency of interest (CI)	0.018 [−0.01; 0.05]	0.002 [−0.003; 0.008]	0.02 [−0.01; 0.05]	0.09
Perseverance of effort (PE)	0.03 [−0.000; 0.045]	0.01 [0.004; 0.019]	0.04 [0.01; 0.08]	0.26

11.13 Discussion

The aim of this study was to assess whether perseverance and consistency of interests can predict long-term outcomes in the desired educational trajectory while controlling for previous educational achievement, aspirations, cognitive abilities, SES and gender. The search for the effects of grit in desired and long-term activities was guided by the theoretical model underlying the Grit scale that specified grit as determination to achieve long-term goals. We hypothesized that if PE and CI are facets of a unified grit construct, we would find consistent patterns in these facets for a range of educational outcomes.

Generally, the results showed that perseverance was a better predictor than interests, although the effects of perseverance were more often indirect. Consistency of interests did not predict educational trajectories or achievement. Accordingly, we failed to find any consistent patterns in perseverance and interests with long-term educational outcomes. We discuss the results in detail.

First, perseverance measured at Grade 9 and with only five items (in the Russian version of Grit scale) could directly predict exam scores in general school and, indirectly, in university, that is, two and six(!) years after it was measured. We consider this fact to be a very promising indication of the predictive strength of goal-oriented and goal-pursuing traits. Indeed, our results are strictly in line with a number of previous findings about the impact of goal-pursuing traits on the successful attainment of established goals (Bowman et al., 2015; Chang, 2014; Rimfeld et al., 2016; Wolters & Hussain, 2014).

However, consistency of interests could not predict any educational achievements. This finding undermines the value of this subscale as part of the Grit scale. Additionally, the fact that perseverance and interests did not show consistent patterns with a range of educational achievements calls into question the existence of the grit construct.

Second, both perseverance and interests predicted trajectories after basic school via educational aspirations, although both measures did not have direct effects. This means that the higher students scored in perseverance and consistency of interests, the more ambition they had about a desired level of education, and this ambition was the main driver to pursue a specific trajectory (specifically, staying in general school vs. obtaining vocational training).

In line with this, there were findings about the roundabout strategy to enter university. In Russia, the most serious educational exam is the USE, which is the main path to enter university. The USE requires serious preparation, especially if a student aims to obtain the highest USE scores and enter a selective university. Staying in general school after ninth grade generally means that a student is going to take this path. A roundabout way to university is to leave general school after Grade 9 for vocational training and to enter university without passing the USE because the USE is not required after completing vocational training. This is the main reason why less academically successful students take this path to enter university. Accordingly, we expected that the facets of grit would play a role in the choice between a straightforward way to university through the demanding USE and a longer but less demanding vocational track. Although we found the expected effects of the facets of grit on the choice of a path to university, these effects were not significant when the covariates and mediators were controlled. Hence, the choice of a trajectory after basic school should be considered mainly in relation to SES and academic aspirations rather than the facets of grit.

Similarly, we did not find any direct effects of the facets of grit on entering university, even selective universities, although perseverance (but not interests) had an indirect effect through USE scores and other factors, such as SES and cognitive abilities.

Generally, the CI subscale showed a lack of predictive validity. This is consistent with previous findings on the weaker associations of CI with different outcomes in comparison with the PE subscale (Bowman et al., 2015; Datu et al., 2015; Tang et al., 2019). Why does consistency of interests fail to predict the choice of educational trajectories and achievements? First, we cannot explain the weak predictive validity of the CI subscale by the participants' young age because the stability of interests, when measured by profiles and rank-order correlations, remains unchanged during much of adolescence and increases significantly during the college years (Low, Yoon, Roberts, & Rounds, 2005). Thus, the problem may be due to how stability is measured, that is, from the content of the CI items. Most of the CI items include terms of time duration, such as "later", "more than a few months", and "a short time", but there is no single criterion for what these terms mean, and it is unknown how much their meaning differs from person to person. A similar problem is the distinction between "new" and "previous" interests. Thus, additional research is needed to understand what people have in mind when they approach this type of item and what improvements should be made to the CI measure.

Alternatively, taking into account that the stability of interests over time is crucial for any significant attainment, as rightly pointed out in the original paper on grit (Duckworth et al., 2009), we should think about capturing this construct more carefully, than just relying on such blurred terms as "different projects" and "often change goals". We suggest, first, defining an interest domain specification to judge the sameness of interests. For example, we could obtain some lists of interests based on the modern interest inventories (e.g. Holland, 1996; Nye & Rounds, 2019) or any other credible framework to identify current interests of respondents. Then, we could ask them to report about their interests on the same interest inventory in some arbitrary retrospect and, in that way, determine changes in interests over some period of time. Surely, this approach would involve much more consideration of the interests domain and an appropriate period of time to assess the stability of interests, than the current approach does. Not until we explore the nature of complex constructs can we measure them.

A more general concern should be raised from our results. Should we continue to think that there is such a psychological trait as the grit construct, or we should accept that there are two independent traits: perseverance and consistency (or stability) of interests? The answer depends on what the term "construct" means and, more specifically, which type of construct we mean when we discuss grit. If we treat grit as a single latent psychological reality that causes perseverance and consistency of interests, as psychologists prefer, the answer would be negative. A significant number of previous studies have failed to find unidimensionality and consistency between the patterns of PE and CI with respect to outcomes. This is also the case in the current results.

If, alternatively, we treat grit as a composite construct in which perseverance and consistency of interests are occasionally brought together and we call this happy combination "grit", the answer might be positive. Indeed, there are many other formative composites or formative constructs that can better account for social reality, such as a socio-economic status index, for example. Indeed, in some studies, there has been found better predictive validity for the "grit" composition than for perseverance alone, although this is also a debated issue (Credé, 2019; Guo et al., 2019; Jachimowicz et al., 2019).

An answer to the question of what we are talking about when we discuss grit is important both technically and theoretically. Technically, based on the answer, different statistical approaches should be applied to measure grit (for a deep discussion of the issue with understanding of the reflective and formative constructs, see Schmittmann et al., 2013). Additionally, before using the total grit score as a composite, it is necessary to justify why and how the total score should be built. Theoretically, answering the question about the nature of the grit construct involves answering the question about a piece of psychological reality, which, we believe, is a priority goal of psychology. Based on the previous findings as well as the current results, we can conclude that grit, as a unique trait conjoining perseverance and stability (or consistency) of interests, rather failed to manifest itself. The findings so far reflect that it is only perseverance that matters. Nevertheless, the consistency of interests construct looks very promising for the future research, but for now it is too ill-defined and cannot be properly measured. Hence, we would suggest seeking systems of traits which, when synergized with each other, can significantly improve our understanding of how a person can manage his or her own life.

Finally, we must note some limitations of our study. Although the study was conducted on a large sample, there was serious attrition of the sample over 6 years, particularly among some vocational students. This was the main reason why we analysed students from university trajectories and moved away from those who did not enter university. We are aware that this imbalance could bias our results, but with no information about the missing part of the sample, we cannot predict this bias. Another limitation may be due to the self-reported measures of student achievement. Although many researchers rely on college students to self-report their academic record, the accuracy of self-reports is not perfect and may involve over-report bias (Caskie, Sutton, & Eckhardt, 2014; Cole & Gonyea, 2010). This could also affect our results, although researchers generally agree that self-reported data are usually highly correlated with official records and can be used when the latter are not available.

Appendix

Table 11.11 Standardized factor loadings

Items	CI	PE
Without irony I am a hard worker		0.56
I have achieved a goal that took years of work		0.59
I have overcome setbacks to conquer an important challenge		0.59
I finish whatever I begin		0.72
At work I am diligent		0.73
I often set a goal but later choose to pursue a different one[a]	0.55	
New ideas and new projects sometimes distract me from previous ones[a]	0.41	
I become interested in new pursuits every few months[a]	0.36	
My interests change from year to year[a]	0.52	
I have been obsessed with a certain idea or project for a short time but later lost interest[a]	0.68	
I have difficulty maintaining my focus on projects that take more than a few months to complete[a]	0.44	
Setbacks discourage me[a]	0.49	

[a]This item's scores were reversed

Table 11.12 Descriptive statistics on predictive and outcome variables

Variable	Options	*N* (%)
Educational trajectories		
Track after Grade 9	Continue education in school	1948 (63%)
	Vocational school	1162 (37%)
Track after Grade 11	University	1325 (89%)
	Vocational school	168 (11%)
Selective universities	Entrance into selective universities	353 (25%)
	Non-selective universities	1015 (75%)
Educational aspirations		
Aspirations at Grade 9	Have plan to get a higher education	1850 (66%)
	Do not have plan to get a higher education	967 (34%)
Aspirations at Grade 11	Have plan to get a higher education	1676 (89%)
	Do not have plan to get a higher education	197 (11%)
Educational achievement in high school	USE scores (for general school graduates)	Mean = 59.19, SD = 13.65
Educational achievement in universities	Have only excellent or good marks	708 (54%)
	Have satisfactory or lower marks	594 (46%)

References

Abuhassàn, A., & Bates, T. C. (2015). Grit. *Journal of Individual Differences, 36*, 205–214.

Arco-Tirado, J. L., Fernández-Martín, F. D., & Hoyle, R. H. (2018). Development and validation of a Spanish version of the grit-S scale. *Frontiers in Psychology, 9*, 96.

Baum, J. R., & Locke, E. A. (2004). The relationship of entrepreneurial traits, skill, and motivation to subsequent venture growth. *The Journal of Applied Psychology, 89*, 587–598. https://doi.org/10.1037/0021-9010.89.4.587.

Bowman, N. A., Hill, P. L., Denson, N., & Bronkema, R. (2015). Keep on truckin' or stay the course? Exploring grit dimensions as differential predictors of educational achievement, satisfaction, and intentions. *Social Psychological and Personality Science, 6*, 639–645. https://doi.org/10.1177/1948550615574300.

Caskie, G. I., Sutton, M. C., & Eckhardt, A. G. (2014). Accuracy of self-reported college GPA: Gender-moderated differences by achievement level and academic self-efficacy. *Journal of College Student Development, 55*(4), 385–390.

Chang, W. (2014). *Grit and academic performance: Is being grittier better*? (Doctoral dissertation). Miami, FL: University of Miami.

Christopoulou, M., Lakioti, A., Pezirkianidis, C., Karakasidou, E., & Stalikas, A. (2018). The role of grit in education: A systematic review. *Psychology, 9*, 2951–2971. https://doi.org/10.4236/psych.2018.915171.

Cole, J. S., & Gonyea, R. M. (2010). Accuracy of self-reported SAT and ACT test scores: Implications for research. *Research in Higher Education, 51*(4), 305–319.

Constantin, T., Holman, A., & Hojbotă, M. A. (2011). Development and validation of a motivational persistence scale. *Psihologija, 45*(2), 99–120.

Cox, C. M. (1926). *Genetic studies of genius: Vol. 2. The early mental traits of three hundred geniuses*. Stanford, CA: Stanford University Press.

Credé, M. (2019). Total grit scale score does not represent perseverance. *Proceedings of the National Academy of Sciences, 116*(10), 3941–3941.

Credé, M., Tynan, M. C., & Harms, P. D. (2016). Much ado about grit: A meta-analytic synthesis of the grit literature. *Journal of Personality and Social Psychology, 113*, 492–511. https://doi.org/10.1037/pspp0000102.

Datu, J. A. D., Valdez, J. P. M., & King, R. B. (2015). Perseverance counts but consistency does not! Validating the short grit scale in a collectivist setting. *Current Psychology, 35*, 121–130. https://doi.org/10.1007/s12144-015-9374-2.

Dobryakova, M. S., & Kuzminov, Y. I. (Eds.). (2016). *Kachestvo priema v rossiyskie vuzyi 2015 [Quality of enrollment in Russian higher education institutes-2015]*. Moscow: Izd. dom VShE.

Duckworth, A. L., Peterson, C., Matthews, M. D., & Kelly, D. R. (2007). Grit: Perseverance and passion for long-term goals. *Journal of Personality and Social Psychology, 92*, 1087–1101. https://doi.org/10.1037/0022-3514.92.6.1087.

Duckworth, A. L., Quinn, P. D., & Seligman, M. E. P. (2009). Positive predictors of teacher effectiveness. *The Journal of Positive Psychology, 4*(6), 540–547. https://doi.org/10.1080/17439760903157232.

Eskreis-Winkler, L., Shulman, E. P., Beal, S. A., & Duckworth, A. L. (2014). The grit effect: Predicting retention in the military, the workplace, school and marriage. *Frontiers in Psychology, 5*, 36. https://doi.org/10.3389/fpsyg.2014.00036.

Galton, F. (1892). *Hereditary genius: An inquiry into its laws and consequences*. London: Macmillan.

Gonzalez, O., Canning, J. R., Smyth, H., & MacKinnon, D. P. (2019). A psychometric valuation of the short grit scale: A closer look at its factor structure and scale functioning. *European Journal of Psychological Assessment*, 1–12. https://doi.org/10.1027/1015-5759/a000535.

Guo, J., Tang, X., & Xu, K. M. (2019). Capturing the multiplicative effect of perseverance and passion: Measurement issues of combining two grit facets. *Proceedings of the National Academy of Sciences, 116*(10), 3938–3940.

Hatchimonji, D. R. (2016). *Grit in Latino middle school students: Construct validity and psychometric properties of the short grit scale* (Master's thesis). New Brunswick, NJ: Rutgers University, Graduate School – New Brunswick.

Hein, V., Kalajas-Tilga, H., Koka, A., Raudsepp, L., & Tilga, H. (2019). How grit is related to objectively measured moderate-to-vigorous physical activity in school student. *Montenegrin Journal of Sports Science and Medicine, 8*(2), 47–53.

Holland, J. L. (1996). Exploring careers with a typology: What we have learned and some new directions. *American Psychologist, 51*(4), 397–406.

Hough, L. M. (1992). The "big five" personality variables construct confusion: Description versus prediction. *Human Performance, 5*(1–2), 139–155.

Jachimowicz, J. M., Wihler, A., Bailey, E. R., & Galinsky, A. D. (2019). Reply to Guo et al. and Credé: Grit-S scale measures only perseverance, not passion, and its supposed subfactors are merely artifactors. *Proceedings of the National Academy of Sciences, 116*(10), 3942–3944.

Kalia, V., Fuesting, M., & Cody, M. (2019). Perseverance in solving Sudoku: Role of grit and cognitive flexibility in problem solving. *Journal of Cognitive Psychology, 31*(3), 370–378.

Kalia, V., Thomas, R., Osowski, K., & Drew, A. (2018). Staying alert? Neural correlates of the association between grit and attention networks. *Frontiers in Psychology, 9*, 1377.

Li, J., Zhao, Y., Kong, F., Du, S., Yang, S., & Wang, S. (2018). Psychometric assessment of the short grit scale among Chinese adolescents. *Journal of Psychoeducational Assessment, 36*(3), 291–296.

Low, K. S. D., Yoon, M., Roberts, B. W., & Rounds, J. (2005). The stability of vocational interests from early adolescence to middle adulthood: A quantitative review of longitudinal studies. *Psychological Bulletin, 131*(5), 713–737.

Lufi, D., & Cohen, A. (1987). A scale for measuring persistence in children. *Journal of Personality Assessment, 51*(2), 178–185.

McClelland, D. C. (1961). *The achieving society*. Oxford, UK: Van Nostrand.

Mega, C., Ronconi, L., & De Beni, R. (2014). What makes a good student? How emotions, self-regulated learning, and motivation contribute to academic achievement. *Journal of Educational Psychology, 106*(1), 121–131.

Meisenberg, G., & Woodley, M. A. (2013). Are cognitive differences between countries diminishing? Evidence from TIMSS and PISA. *Intelligence, 41*(6), 808–816.

Muenks, K., Yang, J. S., & Wigfield, A. (2018). Associations between grit, motivation, and achievement in high school students. *Motivation Science, 4*(2), 158–176.

Nye, C. D., & Rounds, J. (2019). *Vocational interests in the workplace: Rethinking behavior at work*. New York: Routledge.

O'Neal, C. R., Goldthrite, A., Weston Riley, L., & Atapattu, R. K. (2018). A reciprocal, moderated mediation model of grit, engagement, and literacy achievement among dual language learners. *Social Development, 27*(3), 665–680.

Organisation for Economic Co-operation and Development. (2013). *PISA 2012 assessment and analytical framework: Mathematics, reading, science, problem solving and financial literacy*. OECD Publishing.

Reed, A. J., Schmitz, D., Baker, E., Nukui, A., & Epperly, T. (2012). Association of "grit" and satisfaction in rural and nonrural doctors. *The Journal of the American Board of Family Medicine, 25*, 832–839. https://doi.org/10.3122/jabfm.2012.06.110044.

Rimfeld, K., Kovas, Y., Dale, P. S., & Plomin, R. (2016). True grit and genetics: Predicting academic achievement from personality. *Journal of Personality and Social Psychology, 111* (5), 780–789.

Rindermann, H. (2007). Discussion on the g-factor of international cognitive ability comparisons: The homogeneity of results in PISA, TIMSS, PIRLS and IQ-tests across nations. *European Journal of Personality, 21*, 707–765.

Robertson-Kraft, C., & Duckworth, A. L. (2014). True grit: Trait-level perseverance and passion for long-term goals predicts effectiveness and retention among novice teachers. *Teachers College Record (1970), 116*(3), 25364065.

Sadiković, S., Milovanović, I., & Oljača, M. (2018). Another psychometric proof of the abbreviated math anxiety scale usefulness: IRT analysis. *Primenjena Psihologija, 11*(3), 301–323. https://doi.org/10.19090/pp.2018.3.301-323.

Salles, A., Cohen, G. L., & Mueller, C. M. (2014). The relationship between grit and resident well-being. *The American Journal of Surgery, 207*, 251–254. https://doi.org/10.1016/j.amjsurg.2013.09.006.

Saunders-Scott, D., Braley, M. B., & Stennes-Spidahl, N. (2018). Traditional and psychological factors associated with academic success: Investigating best predictors of college retention. *Motivation and Emotion, 42*(4), 459–465.

Schmidt, F. T., Fleckenstein, J., Retelsdorf, J., Eskreis-Winkler, L., & Möller, J. (2017). Measuring grit: A German validation and a domain-specific approach to grit. *European Journal of Psychological Assessment, 35*(3), 436–447. https://doi.org/10.1027/1015-5759/a000407.

Schmittmann, V. D., Cramer, A. O., Waldorp, L. J., Epskamp, S., Kievit, R. A., & Borsboom, D. (2013). Deconstructing the construct: A network perspective on psychological phenomena. *New Ideas in Psychology, 31*(1), 43–53.

Sheehan, K. (2014). *Storm clouds in the mind: A comparison of hope, grit, happiness, and life satisfaction in traditional and alternative high school students* (Doctoral dissertation).

Silvia, P. J., Eddington, K. M., Beaty, R. E., Nusbaum, E. C., & Kwapil, T. R. (2013). Gritty people try harder: Grit and effort related cardiac autonomic activity during an active coping challenge. *International Journal of Psychophysiology, 88*, 200–205. https://doi.org/10.1016/j.ijpsycho.2013.04.007.

StataCorp. (2017). *Stata statistical software: Release 15*. College Station, TX: StataCorp LLC.

Tang, X., Wang, M. T., Guo, J., & Salmela-Aro, K. (2019). Building grit: The longitudinal pathways between mindset, commitment, grit, and academic outcomes. *Journal of Youth and Adolescence, 48*(5), 850–863.

Tedesqui, R. A., & Young, B. W. (2017). Investigating grit variables and their relations with practice and skill groups in developing sport experts. *High Ability Studies, 28*(2), 167–180.

Terman, L. M., & Oden, M. H. (1947). *The gifted child grows up: Twenty-five years' follow-up of a superior group*. Oxford, UK: Stanford University Press.

Tyumeneva, Y., Kardanova, E., & Kuzmina, J. (2019). Grit: Two related but independent constructs instead of one. Evidence from item response theory. *European Journal of Psychological Assessment, 354*(4), 469–478. https://doi.org/10.1027/1015-5759/a000424.

Vazsonyi, A. T., Ksinan, A. J., Jiskrova, G. K., Mikuška, J., Javakhishvili, M., & Cui, G. (2019). To grit or not to grit, that is the question! *Journal of Research in Personality, 78*, 215–226.

Weston, L. C. (2014). *A replication and extension of psychometric research on the Grit scale* (Master's thesis). College Park, MD: University of Maryland.

Wohleber, R. W., Matthews, G., Reinerman-Jones, L. E., Panganiban, A. R., & Scribner, D. (2015). Individual differences in resilience and affective response during simulated UAV operations. *Proceedings of the Human Factors and Ergonomics Society Annual Meeting, 59*(1), 751–755. https://doi.org/10.1177/1541931215591176.

Wolters, C. A., & Hussain, M. (2014). Investigating grit and its relations with college students' self-regulated learning and academic achievement. *Metacognition and Learning, 10*, 293–311. https://doi.org/10.1007/s11409-014-9128-9.

Zhong, C., Wang, M. C., Shou, Y., Ren, F., Zhang, X., Li, M., & Yang, W. (2018). Assessing construct validity of the grit-S in Chinese employees. *PLoS One, 13*(12), e0209319.

Yulia Tyumeneva has obtained Ph.D. in psychology, and is an associate professor and senior research fellow at the National Research University Higher School of Economics in Moscow, Russia. Her area of interests include measurement in cognitive psychology and education. She conducts research in reasoning, learning and problem solving. Her work is concerned with the interaction between learning and cognitive processes, in particular, knowledge acquisition, transfer of learning, analogies in learning and understanding, math education. One of the major themes is also the validity of measurement in cognitive and educational areas. She teaches courses on principles of measurement in education and psychology, research design and methods.

Yulia Kuzmina is a research fellow at the Institute of Education at the National Research University Higher School of Economics and at Psychological Institute of Russian Academy of Education in Moscow, Russia. Her research interests are in math development and precursors of math achievement and math motivation. Her current works are focused on investigation of nonsymbolic, symbolic and verbal magnitude representations, and their developmental trajectories. She teaches courses on cognitive assessment, data analysis and research design and methods.

Tatiana Chirkina is a Junior Research Fellow at the Institute of Education, Higher School of Economics, Moscow. Her research interests include educational inequality, social mobility and the factors associated with success for students of disadvantaged social background.

Chapter 12
Exploring the Grit-Performance and Grit-Career Success Relationship: The Role of Psychological Ownership

Chantal Olckers and Eileen Koekemoer

Abstract Recently, particular attention is being given to grit (as a personality trait) and its associated individual and organisational outcomes. Gritty individuals are more likely to remain interested in achieving their goals over an extended period, despite failure, adversity and setbacks. As a result, literature suggest relationships between grit and outcomes such as career success and performance. However, empirical studies investigating these direct relationships are inconclusive, since findings indicate these relationships as weak to moderate. Although gritty employees might perform better or experience career success, what remains unclear are understanding the theoretical and psychological mechanisms (possible influencing variables) through which grit may lead to performance or career success. Using the distal-proximal framework, the argument are being made that grit as a distal personality trait is unlikely to have a direct effect on work behaviour, but rather indirectly through proximal motivational variables. Thus, for the transformation of distal attributes (e.g. grit) to increase performance, the proximal mechanisms (possible influencing variables) becomes significant. Once such possible proximal- mechanism (influencing variable) that have already been linked with employees' performance and attachment to their careers, is psychological ownership. Psychological ownership is defined as a cognitive-affective state in which an individual feels a sense of ownership for a target that could be tangible or intangible in nature. Through a review of existing literature, we explore the possible associations or the influencing role that psychological ownership may play in the relationship between grit and employees' task performance and perceived subjective career success. Based on the distal-proximal perspective we propose that psychological ownership as a proximate, domain-specific flexible psychological construct which may influence both the grit-performance as well as grit-subjective career success relationship. To date, no research has explored these relationships theoretically based on extant literature. Thus, this chapter aims to contribute to the field of career development and talent management by exploring whether grit, as a trait, could play a role in

C. Olckers (✉) · E. Koekemoer
Department of Human Resource Management, University of Pretoria, Pretoria, South Africa
e-mail: chantal.olckers@up.ac.za; eileen.koekemoer@up.ac.za

L. E. van Zyl et al. (eds.), *Multidisciplinary Perspectives on Grit*,
https://doi.org/10.1007/978-3-030-57389-8_12

enhancing employees' task performance and perceptions of career through psychological ownership within an organisational context providing a possible basis for future empirical studies.

Keywords Grit · Psychological ownership · Subjective career success · Task performance · Talent retention

12.1 Introduction

An intra-personal psychological strength that has received much attention in recent literature is the personality construct *grit* (Credé, Tynan, & Harms, 2017). In the words of Duckworth, Peterson, Matthews, and Kelly (2007, p. 1087), grit is defined as "perseverance and passion for long-term goals". This means that individuals who have grit remain interested in achieving their goals over an extended period of time despite failure, adversity, and setbacks (Credé et al., 2017). Thus, they display willingness and stamina over a long period of time (Kim & Lee, 2015). Nothing distracts them from achieving their goals and they are able to overcome setbacks that might discourage many other people (Akin & Arslan, 2014). Grit comprises two components: consistency of interest and perseverance of effort. Consistency of interest relates to the tendency of individuals to continuously re-engage with and remain focused on specific tasks, goals, and ideas over time. Perseverance of effort relates to putting in continuous hard work to achieve set goals despite setbacks, failures, or stumbling blocks (Duckworth et al., 2007; Duckworth & Quinn, 2009).

Grit has been associated with several positive individual and organisational outcomes. For example, grit has been related to longevity in the workplace and marriage (Eskreis-Winkler, Shulman, Beal, & Duckworth, 2014), commitment to a career (Duckworth & Quinn, 2009), successful aging in the elderly (Kim & Lee, 2015), life satisfaction and harmony in life (Vainio & Daukantaite, 2016), greater psychological well-being (Salles, Cohen, & Mueller, 2014) and less counterproductive behaviour (Ceschi, Sartori, Dickert, & Costantini, 2016).

As mentioned earlier, grit is essentially about holding on to a goal steadfastly even when the road is bumpy and progress towards the goal is slow. In sum, being gritty entails pursuing one's passion by making the choice to invest time and psychological resources in a specific endeavour (e.g. having a successful career) and potentially even dropping many other things to stay steadfast in this pursuit (Bashant, 2014).

Within the context of the new career landscape (e.g., which is characterised by boundaryless and protean careers), the premise of independent, individually driven and subjectively addressed career concepts are being put forward (Arthur & Rousseau, 1996). In this landscape, individuals, rather than their employing organisations, become the architects of their own careers and development, and they take responsibility for managing their careers and transforming their career paths (Baruch, 2004). Already in 2007, Duckworth and colleagues argued that grit, and not intelligence or academic performance, is the most reliable predictor of personal success. The literature has indicated that grit predicts success in a variety of domains (Duckworth et al., 2007; Duckworth, Kirby, Tsukayama, Berstein, & Ericsson, 2011; Duckworth, Quinn, & Seligman, 2009; Eskreis-Winkler et al., 2014).

Numerous studies found that individuals with a lot of grit might overcome various career challenges through their passion and perseverance (i.e. staying engaged with their work) to achieve long-term goals, resulting in their achieving higher success in their careers than individuals with less grit (Duckworth et al., 2007; Duckworth & Quinn, 2009; Eskreis-Winkler et al., 2014; Suzuki, Tamesue, Asahi, & Ishikawa, 2015; Von Culin, Tsukayama, & Duckworth, 2014).

Theoretically speaking, a relationship between grit and career success seems plausible, but only a few studies have investigated this relationship (Clark & Clark, 2016; Duckworth et al., 2007; Duckworth et al., 2009; Eskreis-Winkler et al., 2014). The more recent study of Clark and Clark (2016) investigated grit and career success from both qualitative and quantitative perspectives, but their findings were inconsistent. Clark and Clark (2016, p. 148) proposed the following: "grit may be more important in structured environments; as the environment becomes less structured, grit becomes a foundation on which success is built, and other factors become more prominent in success". According to Danner, Lechner, and Rammstedt's (2020) study conducted across several countries and nationalities, grit's influence on career success depends partly on individual characteristics (e.g. educational attainment), and on contextual factors (e.g. labour market conditions). They emphasised the fact that the interplay between a non-cognitive skill (grit) and the individual as well as contextual factors seems to be much more complex than anticipated.

Although most research has focused on validating grit as a predictor of academic performance (Credé et al., 2017), findings have been inconclusive and beset by contradictory evidence. According to Credé (2018), empirical studies investigating the direct relationship between grit and performance indicated weak to moderate relationships, suggesting grit as a weak predictor of success. Consequently, support for grit as a defining feature of success is limited. Recently, Luthans, Luthans, and Chaffin (2019), posit that these moderate to weak correlations between grit and success may be partially due to the stable, non-cognitive, "trait-like" nature of grit. Another possible reason to the failure of grit to predict performance is related to the measurement of grit. In their meta-analytical study, Credé et al. (2017) raised the issue that several studies, although theoretically sound, suggested flaws in the manner in which items were designed. The validity of the Grit-scale developed by Duckworth et al. (2007) maybe compromised by making use of reverse wording items as well as lengthy items. According to Jachimowicz, Wihler, Bailey, and Galinsky (2018) the measurement of grit is in contrast to its definition. These authors stated that the measurement of grit rather focus on perseverance of effort than a combination of perseverance of effort and consistency of interest.

Using the distal-proximal framework, Luthans et al. (2019) argue that grit as a distal personality trait is unlikely to have a direct effect on work behaviour, but rather indirectly through proximal motivational variables (thus other variables come into play). Such motivational variables/constructs become important in tasks and goals that require sustained effort, the development of new skills, and long-term goal orientation (such as career success). For the transformation of distal attributes (e.g. grit) to increase performance, the proximal mechanisms become significant. It is thus important to have a better understanding of the theoretical and psychological mechanisms through which grit may lead to performance or career success (thus other possible influencing variables). One such possible influencing variable that may play a role in employees' performance (Jakada, 2019; Peng & Pierce, 2015; Sieger, Zellweger, & Aquino, 2013; Torp & Nielsen, 2018) and their attachment to their career (Olckers & Koekemoer, 2017) is psychological ownership (PO).

PO is defined as a cognitive-affective state in which an individual feels a sense of ownership for a target that could be tangible or intangible in nature (Pierce, Kostova, & Dirks, 2001, 2003). PO emerged as a construct when an understanding was gained of the psychological processes that explained why employee stock ownership resulted in positive employee attitudes and performance in some but not all cases (Vandewalle, Van Dyne, & Kostova, 1995; Wagner, Parker, & Christiansen, 2003). Pierce et al. (2003) came to the conclusion that PO can be seen not only as a motivational driver but also as a predictor of desirable employee attitudes (e.g. attachment to one's job or career) and behaviours (e.g. enhanced performance) that can be linked to organisational effectiveness. This chapter aims to provide a better theoretical understanding of how PO as a cognitive-affective state might influence the grit-success and grit-performance relationship.

12.2 Literature Review

12.2.1 Grit and Performance

Duckworth et al. (2011) expressed the opinion that gritty individuals perform better compared to their non-gritty counterparts because they spend more time on their work, put in more effort, and persevere in tedious and frustrating situations. Gritty employees are committed, show extreme stamina, and apply effort to the job tasks they have to perform or the goals they would like to achieve. According to Eskreis-Winkler et al. (2014) gritty individuals are diligent in completing their job tasks and achieve their set goals over an extended period of time. Gritty individuals remain focused on their task and/or goal and work strenuously toward meeting challenges despite possible failures, setbacks and obstacles they might experience. As Duckworth et al. (2007, p. 1088) stated: "The gritty individual approaches achievement as a marathon: his or her advantage is stamina". Individuals who have grit are more likely to perform well because they are better equipped to utilise their capabilities and are less influenced by failures and setbacks. They also seem to be less distracted by short-term goals and more focused on performing their job well.

Studies investigating the grit-performance relationship is well documented in the literature. In the study of Wang et al. (2017)—after controlling for demographic factors, general intelligence and the big-five personality traits—a significant relationship between grit and academic performance was established. In their study among university students, Miller-Matero, Martinez, Maclean, Yaremchuk, and Ko (2018) provided empirical evidence indicating a positive relationship between grit and academic performance. In addition, they established that the students displaying higher levels of grit completed their programme a year in advance of their less gritty classmates. A longitudinal study by Robertson-Kraft and Duckworth (2014), among novice teachers, showed that teachers with higher grit scores performed better and were more effective compared to teachers with lower grit scores. The results of a study conducted by Luthans et al. (2019), in which they explored the mediating effect of psychological capital on the grit-academic performance relationship, indicated a modest yet significant relationship between grit and academic performance.

Conversely, research conducted by Maddi, Matthews, Kelly, Villarreal, and White (2012) and De Vera, Gavino Jr, and Portugal (2015) did not confirm a significant grit-performance relationship. In Maddi et al.'s (2012) study, grit failed to predict the performance of first-year United States Military Academy cadets. In De Vera et al.'s (2015) study among medical sales representatives, grit as a factor predicting superior work performance could not be proved. However, the researchers ascribed this result to the incentive-based performance system that had been used. Other studies (Credé et al., 2017; Eskreis-Winkler et al., 2014; Von Culin et al., 2014) also reported that grit accounts for minor incremental variance in performance and success when controlling for the big five personality factors.

Given aforementioned evidence, grit is at least moderately positively related to performance. What remains unclear are the various possible underlying psychological mechanisms explaining the moderate relationships between grit and performance.

12.2.2 Grit and Subjective Career Success

Career success is generally referred to as "work-related accomplishments/outcomes that individuals achieve through their work experience over time" (Seibert, Kraimer, & Crant, 2001, p. 2). More recently, *subjective career success* has been featuring prominently in research. Subjective career success is described as "employees' perception of how much they have achieved career goals on the basis of an appraisal of past career experiences and anticipated career-related attainments using their personal criteria" (Pan & Zhou, 2015, p. 47). More specifically, Visagie and Koekemoer (2014) described subjective career success as being more than just an ultimate state or destination; it refers to an ongoing process of progress or a lifelong journey towards achieving goals. Given this definition and the inclination of grit being a long-term orientation towards achieving goals, one might argue that if one applies grit in working towards long-term work-related goals, one might experience feelings of perceived subjective career success. This notion is in line with the work of Li, Fang, Wang, Sun, and Cheng (2018) who found that individuals who are passionate about achieving their long-term goals and who display a lot of perseverance in this regard, feel very positive about themselves and evaluate their quality of life as positive. Furthermore, they argued that traits that have been formed over a long period of time will determine the standard of judgement of one's quality of life (or, for example, individuals' evaluation of their career accomplishments and/or outcomes). However, a limited number of studies investigated the grit-career success relationship (Clark & Clark, 2016; Duckworth et al., 2007, 2009; Eskreis-Winkler et al., 2014).

In the qualitative phase of their study, Clark and Clark's (2016) participants considered grit as essential to their career success. However, the study of Eskreis-Winkler et al. (2014), which examined grit within four different contexts (i.e. military, workplace sales, high schools and marriage), are criticised for using quantitative, correlational methods and for using retention as a proxy for career success.

In the qualitative study of Koekemoer (2014), findings indicated that individuals' mind-set and attitude towards their careers (e.g. not attaching importance to putting in enough effort) could actually impede the attainment of career success. Visagie and Koekemoer (2014) described the attainment of subjective career success as the achievement of personal goals, objectives and aspirations, and the establishment of different goals. Gritty individuals or employees are more likely to persevere in performing their duties at work as they keep an eye on longer-term career goals (Kabat-Farr, Walsh, & McGonagle, 2019), which relates to the notion that career success is an ongoing process aimed at achieving career-related goals. According to Caza and Posner (2019), the dogged perseverance and the passionate pursuit of long-term goals of individuals who have grit should make them more willing to stick with, stand up for and live by their principles: therefore, grit may shape behaviour that is directly relevant to the accomplishment of individual goals (which can be either personal or career-related). Thus, if individuals display more grit and make an effort and persevere to achieve their career goals, feelings of subjective career success may follow.

In light of the distal-proximal framework, proximal constructs (such as PO) are more closely related to specific performance outcomes or may influence such outcomes. In terms of performance and career success, relationships and associations with psychological ownership have been established (Jakada, 2019; Peng & Pierce, 2015; Sieger et al., 2013; Torp & Nielsen, 2018).

12.2.3 Psychological Ownership

Pierce et al. (2001, 2003, p. 86) defined PO as "the state in which individuals feel as though the target of ownership or a piece of that target is "theirs" (i.e. "It is mine!"). Grounded in the theory of possession, PO is a construct that describes the psychological connection an individual has with an object, entity or idea and answers the question: "What do I feel is mine?" (Pierce et al., 2003, p. 86). PO is a cognitive-affective state describing not only individuals' cognitive awareness of their beliefs but also their emotional attachment to the targets of ownership. The extent of the attachment is such that the individuals perceive the targets as extensions of themselves.

PO is a state that emerges to satisfy three basic human needs, also called the motives or "roots" of PO. These needs or motives are efficacy and effectance, self-identity, and having a place that feels like "home" (Pierce et al., 2003). The motive of efficacy and effectance refers to the individuals' ability to control a target of ownership in whichever way they prefer. Individuals' ability to control the target will give them the opportunity to develop possessive feelings towards it, which will allow for the psychological experience of ownership to take place. Interacting with and controlling the target of ownership will foster pleasurable feelings of efficacy and satisfaction (Pierce et al., 2001, 2003). The second motive relates to individuals' possession or their targets of ownership and the individuals' self-identity. Through interacting with the targets of ownership and reflecting on their meaning, individuals establish, maintain, and transform their self-identity. Targets of ownership thus serve as descriptors of the individuals' identity, granting them autonomy, pleasure, and meaning (Jussila, Tarkiainen, Sarstedt, & Hair, 2015; Olckers & Van Zyl, 2019). The last motive is associated with individuals' need to have a place where they feel "at home" and where they belong. These feelings of belongingness give individuals pleasure and make them feel comfortable and secure (Dawkins, Tian, Newman, & Martin, 2017).

PO develops via its three paths or so-called "routes," and these are: controlling the ownership target; having an intimate knowledge of the target; and investing the self in the target (Pierce et al., 2001). Having control and influence over a target facilitates satisfying individuals' need for control and self-efficacy (Brown, Pierce, & Crossley, 2014). Controlling the target of ownership gives rise to PO feelings and causes the target to become part of the self. Thus, the more control individuals have over their targets, the more the individuals experience the targets as a part of themselves. Through association with their targets (also referred to as objects), individuals gather more information about these targets or objects, become more familiar with them and get to know them intimately. The more in-depth knowledge individuals gather about their targets or objects, the stronger their connection with the targets or objects becomes, resulting in enhanced feelings of ownership. Only if individuals invest their energy, time, effort, and attention in their targets or objects of ownership, the targets or objects will become part of their selves, resulting in the development of PO. In this way, employees become owners of their targets or objects, of which the nature can be tangible (e.g. the machines they operate or the products they create) (Jussila et al., 2015) or intangible (their jobs or careers). Only if individuals get to know their targets and invest themselves in these targets, will they satisfy their need for self-identity and belongingness. Control over the target, knowledge about the target and investment of the self in the target, build feelings of self-efficacy (Pierce et al., 2001, 2003).

12.2.3.1 Psychological Ownership and Its Implications for Performance

Although Vandewalle et al. (1995) argued that psychological ownership, coupled with a sense of responsibility and pride, will motivate employees to improve their performance in their organisation, they found a non-significant relationship between PO and in-role behaviour or core-task behaviour (i.e. the behaviour described and expected as part of employees' work in an organisation). This result was supported by Mayhew, Ashkanasy, Bramble, and Gardner (2007) who reported a non-significant relationship between PO and in-role behaviour. In contrast to these studies, Park, Kim, and Song (2015) confirmed a significant association between organisation-based PO and in-role behaviour, with PO acting as a mediator between ethical leadership and in-role behaviour. A study conducted by Wagner et al. (2003) confirmed a positive relationship between PO and the financial performance of work groups. Similarly, Torp and Nielsen (2018) established a significant relationship between employee stock ownership, PO and a firm's financial performance, with PO playing a mediating role. Similar to the study of Sieger et al. (2013) that reported a significant influence of organisation-based PO on company performance, the study of Liu, Chow, Xiao, and Huang (2017) found organisation-based PO to be a significant predictor of job performance. By making use of supervisor ratings of job performance, Van Dyne and Pierce (2004) established only a moderate correlation between PO and job performance. Ghafoor, Qureshi, Khan, and Hijazi (2011) found a significant relationship between PO and employee performance, with PO playing a mediating role between transformational leadership and employee performance. Md-Sidin, Sambasivan, and Muniandy (2010) conducted a PO-related study within an educational environment and their findings revealed a significant relationship between job-based PO and the job performance of business school lecturers. Within the health care environment, a study conducted by Kaur, Sambasivan, and Kumar (2013) confirmed a positive relationship between job-based PO and in-role performance, specifically relating to the caring behaviour of nurses. In their study, Brown et al. (2014) explored whether job-based PO would have a mediating effect on the relationship between perceived job complexity and in-role performance, in this case sales performance. Although they established a moderate relation between PO and sales performance, they expressed the belief that its value, is exponential across the organisation. In all the above-mentioned studies, PO acts as a mediating variable. There is, however, a lack of literature indicating the moderating role of PO in previous studies and specifically in relation to performance.

The preceding discussion clearly indicates inconsistent results regarding the PO-performance relationship. Therefore, Pierce and Rodgers (2004) warned that empirical efforts to explain the ownership-performance relationship may be too simple and that several factors need to be taken into consideration. They suggested that a distinction should be made between in-role or so-called task performance and extra-role or so-called contextual performance, as well as between employee declarative knowledge (the knowledge about *what* to do) and procedural knowledge (the knowledge about *how* to perform the task and the *ability* to perform the task).

Research to date seems to focus more on organisation-based PO's relationship to extra-role behaviours or contextual performance than on job-based PO's relationship to in-role behaviours or task performance (Dawkins et al., 2017).

Consequently, the focus of this chapter is on exploring the influence of job-based PO on in-role behaviour (i.e. task performance). Task performance is defined as individuals' capability to perform the core and most important substantive tasks that are central to their jobs (Koopmans et al., 2012). Task performance comprises behaviours that are under the control of the employee; therefore, to perform tasks, employees have the opportunity to utilise the routes to PO at job-task level. For example, employees are likely exercise control over the tasks their jobs require them to perform; they can accumulate intimate knowledge about their jobs and about what is expected of them, and they have the opportunity to invest their time, energy and effort in performing these job tasks.

From the perspective of the social exchange theory (SET), the possible positive relationship between PO and performance can be supported. According to SET, when two parties engage with one another, the party receiving a certain offering often feels obligated to reciprocate in kind (Cropanzano & Mitchell, 2005). Thus, the concept of reciprocity lies at the core of this theory. To illustrate this concept with reference to an employee-employer relationship: A job gives employees the opportunity to satisfy several human needs (self-efficacy, self-identity, belongingness), resulting in the employees fusing their selves with the job. Furthermore, the satisfaction of these needs enhances the development of employees' job-based PO, resulting in the employees feeling a sense of responsibility towards their job. In accordance with the SET's concept of reciprocity, employees will in all likelihood perform desirably in their job in exchange for the opportunity to have their needs satisfied.

12.2.3.2 Psychological Ownership and its Implications for Subjective Career Success

The association between PO and subjective career success could most probably be best described by indicating how the motives of PO (efficacy and effectance, self-identity, and belongingness) can play a role in enhancing subjective career success.

'Effectance' Motive

Individuals develop PO feelings if they feel they have control over objects or targets, which, in turn, allows them to experience self-efficacy and satisfaction (Pierce et al., 2001, 2003). Like studies on PO that found a positive association between one's internal locus of control and the 'effectance' motive of PO, Spector (1982) found a positive relation between one's internal locus of control and career success. Both these relations are formed due to individuals' belief that they can control their environment. Ballout (2007) expressed the opinion that individuals, in order to progress in their careers, take control and thus ownership of their careers and improve their human capital so as to enhance their performance, all of which ultimately lead to their success.

Self-identity Motive
A close connection exists between individuals' ownership targets and their self-identity (Pierce et al., 2003). Through interacting with their targets of ownership and reflecting on their meaning, individuals establish their self-identity. They discover who they are and what they will become (Jussila et al., 2015). For example, if individuals find that they can identify with the work they perform as part of establishing their career and that this is aligned with their values, they will most likely find their careers appealing. In turn, this will allow for the development of PO feelings towards their careers (Avey, Avolio, Crossley, & Luthans, 2009).

Belongingness Motive
All people have an inherent need for a certain place where they feel they "can be" and where they feel they belong (Jussila et al., 2015). Therefore, individuals prefer to work in an environment that is conducive to the development of these feelings (Pierce et al., 2001, 2003). The feeling of being at home is enhanced if there is an alignment between the personal values of the individual and the values of the organisation. Furthermore, if there is a good fit between the individuals' skills and competencies and the job or career requirements (Ballout, 2007), allowing individuals to develop their adaptability in the workplace, it will not only enhance feelings of belongingness but also enhance feelings of career success (Heslin, 2005). In addition, if appreciation is shown for the work they do and the effort they put into it, and if there is a sympathetic understanding of their personal problems and their need to maintain a work-life balance, employees' development of PO feelings might be promoted and their perceptions of their career success would most probably be enhanced.

Moreover, if employees develop PO through control over, knowledge about and investment in the ownership target (i.e. through the so-called three paths), it might assist them in attaining subjective career success.

Control of the Ownership Target
As mentioned previously, an individual will only experience a target or object as "mine" if they feel they can exercise control over it and manipulate it and if they allow it to affect them personally (Pierce et al., 2001, 2003). If employees' workplace allows them to take control over developments and occurrences in their work life, it will satisfy their need for control and give them the opportunity to experience efficacy in their work, which will enhance their PO feelings (Avey et al., 2009) and thus their experience of their career. An organisation could provide its employees with several opportunities to develop their careers, for example, by giving supervisory support and training and making company resources available for development (De Vos, De Clippeleer, & Dewilde, 2009). Although the organisation can provide these opportunities, it remains the responsibility of the employees to be proactive in managing and taking control of their own careers (Colakoglu, 2011). Each individual employee should therefore act as the architect of his or her own career (Ballout,

2007). Being the architect of one's own career will not only enhance one's feelings of self-efficacy and well-being, but will most probably lead to one's experience of satisfaction in one's occupation or career that one is trying to build (Enache, Sallan, Sime, & Fernandez, 2011).

Knowledge of the Ownership Target
To make an object or target become part of the self, an individual needs to gain intimate knowledge of it. By implication, individuals will acquire information about objects and become familiar with them only if they actively participate or associate with the objects (Jussila et al., 2015). It is important for individuals to understand what the objects mean to them because only then will they learn more about themselves and become more aware of their identity and expectations (Jussila et al., 2015). This knowledge of the ownership target is particularly important in the contemporary career landscape. As Ballout (2007) pointed out, individuals need to follow the so-called "knowing why" approach to their careers; to enhance their perceptions of career success they need to know the type of career that they can identify with and that will be personally meaningful to them. Individuals should also adopt the so-called "knowing whom" approach not only to establish and build good relationships with mentors who can provide necessary emotional support but also to network. Last but not least, the "knowing how" approach is important. According to this approach, individuals are responsible for improving their own skills, abilities, and competencies. Thus, employees can apply the "knowing why," "knowing whom" and "knowing how" approaches to their careers to increase their knowledge of their targets (and their careers). By doing that they might create the opportunity to experience their careers as successful.

Investment in the Ownership Target
For a target to become part of themselves, individuals need to not only acquire knowledge about the target but also invest energy, time and effort in it. Investment of the self in the target will satisfy their need for self-identity and their yearning for a place where they belong (Pierce et al., 2003). To achieve success in a career, individuals must invest time, energy, and effort in developing the necessary skills and building the relationships that could enhance their career. They should also gain experience to enable them to perform well in their jobs (Ng & Feldman, 2010). Being experienced and skilful would enhance employees' feelings of self-efficacy, ultimately helping them feel more successful in their careers. Remaining at an organisation for a longer period of time allows employees to increase their knowledge and skills and build good relationships, which can be regarded as investments in their career (Supangco, 2011).

To summarise: employees will, by controlling their target (i.e. taking control of their own career), by knowing their target through close association (i.e. applying the "knowing why," "knowing whom" and "knowing how" approaches), and by immersing themselves into creating and shaping their target of ownership, experience oneness with the target (i.e. PO feelings), and as a result they may experience subjective career success.

12.3 Theoretical Framework

Understanding more clearly how grit relates to career success and performance, we suggest the distal-proximal framework. Based on the distal-proximal framework, a distal motivational force, influences behaviour through proximal performance motivation variables (Barrick & Mount, 2005). By using this framework, we suggest that grit (as a trait) serve as a distal motivational function by influencing behaviours through psychological ownership (a proximal motivational state-like variable).

Proximal constructs operate at the level of purposive actions and focus on the mechanisms that control initiation and execution of actions when performing tasks (Kanfer, 1990). This becomes particularly important in tasks that require sustained effort and when goals are not quickly realised (such as building a career). Proximal mechanisms (such as PO) thus play an important role in how distal attributes (such as grit) are translated into actions for increased performance (as well as career success). Although grittier employees do display perseverance and passion for long-term goals, in light of this framework, individuals need or will use a proximal construct (such as PO) to translate this perseverance into action (meaning performance). Since distal personality traits are known as being more stable and not open to change and development, it is unlikely that they will have a direct effect on work behaviours, although an indirect effect via a proximal construct is possible (Lanaj, Chang, & Johnson, 2012).

Applying this framework, we argue that grit, as a distal personality trait, may influence performance as well as career success via the more proximal mechanism of PO. According to Luthans et al. (2019), grit is likely to direct individuals to identify general intentions and goals as it relates to their performance. Compared to grit that is domain neutral, PO, which is state-like and open to change, is more domain specific. This suggests that grit can be appropriate for various contexts, situation or environments, whereas PO is more related to a specific target of ownership such as your job tasks (which might lead to increased performance or perceptions of career success). Therefore, grit as a general trait-like construct will most probably give rise to state-like motivational cognitive constructs such as PO.

As stated by Kwon (2017), individuals will most likely develop a gritty disposition if they experience a sense of control (for example over their job tasks) and will most probably put in more and consistent effort toward achieving their goals and desired outcomes. This will in the long run, contributes to achievement. If the individual thus believes that he/she is the only one responsible for his/her own life path, he/she will most likely put in more effort to reach his/her long-term life goals. Therefore, employees who display a gritty disposition are more likely to have a sense of responsibility towards and engage with their job tasks and their career.

Taking into consideration our earlier argument that individuals who take psychological ownership of their career are more likely to experience subjective career success, the view of Luthans, Luthans, and Luthans (2004) suggests that having knowledge about one's career and taking ownership of it is not enough. Individuals should also understand themselves and know how this understanding shapes their

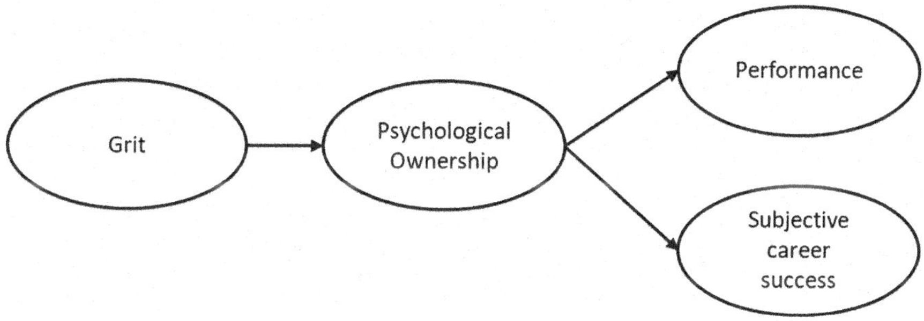

Fig. 12.1 Proposed conceptual model

career experiences and/or outcomes. According to Luthans et al. (2019), while grit may be the source of passion and persistence that assist in achieving long-term goals, individuals also need to believe in their capabilities and be aware of the resources (PO) they need to sustain their efforts over time so as to reach their long-term goals.

According to Eskreis-Winkler et al. (2014), individuals with higher levels of grit are more inclined to pursue their goals and commitments than to quit or drop out, a characteristic which might result in increasing these individuals' perceptions of subjective career success. This view confirms our view that individuals who possesses grit are more inclined to experience subjective career success, and the degree to which the individual take psychological ownership will influence this.

In sum, we thus suggest that gritty individuals in pursuing their passion to establish a successful career and to perform well, will most probably invest time and energy (PO) to stay steadfast in their pursuit (Bashant, 2014). Having grit may thus enable individuals to persist and persevere over a long period of time to reach their career goals (i.e. to achieve subjective career success and to perceive it as such), but only if they take ownership of their careers (i.e. invest time and energy in their careers).

Based on the aforementioned, we propose that PO as a proximate, domain-specific flexible psychological construct may influence the grit-performance as well as grit-subjective career success relationship (as illustrated in conceptual model in Fig. 12.1). Given the limited empirical studies exploring these relationships, based on the proximal-distal framework, more research is recommended to explore the indirect effects of PO.

12.4 Practical Implications

The premise of this chapter was to argue that a state-like variable such as PO can facilitate the strategic and contextual application of grit in relation to performance and career success. This suggest that individuals who take ownership of their careers and persevere in their career-related tasks over long periods of time despite setbacks and failure can improve their task performance and experience feelings of subjective career success. As argued, individuals (as opposed to organisations) should know exactly what is expected of them in the workplace so that they can take charge of their careers (Eby, Butts, & Lockwood, 2003) and set clear career goals and responsibilities for themselves. For their part, organisations should make their employees responsible for completing their tasks and should allow them to take ownership of their own tasks, which may inspire and reinforce employees' self-motivation and self-worth, which, in turn, may increase their experience of psychological ownership feelings towards their task performance and careers.

According to Pierce et al. (2001, 2003), in order to capture individuals' interest and attention, emphasis should be placed on taking ownership of targets (in this instance their task performance or their careers). Given earlier propositions about the influence of grit, this means that employees who have grit (i.e. who persevere and maintain interest in their tasks at work and their careers) and who invest in and take ownership of their job tasks and careers are likely to improve their job performance and experience career success. Therefore, our argument is that grit alone cannot predict job performance or career success. Gritty individuals should play a more active role in managing their job tasks and career by using their psychological resources (PO by specifically taking control, acquiring in-depth insight into and knowledge of and investing in their job tasks and career) as this can assist them to experience increased feelings of performance and career success.

The development of PO might assist employees to apply and relate their grit strategically towards behaviours and attitudes that are likely to enhance their task performance and career goals. This is in line with the suggestions by Visagie and Koekemoer (2014) that various factors could contribute to the attainment of career success, for example, delivering work of a high standard, being open to feedback and constructive criticism for self-development, establishing and maintaining trusting relationships in the work environment and working in organisations that facilitate a culture of shared knowledge and skills development. In addition, employees need to be aware of personal attributes that may influence their perceived attainment of career success. They should take personal responsibility for their success by educating themselves, performing within their organisation and establishing networks.

12.5 Conclusion

To conclude, employees should make use of every opportunity and all available resources in their work environment to ensure that they meet their personal expectations regarding the performance of their work-related tasks and the experience of career success. By implication, individuals need to: exercise control over their tasks at work (targets) and their careers; acquire intimate knowledge about their job tasks and careers; keep up with what exactly is expected of them in their occupations; and make significant personal investments in their career over long periods of time without being discouraged and quitting. Furthermore, individuals (and not organisations) should take ownership of their tasks at work to improve their task performance. Thus, based on this chapter, it seems theoretically plausible that psychological ownership has a role to play in the relationship between grit and employees' task performance and perceived subjective career success. However, future research should investigate such relationships empirically within an organisational context.

References

Akin, A., & Arslan, S. (2014). The relationship between achievement goal orientations and grit. *Education and Science, 39*(175), 267–274. https://doi.org/10.15390/EB.2014.2125.

Arthur, M. B., & Rousseau, D. M. (1996). *The boundaryless career: A new employment principle for a new organizational era* (Vol. 23, pp. 176–178). New York, NY: Oxford University Press. https://doi.org/10.5465/amr.1998.192975.

Avey, J. B., Avolio, B., Crossley, C., & Luthans, F. (2009). Psychological ownership: Theoretical extensions, measurement, and relation to work outcomes. *Journal of Organizational Behavior, 30*, 173–191. https://doi.org/10.1002/job.583.

Ballout, H. I. (2007). Career success: The effects of human capital, person-environment fit and organizational support. *Journal of Managerial Psychology, 22*(8), 741–765. https://doi.org/10.1108/02683940710837705.

Barrick, M. R., & Mount, M. K. (2005). Yes, personality matters: Moving on to more important matters. *Human Performance, 18*(4), 359–372.

Baruch, Y. (2004). *Managing careers: Theory and practice*. Harlow: Prentice Hall.

Bashant, J. (2014). Developing grit in our students: Why grit is such a desirable trait, and practical strategies for teachers and schools. *Journal for Leadership and Instruction, 13*(2), 14–17.

Brown, G., Pierce, J. L., & Crossley, C. (2014). Toward an understanding of the development of ownership feelings. *Journal of Organizational Behavior, 35*, 318–338. https://doi.org/10.1002/job.1869.

Caza, A., & Posner, B. Z. (2019). How and when does grit influence leaders' behavior? *Leadership & Organization Development Journal, 40*(1), 124–134. https://doi.org/10.1108/LODJ-06-2018-0209.

Ceschi, A., Sartori, R., Dickert, S., & Costantini, A. (2016). Grit or honesty-humility? New insights into the moderating role of personality between the health impairment process and counterproductive work behavior. *Frontiers in Psychology, 7*(1799), 1–11. https://doi.org/10.3389/fpsyg.2016.01799.

Clark, R. S., & Clark, V. L. P. (2016). Grit within the context of career success: A mixed methods study. *International Journal of Applied Positive Psychology*, 1–21. https://doi.org/10.1007/s41042-019-00020-9.

Colakoglu, S. N. (2011). The impact of career boundarylessness on subjective career success: The role of career competencies, career autonomy, and career insecurity. *Journal of Vocational Behavior, 79*, 47–59. https://doi.org/10.1016/j.jvb.2010.09.011.

Credé, M. (2018). What shall we do about grit? A critical review of what we know and what we don't know. *Educational Researcher, 47*(9), 606–611. https://doi.org/10.3102/0013189X18801322.

Credé, M., Tynan, M. C., & Harms, P. D. (2017). Much ado about grit: A meta-analytic synthesis of the grit literature. *Journal of Personality and Social Psychology, 113*(3), 492–511. https://doi.org/10.1037/pspp0000102.

Cropanzano, R., & Mitchell, M. S. (2005). Social exchange theory: An interdisciplinary review. *Journal of Management, 31*(6), 874–900. https://doi.org/10.1177/0149206305279602.

Danner, D., Lechner, C. M., & Rammstedt, B. (2020). A cross-national perspective on the associations of grit with career success. *Compare, 50*(2), 185–201. https://doi.org/10.1080/03057925.2019.1617110.

Dawkins, S., Tian, A. W., Newman, A., & Martin, A. (2017). Psychological ownership: A review and research agenda. *Journal of Organizational Behavior, 38*(2), 163–183. https://doi.org/10.1002/job.

De Vera, M. J., Gavino, J. C., Jr, & Portugal, E. J. (2015January). Grit and superior work performance in an Asian context. In *Proceedings of the 11th International Business and Social Science Research Conference, Crowne Plaza Hotel, Dubai*, January 8–9. Retrieved from https://wbiworldconpro.com/pages/paper/dubai-conference-2015-january/2392

De Vos, A., De Clippeleer, I., & Dewilde, T. (2009). Proactive career behaviours and career success during the early career. *Journal of Occupational and Organizational Psychology, 82*, 761–777. https://doi.org/10.1348/096317909x471013.

Duckworth, A. L., Kirby, T., Tsukayama, E., Berstein, H., & Ericsson, K. A. (2011). Deliberate practice spells success: Why grittier competitors triumph at the National Spelling Bee. *Social Psychological and Personality Science, 2*(2), 174–181. https://doi.org/10.1177/1948550610385872.

Duckworth, A. L., Peterson, C., Matthews, M. D., & Kelly, D. R. (2007). Grit: Perseverance and passion for long-term goals. *Journal of Personality and Social Psychology, 92*(6), 1087–1101. https://doi.org/10.1037/0022-3514.92.6.1087.

Duckworth, A., & Quinn, P. D. (2009). Development and validation of the short grit scale (grit-S). *Journal of Personality Assessment, 91*(2), 166–174. https://doi.org/10.1080/00223890802634290.

Duckworth, A. L., Quinn, P. D., & Seligman, M. E. P. (2009). Positive predictors of teacher effectiveness. *Journal of Positive Psychology, 4*(6), 540–547. https://doi.org/10.1080/17439760903157232.

Eby, L. T., Butts, M., & Lockwood, A. (2003). Predictors of success in the era of the boundaryless career. *Journal of Organizational Behavior: The International Journal of Industrial, Occupational and Organizational Psychology and Behavior, 24*(6), 689–708.

Enache, M., Sallan, J. M., Sime, P., & Fernandez, V. (2011). Career attitudes and subjective career success: Tackling gender differences. *Gender in Management: An International Journal, 26*(3), 234–250. https://doi.org/10.1108/17542411111130990.

Eskreis-Winkler, L., Shulman, E. P., Beal, S. A., & Duckworth, A. L. (2014). The grit effect: Predicting retention in the military, the workplace, school and marriage. *Frontiers in Psychology, 5*, 36. https://doi.org/10.3389/fpsyg.2014.00036.

Ghafoor, A., Qureshi, T. M., Khan, M. A., & Hijazi, S. T. (2011). Transformational leadership, employee engagement and performance: Mediating effect of psychological ownership. *African Journal of Business Management, 5*(17), 7391–7403. https://doi.org/10.5897/ajbm11.126.

Heslin, P. A. (2005). Experiencing career success. *Organisational Dynamics, 34*(4), 376–390. https://doi.org/10.1016/j.orgdyn.2005.08.005.

Jachimowicz, J. M., Wihler, A., Bailey, E. R., & Galinsky, A. D. (2018). Why grit requires perseverance and passion to positively predict performance. *PNAS, 115*(40), 9980–9985. https://doi.org/10.1073/pnas.1803561115.

Jakada, M. B. (2019). Moderating effect of psychological ownership on the relationship between job satisfaction and job performance among academic staff of Federal University, Dutse, Nigeria: Conceptual model. *International Journal of Information, Business and Management, 11*(1), 40–46. https://doi.org/10.1016/j.ijinfomgt.2010.11.002.

Jussila, I., Tarkiainen, A., Sarstedt, M., & Hair, J. F. (2015). Individual psychological ownership: Concepts, evidence, and implications for research in marketing. *Journal of Marketing Theory and Practice, 23*(2), 121–139. https://doi.org/10.1080/10696679.2015.1002330.

Kabat-Farr, D., Walsh, B. M., & McGonagle, A. K. (2019). Uncivil supervisors and perceived work ability: The joint moderating roles of job involvement and grit. *Journal of Business Ethics, 156* (4), 971–985. https://doi.org/10.1007/s10551-017-3604-5.

Kanfer, R. (1990). Motivation theory and industrial and organizational psychology. In M. D. Dunette & L. Hough (Eds.), *Handbook of industrial and organizational psychology* (Theory in industrial and organisational psychology) (Vol. 1, pp. 75–170). Palo Alto, CA: Consulting Psychologists Press.

Kaur, D., Sambasivan, M., & Kumar, N. (2013). Effect of spiritual intelligence, emotional intelligence, psychological ownership and burnout on caring behaviour of nurses: A cross-sectional study. *Journal of Clinical Nursing, 22*, 3192–3202. https://doi.org/10.1111/jocn.12386.

Kim, Y. J., & Lee, C. S. (2015). Effects of grit on the successful aging of the elderly in Korea. *Indian Journal of Science and Technology, 8*(57), 373–378. https://doi.org/10.17485/ijst/2015/v8iS7/70421.

Koekemoer, E. (2014). An explorative study on factors influencing the career success of management employees. *SA Journal of Industrial Psychology, 40*(2), 1–10. https://doi.org/10.4102/sajip.v40i2.1204.

Koopmans, L., Bernaards, C., Hildebrandt, V., Van Buuren, S., Van der Beek, A. J., & De Vet, H. C. W. (2012). Development of an individual work performance questionnaire. *International Journal of Productivity and Performance Management, 62*(1), 6–28. https://doi.org/10.1108/17410401311285273.

Kwon, H. W. (2017). The sociology of grit: Exploring grit as a sociological variable and its potential role in social stratification. *Sociology Compass, 11*(12) 13 p. https://doi.org/10.1111/soc4.12544.

Lanaj, K., Chang, C. H., & Johnson, R. E. (2012). Regulatory focus and work-related outcomes: A review and meta-analysis. *Psychological Bulletin, 138*(5), 998–1034. https://doi.org/10.1037/a0027723.

Li, J., Fang, M., Wang, W., Sun, G., & Cheng, Z. (2018). The influence of grit on life satisfaction: Self-esteem as a mediator. *Psychologica Belgica, 58*(1), 51–66. https://doi.org/10.5334/pb.400.

Liu, F., Chow, I. H.-S., Xiao, D., & Huang, M. (2017). Cross-level effects of HRM bundle on employee well-being and job performance. *Chinese Management Studies, 11*(3), 520–537. https://doi.org/10.1108/cms-03-2017-0065.

Luthans, K. W., Luthans, B. C., & Chaffin, T. D. (2019). Refining grit in academic performance: The mediational role of psychological capital. *Journal of Management Education, 43*(1), 35–61. https://doi.org/10.1177/1052562918804282.

Luthans, F., Luthans, K. W., & Luthans, B. C. (2004). Positive psychological capital: Beyond human and social capital. *Business Horizons, 47*(1), 45–50. https://doi.org/10.1016/j.bushor.2003.11.007.

Maddi, S. R., Matthews, M. D., Kelly, D. R., Villarreal, B., & White, M. (2012). The role of hardiness and grit in predicting performance and retention of USMA cadets. *Military Psychology, 24*, 19–28. https://doi.org/10.1080/08995605.2012.639672.

Mayhew, M. G., Ashkanasy, N. M., Bramble, T., & Gardner, J. (2007). A study of the antecedents and consequences of psychological ownership in organizational settings. *Journal of Social Psychology, 147*(5), 477–500. https://doi.org/10.3200/SOCP.147.5.477-500.

Md-Sidin, S., Sambasivan, M., & Muniandy, N. (2010). Impact of psychological ownership on the performance of business school lecturers. *Journal of Education for Business, 85*, 50–56. https://doi.org/10.1080/08832320903217903.

Miller-Matero, L. R., Martinez, S., Maclean, L., Yaremchuk, K., & Ko, A. B. (2018). Grit: A predictor of medical student performance. *Education for Health, 31*(2), 109–113. https://doi.org/10.4103/efh.EfH.

Ng, T. W. H., & Feldman, D. C. (2010). Human capital and objective indicators of career success: The mediating effects of cognitive ability and conscientiousness. *Journal of Occupational and Organizational Psychology, 83*(1), 207–235. https://doi.org/10.1348/096317909X414584.

Olckers, C., & Koekemoer, F. E. (2017). Linking psychological ownership with subjective career success and positive work-related outcomes. In C. Olckers, L. E. van Zyl, & L. van der Vaart (Eds.), *Psychological ownership: Theoretical orientations and practical applications* (pp. 3–20). New York, NY: Springer. https://doi.org/10.1007/978-3-319-70247-6.

Olckers, C., & Van Zyl, L. E. (2019). Psychometric properties of the psychological ownership questionnaire. *Australian Journal of Psychology, 72*(2), 127–136.

Pan, J., & Zhou, W. (2015). How do employees construe their career success: An improved measure of subjective career success. *International Journal of Selection and Assessment, 23*(1), 45–58. https://doi.org/10.1111/ijsa.12094.

Park, H. C., Kim, W., & Song, J. H. (2015). The impact of ethical leadership on employees' in-role performance: The mediating effect of employees' psychological ownership. *Human Resource Development Quarterly, 26*(4), 385–408. https://doi.org/10.1002/hrdq.2121.

Peng, H., & Pierce, J. (2015). Job- and organization-based psychological ownership: Relationship and outcomes. *Journal of Managerial Psychology, 30*(2), 151–168. https://doi.org/10.1108/JMP-07-2012-0201.

Pierce, J. L., Kostova, T., & Dirks, K. T. (2001). Toward a theory of psychological ownership in organizations. *Academy of Management Review, 26*(2), 298–310. https://doi.org/10.5465/amr.2001.4378028.

Pierce, J. L., Kostova, T., & Dirks, K. T. (2003). The state of psychological ownership: Integrating and extending a century of research. *Review of General Psychology, 7*(1), 1–46. https://doi.org/10.1037/1089-2680.7.1.84.

Pierce, J. L., & Rodgers, L. (2004). The psychology of ownership and worker-owner productivity. *Group and Organisation Management, 29*(5), 588–613. https://doi.org/10.1177/1059601103254270.

Robertson-Kraft, C., & Duckworth, A. L. (2014). True grit: Trait-level perseverance and passion for long-term goals predicts effectiveness and retention among novice teachers. *Teachers College Record, 116*(3) http://www.tcrecord.org/Content.asp?Contentid=17352.

Salles, A., Cohen, G. L., & Mueller, C. M. (2014). The relationship between grit and resident well-being. *American Journal of Surgery, 207*(2), 251–254. https://doi.org/10.1016/j.amjsurg.2013.09.006.

Seibert, S. E., Kraimer, M. L., & Crant, J. M. (2001). What do proactive people do? A longitudinal model linking proactive personality and career success. *Personnel Psychology, 54*(4), 845–874. https://doi.org/10.1111/j.1744-6570.2001.tb00234.x.

Sieger, P., Zellweger, T., & Aquino, K. (2013). Turning agents into psychological principals: Aligning interests of non-owners through psychological ownership. *Journal of Management Studies, 50*(3), 361–388. https://doi.org/10.1111/joms.12017.

Spector, P. E. (1982). Behavior in organizations as a function of employee's locus of control. *Psychological Bulletin, 91*(3), 482–497. https://doi.org/10.1037//0033-2909.91.3.482.

Supangco, V. T. (2011). Organisational and individual determinants of career success of MBA students. *Journal of International Business Research, 10*(2), 113–128.

Suzuki, Y., Tamesue, D., Asahi, K., & Ishikawa, Y. (2015). Grit and work engagement: A cross-sectional study. *PLoS One, 10*(9), e0137501. https://doi.org/10.1371/journal.pone.0137501.

Torp, S., & Nielsen, B. B. (2018). Psychological ownership and financial firm performance: The interplay of employee stock ownership and participative leadership. *Australian Journal of Management, 43*(3), 476–492. https://doi.org/10.1177/031289621875551.

Vainio, M. M., & Daukantaite, D. (2016). Grit and different aspects of well-being: Direct and indirect relationships via sense of coherence and authenticity. *Journal of Happiness Studies, 17*(5), 2119–2147. https://doi.org/10.1007/s10902-015-9688-7.

Van Dyne, L., & Pierce, J. L. (2004). Psychological ownership and feelings of possession: Three field studies predicting employee attitudes and organizational citizenship behaviors. *Journal of Organizational Behavior, 25*, 439–459. https://doi.org/10.1002/job.249.

Vandewalle, D., Van Dyne, L., & Kostova, T. (1995). Psychological ownership: An empirical examination of its consequences. *Group and Organization Management, 20*(2), 217–234. https://doi.org/10.1177/1059601195202008.

Visagie, S., & Koekemoer, E. (2014). What it means to succeed: Personal perceptions of career success held by senior managers. *South African Journal of Business Management, 45*(1), 43–54. https://doi.org/10.4102/sajbm.v45i1.116.

Von Culin, K. R., Tsukayama, E., & Duckworth, A. L. (2014). Unpacking grit: Motivational correlates of perseverance and passion for long-term goals. *Journal of Positive Psychology, 9* (4), 306–312. https://doi.org/10.1080/17439760.2014.898320.

Wagner, S. H., Parker, C. P., & Christiansen, N. D. (2003). Employees that think and act like owners: Effects of ownership beliefs and behaviors on organisational effectiveness. *Personnel Psychology, 56*(4), 847–871. https://doi.org/10.1111/j.1744-6570.2003.tb00242.x.

Wang, S., Zhou, M., Chen, T., Yang, X., Chen, G., Wang, M., & Gong, Q. (2017). Grit and the brain: Spontaneous activity of the dorsomedial prefrontal cortex mediates the relationship between the trait grit and academic performance. *Social Cognitive and Affective Neuroscience, 12*(3), 452–460. https://doi.org/10.1093/scan/nsw145.

Chantal Olckers (PhD) is a registered psychologist (Category: Industrial) with the Health Professions Council of South Africa. She has completed a Doctorate degree in the field of Human Resource Management, specialising in psychological ownership. She also holds a Master of Commerce, an Honours and a Bachelor's degree in Personnel Management, which were obtained from the University of Pretoria. Chantal is a respected researcher and published author of various scientific articles in peer-reviewed journals, chapters in international peer-reviewed books and editor of a specialist book on psychological ownership. She has presented several research papers at both national and international conferences. She is employed at the University of Pretoria as an Associate Professor in the Department of Human Resource Management. Chantal is involved with the South African Journal of Human Resource Management as well as the South African Journal of Industrial Psychology as a Section Editor. She has extensive experience within the tertiary educational environment (as a lecturer and researcher), as well as within the private sector (as a consultant). Chantal has a passion for positive organisational behaviour and specifically psychological ownership.

Eileen Koekemoer is an associate Professor at the University of Pretoria in South Africa. She is a registered Industrial Psychologist with the Health Professions Council of South Africa (HPCSA). In 2010, she obtained her PhD in Industrial Psychology at the North-West University in South Africa. Her areas of research include work-life interaction, career success and the wellbeing of employees. She is involved in various research projects investigating the interaction between employees' work and family life and how it influences their career success and/or wellbeing. She is the mother of three daughters and constantly juggles her own work-life balance between her children and her career as academic and researcher.

Chapter 13
Developing Gritty Job Seekers: A Need-Supportive Approach to Grit Interventions

Leoni van der Vaart, Llewellyn Ellardus van Zyl, and Jessica van Wingerden

Abstract Optimizing job search performance of unemployed job seekers remains a priority for unemployment researchers and practitioners alike. Grit, as a non-cognitive personality trait, may play an essential role in optimizing job search performance. However, grit is largely ignored in the context of unemployment. This chapter first contends that grit interventions should be developed for and implemented in the unemployment context. Secondly, it proposes practical strategies on how job seekers could develop the psychological conditions of grit (interest, deliberate practice, hope, meaning and purpose). Thirdly, it provides an overview of strategies which could be employed to develop a growth-mindset within the unemployed. Finally, it argues how self-determination theory (SDT) could be used to create a need supportive environment which is important to facilitate the job seeker's adherence to, engagement with grit intervention strategies. In doing so, the chapter contributes to the limited literature on grit interventions, in general, but also more specifically in the unemployment context. It also contributes to incorporating SDT principles in the delivery of grit interventions.

Keywords Grit · Unemployed · Interventions · Growth-mindset

L. van der Vaart (✉)
Optentia Research Focus Area, School of Industrial Psychology and Human Resource Management, North-West University, Vanderbijlpark, South Africa
e-mail: leoni.vandervaart@nwu.ac.za

L. E. van Zyl
Human Performance Management, University of Universiteit Eindhoven, Eindhoven, the Netherlands

J. van Wingerden
Center of Excellence for Positive Organizational Psychology, Erasmus University Rotterdam, Rotterdam, the Netherlands

L. E. van Zyl et al. (eds.), *Multidisciplinary Perspectives on Grit*,
https://doi.org/10.1007/978-3-030-57389-8_13

13.1 Introduction

Ever-increasing trends like digitization, work automation and the mass adoption of artificial intelligence—commonly referred to as the fourth industrial revolution—change the world of work fundamentally (Hirschi, 2018). Not only does it change the nature of work, but it may also result in the elimination of millions of 'traditional' jobs from the labor market (Peters & Jandrić, 2019) and the creation of new occupations and industries (Hirschi, 2018). Unemployment rates may (temporarily) soar as a result of the shift from current (and possibly redundant) jobs to new ways of working with devastating effects on the psychological-, economic-, political- and societal stability of modern economies. Governments and the private sector), therefore, need not only deal with issues relating to job creation but must invest significantly in aiding the unemployed to transition into new jobs.

At the center of this transitioning process is a psychologically vulnerable individual, engaging in a job search process that is challenging, complex, uncertain and that is often filled with obstacles, setbacks, and rejections (McKee-Ryan, Song, Wanberg, & Kinicki, 2005; Paul & Moser, 2009; Van Hooft, 2014; Wanberg, 2012) in a volatile, uncertain, complex and ambiguous (VUCA)[1] world of work. To secure a high-quality job and to escape the psychological costs of unemployment, individuals need to consistently engage in job search activities, despite the ever-increasing hardships and obstacles which they may face in this process. In effect, successful job seekers are likely to be "gritty" (i.e. showing high levels of Grit). Grit is a non-cognitive, psychological strength that encapsulates passion (i.e. consistency of interest) and perseverance (of effort) in the pursuit of long-term goals (Duckworth, Peterson, Matthews, & Kelly, 2007).

Grit is associated with many positive outcomes, including mastery (i.e. performance) and well-being across a variety of domains and population groups (*c.f.* Credé, Tynan, & Harms, 2017; Datu, Yuen, & Chen, 2017). Individuals who report higher levels of grit are more likely to achieve their goals, can think strategically about failures as learning opportunities, and can seek the necessary resources required to achieve their goals (Park, Yu, Baelen, Tsukayama, & Duckworth, 2018). These individuals are also more likely to report higher levels of emotional-, psychological-, and social well-being (Aswini & Deb, 2017). Consequently, interventions aimed at developing grit can be extremely beneficial but are rarely explored in the literature; despite some researchers arguing that grit is a malleable trait (Duckworth, 2016; Park et al., 2018).

Within the unemployment domain, grit remains mostly unexplored, and interventions to develop gritty job seekers are largely absent. This is unfortunate given that grit may be particularly valuable in adverse, ambiguous and complex situations such as those in which the unemployed find themselves (Credé, 2018). Given that

[1]The acronym VUCA originated in the U.S. military (Whiteman, 1998).

grit is associated with achievement and goal attainment within the general populous and has shown to improve performance in high-stake environments (Credé et al., 2017), a marginal increase in grit could have very meaningful positive effects for the unemployed. However, empirical research (outside of the primary education system) into the ways in which grit could be developed, is largely lacking within the literature (Rhodes, May, Andrade, & Kavanagh, 2018). Duckworth (2016) made some suggestions as to how grit could be developed through external sources and through internal psychological development and argued that grit can be developed through cultivating interest, discovering or defining purpose, instilling hope, and through deliberate skills practice. Further, some have argued that grit could also be fostered through adopting a growth-mindset (Tang, Wang, Guo, & Salmela-Aro, 2019). Grit is also a function of the environment in which an individual function. A gritty organizational or school culture, tends to foster gritty individuals and groups (Cross, 2014). However, none of which have been applied to, translated for or tested within unemployed populations.

As such, the purpose of this chapter is to explore potential grit-development intervention strategies for the unemployed. Specifically, the aim is to highlight how grit can be developed from the inside out (internal psychological development), and from the outside in (through external sources). Further, the current chapter also discusses ways in which grit interventions should be delivered to create a psychological climate that strengthens the effect of grit interventions while enhancing client adherence and engagement. Through self-determination theory (SDT), we will discuss how grit interventions for the unemployed should be delivered in a need-supportive climate. A climate where individuals experience a true sense of ownership over their thoughts, feelings and behaviors (i.e. autonomy), belonging (i.e. relatedness), and efficacy (i.e. competence). In doing so, the chapter contributes to the limited literature on grit interventions, in general, but also more specifically in the unemployment context.

13.2 Conceptualizing Grit

In 2007, Duckworth and colleagues introduced grit as a non-cognitive (personality) trait that matters for performance (Duckworth et al., 2007). Grit, usually operationalized as a higher-order construct, consists of two lower-order (related) dimensions (Credé et al., 2017; Van Zyl, Olckers, & Roll, 2020): Perseverance (of effort) and passion (i.e. consistency of interest). Gritty individuals, those who possess high levels of grit, work consistently and passionately toward meaningful goals even when faced with adversity or confronted by challenges (Duckworth, 2016; Duckworth et al., 2007). Both passion and perseverance are necessary for performance: mastery requires many hours of deliberate practice and are characterized by initial failures through which an individual should persist (Ericsson, Krampe,

& Tesch-Römer, 1993). If an individual does not persist through obstacles or constantly change their interest/s, it is unlikely that they will engage in a deliberate practice that enables performance (Credé et al., 2017). In an unemployment context, job seekers are faced with multiple challenges (Van Hooft, 2014) such as a mismatch between labour market requirements and experience or skills offered and the financial burden associated with job search. Persistence, hard work, determination and readiness for failure (Datu, Yuen, & Chen, 2018) will be important characteristics to portray in an attempt to find (re)employment. In addition, they would need to remain focused, passionate and should set priorities (Datu et al., 2018) during the arduous job-seeking process.

More recently, researchers levelled criticism against the construct and predictive validity of grit. Meta-analytic findings caution against calculating a total grit score (as a higher-order construct) as the width of the credibility interval indicates that the strength of the relation between the grit facets is moderated and because perseverance is a better predictor of performance than passion (Credé et al., 2017). In response, some authors argued that the critique might stem from limitations in the way grit is measured (Jachimowicz, Wihler, Bailey, & Galinsky, 2018). More specifically, Jachimowicz et al. (2018) argue that the grit scale currently only measures persistence and not passion. This is unfortunate because not only does it not reflect the totality of grit as Duckworth and colleagues originally intended but perseverance requires passion for having its intended beneficial effects (Jachimowicz et al., 2018). That is, immersion transpires when perseverance and passion combine, and immersion leads to the cognitive effort and investment into goals required for performance (Credé et al., 2017; Jachimowicz et al., 2018). So, instead of discarding passion as a facet of grit based on weak meta-analytic relations with performance, passion should be clearly defined, operationalised and measured. To this extent, passion is defined as a "strong feeling toward a personally important value/preference that motivates intentions and behaviors to express that value/preference" (Jachimowicz et al., 2018, p. 9981). Unemployed individuals can benefit from internalizing their reasons for job searching to the extent that not only the search activity is personally valuable or important, but also employment.

Whereas the original conceptualization and operationalization of grit included two facets, studies in collectivistic contexts suggested that grit should include a third facet: adaptability to ever-changing situations (Datu et al., 2018). Although these authors argue that adaptability is important in collectivistic societies (because the 'self' is highly context-dependent), it may extend to more individualistic societies to counter the criticism levelled at grit—namely, that it comes at a cost. Grit encapsulates the notion that it is the courage to push through the fear of failure, so less gritty individuals tend to change direction to minimize their losses. In contrast, their grittier counterparts continue on their original path despite their losses (Maddi, Matthews, Kelly, Villarreal, & White, 2012). The cost of grit was confirmed in a recent study by Lucas, Gratch, Cheng, and Marsella (2015). So, appreciating changes, a desire for improvement, flexibility of plans, and maintaining harmonious relationships—key indicators of adaptability (Datu et al., 2018)—may play an important role in facilitating healthy perseverance and passion, even more so within unemployment.

Grit's value lies in its relation to several positive outcomes (Park et al., 2018) in addition to performance, but that also enables performance. Grittier individuals engage in attention-absorbing activities and seek meaning and purpose (Hill, Burrow, & Bronk, 2016; Von Culin, Tsukayama, & Duckworth, 2014). They also tend to perceive their abilities as malleable (Hochanadel & Finamore, 2015; West et al., 2016), demonstrate higher levels of self-efficacy (Muenks, Wigfield, Yang, & O'Neal, 2017), and attribute adversity to specific and changeable causes. Grittier individuals also engage in more self-regulated learning (Wolters & Hussain, 2015). They are also less inclined to quit as demonstrated in several contexts (Eskreis-Winkler, Shulman, Beal, & Duckworth, 2014) and reported higher levels of well-being (Disabato, Goodman, & Kashdan, 2019), also on a daily level (Jiang et al., 2019). Given the value of grit, especially in the unemployment domain, interventions should be developed through which grit can be enhanced.

13.3 Developing Gritty Job Seekers

Personality is often regarded as a stable and unchanged trait. However, only about 40% of someone's personality is due to genetic reasons. This means that about 60% of personality variations are ascribed to environmental influences (Vukasović & Bratko, 2015). In other words, one's personality can be changed, shaped, and cultivated to a large extent (Tang et al., 2019). In line with the notion that grit is a malleable personality trait or strength, Duckworth (2016) discussed possible internal psychological (e.g. interest, deliberate practice, purpose, and hope) and external environmental sources (e.g. career counselors, gritty cultures), that can facilitate the development of grit. Additional internal psychological resources (e.g. growth-mindset) also emerged, from empirical studies, as significant determinants of grit.

13.3.1 Cultivating Sustainable Interest

Aiding the unemployed to discover their interest, aspects of their previous work which they enjoyed or tasks which they found engaging is a valuable way in which to develop grit (Duckworth, 2016). In essence, job seekers should be facilitated to discover their passions and empowered to channel their energies to find job opportunities centered around these enduring interests (Weisskirch, 2019). If passion/interest is present, grit will follow (Duckworth, 2016). When there is alignment between interests/passions, and competencies/strengths, individuals are inclined to exert more effort in achieving the goals flowing from such (Van Zyl, Deacon, & Rothmann, 2010).

However, job seekers may not necessarily have many enjoyable options to choose from when searching for a job. Yet, concerted efforts need to be made to (a) determine enduring interests, (b) experimenting with new skills, tasks or work to discover “new (latent) interests”, (c) translating interests into passions through exploration and (d) cultivate passion through active investment in skill development (Duckworth et al., 2007). Cultivating passion is a time and development intensive process which implies that even though an activity may not be pleasurable in the current moment, it doesn’t mean that it might not be in the future once the skill is mastered (Duckworth, 2016). Job seekers should develop realistic expectations about interests but also need to understand that interests are the seeds needed to develop a passion (Weisskirch, 2019). Discovering and developing interests into passions, and passions into viable job opportunities, requires hard work, dedication and active effort by the job seeker (Cross, 2014).

Latent interests are triggered by practical exposure, exploration or play, and not by mere self-reflection or introspection. Job seekers need to actively and consciously engage with the world and try “new things” in order to discover their interests (Duckworth et al., 2007). Passion develops from discovering and investing in interests; however, it does require a significant amount of time and hard work (Jin & Kim, 2017). It should be noted that interest does not imply discovering a completely new area of expertise or a new functional skill; it could also be found in domains in which one is already competent. Novelty is different for novices (i.e. seeking new interests) and experts (i.e. seeking nuances in current domains of expertise) (Duckworth, 2016). Job seekers need to not only discover new interests but also need to deepen their understanding of their current strengths (O’Keefe, Dweck, & Walton, 2018). Both should be approached in a systematic and structured manner.

Various individual and environmental primers, interventions or techniques could be employed to aid the job seeker to discover his/her interests and to translate such into passions. Table 13.1 provides some practical guidelines or techniques which could be implemented in this regard.

13.3.2 Deliberate Practice

Grit is not just about discovering an interest or passion; it is also about exerting concerted effort to enhance the level of expertise in a given task/skill/interest/hobby (Wolfe & Patel, 2016). Gritty individuals have an innate drive to hone in on the weaknesses of a given skill, isolate the core mistakes, and actively focus on their improvement. In effect, gritty job seekers embody a persistent desire to develop and adopt a “failure as a learning opportunity” mindset. For example, if a job seeker didn’t do well in an interview, he/she would ask for feedback from the organization to determine where he/she could do better the next time around. These job seekers would dissect each failed interview to determine the specific area of concern, develop an active strategy to address such, implement it and engage in repetitive practice to improve. Deliberate practice does not refer to aimless and mindless repetition of a task with the hopes of enhancing performance (i.e. experience does not equate to excellence) (Duckworth et al., 2007).

Table 13.1 Techniques for cultivating interests

Techniques
1. Employ psychometric assessments to discover values, motives, aptitude, strengths and personality preferences and experiment with new activities aligned with these aspects
2. Connect signature strengths to potential domains of work, or fields of interests
3. Listing or exploring tasks and activities which is fun and enjoyable. Determine overarching themes or links between these different types of activities
4. Reflect upon the interests and hobbies of others and determine which you may find interesting 5. Engage in the process of systematic self-reflection on current skills, capabilities, interests or even hobbies to determine which areas could still be improved 6. Discover a niche domain adjacent to your current field of interest and invest time to learn more about it 7. Take up an unpaid internship, or volunteer temporarily in a company which does something subjectively meaningful
8. Attend "free online courses" by reputable institutions through platforms such as Coursera.org
9. Attend free conferences or business meetups relating to domains of interest
10. Find and contract a mentor or a coach
11. Register to participate in social enterprises to be surrounded by gritty individuals who have a passion for a given domain
12. Join social clubs or community-building initiatives hosted by local organisations

Deliberate practice refers to a highly effortful process of purposeful and systematic practice aligned to a desire to improve performance through engaging in specific tasks to overcome current areas of weakness (Miller, Chow, Wampold, & Hubble, 2019). This implies that deliberate practice is not a proverbially pleasurable activity as it requires active effort from job seekers as the desired outcome is beyond his/her current level of skill. This process is painful; it's a challenge, its strenuous and personally stretching. Job seekers should realize that deliberate practice is employed to improve skills, and not to experience flow, pleasure or engagement. Dweck (2012) argued that individuals engaged in deliberate practice should proverbially 'learn to love the burden' of practice and argued that it requires the following:

1. A reasonably developed level of expertise in a given domain or skill, coupled with the motivation needed to improve
2. Clear, well defined, specific, measurable, realistic and attainable goals with clear performance targets
3. A mentor/teacher or coach who could aid in setting clear and specific goals, isolate mistakes and develop activities to aid in enhancing performance
4. Developing skills that have already been mastered by others and that evidence-based practices, training or techniques are available to aid in improving the skill
5. A set (daily) routine and commitment to the process
6. Challenges that are stretching, pushing the individual outside of his/her comfort zone and exceeding current skill levels
7. Active, immediate and constructive feedback from external parties

Fig. 13.1 Deliberate practice model for job seekers

8. Active reflection on progress and performance with a constant refinement of the skill
9. Supporters and encouraging mentors

The conditions for deliberate practice can be clustered into five broad categories (Fig. 13.1). One, job seekers need to set SMART (specific, measurable, attainable, realistic and time-bound) goals associated with the skills or abilities they need to enhance their success of obtaining meaningful employment (Dweck, 2012). These goals need to be aligned to their signature strengths to ensure commitment over time (Van Zyl, Roll, Stander, & Richter, 2020). Job seekers need to perform a gap analyses between their current level of skills/abilities and the level at which they would like to perform (Van Zyl et al., accepted). Two, based on the gap analyses, job seekers need to establish a clear path to bridge the gap between the current and desired state (Oades, Crowe, & Nguyen, 2009). This implies that process of goal attainment needs to be broken down into smaller, sequential steps and tasks which systematically build on one another to achieve the performance goals (Orem, Binkert, & Clancy, 2007). Three, job seekers need to focus on developing the 'right' tasks first (Passmore & Oades, 2015). For example, if a job seeker aims to become a concert pianist, he/she would first need to learn how to read sheet music or notes, before he/she can learn how to hit the right notes, in the correct order and the right time. Four, the job seeker needs to isolate the key moves or areas of active concern and engage in meaningful repetition (Van Zyl, Roll, et al., 2020). Here the focus is on 'micro-skill development' associated with the challenges he/she can't yet meet. Last, the job seeker should actively seek feedback and reflect on his/her performance. Feedback is required to both motivate and empower as well as identify areas of improvement (Duckworth et al., 2007; Dweck, 2012). The type and level of feedback that is being solicited depends on the level of current expertise of the job seeker. When developing a brand-new skill, an individual requires unconditional support and encouragement to fast track mastery (Peláez, Coo, & Salanova, 2019). However, if a specific level of performance is already present, and the aim is to improve a specific aspect, then critical feedback is required. If a novice gets vital feedback, it would be demotivational, and the probability of quitting increases. If a professional only receive supportive feedback, he/she will become stagnant or even bored (Linley, Woolston, & Biswas-Diener, 2009). Job seekers should ensure that they are surrounded by cheerleaders (those who provide unconditional support), supporters (those who empower and encourage) and encouraging mentors (who will provide critical, yet constructive guidance).

13.3.3 Pursuing Purpose and Discovering Meaning

Where interest and deliberate practice is associated with the discovery and development of skills, abilities and competencies, purpose and meaning relate to how such connects to the proverbial bigger picture (Jordan, Ferris, Hochwarter, & Wright, 2019). From Duckworth's (2016) perspective, understanding how one's life, one's work or one's goals are aligned to the service of others, contributes to feelings of contentment. Also, research revealed that experiencing one's work to be meaningful to others is positively related to happiness, work-related well-being, (Van Wingerden & Van der Stoep, 2017), use of strengths and proactive behavior (e.g. job crafting) (Van Wingerden & Van der Stoep, 2018; Van Wingerden, Van der Stoep, & Poell, 2018). Meaning and purpose provide the fuel required to push through difficult situations and to conquer obstacles hindering goal attainment. In other words, individuals are gritty because they perceive their contributions to add value to the lives and well-being of others (Duckworth, 2016). For job seekers, however, understanding the meaning and purpose of their lives are particularly difficult seeing that basic psychological needs (safety and security) aren't being met (Van Zyl & Stander, 2013). However, research suggests that it is the most important aspect to develop to aid individuals to push through times of high uncertainty and disappear (Martela & Steger, 2016).

Meaning and purpose build greater perseverance and enhances commitment to personal goals. Without having meaningful goals, one might be left without clear targets to persevere towards (Duckworth, 2016; Hill et al., 2016; Tang et al., 2019). Albeit its importance, the experience of purpose and meaning differs between individuals making it the most challenging aspect to develop in job seekers (Van Zyl & Stander, 2019). Meaning and purpose is a deeply subjective experience which actively influences how life, work, struggles and failures are interpreted. Although no generic set of guidelines can be provided to aid job seekers in experiencing meaning during the job searching process, Van Zyl and Stander (2019) provided some general techniques which could be used to develop meaning. These are summarized in Table 13.2.

Table 13.2 Techniques for pursuing purpose and discovering meaning

Techniques
1. Exercise autonomy and the freedom to choose
2. Engage in a cognitive recrafting exercise linking the job-seeking behaviors or the unemployment process to something larger than one-self or a bigger goal
3. Contract a mentor who shows a high level of purpose or advocates his work as a calling
4. Reflect upon the meaningful moments during the job searching process and celebrate the small victories
5. Engage in activities that are aligned to personal strengths, and those which contribute to the wellbeing of others
6. List ways in which the job search process has had a positive impact on the self and others
7. Act as a mentor for someone else
8. Deepen social connections with those in one's network
9. Use employment-crafting strategies as a means to optimize demands and to seek resources

Another essential element associated with crafting meaning is to reframe stories of failures (told as a victim) into stories of triumphs (told as a survivor) (Van Zyl, Motschnig-Pitrik, & Stander, 2016). This aids in reframing the victim mentality and builds an internal locus of control (Van Zyl et al., accepted). Van Zyl et al. (accepted) argued that simple strategies such as "finding 15 positive things about the current negative situation" or "looking for the silver lining" could have significant positive effects on the experience of meaning.

13.3.4 Instilling Hope

Like purpose and meaning, hope aids job seekers to keep faith in difficult times. Hope is created by allowing individuals to (a) set personally meaningful goals, (b) developing multiple pathways to achieve these goals and (c) preparing for possible obstacles (Snyder, 2000; Vela, Lu, Lenz, & Hinojosa, 2015). Duckworth (2016) theorized that an expectation that one has control over one's destiny or that one can create a better future through one's efforts may enhance grit. Not only does hope aid in the development of grit, but it also buffers against the onset of psychopathology and decreases the impact of the long-term psychological suffering associated with being unemployed (Van Zyl et al., 2016).

During unemployment, job seekers may over time develop feelings that they are not in control of the situation, which in effect leads to feelings of hopelessness (Van der Vaart & Van den Broeck, 2019). This type of psychological suffering, coupled with feelings of a lack of control, could lead people to experience depression, helplessness and despair (Seligman, 1972; Wanberg, 2012). Once hope is lost, it's particularly difficult to re-establish (Snyder, 2000). In contrast, when individuals are hopeful, and they feel that they have a sense of control over their lives, they tend to persevere even under the harshest of circumstances (Snyder, 2000). As such, it's important to aid job seekers to develop a hopeful disposition.

Although the first two components of Snyder's Hope Theory (Snyder, 2000), goal setting and goal strategizing, has already been discussed in the preceding sections, the final component "preparing for obstacles" (agency) needs further exploration. A major component of hope is the ability to anticipate and prepare for possible challenges and/or negative outcomes associated with goal attainment. Luthans, Avey, Avolio, Norman, and Combs (2006) argued that if an individual is prepared for possible failures, the potential impact it has on well-being and future performance is largely mitigated. Planning and preparing establish a sense of control over one's destiny. But how can this type of behavior be developed?

Although it's beyond the scope of this chapter to go into depth regarding scenario mapping, strategic planning, decision forecasting, SWOT/SOAR analysis and the like, job seekers need to employ a structured technique to identify the possible obstacles and risks which may lead to failures.[2] Besides these practical forecasting tools, on a psychological level, the job seeker could develop hope through:

1. Developing positive, and optimistic self-talk (Furtner, Sachse, & Exenberger, 2012)
2. Drawing a Hope Map, where high expectations of the future are articulated and clear view of how barriers will be approach in achieving such developed (McQuaid, Niemiec, & Doman, 2018)
3. Guided self-reflection through keeping a hope journal focused on artifacts which provide hope (Crain & Koehn, 2012)
4. Clarifying the meaning job seekers attach to hope and what it means to be hopeful (Van Zyl et al., 2016)
5. Showing a willingness to ask for help before things become too difficult to bear (Van Zyl & Stander, 2019)
6. Praise and celebrate EFFORT and not just successes (Duckworth, 2016)
7. Develop a growth-mindset (Dweck, 2012)

13.3.5 Fostering a Growth-Mindset

The job seeker's mindset is another factor which influences the potential success of his/her job seeking endeavors. Dweck (2012) argued that mindsets encapsulate one's belief about the developmental or fixed nature of the human condition. In her research, Dweck (2012) distinguishes between two types of mindsets: (a) a fixed mindset (i.e. people's talents, behavior and capacity to grow are static and cannot be significantly changed) and (b) a growth-mindset (i.e. individuals have the capacity to grow, develop and change). According to Dweck (1986), people with a growth-mindset tend to have a mastery goal-orientation and view challenges as learning opportunities. They are open to and embrace failures and persists despite difficulties and setbacks. They actively learn and grow from critiques and find lessons in the successes or/victories of others (Stoycheva & Ruskov, 2015). Duckworth (2016)

[2]For a non-technical primer on these tools, the reader is urged to consult Schoemaker (2004).

Table 13.3 Techniques for fostering a growth-mindset

Techniques
1. Get comfortable with imperfection and embrace uncertainty
2. Reframe failures as learning opportunities
3. Develop and test alternative strategies for approaching re-occurring problems
4. Avoid social-comparison and celebrate the achievements of others
5. Praise one's own effort towards goal achievement
6. Take calculated risks
7. Adopt a positive approach to both self-talk and communication with others (words create worlds)
8. Avoid attaching personal worth to failures in the job-seeking process
9. Learn from critiques
10. Know your current skill limits and don't push yourself till exhaustion
11. Actively request feedback on own growth and job-seeking strategies
12. When reflecting on failures, focus on the process, not on the self
13. Share mistakes and failures openly
14. Challenge own assumptions about personal value and the attributing factors to the unsuccessful job search process
15. Read up on brain plasticity (to help solidify the fact that even intelligence can change over time)

argued that gritty individuals adopt a growth-orientated mindset (Duckworth, 2016) which has subsequently been empirically confirmed (Tang et al., 2019).

Job seekers, therefore, need to actively work on the establishment and maintenance of a growth-mindset to aid them in finding meaningful employment. Hymer and Gershon (2014) provided several practical suggestions on how a growth-mindset can be developed and maintained. These are partially summarized in Table 13.3.

13.4 Need Satisfaction in the Context in which Gritty Job Seekers Are Developed

Grit interacts with situational characteristics to determine success or performance (Credé, 2018; Jordan, Ferris, et al., 2019). In the absence of such characteristics, grit's influence may be nonlinear or nonsignificant (Jordan, Ferris, et al., 2019). One such characteristic is the environment or the climate in which grit is developed (Duckworth, 2016). Van der Vaart and Van den Broeck (2019) argue that unemployment interventions should be delivered in a need-supportive climate—a climate where individuals experience a true sense of ownership over their thoughts, feelings and behaviors (i.e. autonomy), belonging (i.e. relatedness), and efficacy (i.e. competence). Need support is guided by the SDT and, hence, an overview of the theory is provided before illustrating how career counsellors (and significant others) can create a need-supportive psychological climate to in which gritty job seekers can flourish.

13.4.1 Self-Determination Theory

SDT is a prominent theory of motivation that proved to be effective in identifying psychological determinants and the processes through which they affect attitudinal, behavioural and well-being in multiple contexts (Ryan & Deci, 2017), including in the unemployment context (Van der Vaart, Van den Broeck, Rothmann, & De Witte, 2019). SDT holds that the kind of motivation one holds, alongside the amount of motivation, matters for behavioural and well-being outcomes. More specifically, the theory distinguishes between engaging in an activity because one ought to vs engaging in an activity because one considers it valuable or enjoyable (Deci & Ryan, 2000; Ryan & Deci, 2017). The former is referred to as controlled (and means the unemployed search because they have to) whereas the latter is autonomous (and means the unemployed search because it is important or interesting) motivation (Vansteenkiste & Van den Broeck, 2018). Autonomous motivation is self-determined—as the reasons for performing an activity is congruent with the self—and results in more positive attitudinal, behavioural and well-being outcomes as compared to controlled motivation (Deci & Ryan, 2000; Ryan & Deci, 2017). The third category is amotivation—amotivated persons lack the motivation to engage in an activity because they do not value the activity, they see no positive outcomes or resist the activity (Ryan & Deci, 2017; Ryan, Lynch, Vansteenkiste, & Deci, 2011). Amotivation predicts the worst outcomes for individuals (Ryan, Deci, & Grolnick, 1995). In the unemployment context, different kinds of motivation are also associated with differential outcomes in line with theory (Vansteenkiste & Van den Broeck, 2018). Although SDT categorises these different kinds of motivation and posits that it exists on a continuum, researchers acknowledge that they co-exist for behaviour to be multi-determined (Howard, Gagné, Morin, & Forest, 2018; Vansteenkiste & Mouratidis, 2016).

13.4.2 Basic Need Satisfaction

SDT further holds that the development of these different kinds of motivation is influenced by the satisfaction of three basic psychological needs: the need for autonomy, the need for competence and the need for relatedness.[3] The need for autonomy is defined as individuals' inherent desire to act with a sense of choice and volition, that is, to be the author of one's actions and to feel psychologically free (Deci & Ryan, 2000). For example, when feeling satisfied in the need for autonomy,

[3]In order to be classified as a *psychological* need, a need must consistently promote psychological growth, internalisation, and well-being across different cultures—beyond the variance explained by other proposed needs (Deci & Ryan, 2000). Thus far, empirical research provided evidence for the essential role of the three needs for autonomy, competence and relatedness (Sheldon, Elliot, Kim, & Kasser, 2001).

the unemployed would experience a sense of control over decisions to apply for a job such that their decisions reflect their wishes (Van der Vaart & Van den Broeck, 2019). However, on average, the unemployed may be more prone to low need satisfaction. Their daily activities may feel more like a chain of 'musts' and 'shoulds', undermining their need for autonomy (Vansteenkiste & Van den Broeck, 2018). The need for competence is the desire to feel capable of mastering the environment and to bring about desired outcomes (Deci & Ryan, 2000). Actively seeking out challenges helps people to develop their skills and adapt to complex and changing environments. For example, when they would feel competent, the unemployed experience a sense of confidence and feel capable and energised to pursue an activity (e.g., going for an interview) (Van der Vaart & Van den Broeck, 2019). However, continually facing rejections, the unemployed may experience rather low levels of competence satisfaction (Vansteenkiste & Van den Broeck, 2018). Finally, the need for relatedness is the inherent propensity to feel connected to others, that is, to be a member of a group, to love and care and be loved and cared for (Deci & Ryan, 2000). The need for relatedness is satisfied if people experience a sense of communion and maintain close and intimate relationships. For example, unemployed who would experience a sense of closeness and being connected to those who support them in coping with the frustrations accompanying unemployment would feel related (Van der Vaart & Van den Broeck, 2019). However, after a while, most unemployed feel isolated from external networks and may experience little satisfaction of their need for relatedness (Vansteenkiste & Van den Broeck, 2018).

The three needs are, in turn, influenced by the interpersonal environment in which a person finds themselves (Deci & Ryan, 2000). A need supportive interpersonal environment where individuals experience a true sense of ownership over their thoughts, feelings and behaviours (i.e. autonomy), belonging (i.e. relatedness), and efficacy (i.e. competence) leads to optimal outcomes indirectly via the different kinds of motivation (Deci, Olafsen, & Ryan, 2017; Ryan & Deci, 2017) but also directly (Van den Broeck, Ferris, Chang, & Rosen, 2016). A study by Van Wingerden, Bakker, and Derks (2017) revealed that the satisfaction of the three basic needs predicts employees' proactive behaviour (job crafting). This positive relationship between basic need satisfaction and proactive behaviour may also be relevant to the unemployed. Evidence in the unemployment context supports the importance of providing autonomy and enabling the unemployed to feel competent and a sense of belonging because it influences their motivation, job search behaviours, well-being and re-employment quality (Ellingsen-Dalskau, Morken, Berget, & Pedersen, 2016; Koen, Klehe, Van Vianen, Zikic, & Nauta, 2010; Koen, Van Vianen, Van Hooft, & Klehe, 2016; Van der Vaart et al., 2019). Preliminary evidence also hints at the importance of relatedness and competence in the development of grit. For example, Park et al. (2018) showed that when students perceive their school environment as mastery-oriented, higher levels of grit transpires (Park et al., 2018). Datu et al. (2017) showed that a sense of relatedness is positively associated with grit (Datu, 2017). Duckworth (2016) recommends that significant others strike a balance between being supportive (i.e. being warm and respectful) and firmly enforcing expectations when developing grit. Taken together, basic need satisfaction potentially boost grit and can be nurtured through interpersonal sources.

13.4.3 Autonomy-Supportive Behaviors

Autonomy-supportive behaviors include (a) acknowledging others' feelings and ideas, (b) providing reasons for rules and expectations, and (c) offering of choice and opportunities for others to take initiative (Mageau et al., 2015; Rocchi, Pelletier, Chueng, & Desmarais, 2017; Williams, Whipp, Jackson, & Dimmock, 2013). Autonomy-supportive counsellors, for example, would give the unemployed as much choice as possible and provide a rationale when necessary.

13.4.4 Competence-Supportive Behaviors

Competence-supportive behaviors include (a) structuring tasks in a way that individuals can expand their knowledge and capabilities (Niemiec & Ryan, 2009), (b) acknowledging improvement, (c) believing in others' abilities to succeed, and (d) providing constructive and valuable feedback (Rocchi et al., 2017; Sheldon & Filak, 2008). Competence-supportive counsellors, for example, would acknowledge the improvement in competency development and provide positive feedback on areas of growth.

13.4.5 Relatedness-Supportive Behaviors

Relatedness-supportive behaviors include (a) showing unconditional positive regard, (b) being warm and empathetic, (c) having a genuine interest in them and their activities (Jones, Armour, & Potrac, 2004; Rocchi et al., 2017). Relatedness-supportive counsellors should not only engage in interactions in a warm, empathic and compassionate way but may also encourage them to seek social support when engaging in activities that are aimed at developing grit.

13.4.6 Grit and Self-Employment

Grit not only matters for job seekers that aim to find employment, but also for those who wish to be self-employed (or entrepreneurs) (Wolfe & Patel, 2016). Authors argue that self-employment and employment are both characterised by goal setting and achievement (Baum & Locke, 2004; Wolfe & Patel, 2016) and for this reason, grit plays an important role in not only the decision to engage in self-employment or entrepreneurship but also to be a successful entrepreneur (Arco-Tirado, Bojica, Fernández-Martin, & Hoyle, 2019; Wolfe & Patel, 2016). For this reason, and because of the role of self-employment and entrepreneurship in combating unemployment, interventions can be equally beneficial for those wishing to pursue entrepreneurial aspirations instead of employment.

13.5 Conclusion and Future Directions

To reap the benefits of gritty job seekers, stakeholders (i.e. career counsellors, government, organizational psychologists) should actively invest in interventions. However, developing gritty job seekers remain a challenge; even more so in the absence of scientific evidence of grit's benefit in the unemployment context and intervention research in the grit domain. The current chapter theoretically argued the relevance of grit in the unemployment context and provided theoretically grounded ways in which gritty job seekers can be developed. The chapter also illustrated how a need-supportive psychological climate can be created that would enhance the success of grit interventions. Recommendations for future research include intervention studies to determine the effectiveness of these interventions in a variety of countries.

References

Arco-Tirado, J. L., Bojica, A., Fernández-Martin, F., & Hoyle, R. H. (2019). Grit as predictor of entrepreneurship and self-employment in Spain. *Frontiers in Psychology, 10*, 389. https://doi.org/10.3389/fpsyg.2019.00389.

Aswini, S., & Deb, A. (2017). Flourishing among postgraduate students: The role of resilience, meaningfulness and grit. *Indian Journal of Community Psychology, 13*(1), 24.

Baum, J. R., & Locke, E. A. (2004). The relationship of entrepreneurial traits, skill, and motivation to subsequent venture growth. *Journal of Applied Psychology, 89*(4), 587–598. https://doi.org/10.1037/0021-9010.89.4.587.

Crain, M., & Koehn, C. (2012). The essence of hope in domestic violence support work: A hermeneutic-phenomenological inquiry. *Journal of Mental Health Counseling, 34*(2), 170–188.

Credé, M. (2018). What shall we do about grit? A critical review of what we know and what we don't know. *Educational Researcher, 47*(9), 606–611. https://doi.org/10.3102/0013189X18801322.

Credé, M., Tynan, M. C., & Harms, P. D. (2017). Much ado about grit: A meta-analytic synthesis of the grit literature. *Journal of Personality and Social Psychology, 113*(3), 492–511. https://doi.org/10.1037/pspp0000102.

Cross, T. M. (2014). The gritty: Grit and non-traditional doctoral student success. *Journal of Educators Online, 11*(3), n3.

Datu, J. A. D. (2017). Sense of relatedness is linked to higher grit in a collectivist setting. *Personality and Individual Differences, 105*, 135–138. https://doi.org/10.1016/j.paid.2016.09.039.

Datu, J. A. D., Yuen, M., & Chen, G. (2017). Grit and determination: A review of literature with implications for theory and research. *Journal of Psychologists and Counsellors in Schools, 27*(2), 168–176. https://doi.org/10.1017/jgc.2016.2.

Datu, J. A. D., Yuen, M., & Chen, G. (2018). Exploring determination for long-term goals in a collectivist context: A qualitative study. *Current Psychology, 37*, 263–271. https://doi.org/10.1007/s12144-016-9509-0.

Deci, E. L., Olafsen, A. H., & Ryan, R. M. (2017). Self-determination theory in work organizations: The state of a science. *Annual Review of Organizational Psychology and Organizational Behavior, 4*(1), 19–43. https://doi.org/10.1146/annurev-orgpsych-032516-113108.

Deci, E. L., & Ryan, R. M. (2000). The 'what' and 'why' of goal pursuits: Human needs and the self-determination of behavior. *Psychological Inquiry, 11*(4), 227–268.

Disabato, D. J., Goodman, F. R., & Kashdan, T. B. (2019). Is grit relevant to well-being and strengths? Evidence across the globe for separating perseverance of effort and consistency of interests. *Journal of Personality, 87*, 194–211. https://doi.org/10.1111/jopy.12382.

Duckworth, A. L. (2016). *Grit: The power of passion and perseverance*. New York, NY: Scribner.

Duckworth, A. L., Peterson, C., Matthews, M. D., & Kelly, D. R. (2007). Grit: Perseverance and passion for long-term goals. *Journal of Personality and Social Psychology, 92*(6), 1087–1101. https://doi.org/10.1037/0022-3514.92.6.1087.

Dweck, C. S. (1986). Motivational processes affecting learning. *American Psychologist, 41*(10), 1040–1048. https://doi.org/10.1037/0003-066X.41.10.1040.

Dweck, C. (2012). *Mindset: Changing the way you think to fulfil your potential*. London: Little, Brown Book Group.

Ellingsen-Dalskau, L. H., Morken, M., Berget, B., & Pedersen, I. (2016). Autonomy support and need satisfaction in prevocational programs on care farms: The self-determination theory perspective. *Work, 53*(1), 73–85. https://doi.org/10.3233/WOR-152217.

Ericsson, K. A., Krampe, R. T., & Tesch-Römer, C. (1993). The role of deliberate practice in the acquisition of expert performance. *Psychological Review, 100*, 363–406. https://doi.org/10.1037/0033-295X.100.3.363.

Eskreis-Winkler, L., Shulman, E. P., Beal, S. A., & Duckworth, A. L. (2014). The grit effect: Predicting retention in the military, the workplace, school and marriage. *Frontiers in Psychology, 5*(36), 1–12. https://doi.org/10.3389/fpsyg.2014.00036.

Furtner, M. R., Sachse, P., & Exenberger, S. (2012). Learn to influence yourself: Full range self-leadership training. *Journal of the Indian Academy of Applied Psychology, 38*(2), 294–304.

Hill, P. L., Burrow, A. L., & Bronk, K. C. (2016). Persevering with positivity and purpose: An examination of purpose commitment and positive affect as predictors of grit. *Journal of Happiness Studies, 17*, 257–269. https://doi.org/10.1007/s10902-014-9593-5.

Hirschi, A. (2018). The fourth industrial revolution: Issues and implications for career research and practice. *The Career Development Quarterly, 66*(3), 192–204. https://doi.org/10.1002/cdq.12142.

Hochanadel, A., & Finamore, D. (2015). Fixed and growth mindset in education and how grit helps students persist in the face of adversity. *Journal of International Education Research, 11*(1), 47–50.

Howard, J. L., Gagné, M., Morin, A. J. S., & Forest, J. (2018). Using bifactor exploratory structural equation modeling to test for a continuum structure of motivation. *Journal of Management, 44*(7), 2638–2664. https://doi.org/10.1177/0149206316645653.

Hymer, B., & Gershon, M. (2014). *Growth mindset pocketbook*. Hampshire: Management Pocketbooks.

Jachimowicz, J. M., Wihler, A., Bailey, E. R., & Galinsky, A. D. (2018). Why grit requires perseverance and passion to positively predict performance. *PNAS, 115*(40), 9980–9985. https://doi.org/10.1073/pnas.1803561115.

Jiang, W., Jiang, J., Du, X., Gu, D., Sun, Y., & Zhang, Y. (2019). Striving and happiness: Between- and within-person-level associations among grit, needs satisfaction and subjective well-being. *The Journal of Positive Psychology, 15*, 543–555. https://doi.org/10.1080/17439760.2019.1639796.

Jin, B., & Kim, J. (2017). Grit, basic needs satisfaction, and subjective well-being. *Journal of Individual Differences, 38*, 29–35. https://doi.org/10.1027/1614-0001/a000219.

Jones, R., Armour, K., & Potrac, P. (2004). *Sports coaching cultures: From practice to theory*. London: Routledge.

Jordan, S. L., Ferris, G. R., Hochwarter, W. A., & Wright, T. A. (2019). Toward a work motivation conceptualization of grit in organizations. *Group & Organization Management, 44*(2), 320–360. https://doi.org/10.1177/1059601119834093.

Koen, J., Klehe, U.-C., Van Vianen, A. E. M., Zikic, J., & Nauta, A. (2010). Job-search strategies and reemployment quality. *Journal of Vocational Behavior, 77*(1), 126–139. https://doi.org/10.1016/j.jvb.2010.02.004.

Koen, J., Van Vianen, A. E. M., Van Hooft, E. A. J., & Klehe, U.-T. (2016). How experienced autonomy can improve job seekers' motivation, job search, and chance of finding reemployment. *Journal of Vocational Behavior, 9–96*, 31–44. https://doi.org/10.1016/j.jvb.2016.07.003.

Linley, P. A., Woolston, L., & Biswas-Diener, R. (2009). Strengths coaching with leaders. *International Coaching Psychology Review, 4*(1), 37–48.

Lucas, G. M., Gratch, J., Cheng, L., & Marsella, S. (2015). When the going gets tough: Grit predicts costly perseverance. *Journal of Research in Personality, 59*, 15–22. https://doi.org/10.1016/j.jrp.2015.08.004.

Luthans, F., Avey, J. B., Avolio, B. J., Norman, S. M., & Combs, G. J. (2006). Psychological capital development: Toward a micro-intervention. *Journal of Organizational Behavior, 27*, 387–393. https://doi.org/10.1002/job.373.

Maddi, S. R., Matthews, M. D., Kelly, D. R., Villarreal, B., & White, M. (2012). The role of hardiness and grit in predicting performance and retention of USMA cadets. *Military Psychology, 24*(1), 19–28. https://doi.org/10.1080/08995605.2012.639672.

Mageau, G. A., Ranger, F., Joussemet, M., Koestner, R., Moreau, E., & Forest, J. (2015). Validation of the perceived parental autonomy support scale (P-PASS). *Canadian Journal of Behavioural Science, 47*(3), 251–262.

Martela, F., & Steger, M. F. (2016). The three meanings of meaning in life: Distinguishing coherence, purpose, and significance. *The Journal of Positive Psychology, 11*(5), 531–545. https://doi.org/10.1080/17439760.2015.1137623.

McKee-Ryan, F., Song, Z., Wanberg, C. R., & Kinicki, A. J. (2005). Psychological and physical well-being during unemployment: A meta-analytic study. *Journal of Applied Psychology, 90*(1), 53–76. https://doi.org/10.1037/0021-9010.90.1.53.

McQuaid, M., Niemiec, R., & Doman, F. (2018). A character strengths-based approach to positive psychology coaching. In S. Green & S. Palmer (Eds.), *Positive psychology coaching in practice* (pp. 93–106). New York, NY: Routledge.

Miller, S. D., Chow, D., Wampold, B., & Hubble, M. A. (2019). "You say tomatoe, I say tomawto": The importance of deliberate practice for improved performance. *High Ability Studies, 30*(1–2), 288–290. https://doi.org/10.1080/13598139.2019.1652542.

Muenks, K., Wigfield, A., Yang, J. S., & O'Neal, C. R. (2017). How true is grit? Assessing its relations to high school and college students' personality characteristics, self-regulation, engagement, and achievement. *Journal of Educational Psychology, 109*(5), 599–620. https://doi.org/10.1037/edu0000153.

Niemiec, C. P., & Ryan, R. M. (2009). Autonomy, competence, and relatedness in the classroom: Applying self-determination theory to educational practice. *Theory and Research in Education, 7*(2), 133–144. https://doi.org/10.1177/1477878509104318.

O'Keefe, P. A., Dweck, C. S., & Walton, G. M. (2018). Implicit theories of interest: Finding your passion or developing it? *Psychological Science, 29*(10), 1653–1664. https://doi.org/10.1177/0956797618780643.

Oades, L. G., Crowe, T. P., & Nguyen, M. (2009). Leadership coaching transforming mental health systems from the inside out: The collaborative recovery model as person-centred strengths based coaching psychology. *International Coaching Psychology Review, 4*(1), 25–36.

Orem, S. L., Binkert, J., & Clancy, A. L. (2007). *Appreciative coaching: A positive process for change*. San Francisco, CA: Wiley.

Park, D., Yu, A., Baelen, R. N., Tsukayama, E., & Duckworth, A. L. (2018). Fostering grit: Perceived school goal-structure predicts growth in grit and grades. *Contemporary Educational Psychology, 55*, 120–128. https://doi.org/10.1016/j.cedpsych.2018.09.007.

Passmore, J., & Oades, L. (2015). Positive psychology techniques: Positive case conceptualisation. *The Coaching Psychologist, 11*(1), 43–45.

Paul, K. I., & Moser, K. (2009). Unemployment impairs mental health: Meta-analyses. *Journal of Vocational Behavior, 74*(3), 264–282. https://doi.org/10.1016/j.jvb.2009.01.001.

Peláez, M. J., Coo, C., & Salanova, M. (2019). Facilitating work engagement and performance through strengths-based micro-coaching: A controlled trial study. *Journal of Happiness Studies, 1*, –20. https://doi.org/10.1007/s10902-019-00127-5.

Peters, M. A., & Jandrić, P. (2019). Education and technological unemployment in the fourth industrial revolution. In G. Redding, A. Drew, & Crump, S. (Eds.), *The Oxford handbook of higher education systems and university management*. Retrieved from https://bib.irb.hr/datoteka/1010913.oxfordhb-9780198822905-e-27.pdf

Rhodes, J., May, J., Andrade, J., & Kavanagh, D. (2018). Enhancing grit through functional imagery training in professional soccer. *The Sport Psychologist, 32*(3), 220–225. https://doi.org/10.1123/tsp.2017-0093.

Rocchi, M., Pelletier, L., Chueng, S., & Desmarais, D. (2017). Assessing need-supportive and need-thwarting interpersonal behaviours: The interpersonal Behaviours questionnaire (IBQ). *Personality and Individual Differences, 104*, 423–433. https://doi.org/10.1016/j.paid.2016.08.034.

Ryan, R. M., & Deci, E. L. (2017). *Self-determination theory: Basic psychological needs in motivation, development, and wellness*. New York, NY: The Guilford Press.

Ryan, R. M., Deci, E. L., & Grolnick, W. S. (1995). Autonomy, relatedness, and the self: Their relation to development and psychopathology. In D. Cicchetti & D. J. Cohen (Eds.), *Developmental psychopathology: Theory and methods* (Vol. 1, pp. 618–655). New York, NY: Wiley.

Ryan, R. M., Lynch, M. F., Vansteenkiste, M., & Deci, E. L. (2011). Motivation and autonomy in counseling, psychotherapy, and behavior change: A look at theory and practice. *The Counseling Psychologist, 39*(2), 193–260.

Schoemaker, P. J. (2004). Forecasting and scenario planning: The challenges of uncertainty and complexity. In D. J. Koehler & N. Harvey (Eds.), *Handbook of judgment and decision-making* (pp. 274–296). Oxford: Blackwell.

Seligman, M. E. (1972). Learned helplessness. *Annual Review of Medicine, 23*(1), 407–412.

Sheldon, K. M., Elliot, A. J., Kim, Y., & Kasser, T. (2001). What is satisfying about satisfying events? Testing 10 candidate psychological needs. *Journal of Personality and Social Psychology, 80*(2), 325–339. https://doi.org/10.1037//O022-3514.80.2.325.

Sheldon, K., & Filak, V. (2008). Manipulating autonomy, competence, and relatedness support in a game-learning context: New evidence that all three needs matter. *British Journal of Social Psychology, 47*, 257–283. https://doi.org/10.1348/014466607X238797.

Snyder, C. R. (2000). *Handbook of hope*. San Diego, CA: Academic Press.

Stoycheva, M., & Ruskov, P. (2015, July). Growth mindset development pattern. Paper present at the *20th European Conference on Pattern Languages of Programs*.

Tang, X., Wang, M., Guo, J., & Salmela-Aro, K. (2019). Building grit: The longitudinal pathways between mindset, commitment, grit, and academic outcomes. *Journal of Youth and Adolescence, 48*, 850–863. https://doi.org/10.1007/s10964-019-00998-0.

Van den Broeck, A., Ferris, D. L., Chang, C.-H., & Rosen, C. C. (2016). A review of self-determination theory's basic psychological needs at work. *Journal of Management, 42*(5), 1195–1229. https://doi.org/10.1177/0149206316632058.

Van der Vaart, L., & Van den Broeck, A. (2019). Self-determination and positive psychology interventions: A extension of the positive activity model in the context of unemployment. In L. E. van Zyl & S. Rothmann (Eds.), *Theoretical approaches to multi-cultural positive psychological interventions* (Vol. 1, pp. 51–67). Cham, Switzerland: Springer.

Van der Vaart, L., Van den Broeck, A., Rothmann, S., & De Witte, H. (2019). Experiences, attitudes, and behaviors of the unemployed: The role of motivation and psychological needs. *Psychological Reports., 123*, 1117–1144. https://doi.org/10.1177/0033294119849020.

Van Hooft, E. A. J. (2014). Motivating and hindering factors during the reemployment process: The added value of employment counselors' assessment. *Journal of Occupational Health Psychology, 19*(1), 1–17. https://doi.org/10.1037/a0035118.

Van Wingerden, J., Bakker, A. B., & Derks, D. (2017). Fostering employee well-being via a job crafting intervention. *Journal of Vocational Behavior, 100*, 164–174. https://doi.org/10.1016/j.jvb.2017.03.008.

Van Wingerden, J., & Van der Stoep, J. (2017). The role of meaningful work in employees' work-related and general Well-being. *International Journal of Human Resource Studies, 7*(4), 23–37. https://doi.org/10.5296/ijhrs.v7i4.11611.

Van Wingerden, J., & Van der Stoep, J. (2018). The motivational potential of meaningful work: Relationships with strengths use, work engagement, and performance. *PLoS One, 13*(6), e0197599. https://doi.org/10.1371/journal.pone.0197599.

Van Wingerden, J., Van der Stoep, J., & Poell, R. (2018). Meaningful work and work engagement: The mediating role of perceived opportunities to craft and job crafting behavior. *International Journal of Human Resource Studies, 8*(2), 1–15. https://doi.org/10.5296/ijhrs.v8i2.12635.

Van Zyl, L. E., Deacon, E., & Rothmann, S. (2010). Towards happiness: Experiences of work-role fit, meaningfulness and work engagement of industrial/organisational psychologists in South Africa. *SA Journal of Industrial Psychology, 36*(1), 890. https://doi.org/10.4102/sajip.v36i1.890.

Van Zyl, L. E., Motschnig-Pitrik, R., & Stander, M. W. (2016). Exploring positive psychology and person-centred psychology in multi-cultural coaching. In *Coaching psychology: Meta-theoretical perspectives and applications in multicultural contexts* (pp. 315–355). Cham, Switzerland: Springer.

Van Zyl, L. E., Olckers, C., & Roll, L. C. (2020). The psychometric properties of the grit-O scale within the Twente Region in the Netherlands: An ICM-CFA vs. ESEM Approach. *Frontiers in Psychology, 11*, 796. https://doi.org/10.3389/fpsyg.2020.00796.

Van Zyl, L. E., Roll, L. C., Stander, M. W., & Richter, S. (2020). Positive psychological coaching definitions and models: A systematic literature review. *Frontiers in Psychology, 11*, 793. https://doi.org/10.3389/fpsyg.2020.00793.

Van Zyl, L. E., & Stander, M. W. (2013). A strengths-based approach towards coaching in a multicultural environment. In J. White, R. Motching, & M. Lux (Eds.), *Theory and practice of the person-centred approach – Interconnections beyond psychotherapy* (pp. 245–257). Cham, Switzerland: Springer.

Van Zyl, L. E., & Stander, M. W. (2019). Flourishing interventions 2.0: A practical guide to student development. In L. E. van Zyl & S. Rothmann (Eds.), *Positive psychological intervention design and protocols for multi-cultural contexts*. Cham, Switzerland: Springer.

Vansteenkiste, M., & Mouratidis, A. (2016). Emerging trends and future directions for the field of motivation psychology: A special issue in honor of Prof. Dr Willy Lens. *Psychologica Belgica, 56*(3), 317–341. https://doi.org/10.5334/pb.354.

Vansteenkiste, M., & Van den Broeck, A. (2018). Understanding the motivational dynamics among unemployed individuals: Refreshing insights for the self-determination theory perspective. In U. Klehe & E. A. J. van Hooft (Eds.), *The Oxford handbook of job loss and job search*. Oxford: Oxford University Press.

Vela, J. C., Lu, M. P., Lenz, A. S., & Hinojosa, K. (2015). Positive psychology and familial factors as predictors of Latina/o students' psychological grit. *Hispanic Journal of Behavioral Sciences, 37*(3), 287–303. https://doi.org/10.1177/0739986315588917.

Von Culin, K. R., Tsukayama, E., & Duckworth, A. L. (2014). Unpacking grit: Motivational correlates of perseverance and passion for long-term goals. *The Journal of Positive Psychology, 9*(4), 306–312. https://doi.org/10.1080/17439760.2014.898320.

Vukasović, T., & Bratko, D. (2015). Heritability of personality: A meta-analysis of behavior genetic studies. *Psychological Bulletin, 141*(4), 769–785. https://doi.org/10.1037/bul0000017.

Wanberg, C. R. (2012). The individual experience of unemployment. *Annual Review of Psychology, 63*, 369–396. https://doi.org/10.1146/annurev-psych-120710-100500.

Weisskirch, R. S. (2019). Grit applied within: Identity and well-being. *Identity, 19*(2), 98–108. https://doi.org/10.1080/15283488.2019.1604345.

West, M. R., Kraft, M. A., Finn, A. S., Martin, R. E., Duckworth, A. L., Gabrieli, C. F., & Gabrieli, J. D. (2016). Promise and paradox: Measuring students' non-cognitive skills and the impact of schooling. *Educational Evaluation and Policy Analysis, 38*(1), 148–170. https://doi.org/10.3102/0162373715597298.

Whiteman, W. E. (1998). *Training and educating army officers for the 21st century: Implications for the United States Military Academy*. Fort Belvoir, VA: Defense Technical Information Center.

Williams, N., Whipp, P., Jackson, B., & Dimmock, J. (2013). Relatedness support and the retention of young female golfers. *Journal of Applied Sport Psychology, 25*, 412–430. https://doi.org/10.1080/10413200.2012.749311.

Wolfe, M. T., & Patel, P. C. (2016). Grit and self-employment: A multi-country study. *Small Business Economics, 47*(4), 853–874. https://doi.org/10.1007/s11187-016-9737-6.

Wolters, C. A., & Hussain, M. (2015). Investigating grit and its relations with college students' self-regulated learning and academic achievement. *Metacognition and Learning, 10*(3), 293–311. https://doi.org/10.1007/s11409-014-9128-9.

Leoni van der Vaart completed her Master's degrees in Human Resource Management and Industrial/Organisational Psychology and a joint PhD in the field of Industrial/Organisational Psychology with KU Leuven (Belgium) and the North-West University (South Africa). She is a senior lecturer and researcher at the North-West University and has a passion for understanding employee/job seeker attitudes and behaviour from a motivational perspective. Leoni is an active researcher with publications in peer-reviewed journals and presentations at international conferences and has experience in the tertiary education environment, both as lecturer and researcher. She is a registered psychological counsellor (category: independent practitioner), a registered psychologist (category: organisational psychology) with the Health Professions Council of South Africa (HPCSA), and human resource professional (category: learning and development) with the South African Board of People Practices (SABPP).

Llewellyn E. van Zyl (Ph.D.) is an assistant professor of work and organisational psychology with the University of Eindhoven in the Netherlands and holds an Extraordinary professorship with the North-West University in South Africa. He is a respected academic, published author and talent management consultant specializing in talent analytics, -assessment and -development. During the past decade he has gained extensive experience in the development, implementation and evaluation of strategic talent development initiatives for multi-national corporations spanning from the Netherlands and Saudi Arabia to South Africa. He has a passion for developing strengths-based, fit-for-purpose leadership development solutions aimed at the optimization of leaders' capability.

Jessica van Wingerden Ph.D. is Executive Vice President Human Resources at Rabobank, Member of the Supervisory Board in the field of education and Research Fellow at Erasmus University Rotterdam, the Center of Excellence for Positive Organizational Psychology, Rotterdam, The Netherlands. During the past decade she has gained extensive experience in the development, implementation and evaluation of organizational development and change within multi-national corporations. Her research interests include organizational conditions for work engagement and employee performance such as climate for work engagement, meaningful work, job crafting and positive organizational interventions.

Printed by Printforce, United Kingdom